Development of Complex Societies in Southeastern Shandong, China

YALE UNIVERSITY PUBLICATIONS IN ANTHROPOLOGY

The Yale University Publications in Anthropology series, published by the Yale University Department of Anthropology and the Peabody Museum of Natural History at Yale University, is supported by the Theodore and Ruth Wilmanns Lidz Endowment Fund for Excellence in Scholarly Publications, dedicated to the dissemination of scholarly research and study of the world and its cultures.

The Yale University Publications in Anthropology series embodies the results of researches in the general field of anthropology directly conducted or sponsored by the Yale University Department of Anthropology and the Yale Peabody Museum of Natural History Division of Anthropology. Occasionally other manuscripts of outstanding quality that deal with subjects of special interest to the faculty of the Department of Anthropology may also be included.

Distributed by Yale University Press
NEW HAVEN AND LONDON

For quantity purchases and exam copies for coursework, and a complete list of available titles in this series visit www.yalebooks.com or yalebooks.co.uk.

Development of Complex Societies in Southeastern Shandong, China

Settlement Patterns from the Neolithic to the Han Period

Hui Fang
Anne P. Underhill
Gary M. Feinman
Linda M. Nicholas
Fengshi Luan
Haiguang Yu

Number 97

Published by
the Yale University Department of Anthropology
and the Yale Peabody Museum of Natural History

Distributed by
Yale University Press
NEW HAVEN AND LONDON

Yale

YALE UNIVERSITY PUBLICATIONS IN ANTHROPOLOGY
NUMBER 97

Rosemary Volpe
Publications Manager

Sally H. Pallatto
Graphic Designer
Cover Design

Huanzhen Cao
Project Assistant

Index by Judy A. Hunt

Front cover: Gary Feinman collecting sherds from the surface of the Shang-Zhou site WL-YG-1 (Year 3, 1998).

Back cover: Professor Fang Hui scrapes an exposed profile at the Longshan site JN-ZJDZ-3 (Year 7, 2001).

Title page illustration by Sally H. Pallatto.

Photographs in this book are from *Ludongnan yanhai diqu xitong kaogu diaocha baogao* [*Report of the systematic archaeological regional survey in the coastal region of southeastern Shandong*] by Fang Hui, Anne Underhill, Gary M. Feinman, Linda M. Nicholas, Fengshi Luan, Haiguang Yu, and Fengshu Cai (Wenwu Press, Beijing, 2012) and are reprinted with permission of the publisher.

Peabody Museum of Natural History
Yale University
P. O. Box 208118
New Haven CT 06520-8118 USA
peabody.yale.edu

Distributed by Yale University Press
NEW HAVEN AND LONDON
www.yalebooks.com | yalebooks.co.uk

ISBN 978-0-913516-33-1
ISSN 1535-7082

Printed in the United States of America

Library of Congress Control Number: 2022939548

∞ This paper meets the requirements of ANSI/NISO Z39.48-1992 (Permanence of Paper).
10 9 8 7 6 5 4 3 2 1

Our long-term collaborative project would not have been possible without the enthusiastic support of the late Shandong University professor Cai Fengshu.

We dedicate our book to his memory.

Contents

viii List of Figures

xiv List of Tables

xv Preface

1 One — **The Survey Region, Prior Investigations, and the Research Process**

13 Two — **The Value of Systematic, Full-coverage Regional Survey**

69 Three — **Descriptions of Major Sites and Collections**

269 Four — **Regional Settlement Patterns and the Development of Complex Societies**

307 References

323 Index

Figures

Chapter One

3 Figure 1.1. Area surveyed in southeastern Shandong Province, China.
10 Figure 1.2. Administrative boundaries and areas covered in each field season.

Chapter Two

16 Figure 2.1. Crew members survey the Dantu site in Year 1.
17 Figure 2.2. Schematic key for the topographic maps used on survey by year.
19 Figure 2.3. Crew members examine a profile at DG-LCZ-3.
26 Figure 2.4. Longshan sites in the Donggang, Wulian, and Jiaonan Districts, Year 1 and Year 2.
27 Figure 2.5. Zhou sites in the Donggang, Wulian, and Jiaonan Districts, Year 1 and Year 2.
28 Figure 2.6. Han sites in the Donggang, Wulian, and Jiaonan Districts, Year 1 and Year 2.
29 Figure 2.7. Longshan sites in the Donggang, Wulian, and Jiaonan Districts, Year 3.
30 Figure 2.8. Zhou sites in the Donggang, Wulian, and Jiaonan Districts, Year 3.
31 Figure 2.9. Han sites in the Donggang, Wulian, and Jiaonan Districts, Year 3.
32 Figure 2.10. Longshan sites in the Donggang District, southern survey area, Year 4.
32 Figure 2.11. Zhou sites in the Donggang District, southern survey area, Year 4.
32 Figure 2.12. Han sites in the Donggang District, southern survey area, Year 4.
33 Figure 2.13. Longshan sites in the Wulian and Jiaonan Districts, northern survey area, Year 4.
33 Figure 2.14. Zhou sites in the Wulian and Jiaonan Districts, northern survey area, Year 4.
34 Figure 2.15. Han sites in the Wulian and Jiaonan Districts, northern survey area, Year 4.
34 Figure 2.16. Longshan sites in the Donggang District, Year 5.
35 Figure 2.17. Zhou sites in the Donggang District during Year 5.
35 Figure 2.18. Han sites in the Donggang District during Year 5.
36 Figure 2.19. Longshan sites in the Jiaonan District, northern survey area, Year 6.
37 Figure 2.20. Zhou sites in the Jiaonan District, northern survey area, Year 6.
38 Figure 2.21. Han sites in the Jiaonan District, northern survey area, Year 6.
39 Figure 2.22. Longshan sites in the Donggang District, southern survey area, Year 6.
39 Figure 2.23. Zhou sites in the Donggang District, southern survey area, Year 6.
40 Figure 2.24. Han sites in the Donggang District, southern survey area, Year 6.
41 Figure 2.25. Longshan sites in the Jiaonan District, northern survey area, Year 7.
42 Figure 2.26. Zhou sites in the Jiaonan District, northern survey area, Year 7.
43 Figure 2.27. Han sites in the Jiaonan District, northern survey area, Year 7.
44 Figure 2.28. Longshan sites in the Donggang District, southern survey area, Year 7.
45 Figure 2.29. Zhou sites in the Donggang District, southern survey area, Year 7.
46 Figure 2.30. Han sites in the Donggang District, southern survey area, Year 7.
47 Figure 2.31. Longshan sites in the Donggang District, southern survey area, Year 8.

48 Figure 2.32. Zhou sites in the Donggang District, southern survey area, Year 8.
49 Figure 2.33. Han sites in the Donggang District, southern survey area, Year 8.
50 Figure 2.34. Longshan sites in the Jiaonan District, northern survey area, Year 8.
50 Figure 2.35. Zhou period sites in the Jiaonan District, northern survey area, Year 8.
50 Figure 2.36. Han sites in the Jiaonan District, northern survey area, Year 8.
51 Figure 2.37. Longshan sites in the Lanshan and Donggang Districts during Year 9.
52 Figure 2.38. Zhou sites in the Lanshan and Donggang Districts during Year 9.
53 Figure 2.39. Han sites in the Lanshan and Donggang Districts during Year 9 (2003).
54 Figure 2.40. Longshan sites in the Lanshan and Donggang Districts during Year 10.
55 Figure 2.41. Zhou sites in the Lanshan and Donggang Districts during Year 10.
56 Figure 2.42. Han sites in the Lanshan and Donggang Districts during Year 10.
57 Figure 2.43. Longshan sites in the Lanshan and Donggang Districts during Year 11.
58 Figure 2.44. Zhou sites in the Lanshan and Donggang Districts during Year 11.
59 Figure 2.45. Han sites in the Lanshan and Donggang Districts during Year 11.
60 Figure 2.46. Longshan sites in the Lanshan District during Year 12.
61 Figure 2.47. Zhou sites in the Lanshan District during Year 12.
62 Figure 2.48. Han sites in the Lanshan District during Year 12.
63 Figure 2.49. Longshan sites in the Lanshan District during Year 13.
63 Figure 2.50. Zhou sites in the Lanshan District during Year 13.
64 Figure 2.51. Han sites in the Lanshan District during Year 13.
64 Figure 2.52. Longshan sites in the Donggang District during Year 13.
65 Figure 2.53. Zhou sites in the Donggang District during Year 13.
65 Figure 2.54. Han sites in the Donggang District during Year 13.
66 Figure 2.55. Longshan sites in the Jiaonan and Zhucheng Districts during Year 13.
66 Figure 2.56. Zhou sites in the Jiaonan and Zhucheng Districts during Year 13.
67 Figure 2.57. Han sites in the Jiaonan and Zhucheng Districts during Year 13.
67 Figure 2.58. Han sites in the Wulian District during Year 13.

Chapter Three
74 Figure 3.1. Cultural layer with Han ceramics at Chengzigou (DG-CZG-1/HSD-7).
76 Figure 3.2. Dagucheng (DG-DGC-1/XSLP-2/QEZ-1, 3, 4, 5) with Han tombs and platforms.
77 Figure 3.3. Shang ceramics from Dagucheng (DG-DGC-1/XSLP-2[CAF]/QEZ-1, 3, 4, 5).
78 Figure 3.4. View of DG-DGZ-5.
79 Figure 3.5. Western Donghaiyu (DG-DHY-1).
79 Figure 3.6. Late Dawenkou and Longshan cultural layers at Donghaiyu (DG-DHY-1).
80 Figure 3.7. Late Dawenkou and Early Longshan sherds from Donghaiyu (DG-DHY-1 [CABB]).
81 Figure 3.8. Stone *dao* (刀) knife from Donghaiyu (DG-DHY-1[CABB]).
81 Figure 3.9. Luan Fengshi and Linda Nicholas surveying at DG-DJP-2.
84 Figure 3.10. Searching for diagnostic sherds at Donglianghe (DG-DLH-1).
84 Figure 3.11. Early Beixin pottery sherds from Donglianghe (DG-DLH [CAA]).
86 Figure 3.12. DG-DNZ-2 on a piedmont spur above a small reservoir.

87 FIGURE 3.13. DG-DSQ-2 on piedmont ridges near a modern reservoir.
88 FIGURE 3.14. Dataoyuan (DG-DTY-1/DJZ-3, 5) in fields on the west side of the village.
89 FIGURE 3.15. Exposed Longshan burial outlined by stones at Dataoyuan (DG-DTY-1/DJZ-3, 5).
90 FIGURE 3.16. Longshan ceramic and stone artifacts from Dataoyuan (DG-DTY-1 [CAA]/DJZ-3, 5).
90 FIGURE 3.17. Longshan white body sherds from Dataoyuan (DG-DTY-1[CAA]/DJZ-3, 5).
93 FIGURE 3.18. Fanjiahe (DG-FaJH-1/LJC-6) on a low rise in the alluvium.
95 FIGURE 3.19. Eastern Zhou weight and Western Zhou sherd from Guheya (DG-GHA-2 [CAG]).
96 FIGURE 3.20. Guanjiacun (DG-GJC-1) from the east.
96 FIGURE 3.21. Gaojiagou (DG-GJG-2) on a low piedmont ridge.
98 FIGURE 3.22. Large, flat stone at Houguzi (DG-HGZ-1).
101 FIGURE 3.23. Gary Feinman surveying at Huangjiahe (DG-HJH-2, 3).
101 FIGURE 3.24. Cai Fengshu, Linda Nicholas, and Luan Fengshi surveying Longshan site DG-HQC-5.
104 FIGURE 3.25. Eastern Zhou ceramic fishing weight from Jiaokezhuang (DG-JKZ-8, 9 [CAC]).
105 FIGURE 3.26. Rammed earth layers at a Han tomb at Liangchengzhen (DG- LCZ-1 [CAAA]).
109 FIGURE 3.27. Multicomponent site Majiacun near modern shrimp ponds (DG-MaJC-1).
109 FIGURE 3.28. Ceramic sherds from Majiacun (DG-MaJC-1[CAB]).
111 FIGURE 3.29. Western Zhou sherds from Miaojiacun (DG-MJC-1[CAJ]).
113 FIGURE 3.30. Majiazhuang (DG-MJZ-3) on a terraced piedmont spur above a modern reservoir.
113 FIGURE 3.31. The Longshan and Zhou site DG-MSH-1 on a low piedmont slope above a modern reservoir.
115 FIGURE 3.32. Fang Hui and Linda Nicholas surveying Nantunling (DG-NTL-4).
115 FIGURE 3.33. Beixin and Dawenkou ceramic artifacts from Nantunling (DG-NTL-4).
119 FIGURE 3.34. A partially destroyed Han tomb at Qinjiaguanzhuang (DG-QJGZ-1).
121 FIGURE 3.35. Surveying an exposed cultural layer in Qianlianghe (DG-QLH-1).
122 FIGURE 3.36. Early Longshan sherds from Qianwulihe (DG-QWLH-1).
122 FIGURE 3.37. An ancient pit exposed at Qianwulihe (DG-QWLH-1).
124 FIGURE 3.38. Qianzhucun (DG-QZC-1/WLZ-2) on low piedmont ridges and alluvial terraces.
126 FIGURE 3.39. Surveying at the Longshan site Suijiaguanzhuang (DG-SJGZ-1).
126 FIGURE 3.40. Early Longshan ceramic and stone artifacts from Suijiaguanzhuang (DG-SJGZ-1).
128 FIGURE 3.41. DG-SJP-6/WLZ-5 located on a low piedmont rise.
128 FIGURE 3.42. Gary Feinman collecting in a Longshan cultural layer at DG-SJP-6/WLZ-5.
129 FIGURE 3.43. Small Zhou site DG-SKC-1 completely within an apple orchard.
131 FIGURE 3.44. DG-SNG-1 on a low piedmont spur above a modern reservoir.
132 FIGURE 3.45. Zhou site Taojiacun (DG-TJC-1) at the base of a low mountain.
133 FIGURE 3.46. Survey crew members examine the Han cultural layer at DG-TL-5.

134 Figure 3.47. Wujiatai (DG-WJT-1) on a low alluvial terrace above the sea.
137 Figure 3.48. Gary Feinman collecting from an exposed cultural layer at DG-XCWA-9.
139 Figure 3.49. Crew surveying Xiangjiagou (DG-XJG-1).
141 Figure 3.50. Crew surveying Xilinzitou (DG-XLZT-1).
141 Figure 3.51. Late Dawenkou and Longshan ceramics from Xilinzitou (DG-XLZT-1 [CAA]).
142 Figure 3.52. Longshan stone tools from Xilinzitou (DG-XLZT-1[CAA]).
144 Figure 3.53. A ceramic roof tile from Han site DG-XXD-1.
145 Figure 3.54. Crew members examining an exposed cultural layer at DG-YJAT-2.
147 Figure 3.55. Eastern Zhou bronze sword from a tomb at DG-YJC-6.
148 Figure 3.56. Zhengjiadingzi (DG-ZJDZ-1) on piedmont slopes.
151 Figure 3.57. Early Longshan sherds from Caiyuan (JN-CY-1[CAA]).
152 Figure 3.58. Han period tombs at Dagou (JN-DG-1, 4).
153 Figure 3.59. A Longshan cultural layer exposed at JN-DJLG-3.
154 Figure 3.60. Crew surveying Dongjiawa (JN-DJW-4).
155 Figure 3.61. JN-DS-4 located on an alluvial terrace.
156 Figure 3.62. Remnant of a Han tomb at Dongsi (JN-DS-11).
157 Figure 3.63. Dawenkou *ding* tripod feet and Early Longshan sherds from JN-DSHK-3 [CAA].
159 Figure 3.64. The large, multicomponent site Fengduncun (JN-FDC-1).
161 Figure 3.65. Crew checking cultural layers at Huanggudunling (JN-HGDL-3).
161 Figure 3.66. Early Longshan sherds from JN-HGDL-3[CAA].
163 Figure 3.67. JN-HQ-10 in area cleared for apple orchards.
164 Figure 3.68. Survey crew and visitors at JN-JGZ-11.
165 Figure 3.69. Survey crew members at the Han tomb at JN-JJC-1.
167 Figure 3.70. Remnants of Han tombs at Jilihe (JN-JLH-4, 5, 6, 8).
168 Figure 3.71. One of the Han tombs at Jiawangdun (JN-JWD-2/LHQ-1).
169 Figure 3.72. Longshan sherds from Liuhangdazhuang (JN-LHDZ-3[CAA]).
173 Figure 3.73. Han tombs on top of the piedmont ridge at JN-QGD-1.
176 Figure 3.74. JN-SH-11 situated on a long rise in the alluvium.
179 Figure 3.75. Longshan sherds from JN-TS-4[CAG].
181 Figure 3.76. A U-shaped marker stone at JN-XDZ-3, 5.
181 Figure 3.77. Possible cut stone markers at JN-XDZ-6.
184 Figure 3.78. JN-XJY-7 in fields just beyond the row of small trees.
185 Figure 3.79. One exposed cultural layer at the multicomponent Xisi site (JN-XS-1).
186 Figure 3.80. Longshan ceramic and stone artifacts from Xisi (JN-XS-1[CACC]).
186 Figure 3.81. Yueshi ceramics from Xisi (JN-XS-1[CAAA]).
187 Figure 3.82. Longshan cup fragment and bowl from Xisi (JN-XS-1).
191 Figure 3.83. Fang Hui examining a Longshan cultural layer at Zhangjiadazhuang (JN-ZJDZ-3).
191 Figure 3.84. Dawenkou and Longshan sherds from Zhangjiadazhuang (JN-ZJDZ-3 [CAG]).
194 Figure 3.85. Survey crew checking for sherds at LS-BY-4.
196 Figure 3.86. Small Western Zhou site LS-DPD-2.

197 FIGURE 3.87. The modern serpentine quarry near LS-DPD-2.
198 FIGURE 3.88. Shang and Zhou site LS-DQL-1.
200 FIGURE 3.89. Crew surveying cultural layer in the center of Datushan (LS-DTS-5/CG-9).
201 FIGURE 3.90. Han sherds and tile end from Datushan (LS-DTS-5/CG-9[CAI]).
201 FIGURE 3.91. Han ceramics from Datushan (LS-DTS-5[CAZ]/CG-9).
202 FIGURE 3.92. Longshan sherds and stone axe from Datushan (LS-DTS-5[CAX]/CG-9).
203 FIGURE 3.93. Middle Longshan white sherd from Datushan (LS-DTS-5[CAZ]/CG-9).
204 FIGURE 3.94. Gary Feinman examining Han sherd in a quarry wall at LS-DZZ-5.
206 FIGURE 3.95. Gouwa (LS-GW-1) in the alluvium above a tributary of the Zhuzi River.
206 FIGURE 3.96. Yueshi and Longshan ceramic and stone artifacts from Gouwa (LS-GW-1 [CAA]).
209 FIGURE 3.97. Burnt soil in a cultural layer at Jinggou (LS-JG-3/DXQH-1).
210 FIGURE 3.98. Late Dawenkou *bei* cup from Jinggou (LS-JG-3/DXQH-1).
211 FIGURE 3.99. Stone tools and Early Longshan ceramic *bei* cup from Jinggou (LS-JG-3/ DXQH-1).
211 FIGURE 3.100. Ceramics from Jinggou (LS-JG-3[CAG]/DXQH-1).
213 FIGURE 3.101. Survey crew collecting sherds from Zhou site Jijiagou (LS-JJG-4).
213 FIGURE 3.102. Zhou sherds from Jijiagou (LS-JJG-4[CAA]).
214 FIGURE 3.103. LS-LCG-1 in plowed fields in the alluvium.
215 FIGURE 3.104. Yueshi sherds from LS-LCG-1[CAA].
217 FIGURE 3.105. Gary Feinman collecting sherds at Liujiagou (LS-LJG-4).
218 FIGURE 3.106. LS-LZD-1 between the water channel and the piedmont ridge.
219 FIGURE 3.107. Crew surveying Matuan (LS-MT-7) on top of alluvial terrace.
220 FIGURE 3.108. Sherds from Matuan (LS-MT-7[CAE]).
220 FIGURE 3.109. Longshan stone *dao* knife and *fu* axe from Matuan (LS-MT-7[CAC]).
222 FIGURE 3.110. Qinjiajiezhuang (LS-QJJZ-3) on a gradual slope in the alluvium.
222 FIGURE 3.111. Western Zhou sherds from LS-QJJZ-3[CAB].
223 FIGURE 3.112. Western Zhou stone *fu* axes from LS-QJJZ-3[CAA].
224 FIGURE 3.113. Stone ornament, Western Zhou vessel handle, and Late Shang *li* tripod rim from Qulingnantou (LS-QLNT-2[CAA]).
224 FIGURE 3.114. Qianshuichegou (LS-QSCG-1) on low rise in the alluvium.
226 FIGURE 3.115. Late Dawenkou and Early Longshan sherds from Qianshuichegou (LS-QSCG-1[CAA]).
227 FIGURE 3.116. Longshan stone *zao* chisel from Qianshuichegou (LS-QSCG-1[CAA]).
229 FIGURE 3.117. Crew members surveying at Xiaocun (LS-XC-2, 4).
230 FIGURE 3.118. Xiaodaituan (LS-XDT-3) under modern town, extending up piedmont.
231 FIGURE 3.119. Longshan sherds from Xiaodaituan (LS-XDT-3[CAD]).
231 FIGURE 3.120. Stone tools from Xiaodaituan (LS-XDT-3[CAD]).
233 FIGURE 3.121. Western Zhou sherds from LS-XJC-1[CAA].
234 FIGURE 3.122. Crew members checking deposits in road cut at Xujiacun (LS-XJC-2, 3).
235 FIGURE 3.123. Early Dawenkou *dou* stemmed dish rim and *bo* footed bowl from Xujiacun (LS-XJC-2, 3[CAD]).
235 FIGURE 3.124. Early Dawenkou rims and body sherd from Xujiacun (LS-XJC-2, 3 [CAD]).

236 Figure 3.125. Early Dawenkou sherds from Xujiacun (LS-XJC-2, 3[CAA]).
236 Figure 3.126. Dawenkou period *fanglun* spindle whorls from Xujiacun (LS-XJC-2, 3 [CAD]).
237 Figure 3.127. Early Dawenkou stone tools from Xujiacun (LS-XJC-2, 3[CAD]).
238 Figure 3.128. Northwestern Xinliu (LS-XL-1–7) on top and slopes of piedmont ridge.
238 Figure 3.129. Zhou sherds from Xinliu (LS-XL-1–7[CAJ]).
239 Figure 3.130. Zhou sherds from Xinliu (LS-XL-1–7[CAL]).
239 Figure 3.131. Broken Western Zhou stone point and *li* tripod foot from Xinliu (LS-XL-1 –7[CAX]).
241 Figure 3.132. Crew members examining an cultural layer at Yangjiazhuang (LS-YJZ-1).
243 Figure 3.133. The large Yaowangcheng site (DG-YWC-1/GaJL-1).
244 Figure 3.134. Rammed earth exposed at Yaowangcheng (DG-YWC-1/GaJL-1).
246 Figure 3.135. Longshan sherds from Yaowangcheng (DG-YWC-1[CAAI]/GaJL-1).
246 Figure 3.136. Artifacts from Yaowangcheng (DG-YWC-1[CAAI]/GaJL-1).
248 Figure 3.137. Crew surveying Zhengjiajiezhuang (LS-ZJJZ-4).
248 Figure 3.138. Western Zhou sherds from Zhengjiajiezhuang (LS-ZJJZ-4[CAP]).
252 Figure 3.139. Crew surveying Donghuaya (WL-DHY-6).
254 Figure 3.140. Western Zhou *li* tripod feet from WL-GST-1[CAC].
254 Figure 3.141. Zhou site WL-GST-1 on top of low piedmont spur.
256 Figure 3.142. WL-LQ-2, 6 on the top and upper slopes of a low piedmont spur.
257 Figure 3.143. Luan Fengshi and Fang Hui examining exposed profile at Wangshitou (WL-WST-1).
257 Figure 3.144. Early Longshan period *ding* tripod feet from Wangshitou (WL-WST-1).
258 Figure 3.145. Western Zhou period *li* tripod feet from Wangshitou (WL-WST-1).
258 Figure 3.146. Unfinished stone tools from Wangshitou (WL-WST-1).
260 Figure 3.147. Crew surveying the eastern section of Xiajiazhuang (WL-XJZ-1).
260 Figure 3.148. Exposed Longshan cultural layers at Xiajiazhuang (WL-XJZ-1).
262 Figure 3.149. Yaogou (WL-YG-1) on the top and terraced slopes of the piedmont rise.
262 Figure 3.150. Luan Fengshi and Fang Hui examining cultural layer at Yaogou (WL-YG-1).
264 Figure 3.151. A Han boundary stone from site ZC-DTY-3.
265 Figure 3.152. A partially visible eroded inscription at site ZC-DTY-3.
267 Figure 3.153. Crew surveying the alluvial terrace where ZC-XCJZ-1, 2, 4 is situated.

Chapter Four
273 Figure 4.1. Beixin and Dawenkou sites in southeastern Shandong.
275 Figure 4.2. All Longshan period sites in southeastern Shandong.
278 Figure 4.3. Early Longshan sites in southeastern Shandong.
281 Figure 4.4. Middle Longshan sites in southeastern Shandong.
288 Figure 4.5. Late Longshan, Yueshi, and Shang sites in southeastern Shandong.
290 Figure 4.6. All Zhou sites in southeastern Shandong.
292 Figure 4.7. Western Zhou sites in southeastern Shandong.
294 Figure 4.8. Eastern Zhou sites in southeastern Shandong.
300 Figure 4.9. Han sites in southeastern Shandong.

Tables

Chapter One

4 Table 1.1. Prehistoric and early historical northern China periods relevant to southeastern Shandong.

6 Table 1.2. Rizhao area administration after Han and before Shandong Province was established.

Chapter Two

22 Table 2.1. The thirteen seasons of the Rizhao area survey from 1995 to 2007.

Chapter Four

274 Table 4.1. Beixin and Dawenkou sites in the survey region.

276 Table 4.2. All Longshan sites in the survey region by settlement hierarchy tier.

279 Table 4.3. Longshan sites with diagnostic pottery.

279 Table 4.4. Early and Middle Longshan sites by settlement hierarchy tier.

282 Table 4.5. Ceramics collected for the Longshan and Zhou periods in the survey region.

291 Table 4.6. All Zhou sites in the survey region by settlement hierarchy tier.

293 Table 4.7. Zhou sites with diagnostic pottery.

293 Table 4.8. Western and Eastern Zhou sites by settlement hierarchy tier.

296 Table 4.9. Defendable sites for the Longshan period through Han.

302 Table 4.10. All Han sites in the survey region by settlement hierarchy tier.

Preface

This report presents the findings of thirteen seasons of a systematic, full-coverage regional survey in southeastern Shandong, China, from 1995 to 2007. Our Sino-American team covered more than 1,400 km^2 within the modern districts of Rizhao City and Qingdao City, as well as a small part of Zhucheng, a county-level city administered by Weifang City. Before our collaborative regional survey, there had been pioneering research on important archaeological sites in the area, including at Liangchengzhen, Dantu, Donghaiyu, and Yaowangcheng. At the outset, the focus of our team was to understand the regional context of Liangchengzhen, which previous fieldwork had suggested was the largest settlement in southeastern Shandong dating to the Longshan period (c. 2500–1900 BC) of the late Neolithic.

This monograph reports the results of our regional survey. This survey was the first to clarify the nature of settlements from the Longshan and other periods in the immediate area, including Liangchengzhen, through a gradual expansion of coverage to the north, west, and south. We include detailed descriptions of the relatively large settlements discovered and assessed by the field crews, along with an expanded discussion of our methodology. This report also places the multi-year survey project in context by discussing the development of survey projects in other areas of China and relevant research in southeastern Shandong after 2007. It provides a more detailed account of the history of research in southeastern Shandong and significantly expands archaeological knowledge of the region beyond what has previously been presented in English-language publications.

Our collaborative project was made possible after China's State Administration of Cultural Heritage announced its policy "The Regulation of the People's Republic of China on Archaeological Work Involving Foreign Affairs" on 22 February 1991. This policy change prompted Anne Underhill (then a visiting assistant professor at McGill University), at a 1992 Sino-American workshop on ceramic analysis in Linzi, Shandong, organized by the National Museum of China, to discuss with Cai Fengshu, professor in the School of History and Culture at Shandong University, the possibility of an international collaboration. Underhill had met Cai in 1987 when she was researching ceramics as a doctoral student at the University of British Columbia. In 1994, on returning to Shandong University from her ethnoarchaeological research on ceramics in Guizhou Province, Underhill discussed a collaborative archaeological survey focusing on the Longshan period in Shandong. She gratefully agreed to plan a survey around the well-known site of Liangchengzhen in the Rizhao area as suggested by Yu Haiguang. At Underhill's request to include an archaeologist with expertise in systematic, full-coverage regional surveys, the Shandong University archaeologists invited Gary Feinman and Linda Nicholas, who had directed regional surveys in Oaxaca, Mexico, to join the project.

With approval from the National Cultural Heritage Bureau, the formal Sino-American collaboration began on 4 December 1995 with Cai and Underhill as the team leaders. The Shandong University professors trained the American participants to recognize sherds from different periods of the Rizhao area and several aspects of Rizhao history. At the same time,

Feinman and Nicholas taught the survey methods they had used successfully in Mexico to the initial American participants (Underhill and Gwen Bennett, then a graduate student at UCLA).

During the first year of fieldwork we found that methods successfully used in Oaxaca also worked well in the vicinity of Liangchengzhen, north of Rizhao City. Field seasons in the fall and early winter made it possible to find pottery sherds and stone tools on the surface and to examine exposed stratigraphic profiles. We investigated previously identified sites in the area and documented a large number of new sites. At each site, we searched for intact cultural layers. We include here a detailed account of the specific methods that we used during this fieldwork, in addition to the methods for preparing maps that display the settlement pattern for each period of occupation. We also provide our specific observations about cultural materials on the surface and from exposed deposits at relatively large sites and describe major characteristics of the local environment. To our knowledge regional surveys that systematically use such methods had not taken place in China before our project.

Gradually expanding our survey area each year resulted in the discovery of hundreds of new sites from the Longshan period, as well as from earlier (Beixin and Dawenkou) and later (Yueshi, Shang, Zhou, and Han) eras. Publishing the data for these sites became even more important, because rapid economic development in the Rizhao area has destroyed many sites over the years. The data presented here should be useful for future assessments of extant sites. Although previous researchers had identified some of these sites, most are new to the archaeological record of southeastern Shandong.

After we illustrated the value of systematic, full-coverage regional survey in papers published in Chinese and English, similar survey projects were begun in more than one area of Shandong and Henan Provinces. While a detailed comparison of the specific methods used for each project is worthy of another volume, we present the methods that worked well for us in southeastern Shandong. As we endeavor to show here, the survey methodology we used made possible more than one significant conclusion about the prehistoric and early historical periods of southeastern Shandong. These include identification of an earlier Neolithic occupation in the area than previously recognized, discovery of multiple late prehistoric centers of different sizes in the northern and southern sectors of the survey region (including the unexpected large size of Yaowangcheng), and uncovering evidence for an increasingly strong state presence during the Zhou and early imperial eras. These data show the value of systematic, full-coverage regional survey for revealing important regional variation in settlement organization within northern China.

We thank our dedicated survey crew members from several different institutions (named in Chapter 2). The institutional home from 1999 to 2007 of the Chinese team members (Cai, Yu, Luan, and Fang) has remained Shandong University. At the outset of the project Feinman and Nicholas were at the University of Wisconsin–Madison and Underhill was at Yale University; all three later moved to the Field Museum of Natural History, Chicago, for the duration of the survey work described in this book (in 2010 Underhill returned to Yale). Several colleagues in Rizhao participated in the survey, including Sun Chengfu from the Rizhao City Museum.

Our work would not have been possible without generous funding from the US National Science Foundation High Risk Exploratory Research Program for the 1995 survey (Underhill, Feinman, and Cai); the Wenner-Gren Foundation for Anthropological Research for the 1996 survey (Underhill, Cai, and Feinman); the Henry Luce Foundation to support both the survey from 1997 to 1999 and the Liangchengzhen excavations (Underhill,

Feinman, and Lothar von Falkenhausen, faculty advisor for Gwen Bennett's dissertation research at UCLA); US National Science Foundation for support of both the survey from 2000 to 2001 and the Liangchengzhen excavations, along with analysis of excavated materials from 2000 to 2005 (Underhill and Feinman, grant no. BCS-9911128); the National Geographic Society to support the survey from 2002 to 2004 (Underhill, grant no. 7335-02); the Cyrus Tang Foundation (Underhill and Feinman) to support the survey from 2005 to 2007; the Civilization Exploration Project of China II (Fang); the 111 Project of China (Fang, grant no. 111-2-09), and the Translation Project of the National Social Science Foundation of China (project no. 13WKG002, Fang, 2013).

We take this opportunity to extend our tremendous gratitude to the government of Rizhao City for its exceptional support over the years, the Rizhao City Museum, the State Administration of Cultural Heritage, the Shandong Provincial Cultural Relics Bureau, and countless colleagues at Shandong University. We also thank Li Feng for generously sharing his valuable, previously unpublished data on the Western Zhou and for his insightful comments. In addition, we are very grateful to the many Shandong University and American graduate students who participated in the survey. We owe a special thank you to Jill Seagard for her skill in helping produce our maps and to Field Museum volunteers for their varied assistance, especially Kristen Buskirk, Lacey Carpenter, Stephen Feinman, Hilary Leathem, Christina Pannos, Carolyn Rauh, and Katie Warden. Finally, we thank Fan Rong, former PhD student at Yale University, for her great help in preparing this manuscript; Wang Ya, former visiting student at Yale from Shandong University, for her valuable assistance with historical references; Rosemary Volpe for her extensive editorial assistance, and Sally Pallatto for her expertise with our photographs. The late Cai Fengshu prepared the first draft of Chapter 1.

Hui Fang
Shandong University

Anne P. Underhill
Yale University

Gary M. Feinman
Field Museum of Natural History

Linda M. Nicholas
Field Museum of Natural History

Fengshi Luan
Shandong University

Haiguang Yu
Shandong University

CHAPTER ONE

The Survey Region, Prior Investigations, and the Research Process

Our collaborative systematic survey of the Rizhao area of Shandong Province in the People's Republic of China (中华人民共和国), from 1995 to 2007, focused on understanding the regional context of the important archaeological site of Liangchengzhen (两城镇), initially regarded as the largest late prehistoric settlement in southeastern Shandong. Earlier pioneering research and fieldwork had dated Liangchengzhen to the late Neolithic Longshan period.

Introduction to the Rizhao Area and Liangchengzhen

The coastal area of southeastern Shandong (山东) (lat 35°04′N, long 119°06′E to 35°45′N, 119°44′E) has a humid continental monsoon climate with an average annual temperature of 12 °C to 13 °C and four distinct seasons (Figure 1.1). There are 213 frost-free days per year, with the most precipitation falling in the summer months. The annual precipitation is 800–900 mm (averaging more than 841 mm), surpassing the average for Shandong Province as a whole. The area has a mild climate, with an average temperature of 12.7 °C.

This coastal area centered in the Donggang District (东港区) of Rizhao City (日照市) is located between Jiaonan County (胶南县) to the north and the Lanshan District (岚山区) in the south, on the border of Shandong and Jiangsu Provinces. The area is relatively long from north to south and narrow from west to east. It faces the Yellow Sea in the east (Haizhou Bay [海州湾] and Huangjiatang Bay [黄家塘湾]) and the Wulian Mountains (五莲山) to the west. The North Jiangsu Plain lies to the south, and the Tiejue Mountains (铁橛山) to the north. The topography, dominated by low hills that are higher in the west and northwest than in the east and south, includes river valleys, piedmont areas, and coastal plains. The highest mountains in the area are Ma'er (马耳山) at 706 m above sea level, Wulian (五莲山) (674 masl), and He Shan (河山) (629 masl). There are several relatively large rivers in the region, along with non-navigable, intermittent, and seasonal rivers. The main rivers in the south are the Futuan (傅疃河) (71 km long) and the Zhuzi (竹子河); the rivers in the north are the Chao (潮河), Jili (吉利河), and Baima (白马河). Today there are mainly secondary, deciduous broad-leaved forests in the area.

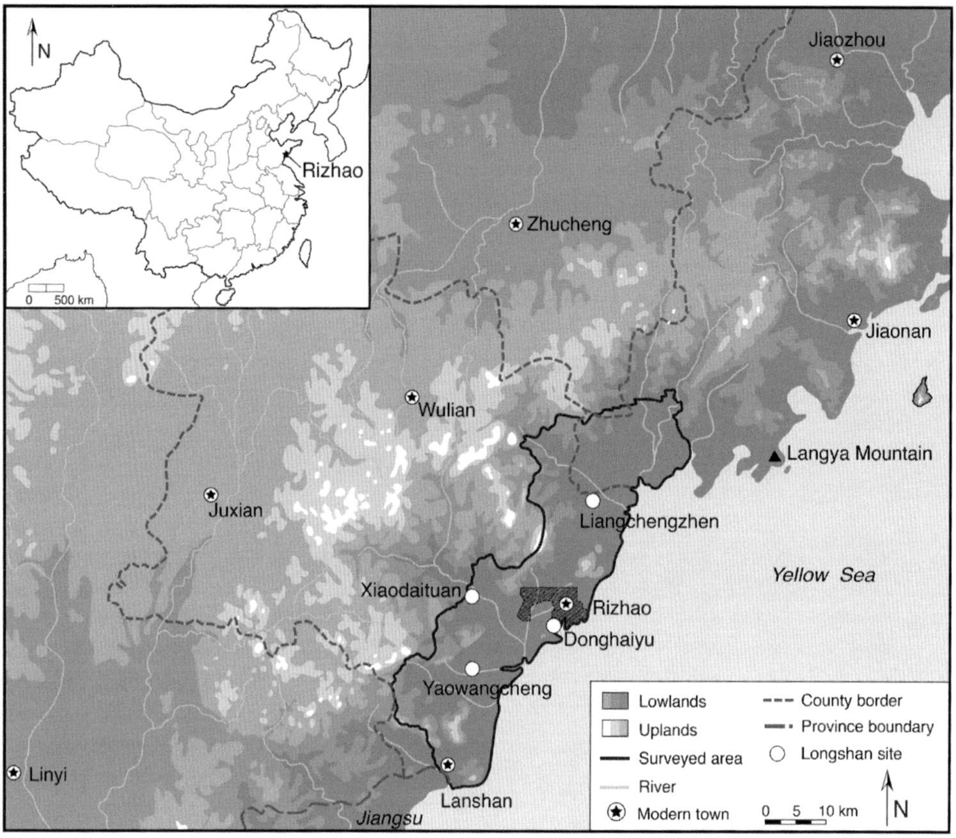

Figure 1.1. The area in coastal, southeastern Shandong Province, China, surveyed from 1995 to 2007, with known Longshan sites in the Rizhao area.

From northeast to southeast, along the arc-shaped Wulian mountain range, the coastal area is separated into three parts: north, south, and central. The central area, which includes two extensions of the Wulian Mountains (He Shan [河山] and Si Shan [丝山]), has two distinct areas of roughly equal size. Rivers flowing through each of these two areas form fan-shaped alluvial basins toward the sea. This book compares and contrasts the trajectories of settlement patterns over time in these two basins from the early Neolithic to the early imperial era (Table 1.1). Our assessment includes consideration of variation in local environments and possible differences in subsistence practices for the northern and southern basins. The agricultural and fishing industries in the Rizhao area today are quite developed. Currently Rizhao produces the most tea in northern China. Other important crops are wheat, corn, rice, soybeans, sweet potatoes, and peanuts. Fishery resources include marine fish, shrimp and other shellfish, and sea cucumbers. There are a variety of rock and mineral sources, including serpentine (abundant at Suluoshu [梭罗树]), granite (at Shijiu [石臼]), and rhyolite (see Cunnar [2007, 2014], China–U.S. Cooperative Archaeological Team [2016], and Underhill et al. [2021] for research on raw materials for stone tools).

Table 1.1. The prehistoric and early historical periods of northern China that are relevant to early settlement in southeastern Shandong.

Chronological period	Phase	Subphase	Date range
Han	Eastern	—	AD 25–220
Han	Western	—	206 BC–AD 25
Qin	—	—	221–206 BC
Zhou	Eastern	Warring States	c. 475–221 BC
		Spring and Autumn	c. 771–475 BC
Zhou	Western	—	c. 1045–771 BC
Shang	Late	—	c. 1300–1045 BC
Shang	Early–Middle	—	c. 1600–1300 BC
Yueshi	—	—	c. 1800–1450 BC
Longshan	Middle–Late	—	c. [2500 2300] to [1900–1800] BC
Longshan	Early	—	c. 2500–2300 BC
Dawenkou	Late	—	c. 2500–2300 BC
Dawenkou	Early–Middle	—	c. 4200–2500 BC
Beixin	—	—	c. 5300–4200 BC

Note: There is limited information at present for the chronology of archaeological sites in southeastern Shandong. This table presents general date ranges for northern China as a whole. See the discussions of dating sites on the basis of diagnostic ceramic sherds in Chapters 1 and 2 and the interpretations for individual temporal periods in Chapters 3 and 4.

The History and Administration of the Rizhao Area

Historical records provide some information about the pre-modern settlement of the Rizhao area, although details are scarce for the early periods. Records mention the legendary Sage Rulers Yao (帝尧), Shun (舜), and Yu (禹). They also refer to an Eastern Yi or Dongyi (东夷) people who are said to have formed the dominant polities in the area before the Xia and Shang periods. Historical records are more specific for Eastern Zhou (770–221 BC). The Rizhao area was ruled by the Ju (莒国) state, followed by the Lu (鲁), Yue (越), Chu (楚), and Qin (秦) states. Our systematic regional survey, in contrast, revealed many settlements during the late Neolithic and early Bronze Age. The earliest mention of the Rizhao area is found in the ancient work *Yugong* (禹贡) (see Underhill and Fang 2004), where Rizhao is described as located in the northeastern part of an area called Xuzhou (徐州) during an era many have interpreted as equivalent to the Xia dynasty (夏代) during the second millennium BC (see L. Liu and Chen [2012], Barnes [2015], and Shelach-Lavi [2015] for more research on the Xia dynasty). During the Zhou period the Rizhao area was part of the Ju state (莒国) and later of the Chu state (楚国), followed by incorporation in the Langya Commandery (琅琊郡) of the Qin period (秦代). During Western Han (西汉) (206 BC–AD 9), Rizhao was administered by the Langya (琅琊) Prefecture and was called Haiqu County (海曲县). According to an annotation by Yan Shigu (颜师古) of the Tang dynasty (唐代) (AD 581–645) to the *Han Shu Xuan* (汉书选, *Selections of the Han histories*; Ran and Chen 1962), during the Xinmang (新莽) period (AD 9–23) Haiqu was then called Haiting (海亭). During Eastern Han (东汉) (AD 25–220), the Rizhao area was called Xihai County (西海县) and still governed by the Langya Prefecture. Our survey results also provide rich new settlement data that add to these records about the early Bronze Age.

Post-Han written records about the Rizhao area (see Editing Committee of Rizhao 1994; Chen, Zhen, and Li 2004) are more abundant and show multiple administrating units during later historical phases (Table 1.2). During the very end of the Eastern Han dynasty, Rizhao was part of the Chengyang Commandery (城阳郡) of the Ju state (莒国). During the early phase of the Jin dynasty (晋朝) (AD 266–420), Rizhao was part of Chengyang Commandery (城阳郡) in the Qingzhou (青州) area, and later it was controlled by the Dongguan Commandery (东莞郡) of Xuzhou (徐州). Rizhao County was established during the Jin (金朝) dynastic period (AD 1115–1234). Our survey region lies within roughly the same area. During the Ming (明代) and early Qing (清代) dynastic periods, Rizhao was under the administration of Ju (莒), Qingzhou (青州), and the Shandong provincial government. In 1730, the eighth year of Emperor Yongzheng (雍正), Rizhao was managed directly by Ju Prefecture (莒州) (Chen, Zhang, and Li 2004:359–360).

During the Republican era (中华民国时期) (AD 1912–1949), the modern city of Rizhao was part of the Jiaozhou (胶州) District. In 1940 the Communist Anti-Japanese Democratic Government of Rizhao was established. After the founding of the People's Republic of China in 1949, Rizhao was administered by Yishui (沂水), Jiaozhou (胶州), and then Linyi (临沂) City. In 1984, the Shijiugang administrative office (石臼港办事处) of Linyi was established. In 1985, this administrative district merged with Rizhao County and became the new Rizhao City. Since 1989, it has been a prefecture-level city (Editing Committee of Rizhao 1994:44). The archaeological site of Liangchengzhen, the initial focus of our regional survey, is located within the modern town with the same name. The site is currently under the administration of the Donggang District (东港区) of Rizhao City, and the area borders Jiaonan County (胶南县) to the north. During China's Republican period Liangchengzhen was governed in part by Jiaozhou County. After 1949, Liangchengzhen was administered by Qingdao (青岛) City. It is said that there was a period when the town was divided into two parts, separately governed by Jiaonan and Rizhao. Later the town became known as Liangchengzhen, with a meaning in Chinese referring to the two former parts.

Characteristics of the Modern City of Rizhao

The modern city of Rizhao is known for the port of Shijiusuo (石臼所), one of the best seaports in northern China for shipping to other cities in Shandong, such as Qingdao and Yantai (烟台) in the north, Lianyungang (连云港) and Shanghai (上海) in the south, and to ports overseas. Today Rizhao's railways and expressways are important transportation routes from eastern China to areas farther west. Historical records mention the significance of Rizhao as a location along roadways during different periods. According to local chronicles, during the Ming (明朝) (AD 1368–1644) and Qing (清朝) (AD 1644–1911) eras two official roads (官道) included Rizhao, linking it to other areas of these realms. One of these roads connected Rizhao to the city of Zhucheng (诸城) at the border of Zhucheng County; the other to the south connected with the border of a city called Ganyu (赣榆). The records state that

Table 1.2. Administrative units governing the Rizhao area after the Han period ended in AD 221 and before Shandong Province was established in 1928.

Era	Date range (AD)	Administrative unit	Established (AD)
Republic Period	1912–1949	Langya (琅琊) Prefecture	1925
Republic Period	1912–1949	Jiaodong (胶东) Prefecture	1913
Qing Dynasty (清代)	1644–1911	Yizhou (沂州) Prefecture	1730, 8th year of Emperor Yongzheng (雍正)
		Zhili (直隶) Prefecture	Unknown
		Ju (莒) Prefecture	Unknown
		Qingzhou (青州) Prefecture	Unknown
Ming Dynasty (明代)	1368–1644	Ju (莒) Prefecture	Unknown
		Qingzhou (青州) Prefecture	Unknown
Yuan Dynasty (元代)	1279–1368	Ju (莒) Prefecture	Unknown
		Yi (沂) Prefecture	Unknown
Jin Dynasty (金代)	1115–1234	Rizhao County (日照县) established as part of Ju (莒) Prefecture	1184, 24th year of Emperor Dading (大定), regnal title of Emperor Shizong
Song Dynasty (宋代)	960–1279	Mi (密) Prefecture of Jingdongdong (京东东)	Unknown
		Rizhao Township (日照镇) established as part of Ju County (莒县) and then Jiaoxi County (胶西县)	1087, Yuanyou (元祐), Emperor Zhezong
Five Dynasties (五代) Period	907–960	Gaomi (高密) Commandery in Mi (密) Prefecture, part of Henan (河南)	Unknown

Continued

TABLE 1.2 CONTINUED.

Era	Date range (AD)	Administrative unit	Established (AD)
Tang Dynasty (唐代)	618–907	Gaomi (高密) Commandery in Mi (密) Prefecture, part of Henan (河南)	Unknown
Sui Dynasty (隋代)	581–618	Langya (琅琊) Commandery in Yi (沂) Prefecture	
Six Dynasties (六朝) Period	220–589	Yitang (义塘) Commandery in Ju (莒) Prefecture	Northern Zhou (北州) phase
		Yitang (义塘) Commandery in southern Qingzhou (青州) Prefecture	Northern Qi (北齐) phase
		Dongwu (东武) Commandery in Liangxiang County (梁乡县) of Jiao (胶州) Prefecture and	Northern Wei (北魏) phase
		Dongwan (东莞) Commandery of south Qingzhou (青州) Prefecture	529, 2nd year of Yongan (永安), Emperor of Xiaozhuang in Northern Wei

the road was vital as both north–south and east–west transportation routes from Shijiusuo (石臼所) in the east to Ju County (莒县) in the west. This road then linked Rizhao to the capitals of districts in Shandong in the northwest and to Linyi (临沂) and Yanzhou (兖州) in the southeast. The Ming and Qing records also mention two smaller roads, one from the port of Taoluo (涛雒) to Pingshang (坪上) (now located in Junan County [莒南县]) and the other from the port of Lanshan (岚山) to Pingshang. Seafood and salt were important coastal products transported here in exchange for various external goods. By the 1920s there were four provincial roads to Rizhao. One road connected Jiaoxian to Lanshantou (岚山头) (through Liangchengzhen), Taoluo, and Andongwei (安东卫). The second road connected Linyi, Jufeng (巨峰), and Taoluo. The third connected Zhucheng, Liangchengzhen, and Rizhao, while the fourth connected Rizhao to Juxian (莒县) by way of Shuqi (竖旗), Sanzhuang (三庄), and Shentuan (沈疃) (Editing Committee of Rizhao 1994:205–206). Today, provincial highways No. 335 and No. 334 and the Rizhao expressway traverse along the Futuan (傅疃河) and Chao (潮河) Rivers. National Highway No. 204 and the Tongsan Expressway (同三高速公路) parallel the coast and link the northern coastal basin, including Liangchengzhen, with the southern basin. In later chapters we discuss the possibility of such transportation routes serving as important lines of communication as early as the Longshan period.

History of Research in the Area

Even before our 1995–2007 collaborative archaeological survey, the diverse and rich cultural heritage of the Rizhao area had been evident to scholars for quite some time. One famous native of Rizhao was the epigrapher Xu Han (许瀚), who lived during the late Qing dynastic and early Republican period (Yuan 1983). Xu Han's influence on later scholarship about Chinese culture has been immense, including on the work of Wang Xiantang (王献唐) (see S. Wang 1994). Wang Xiantang and Fu Sinian (傅斯年) carried out the first archaeological survey in the Rizhao area during the spring of 1934 (Fang 2009).

This inaugural research in southeastern Shandong was inspired in part by initial excavations at Longshan sites farther north in the Licheng area (历城区) of Jinan (济南) City at Chengziya (城子崖) and reconnaissance surveys at the town of Longshan (龙山镇). In 1930, Wang Xiantang, the secretary of the Shandong Ancient Relics Committee (山东古迹研究会), and Fu Sinian, dean of the Institute of History and Philology at the Academia Sinica (中研院史语所), began planning their archaeological research in the Rizhao area. Scholars Wang Xiantang, Li Ji (李济), and Dong Zuobin (董作宾) also assisted with arrangements. The survey was carried out by Wang Xiang (王湘) and Qi Yanpei (祁延霈), also of the Institute of History and Philology at the Academia Sinica. Records differ about the total duration and dates of this pioneering survey, but one can conclude it lasted roughly two months. The records of Wang Xiantang and Fu Sinian state that the survey lasted two months and two days and was completed by 23 May 1934 (Y. Li 2005). If so, the survey would have begun around 20 March 1934. Newly discovered letters, however, state that Wang Xiang and Qi Yanpei conducted their survey from 22 April to 5 May 1934. The specific dates cannot be resolved, but it is possible Wang and Qi continued their survey in Jiaoxian County (胶县) and Zhucheng County (诸城县) northward along the coastline and returned to Jinan from Qingdao. Another possibility is that Wang and Qi began their survey at Qingdao instead of Jinan, traveling all the way down to Rizhao and then north back to Jinan.

The archaeological survey by Wang and Qi was one of the very few conducted in China before 1949 and resulted in the discovery of Liangchengzhen and several other important sites: Dantu (丹土), Yaowangcheng (尧王城), Anjialing (安家岭), Linzitou (林子头), Chengzicun (城子村), Dawacun (大洼村), Taizhuang (台庄), Xiaonuozhuang (小挪庄), Chouqiyuan (臭杞园), Qinguanzhuang (秦官庄), Liujialou (刘家楼), and Langyatai (琅玡台). Four of these sites, in addition to Liangchengzhen (Dantu, Yaowangcheng, Anjialing, and Linzitou), were investigated by our team (see the discussions in Chapter 3). This first survey also was important for the history of archaeology in China as the motivation for the first excavation at Liangchengzhen.

In early May 1936 the Academia Sinica's Institute of History and Philology (in Nanjing) prepared to excavate at Liangchengzhen. The work was directed by Liang Siyong (梁思永) and implemented by Yin Da (尹达, whose original name is Liu Yao [刘燿]), and Qi Yanpei (祁延霈). The fieldwork took place from 17 May to 22 June, first in the northern part of Wawucun (瓦屋村) village and then on the east side of the earthen mound Dagudui (大孤堆) thought to be a Han tomb (Editing Committee of Rizhao 1994:44). This important early work resulted in the discovery of fifty-nine burials identified as belonging to the Longshan culture. They contained many pottery vessels, stone tools, and other artifacts. During the second year, the team completed much of the excavation report (Y. Li 2005), but unfortunately Japanese aggression in north China after 7 June 1937 prevented publication. Some archaeological remains were destroyed during the war and some were transported to the Nanjing Museum (南京博物院), but Nanjing (南京) City suffered tremendous damage during the next eight years of the War of Resistance Against Japan (抗日战争). The entire Institute of History and Philology was moved to Taiwan, including many of the recovered artifacts from Liangchengzhen and the unpublished excavation report.

For quite some time only general summaries about the results of the 1936 Liangchengzhen excavation were available (S. Liang 1954, 1959; Yin 1955). In 1985 the Nanjing Museum published a catalogue of pottery vessels recovered from Liangchengzhen (Nanjing Museum 1985). The political separation, however, has long delayed publication of the final report. A major breakthrough took place in 2009 when the Oriental Archaeology Research Center at Shandong University published *Research on the Liangchengzhen Site* (Luan 2009). With the consent of the Institute of History and Philology, Academia Sinica, in Taipei, Taiwan, this book included Liu Yao's *Prehistoric Sites in the Vicinity of the Liangchengzhen Site in Rizhao, Shandong* (Y. Li 2009). This was the first major archaeological publication about the Rizhao area in seventy years.

After 1949, several more archaeological surveys were organized by the Shandong Provincial Office for the Protection of Cultural Relics (山东省文物管理处), the History Department at Shandong University (山东大学历史系), the Linyi Cultural Affairs Bureau (临沂地区文管会), and the Rizhao Cultural Affairs Office (日照市文化局). During the spring and summer of 1954, the Shandong Provincial Office for the Protection of Cultural Relics conducted a survey at Liangchengzhen and several other nearby sites, including Yaowangcheng, Dataoyuan (大桃园), Dantu, Liujialou, Dawacun (大洼村), and Tianjiayuan (田家园) (M. Yuan 1955). Later it was evident that this significant early survey was arranged by the Provincial Office's director Zhang Jingzhai (张敬斋) and vice director Wang Xiantang (Fang 2009). Our survey area includes the sites of Yaowangcheng, Dataoyuan, Dantu, and Liujialou, in addition to Liangchengzhen. Then, from 1957 to 1963, another significant survey by archaeologists at Shandong University attracted much international attention. Several reports were published in *Kaogu Xuebao* (考古学报), *Kaogu* (考古), *Wenwu* (文物), and other national journals. In 1958, the Provincial Office carried out comprehensive exploration and test excavations at Liangchengzhen (Shandong Provincial Office 1960).

Another important chapter in the history of archaeological research in the Rizhao area involves the contributions of Liu Dunyuan (刘敦愿) and his student, Zhang Zhihan (张知寒). During this period of fieldwork in the 1950s by Liu and Zhang, Liu was teaching in the History Department at Shandong University, located at the time in Qingdao City. On their own time they conducted an archaeological survey in the Rizhao area. Their most remarkable achievements were during their spring breaks in 1955 and 1957 (see D. Liu 1956, 1958a, 1958b). Liu's report (D. Liu 1972) on the famous jade *ben* (锛) adze with *taotie* (饕餮) animal mask from Liangchengzhen is still highly regarded across the world. His later work (D. Liu 1988) on the rare jade objects at Liangchengzhen enriched research on Longshan culture in Shandong. Researchers found many jade objects at Dantu in Wulian County, some of which date back to late Dawenkou (大汶口), the period preceding Longshan (Shandong Provincial Office and Shandong Provincial Museum 1959). Later, scholars deposited some of these jade objects in the Shandong Provincial Museum (山东省博物馆) (see B. Yang 1996).

Other significant early archaeological fieldwork in the Rizhao area informed later teams such as ours. It was fortunate that during the late phase of the Cultural Revolution when little archaeological fieldwork was permitted, excavations by the Shandong Provincial Museum took place at Donghaiyu (东海峪) in 1973 and 1975. A team from Shandong University, including Cai Fengshu (蔡凤书) and Yu Haiguang (于海广), participated in the later excavation and subsequently prepared a pioneering report (Donghaiyu Excavation Team 1976). From the winter of 1978 to the spring of 1979 the Cultural Heritage Administration Office of Linyi conducted test excavations at Yaowangcheng (Linyi District Office and Rizhao County Library 1985). Their 200 m^2 excavation revealed forty-nine small graves containing pottery vessels and also house foundations with walls constructed of adobe, similar to those found during excavations at Donghaiyu. Another important discovery at Yaowangcheng was a piece of copper, possibly indicative of bronze smelting during the Longshan period (Rizhao City Library and Linyi District Committee 1986). During the 1980s, archaeological surveys focused more on Longshan sites in the Rizhao area. The next major publication (Rizhao City Library and Linyi District Committee 1986) describes nine sites, including Xilinzitou (西林子头), a site discovered in 1934. Another significant development for the history of archaeology in the Rizhao area occurred in 1977 when Liangchengzhen was designated a major provincial historical and cultural site (省级文物保护单位) by the Shandong provincial government.

Although knowledge of the prehistoric period in the Rizhao area was greatly expanded through fieldwork from the 1930s to the 1980s, few early Bronze Age sites were identified. The early Bronze Age in the Rizhao area was largely unknown, despite major advances in knowledge in other areas of China. Before our survey the only known site from the Yueshi (岳石) period, regarded as roughly contemporary with the Xia dynasty, was Songzhucun (松竹村) (Yang, Hu, and Xu 1990). In 1934 Yin Da perceptively remarked that it was important to understand whether settlements from the Shang dynasty were present in the Rizhao area or not (see Fang 2009). In the 1980s more information was available about the location of Zhou period sites, but few had been excavated (Yang, Hu, and Xu 1990). Two burials containing bronze vessels provided the most information about the Zhou period at that time. In 1976 and 1983, excavators discovered two burials at Guheya (崮河崖) in the Donggang District of Rizhao. There were fourteen bronze vessels in burial M1, forming a set (two tripods, *ding* [鼎] and *li* [鬲]; a jar, *hu* [壶]; a basin, *pen* [盆]; a plate, *pan* [盘]; and a spouted vessel, *yi* [匜]). Inscriptions, with characters missing, on the rims of four *li* tripods (釐伯[ ]女子乍宝鬲, "Precious *li* made for the daughter of Libo") indicated a link to the ancient Lai state (莱国) mentioned in historical texts. Scholars estimated the date of burial M1 as late Western Zhou to the early Spring and Autumn era (see Table 1.1; S. Yang 1984; see F. Li [2006] and F. Li and Liang [2018] for additional information about the Lai state).

During the 1990s and later, more archaeological surveys were conducted in China by local cultural heritage administrative units. An especially important development was the beginning of national cultural relics surveys. The second survey of this kind yielded especially important results, although the full results were not reported until publication of *Atlas of Cultural Relics in China, Shandong Volume* (中国文物地图集, 山东分册) (China Cultural Heritage Bureau 2007). According to this book, there are approximately eighty-five medium-sized and large sites dating from the Neolithic to the Han period in the coastal region of southeastern Shandong (seventy in the Donggang and Lanshan Districts, eight in Wulian County, and seven in Jiaonan City). Other important developments were additional survey and excavation at Yaowangcheng (Shandong Archaeological Team 1994; Shandong Archaeological Team, Shandong Provincial Institute, and Rizhao Bureau 2015) and excavations at Dantu (see Y. Liu and X. Wang 2002; Shandong Provincial Institute of Archaeology 2001). Shandong University also conducted important fieldwork at Neolithic sites in other areas of Shandong, including at the Longshan settlement of Yinjiacheng (Shandong University 1990).

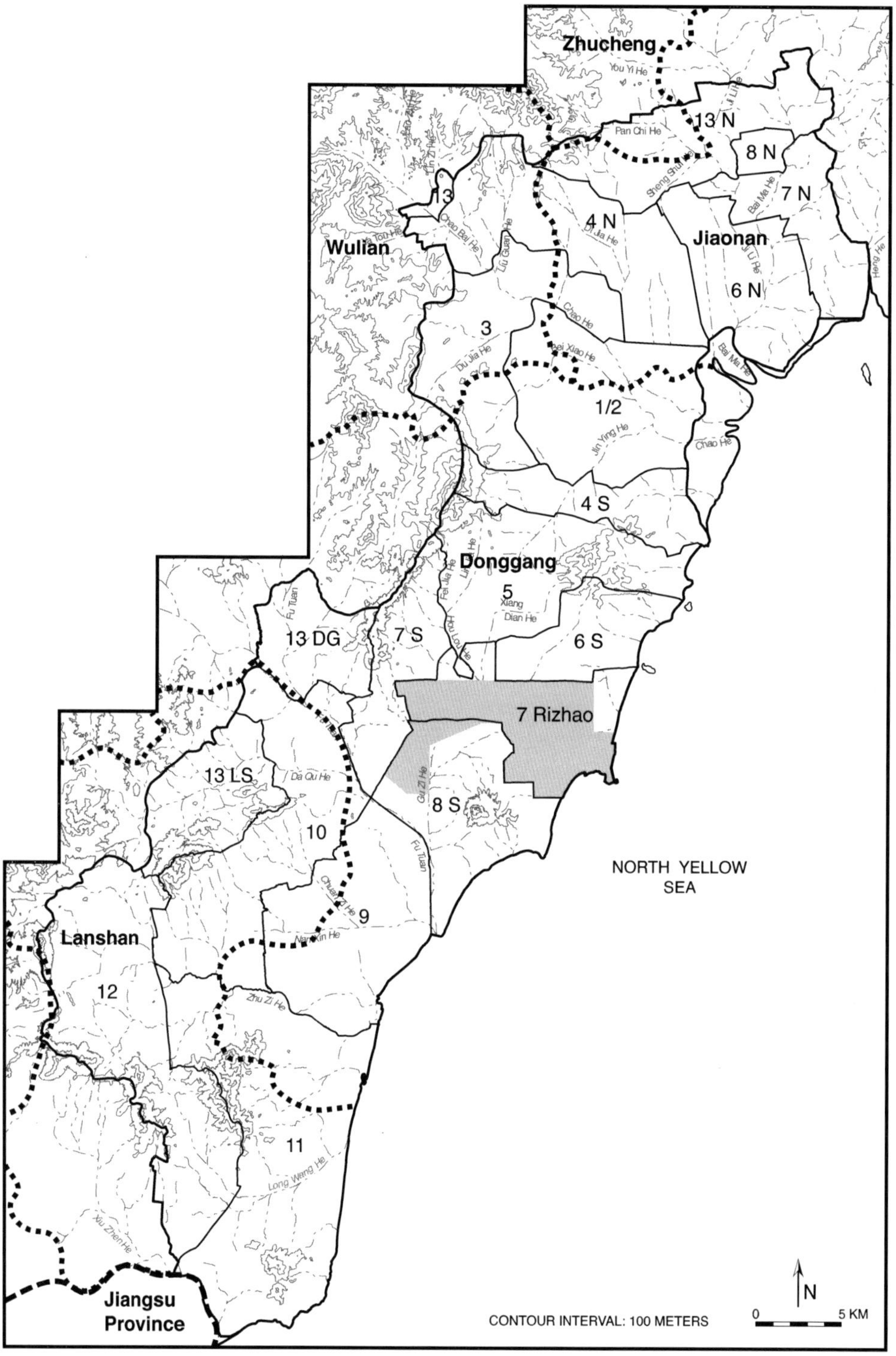

FIGURE 1.2. The surveyed region in coastal, southeastern Shandong, showing administrative district boundaries and the areas covered in each of the thirteen field seasons.

Well before the onset of our collaborative survey, the significance of Shandong archaeology was clear to English readers, thanks to K.-C. Chang (1987), former professor of anthropology at Yale University. Chang's valuable book mentions the important late Dawenkou site of Donghaiyu (Tung-hai-yu, 东海峪) in the Rizhao (Jih-chao) area (Chang 1987:158), but his discussion focuses on other sites in Shandong and neighboring areas. For the Longshan period, Chang mentions the significance of the 1936 Liangchengzhen excavation and notes the quality of its black pottery vessels in comparison to those from other areas. As early as 1939, scholars recognized the distinctiveness and significance of the Longshan cultural remains in coastal Shandong (Chang 1987:246).

As we describe in this volume, our project provided new data that shed light on the occupation of southeastern Shandong during the prehistoric and early historical eras. We identified evidence for Beixin period (Table 1.1) sites for the first time. We also expanded the archaeological record for the Dawenkou period (see Chapter 4). We documented the large size of Liangchengzhen relative to other Longshan sites in the northern sector of our survey region and greatly expanded the archaeological record for the Longshan period in southeastern Shandong. Specific time ranges for the earlier versus later Longshan phases continue to be debated (evident in Table 1.1), including comparison of dates for the end of the Dawenkou period and the beginning of the Longshan period. We characterized Longshan period sites as Early Longshan or Middle Longshan using diagnostic ceramics (see Chapter 4). Our survey revealed the large size of Yaowangcheng, discovered multiple smaller centers, and identified different patterns of Longshan settlement for the northern and southern sectors.

We discovered relatively few sites dating to the Yueshi and Shang periods (see Chapter 4). We found many Zhou period sites and our results revealed a dramatic increase in settlements by Eastern Zhou and early imperial eras, with evidence of increased efforts for control by state authorities. At the outset of our fieldwork in 1995, our team agreed that our primary goals were to understand the regional context of Liangchengzhen and to investigate the development of complex societies in Shandong. The method of systematic, full-coverage regional survey enabled us to provide an expanded long-term perspective, documenting settlements in southeastern Shandong well before, and after, the occupation of Liangchengzhen.

The following chapters provide a detailed account of the results from each of the thirteen seasons (Figure 1.2) of our systematic, full-coverage regional survey in southeastern Shandong from 1995 to 2007. This book complements our publication in Chinese (Fang et al. 2012) and is a significant expansion of results provided in English by Underhill et al. (2008). This report also places the multi-year survey project in context by discussing the development of survey projects in other areas of China and relevant research in southeastern Shandong after 2007. Three team members (Fang, Feinman, and Nicholas) completed the survey of the northern coastal basin (see Feinman, Nicholas, and Fang 2010; Fang, Feinman, and Nicholas 2015; Feinman, Fang, and Nicholas 2019a, 2019b). There were excavations at Liangchengzhen from 1998 to 2001 (Luan et al. 2004, 2021; Luan 2009, 2019; China–U.S. Cooperative Archaeological Team 2016; Underhill et al. 2021; see also Druc et al. 2018, 2021) and again in 2018 (Shandong University and Shandong Provincial Institute of Archaeology 2021). Subsequent chapters mention relatively recent excavations at other sites in southeastern Shandong as well.

Here we update the published results of eleven years of survey (Fang et al. 2008; Underhill et al. 2008) and further reflect on the development of complex societies as expressed by Fang et al. (2012) after thirteen years of survey. Along with information on sites discovered during two additional survey seasons (2006 and 2007), this report provides revised site-size hierarchies that resulted from the discovery of additional large sites and a reconsideration of some of our earlier site-size estimates. As we gained more experience with the conditions of the local landscape and their effect on the visibility of archaeological remains, we realized that during the early years of the survey we had been at times too conservative in defining the limits of larger sites that are now adjacent to or covered by modern towns, or are near larger rivers where more recent eluviation has made surface ceramics harder to find (see Chapter 4).

Chapter 2 describes the specific methods we used to identify, record, and assess archaeological sites in the Rizhao area. The method of systematic, full-coverage regional survey allowed us to identify many sites from the prehistoric and early historical periods during our thirteen seasons of fieldwork. The survey methodology was taught to the team by Gary Feinman and Linda Nicholas, who had extensive survey experience in Oaxaca, Mexico (e.g., Feinman and Nicholas 2013; Feinman 2017). At the same time, all the American participants learned from the local archaeological expertise of Cai Fengshu, Fang Hui, Yu Haiguang, and Luan Fengshi. It was possible to adapt the survey methods pioneered by more than one team in Mexico to the particular conditions of southeastern Shandong. The detailed site descriptions in Chapter 3 are drawn from the team's field observations and additional analyses led by Feinman, Nicholas, and Fang. This chapter provides descriptions for sites that are 10 ha or larger in at least one period of occupation, sites that have cultural layers or other physical remains of ancient features, and smaller sites with significant characteristics. For a complete listing of all sites discovered during the 1995–2007 survey, see Fang et al. (2012). Nicholas prepared the initial maps for every site in the field and completed them for publication. She also prepared the tables in Chapter 4. Chapter 4 considers our survey results in light of relatively recent work in southeastern Shandong and elsewhere in China on the development of complex societies.

Although the first survey season, from 1995 to 1996, was only twenty-two days in duration, it demonstrated the expected effectiveness of systematic, full-coverage survey for the Rizhao area. In an area of 38 km^2 we found more than fifty sites, thirty of which had Longshan period remains. We began to notice a pattern of clusters of sites of different sizes. Also, we established that Liangchengzhen was the largest site in the northern part of the coastal basin. From 1996 to 2000, we expanded the survey coverage to more than 400 km^2, including areas administered by Qingdao City, and discovered more than 750 sites, many of which had occupations dating to the Longshan period. By our thirteenth season in 2007, having covered an area of more than 1,400 km^2, we had discovered a large corpus of sites from the Longshan period and earlier (Beixin and Dawenkou) and later periods (Zhou and Han).

CHAPTER TWO

The Value of Systematic, Full-coverage Regional Survey

Systematic, full-coverage regional survey is a method that has provided valuable data on the development of complex societies in several areas of the world (Sanders, Parsons, and Santley 1979; Wright 1986; Fish and Kowalewski 1989; Kowalewski et al. 1989; Feinman and Nicholas 1990, 1999, 2013, 2017; Kowalewski 1990, 2008; Marcus and Flannery 1996; Billman and Feinman 1999; Blanton et al. 1999; Wilkinson 2000; Feinman 2001, 2015; Blanton 2004; Spencer and Redmond 2004). It has facilitated diverse methods of regional analysis for investigating the development of complex societies (Kantner 2008; Kowalewski 2008) and urban landscapes (M. Smith 2014). Other survey teams in China have recognized the value of this method of surveying entire landscapes (Murowchick 1997; L. Liu and Chen 2001a, 2006, 2012; Shelach-Lavi 2015), which has resulted in the discovery of sites in unexpected locations. In southeastern Shandong we often found sites at higher elevations than we had expected at the beginning of the survey.

At the time we began the survey in 1995, reconnaissance survey methods focusing on the identification of large sites in alluvial zones were predominant in China. Since then, several survey teams have provided abundant new data on changes in settlement patterns during the Neolithic period and early Bronze Age. These areas include the Huan He (洹河) River area of eastern Henan (Huan He River Team 1998), the Chifeng (赤峰) area of northeastern China (Shelach 1998, 1999; Chifeng Project 2003, 2011; Linduff, Drennan, and Shelach 2004; Peterson and Drennan 2005; Peterson et al. 2014), the Yi-Luo River (伊洛河) area of west-central Henan (Lee 2004; L. Liu et al. 2004, 2019), the Qixing River (七星河) valley of Shaanxi (Zhouyuan Archaeological Team 2005), the Xue River (薛河) valley of south-central Shandong (National Museum of China and Shandong University 2016), and the Jiaodong Peninsula (胶东半岛) (F. Li and Z. Liang 2018). There is growing interest in regional analysis (Luan, Fang, and Jin 2002; Xu, Chen, and Zhao 2004; Peterson and Drennan 2005; Drennan and Dai 2010; Peterson et al. 2014). Systematic regional survey has provided valuable new information on population nucleation and regional-level settlement shifts, the development of settlement hierarchies, and the clustering of settlements. Such foundational data are essential for evaluating debates about the development of complex societies in different areas of China that involve such issues as modes of rulership and governance, state formation, and the nature of urbanism (see L. Liu 2004, 2009; Shelach and Jaffe 2014; Underhill 2017).

More systematic regional surveys in northern China should shed light on variation in the nature of sociopolitical change, given research in other parts of the world such as Mesopotamia (Rothman 2001, 2004), the American Midwest (Emerson 1997; Cobb 2003), and Mesoamerica (Blanton et al. 1993, 1996). Within broad areas, we should not be surprised to find significant regional variation in the ways that complex societies were developed and organized (Feinman and Marcus 1998; Stein 1998, 2001; Wright 2005; Underhill 2013). An assessment of the specific strategies that were used to increase power requires large-scale regional data to estimate the nature and extent of sociopolitical units over time. Only with such data can the basis of change in intercommunity relations begin to be addressed.

Systematic, full-coverage regional survey is also an essential means for investigating population nucleation and associated settlement shifts at the regional scale (Feinman and Nicholas 2018). Through this approach, it becomes possible to examine both the growth of single settlements and the range of variation in political landscapes. Although most authors define cities as single settlements (see M. Smith 2003), other scholars (McIntosh 1991, 1999, 2005; McIntosh and McIntosh 2003) argue that complexes of settlements constitute urbanism, as in the Middle Niger of western Africa, and other areas. There is agreement, however, that investigating a city requires consideration of the rural areas surrounding it (e.g., Blanton 1976; M. Smith 2014).

Given that differences in survey methods affect the intensity of coverage (Cowgill 2004:543), this chapter presents the methods we used in the Rizhao area survey in detail. We explain our methods for identifying sites in a broad, contiguous area and argue that survey data are crucial for illuminating possible control strategies, changes in sociopolitical organization, and degrees of settlement nucleation. We hope the information about our methods will be useful for future surveys in Shandong and other areas. In each year of our survey we used the same methods for locating, collecting, and recording sites. We followed the basic procedures used in the Valley of Oaxaca, Mexico, settlement pattern surveys (see Kowalewski et al. 1989; Feinman and Nicholas 1990, 2013), with some modifications for the local conditions in Shandong.

Our survey region lies within two coastal basins ringed and physiographically defined by craggy mountains in southeastern Shandong Province (see Figure 1.1). These relatively flat basins comprise low slopes and floodplains that hug a series of rivers that descend from the rocky ridges to the coast of the north Yellow Sea. These two basins are distinguished from the broader floodplains to the south across the modern political boundary in Jiangsu Province and from the hilly, but less bounded, terrain to the north near the port city of Qingdao. Below we describe the methods that we adapted for the Rizhao survey region.

General Survey Methods for the Rizhao Area

Throughout our survey we consistently used the same methods for locating, collecting, and recording sites. We conducted the surveys in the fall and early winter when there were few crops in fields and many fields were fallow. During these seasons the visibility of surface artifacts and buried profiles was optimal. Ceramic sherds and stone tools also were visible in areas where winter wheat and cabbage were grown. Our crews covered as much of the landscape as possible, including terrain as diverse as terraced fields, apple orchards, rice fields, vegetable gardens, shrimp ponds, piedmont ridges, and alluvial areas. We found sites in all

Figure 2.1. Crew members survey the Dantu site in Year 1 of the regional survey.

these areas. Some locations were impossible to survey, such as high slopes and mountaintops; there we surveyed up to the base of the mountains where the steep slopes began. In many cases we decided not to survey alluvial areas between levees on either side of large river channels that flooded repeatedly. Occasionally some areas were inaccessible, such as orchards within locked gates, rock quarries on steep mountain slopes, slopes with large tea plants, and places inside newly constructed walls enclosing factories. In those cases, we walked along the edges of the features to check for any openings or surface remains that could provide some information about the area.

We covered the terrain systematically to ensure that the area covered during each season was contiguous with previously surveyed areas; we walked soggy rice fields, tightly packed apple orchards, and forested hills. The survey crews averaged five to six people walking across the landscape in a line and spaced roughly 50 m apart, although the distance between crew members fluctuated depending on the kind of terrain and artifact density. We found that crews of three to four also are effective, but seven or more can be unwieldy. When we trained new people, each inexperienced person walked with an experienced crew member.

On survey, crew members check the immediate ground surface while frequently looking for the two people on either side to keep an even pace with them and to cover the area for which they are responsible. The person in the center of the line walks with a map recording sites and marking off the surveyed areas (this was Linda Nicholas). The mapper keeps track of where the crew members are walking—especially the two individuals on the ends. These two people must study the landscape carefully so they can follow their previous passes during subsequent transects. This work is made easier by following natural features on maps, such as river channels, as much as possible to define one end of a given transect (Figure 2.1).

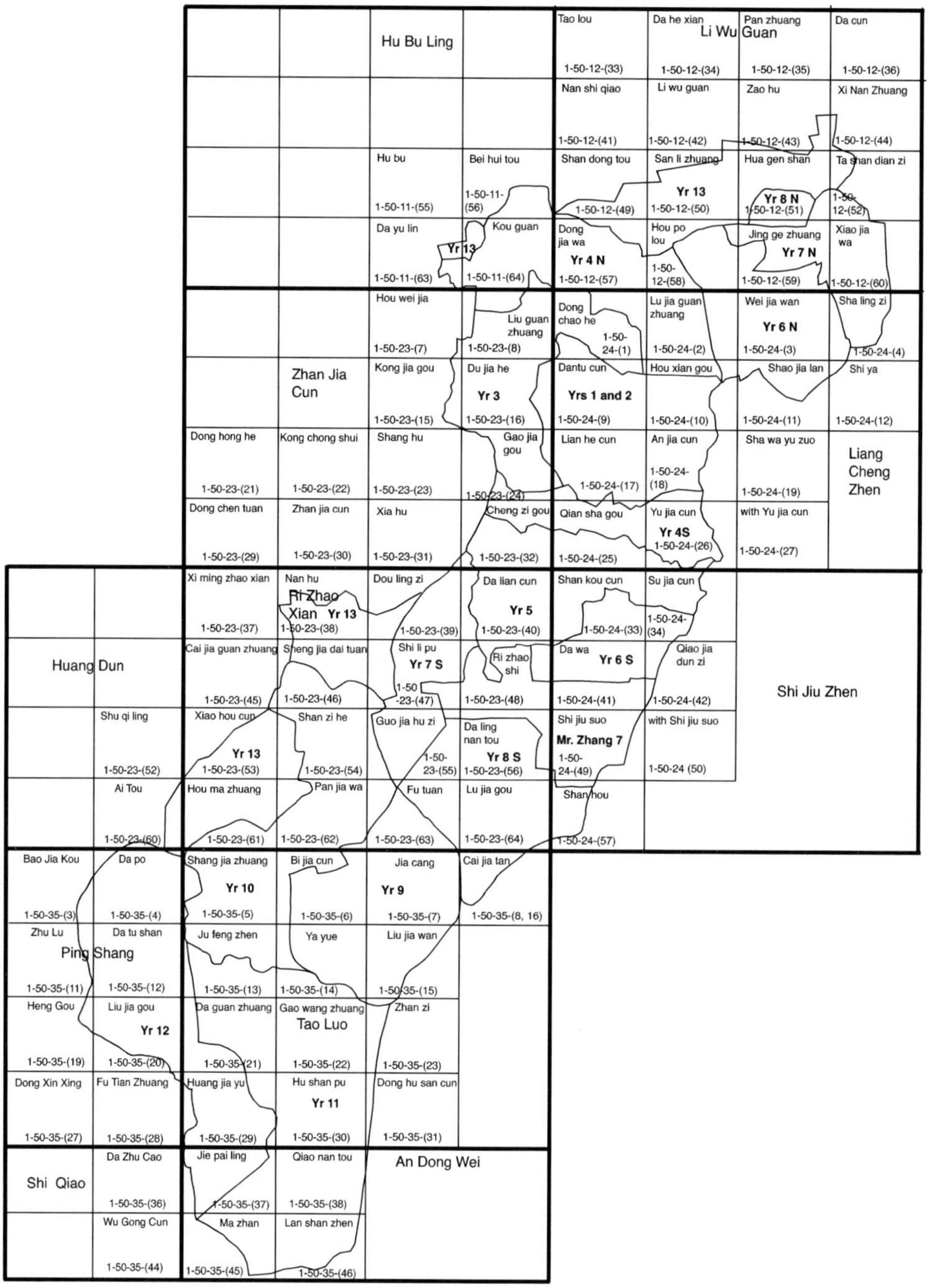

FIGURE 2.2. Schematic key for the topographic maps used on survey in southeastern Shandong Province, China. Bold lines indicate 1:50,000 scale maps and thin lines indicate 1:10,000 scale maps. The 1:50,000 maps are labeled by name, and the 1:10,000 maps are labeled by name and index number. The surveyed areas are shown by year.

Crew members sometimes become separated in heavily dissected terrain, orchards, villages, tree-covered slopes, and other places with physical obstacles that can limit visibility. It is important then to immediately look for at least one of the two people walking on either side and wait when necessary. While waiting, the crew members try to place themselves in an easily visible location, such as the highest spot on a road or other open area. The survey crew all carried whistles for getting the attention of other team members, especially helpful on windy days (cell phones were not yet widely available before 2007).

It is not possible to cover every inch of ground, so each person scans areas on his or her transects looking for the most likely places where sites might be located, such as slightly raised areas in otherwise flat landscapes, and ashy or gray soil. We also checked places where sherds are likely to be most visible, such as fallow areas in fields, pits dug for storing cabbage, exposed stratigraphic cuts in areas with road construction, and areas with newly constructed housing. When feasible we asked local people about sites near their communities. Sometimes they were aware of relatively large sites in the vicinity.

We were given permission to use 1:10,000 scale topographic maps from the Shandong Bureau of Survey and Mapping (Figure 2.2; the location of all maps listed in Chapter 3 are shown in this figure). This scale (1 cm equals 100 m) allows precise placement of site locations during the survey. Most of these maps had 2.5 m contour lines. Some maps with large areas of low relief had 1 m contour lines, and those with mountainous terrain had 5 m contours. These topographic maps were printed in the late 1980s. In most areas, changes in the surveyed locations since then were not significant and did not impede our survey. In other areas, though, some towns had expanded or new roads were present. In those instances, Nicholas drew the new buildings and roads directly on the maps.

Every evening we planned the transects for the next day, building in flexibility to adjust to the nature of the sites that were discovered. Nicholas placed the map for the day on a solid board approximately 50 by 60 cm, holding it in place with large binder clips. We found that around 3 km is a workable length for each transect, especially if the people on the ends of the crew lines do not have clearly defined passes to follow. At the beginning of each pass the mapper discusses the intended pass with the crew, especially the two people on the ends. It is helpful for each person to know what to expect about the terrain ahead. At the beginning of each pass, the crew lines up along a prior boundary and begins the transect. At the end of each transect, the crew turns around and walks back in the opposite direction, with one end person finishing the earlier pass in reverse. At the end of that pass the person on the opposite end will then follow his or her pass.

Finding and Investigating Sites in the Field

We did not require a minimum quantity of surface artifacts to indicate the presence of a site. We found that in the Rizhao area a site with a single sherd on the surface could be associated with discovery of a buried deposit, or the finding of additional sherds on the return pass. At each site we checked for exposed deposits revealed by digging by farmers, riverine cuts, or recent construction. Our site descriptions (see Chapter 3) include the presence of buried cultural deposits. We did not take the time to probe each discovered site, since our goal was to cover as much of the two coastal basins as possible. The Rizhao area has experienced rapid economic development each year. When we returned for another season of survey we often found that previously surveyed areas were now under concrete. We defined a new site if there was a 100 m or larger gap between collection areas. Our system for naming sites includes abbreviations for the names of the county or district and nearest town. If we found more than one site near a town, we numbered them consecutively. For example, DG-LCZ-1, DG-LCZ-2, and DG-LCZ-3, where DG stands for Donggang (东港), the harbor district of Rizhao.

It is not possible for any survey to find every single surface sherd. Our goal was to find and define the extent of each site as much as possible. This was more feasible with relatively large sites. At small sites with sparse sherd scatters, we collected all the diagnostic ceramics that we could find. At sites with denser concentrations of ceramics, we collected the most diagnostic sherds and a representative sample of what was seen on the surface. Stone tools were not common, so we collected all those we found. Following Peterson and Drennan (2005) on the importance of ceramic density, we recorded the relative sherd density at each site as a whole or within specific areas of a site. In our experience, the relative density of surface sherds in the Rizhao area is affected by post-depositional factors such as the degree of soil erosion and farming activities over the years. We agree also with Peterson and Drennan (2005) that there may not be a one-to-one correspondence between sites and communities. There were some cases (see Chapter 3) where, because of modern buildings, collection areas with similar ceramics were separated by more than 100 m. We then made the judgment that the remains represent a single community rather than two.

For dispersed sites with sherds from only one time period, relatively large collection areas were sufficient. The mapper (Nicholas) marks locations on the map where crew members noted sherds. After finding sherds, crew members communicate with the mapper (using whistles if necessary and shouting out the time period when possible). At larger sites we collected sherds in smaller areas that we called collection areas (CA), each of which was drawn on the map. We found that a collection area of around 1 ha is useful for analytical purposes, although in practice the number and size of collections depend on the size of the site, the density of sherds, and the number of time periods represented. The crew members also inform the mapper when they are no longer finding ceramics; the mapper can then draw the site boundary on the map.

We collected at all locations with at least one diagnostic sherd and marked these locations on the map. Other researchers can refine our corpus of sites with further investigations if they wish. We systematically collected as many diagnostic sherds as possible, and all lithics, but the range of ceramic variation in southeastern Shandong is not known.

The most efficient way to collect at a large site is to identify visible surface features on the map, or that can be placed on the map, and use these features to delimit collection areas. For example, a collection area can be defined as the space between two small roads or the fields adjacent to a stream. Each collection area is given a letter designation, such as CAA, CAB, and so on. Whenever possible identified cultural layers or other features were designated as separate collection areas and marked on the map (Figure 2.3).

When small sites were discovered, our usual method was to finish a transect before giving each site a label. Crew members who found more than one site would number their bags consecutively and these would later receive a proper label. In the meantime, each location where crew members were observed collecting sherds would be marked by the mapper. For dispersed sites, in some cases, bags of sherds can later be combined if the sherds belong to the same time period and were found within 100 m of one another.

The tag on each bag was labeled with the site number, collection area (if any), time periods represented (if known before the sherds are washed), the date, and the name of the

Figure 2.3. Crew members examine a profile at DG-LCZ-3 near Liangchengzhen in Year 1 of the survey.

collector(s). For long passes with many new sites, it was better to complete some of the labeling mid-transect instead of waiting until the end.

As noted previously (see Chapter 1), our accumulated experience in understanding the visibility of sites in the local landscape led to a reexamination of the sizes of sites discovered in earlier years of the survey. For example, clusters of large sherd scatters within an 8–10 ha area around a town or in an alluvial setting that are separated by a bit more than 100 m, especially with modern buildings between the clusters, was in the past most likely one large community and not several, small, separate communities. Or if pottery was found on all four sides of a modern community, the entire location, including the inaccessible areas under pavement and modern buildings, was likely one large site instead of four separate, smaller ones.

For this report we reexamined some of the larger concentrations of sites mapped in earlier years and have combined what we then considered to be separate sites. While these changes do affect the number of sites that we consider to be primary, secondary, and tertiary centers in each period (see Chapter 4), they do not change our overall characterization of the site hierarchies and how these changed over time. There is little change to our interpretation of the Longshan settlement pattern. The more significant changes we discuss here are for Western Zhou and the Han period. The revised data, however, even more clearly underscore our published data (Fang et al. 2008; Underhill et al. 2008; Fang et al. 2012) for the patterns in the Zhou and Han periods.

Recording Site Information, Basic Lab Analysis, and Map Preparation

At the end of each day the team met to write up field notes for each site and to ensure that we had all the artifact bags for each site found that day (and none were still in a backpack). We also recorded which sites were on each map from the Shandong Bureau of Survey and Mapping and kept a list of all the field site names used to date, including map and county names. This list was typed into an electronic spreadsheet file to facilitate ceramic analysis at the end of each field season. We recorded the following information for each site: the site's name; the name of the nearest town; the date of the survey; the cultural period(s) represented; the type of environmental zone (alluvial, piedmont, or mountainous area); the physical setting (such as a low rise in a floodplain, vegetable gardens on the edge of town, or the lower slope of a piedmont ridge); a description of the soil (type, color, and estimated depth); and the type of modern land use (such as town, orchard, or fallow field).

From the map we noted the site elevation and distance to the nearest water source (such as a main river, tributary, or small stream). In addition, we recorded the relative density of sherds, the approximate site size, the presence of significant artifacts, and information about any identified cultural layers or features, such as graves. We also described the visibility of artifacts, such as whether there were sherds eroding from a stream bank or whether artifacts could be seen inside a pit dug by a farmer. It also was important to note where ground conditions hampered visibility.

After each day in the field, Nicholas used a light table to trace all sites to a clean map. Maps in the field tend to become worn, so leaving a clean copy in a hotel room safeguarded the findings. Nicholas also marked off the area surveyed every day on a 1:50,000 scale map to track our areal coverage. After the area on a map had been completely surveyed, Nicholas carefully traced all the sites on the map (including individual collection areas) onto a large piece of vellum on the light table, labeling each site and collection area. The boundaries of surveyed areas were also drawn on these tracings. After completion of the ceramic analysis, these maps were used to draw the boundary of each site for each time period.

After all the collected artifacts were carefully washed to ensure segregation by bag, it was possible to more closely examine them and identify the cultural period for each. For the ceramics, we recorded vessel form (if known), vessel part (such as rim, body, or base), type of paste (especially if unusual, such as for white wares), and the type of surface decoration. For stone tools we recorded the raw material (if known) and the form.

At the end of each field season we prepared two spreadsheets summarizing data from the survey season: a site data file and a ceramics data file. The site data file includes the basic site information from the field notebooks, including the name of the map from the Shandong Bureau and the administrative district (such as Donggang). This file has one line for each occupation period at a site (see below), which allows information specific to only one period at multicomponent sites, such as site size or presence of a cultural layer or other feature, to be recorded.

The second spreadsheet has detailed ceramic data for each site. For this file each line represents the smallest reducible detail, so the number of lines for each collection varies based on the size of the collection and the nature of the materials. For example, if the pottery in one collection consisted of five Longshan body sherds, one Early Longshan *gui* (鬶) tripod foot, one Western Zhou body sherd, one Eastern Zhou body sherd, and one Han period tile, there would be five lines in the spreadsheet for the collection. In another example, in the case of five body sherds from an unknown phase of the Longshan period, including one with sandy paste and one with cord marking, there would be three lines in the file for the collection (with three Longshan body sherds on one line). This method allowed for the maximum retrieval of information at various scales, including preparing pivot tables.

After finalizing the temporal information about each collection, the mapper records the data on the vellum maps, using a different color for each time period. Nicholas also traced principal topographic features from the original 1:10,000 scale maps, including major contour lines and rivers, to provide geographic context for the sites. For sites occupied during only one period, she used a colored pencil for that period to trace the site boundary on the vellum map. For sites with many collections, each period is represented by a colored dot inside the collection area. The respective color was then used for each period to draw a boundary around all the collections (all the collection areas together) that had ceramics from that period. The next step was to use a compensating polar planimeter to measure site size in hectares for each time period.

Nicholas prepared the final maps by reducing the tracings by 50% to a manageable size and taping the copies together so that all sites for each period could be traced onto a single large sheet of vellum. The composite maps were then further reduced to a size that could be scanned into a computer. For analytical purposes, each site was given a unique number by period (beginning with one; the sequence of numbers for any one period is independent of the sequence for other periods). This unique number was added to all sites on the composite vellum maps and is included in the site data and ceramic data files. For the final maps, Field Museum illustrator Jill Seagard used Adobe Illustrator with a drawing tablet to trace all the scanned maps into one electronic file, with elements such as topographic features and sites by time period, placed in separate layers.

In the years since the first survey in 1995 many new methods have been developed in world archaeology for recording data during survey and for preparing maps of regional settlement patterns. Continuing our same, effective methods from year to year provided consistency as we expanded our regional coverage and produced comparable results for subregions.

The Survey Process from 1995 to 2007

Year 1: 28 December 1995–12 January 1996

The first field season, described in our first report (Cai et al. 1997), in the vicinity of Liangchengzhen in the Donggang (东港) District, together with a small area in Wulian County and Jiaonan City (Table 2.1), documented that systematic regional survey was quite effective in the Rizhao area. Newly discovered Longshan sites that season included Anjialing (安家岭, DG-ANJ-1) and Xiangjiagou (相家沟, DG-XJG-1). During our initial inspection of Yaowangcheng, we hypothesized that the traces of rammed earth on an L-shaped pit wall that we noted in the northwestern corner of Yaowang village were part of an ancient city wall.

Year 2: 26 December 1996–14 January 1997

During the second field season in the Donggang District of Rizhao, the Chaohezhen (潮河镇) area of Wulian County, and the Haiqingzhen (海青镇) area of Jiaonan County, we discovered several important Longshan period sites (see Figure 2.4), including Suijiaguanzhuang (隋家官庄, DG-SJGZ-1), Wangjiayao (王家窑, WL-WJYa-10), and Wangjiayao (WL-

TABLE 2.1. Summary of the thirteen seasons of the Rizhao area survey from 1995 to 2007.

Year	Survey season dates	Area surveyed (km^2)	Focus	Major findings	Survey participants*
1	28 December 1995 to 12 January 1996	36	Liangcheng River and its branches, Beixiao and Jinyin Rivers Survey of known sites Liangchengzhen, Dantu Survey of neighboring areas	Systematic, full coverage regional survey worked well in the Rizhao area; new Longshan period sites discovered	Cai Fengshu (SDU) Yu Haiguang (SDU) Luan Fengshi (SDU) Fang Hui (SDU) Sun Chengfu (RCG) Anne Underhill (YU) Gary Feinman (UWM) Linda Nicholas (UWM) Gwen Bennett, PhD student (UCLA)
2	26 December 1996 to 14 January 1997	60	Donggang, Wulian, Jiaonan Districts; Liangcheng River area and its branches Beixiao and Jinyin Rivers	Several new Longshan, Zhou, and Han period sites discovered; a Yueshi component found at site DG-SMZ-3, (Shimiaozicun)	Cai Fengshu Yu Haiguang Luan Fengshi Fang Hui Sun Chengfu Anne Underhill Gary Feinman Linda Nicholas Gwen Bennett
3	21 December 1997 to 15 January 1998	About 60	Enlarged the survey area to the west in the Chao River basin and its branches	Several new Longshan, Zhou, and Han period sites discovered	Cai Fengshu Yu Haiguang Luan Fengshi Fang Hui Liu Hongjun (RCG) Anne Underhill Gary Feinman Linda Nicholas Gwen Bennett

* Affiliations for individuals are given at first mention and for changes in affiliation during the survey. Institutional abbreviations are as follows:

FM, Field Museum of Natural History, Chicago, USA;
Kokugakuin, Kokugakuin University, Tokyo, Japan;
Kyushu, Kyushu University, Fukuoka, Japan;
NH, New Haven, Connecticut, USA;
RC, Rizhao City, Shandong Province, China;
RCG, Rizhao City Government, Shandong Province, China;
RM, Rizhao Museum, Shandong Province, China;
SDU, Shandong University, Qingdao, China;
UBC, University of British Columbia, Vancouver, Canada;
UC, University of Chicago, Illinois, USA;
UCLA, University of California, Los Angeles, USA;
UIC, University of Illinois, Chicago, USA;
UWM, University of Wisconsin, Madison, USA;
YU, Yale University, New Haven, Connecticut, USA.

Continued

TABLE 2.1 CONTINUED.

Year	Survey season dates	Area surveyed (km^2)	Focus	Major findings	Survey participants*
4	11 November 1998 to 28 December 1998	About 130	Enlarged the survey area to the north by 90 km^2 (Chao River and Baima River basins) and south by 40 km^2 (Jinyin River basin)	Several new Longshan, Zhou, Han period sites discovered in the northern and southern areas; Yueshi layer found at the Wangshitou site in the north (WL-WST-1); in the south the Shang period site (DG-CZG-1/ DG-HSD-7) and Zhou and Han period sites discovered	Cai Fengshu Yu Haiguang Luan Fengshi Fang Hui Liu Hongjun Anne Underhill Gary Feinman Linda Nicholas Gwen Bennett Christianne Cunnar (NH) Kato Satomi (Kokugakuin) Li Min, MA student (UBC)
5	14 December 1999 to 4 January 2000	About 90	Enlarged the survey area to the south in the Chao River and Jinyin River basins, and Guzi River area (branch of Futuan River)	Discovery of new sites from the Longshan, Yueshi, Shang, Zhou, and Han periods; investigated known sites Sujiacun (DG-SJC-1) and Dataoyuan (DG-DTY-1)	Luan Fengshi Fang Hui Gao Jixi Cao Yanfang Anne Underhill (FM) Gary Feinman (FM) Linda Nicholas (FM) Christianne Cunnar Christopher Needs, PhD student (UIC)
6	10 December 2000 to 15 January 2001	70	Enlarged the southern area around the Guzi River by 35 km^2, and the northern area to the east of the season 4 survey area around the Baima and Jili Rivers by 35 km^2	Longshan, Zhou, and Han period sites found in each area; survey within Rizhao City development areas by Zhang Zhibo (31 January to 1 March 2001) also yielded sites from each period	Fang Hui Wang Jianhua, PhD student (SDU) Zhang Zhibo (RC) Anne Underhill Gary Feinman Linda Nicholas

Continued

TABLE 2.1 CONTINUED.

Year	Survey season dates	Area surveyed (km^2)	Focus	Major findings	Survey participants*
7	10 December 2001 to 5 January 2002	100	Enlarged the southern area to the southwest of the season 5 area around the Futuan River by 50 km^2; northern area enlarged to the northeast of the season 6 survey area in the Jili River basin by 50 km^2	Sites from the Longshan, Zhou, and Han periods found in northern and southern areas; Dawenkou component discovered at Tasha (JN-TS-4)	Fang Hui Wang Fen, PhD student (SDU) Qian Yihui, PhD student (SDU) Anne Underhill Gary Feinman Linda Nicholas
8	25 November 2002 to 18 December 2002	80	The southern area enlarged to the south of the Rizhao urban area around the Guzi River by 70 km^2; northern area enlarged to the north of the season 7 survey area in Jili River and Baima River areas by 10 km^2	Sites from the Longshan, Zhou, Han periods found in both areas; southern area revealed Beixin and early Dawenkou components at Nantunling-4 (DG-NTL-4) and Donglianghe (DG-DLH-1); previously known site of Donghaiyu (DG-DHY-1) surveyed	Fang Hui Luan Fengshi Chen Xuexiang (SDU) Lan Yufu (SDU) Zhai Shaodong, PhD student (SDU) Anne Underhill Gary Feinman Linda Nicholas
9	27 November 2003 to 21 December 2003	70	Exclusive focus on the southern area, south of the season 8 survey area along the coast at the southern bank of the Futuan River	New sites from the Longshan, Zhou, and Han periods discovered; important finding that at 300 ha Yaowangcheng is much larger than the previous estimate of 52 ha	Fang Hui Song Aiping (RC) Chen Xuexiang (SDU) Wang Hua, PhD student (SDU) Qian Yihui, PhD student (SDU) Jin Hanbo, PhD student (SDU) Tanba Takashi, SDU exchange student (Kyushu) Anne Underhill Gary Feinman Linda Nicholas

Continued

Table 2.1 continued.

Year	Survey season dates	Area surveyed (km²)	Focus	Major findings	Survey participants*
10	25 November 2004 to 25 December 2004	About 100	Exclusive focus on the south, in areas of the Zhuzi, Chuanzi, and Futuan Rivers west of Yaowangcheng	Many prehistoric sites discovered; previously known sites of Jinggou and Xiaodaituan surveyed; some new Shang, Zhou, Han period sites found	Fang Hui Lu Jianying, PhD student (SDU) Wang Hua Liu Hongjun (RM) Anne Underhill Gary Feinman Linda Nicholas
11	28 October 2005 to 2 December 2005	150	Exclusive focus south of season 9 and 10 survey areas to clarify settlement patterns south of the Futuan River basin	More than 200 sites from Dawenkou to Han periods found, including 2 sites about 8–12 km from Yaowangcheng; early Dawenkou site discovered at LS-Xujiacun-2/ LS-Xujiacun-3 (LS-XJC-2/LS-XJC-3)	Fang Hui Jin Hanbo Cui Yingjie, PhD student (SDU) Hui Xiping, PhD student (SDU) Anne Underhill Gary Feinman Linda Nicholas
12	10 November 2006 to 13 December 2006	About 150	Focused on the mountainous areas in the southern Rizhao City and western Langshan districts along the Xiuzhen, Longwang, and Zhuzi Rivers and their branches	Over 100 new sites from the Dawenkou to the Han periods found; more Yueshi sites found than in other areas; systematic survey done of known sites Qiashuichegou-1 (LS-QSCG-1), Xinliu (LS-XL-1-7), and Datushan (LS-DTS-5/ LS-CG-9); visible cultural layers at more than 10 sites	Fang Hui Hui Xiping Xia Huogen, PhD student (SDU) Zhao Guangguo, PhD student (SDU) Anne Underhill Gary Feinman Linda Nicholas Adam Schwartz, PhD student (UC)
13	1 November 2007 to 5 December 2007	About 150 total	Survey of Lanshan and Donggang Districts in the south along the Futuan River and its branches (70 km²); Jiaonan and Wulian Districts in the north in the Jili River and the Baima River areas; part of the southeastern Zhucheng area (about 80 km²)	Longshan, Zhou, and Han period sites found in the southern and northern areas; more sites found in the alluvial plain of the Jili and Baima Rivers in the north; a Shang component discovered in the north at Xiejiazhuangzi-1 (ZC-XJZZ-1) and a Zhou component at Nanzhangjiazhuang-1 (ZC-ZNJZ-1)	Fang Hui Wang Di, PhD student (SDU) Xu Bo, PhD student (SDU) Guo Mingjian, PhD student (SDU) Qiao Zhuojun, PhD student (SDU) Hui Xiping, PhD student (SDU) Yin Fengchao, PhD student (SDU) Anne Underhill Gary Feinman Linda Nicholas

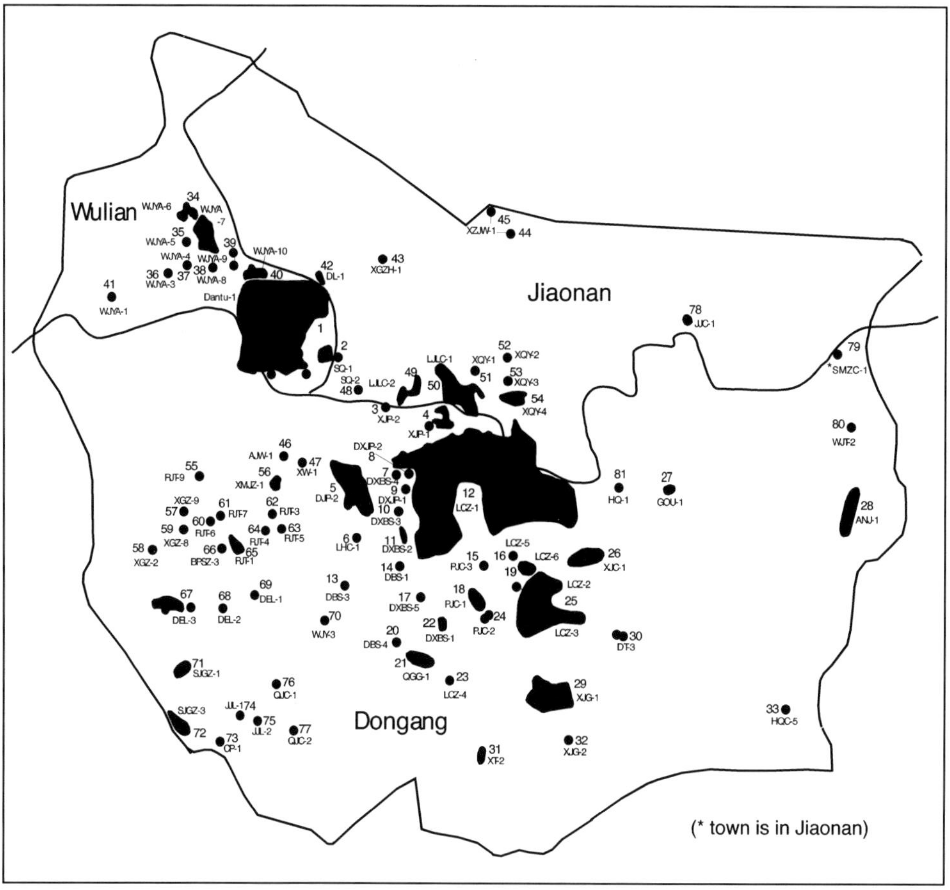

FIGURE 2.4. Longshan period sites found in the Donggang, Wulian, and Jiaonan Districts during survey Year 1 (1995–1996) and Year 2 (1996–1997).

WJYa-6, 7). We found a Zhou site at Anjialing (DG-ANJ-4) and important sites with Zhou and Han period remains, including Qianbianzhuang (前卞庄, DG-QBZ-2), Shimiaozicun (石庙子村, JN-SMZC-3), and Xiuqiyuan (修齐园, JN-XQY-4) (see Cai et al. 1997; Underhill et al. 1998). It was significant to find Yueshi period sherds at Shimiaozicun (DG-SMZ-3). The survey areas and distribution of sites during the first two seasons are presented in Figures 2.4, 2.5, and 2.6.

Year 3: 21 December 1997–15 January 1998

We discovered several important sites during the third field season farther to the northwest in Chaohezhen in Wulian County and parts of the Donggang and Jiaonan Districts. The Longshan period sites include Donghuaya (东花崖, WL-DHY-1), Chaohezhen (WL-CHZ-12), Gaojiagou (高家沟, DG-GJG-2), Luohuaqian (萝花前, DG-LHQ-4), and Xujiawa (徐家洼, JN-XJW-4). Major sites with Zhou and Han period remains are Caiyuan (菜园, WL-CY-1), Chaohezhen (WL-CHZ-14, 8, 9), Yaogou (尧沟, WL-YG-1), and Linquan (林泉, WL-LQ-6, 2) (Figures 2.7, 2.8, and 2.9).

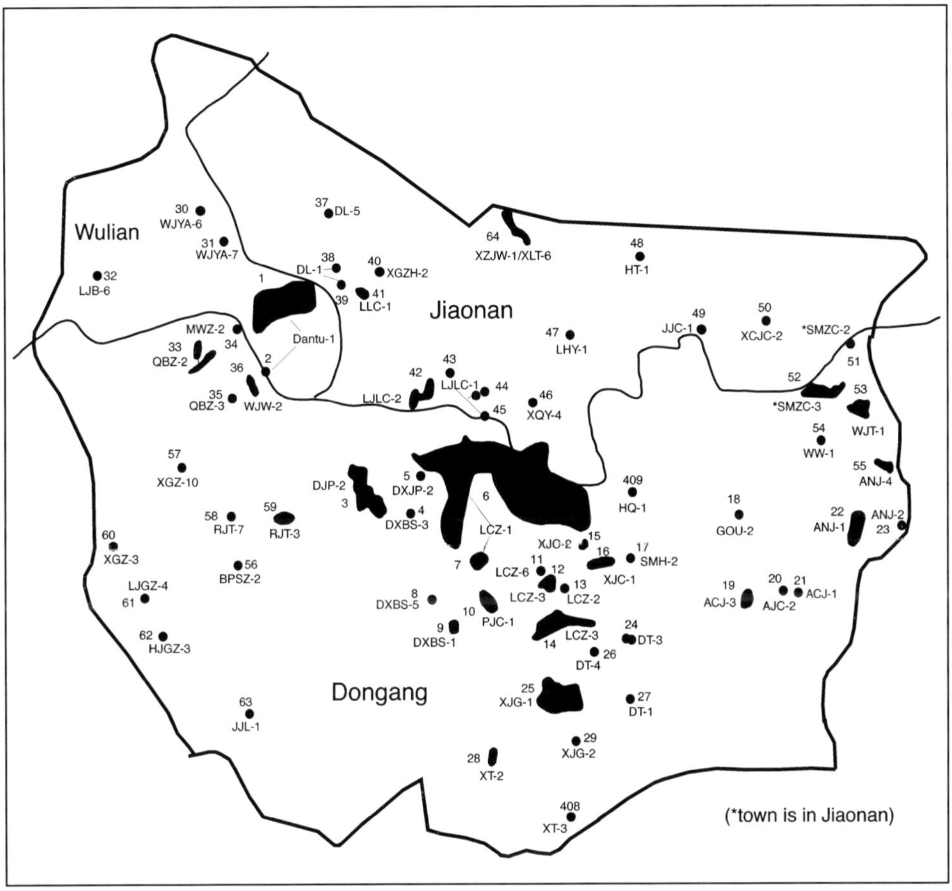

Figure 2.5. Zhou period sites found in the Donggang, Wulian, and Jiaonan Districts during survey Year 1 (1995–1996) and Year 2 (1996–1997).

Year 4: 11 November 1998–28 December 1998

The fourth field season involved investigation of one area in the south and another in the north. The southern area included the Liangchengzhen and Heshanzhen (河山镇) areas of Donggang in the Jinyin River basin. The northern area included the Haiqingzhen and Dachangzhen (大场镇) areas of Jiaonan and the Kouguanzhen (叩官镇) and Chaohezhen areas of Wulian in the Chao River and Baima River basins. Important sites discovered in the north include Jiawangdun (贾王墩, JN-JWD-2/HLQ-1), Dongjiawa (董家洼, JN-DJW-4), Xiajiazhuang (夏家庄, WL-XJZ-1), Yatou (崖头, WL-YT-1), and Wangshitou (王石头, WL-WST-1). It was significant to find a layer of Yueshi material remains at Wangshitou. Important sites with Zhou and Han period remains include Houlaowo (后老窝, JN-HLW-2), Jingzhuang (京庄, WL-JZ-6), Xiajiazhuang (夏家庄, WL-XJZ-1), and Qianpolou (前坡楼, JN-QPL-1). Notable sites in the southern area are the Longshan site of Heshandian (河山店, DG-HSD-10) and the sites of DG-CZG-1/HSD-7 (Shang, Zhou, and Han periods), DG-CZG-2/GZ-2, 3 (Zhou and Han periods), Wujiatai (吴家台, DG-WJT-1, Zhou and Han periods), and Majiazhuang (马家庄, DG-MJZ-3, Zhou and Han periods) (see Figures 2.10 through 2.15).

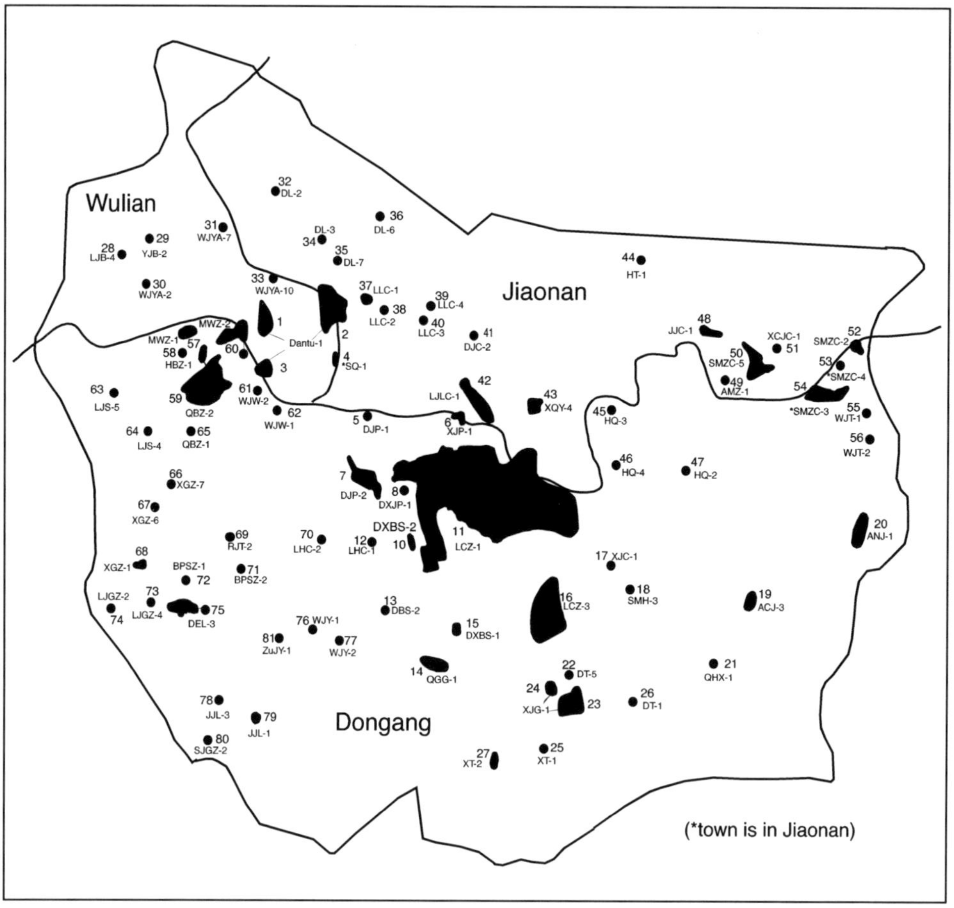

FIGURE 2.6. Han period sites found in the Donggang, Wulian, and Jiaonan Districts during survey Year 1 (1995–1996) and Year 2 (1996–1997).

Year 5: 14 December 1999–4 January 2000

The fifth season involved moving south from Heshanzhen and Qinjialouxiang (秦家楼乡), across the watershed of the Heshan Mountains (河山) and Sishan Mountains (丝山) in the basins of branches of the Chao River (潮河), Jinyin River (金银河, a branch of the Chao River), Futuan River (傅疃河), and the Guzi River (崮子河, a branch of the Futuan River). We systematically surveyed the known sites of Sujiacun (苏家村, DG-SJC-1, 12) and Dataoyuan (大桃园, DG-DTY-1/DJZ-3, 5). Important new Longshan period sites included Yingzi (营子, DG-YZ-1) and Huangjiahe (黄家河, DG-HJH-2, 3). Sites from the Yueshi, Shang, and Zhou periods include Qinjiaguanzhuang (秦家官庄, DG-QJGZ-1) and Xinzhuangzi (辛庄子, DG-XZZ-1). Important Zhou period sites are Qianzhucun (前竹村, DG-QZC-1/WLZ-2), Qianlianghe (前两河, DG-QLH-1), and Dingjiazhuang (丁家庄, DG-DJZ-1). We also found a major Han period site, Fanjiaguanzhuang (范家官庄, DG-FJGZ-2) (Figures 2.16, 2.17, and 2.18). By the end of five seasons we had surveyed about 400 km^2 and discovered more than 750 sites (see Fang et al. 2002; Underhill et al. 2002).

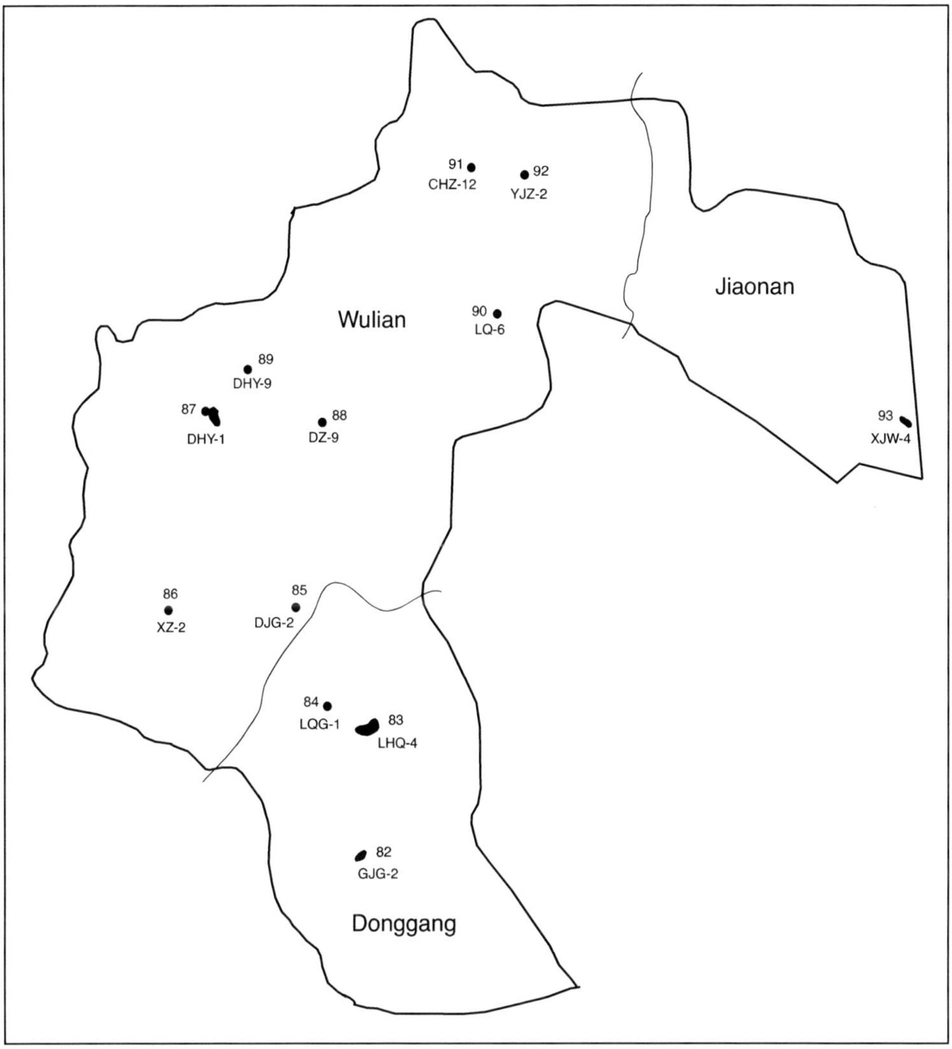

Figure 2.7. Longshan period sites found in the Donggang, Wulian, and Jiaonan Districts during survey Year 3 (1997–1998).

Year 6: 10 December 2000–15 January 2001

During the sixth season we continued the survey in the southern and northern areas (Figures 2.19 through 2.24). In the south we focused on the Qinjialouxiang area of Donggang near the Guzi River and surrounding areas. The northern area was mainly the Xinyangzhen (信阳镇) and Dachangzhen (大场镇) areas of Jiaonan and areas surrounding the Baima (白马河) and Jili (吉利河) Rivers. Important Longshan period sites in the south include Dongwangjiacun (东王家村, DG-DWJC-1) and Fengjiagou (冯家沟, DG-FJG-2). Sites with Zhou period remains are Miaojiacun (苗家村, DG-MJC-1), Tianjiacun (田家村, DG-TiJC-1), and Taojiacun (陶家村, DG-TJC-1). Important Longshan sites in the north are Fengduncun (凤墩村, JN-FDC-1), Caiyuan (JN-CY-1), and Zhoujiacun (周家村, JN-ZJC-4). Major sites

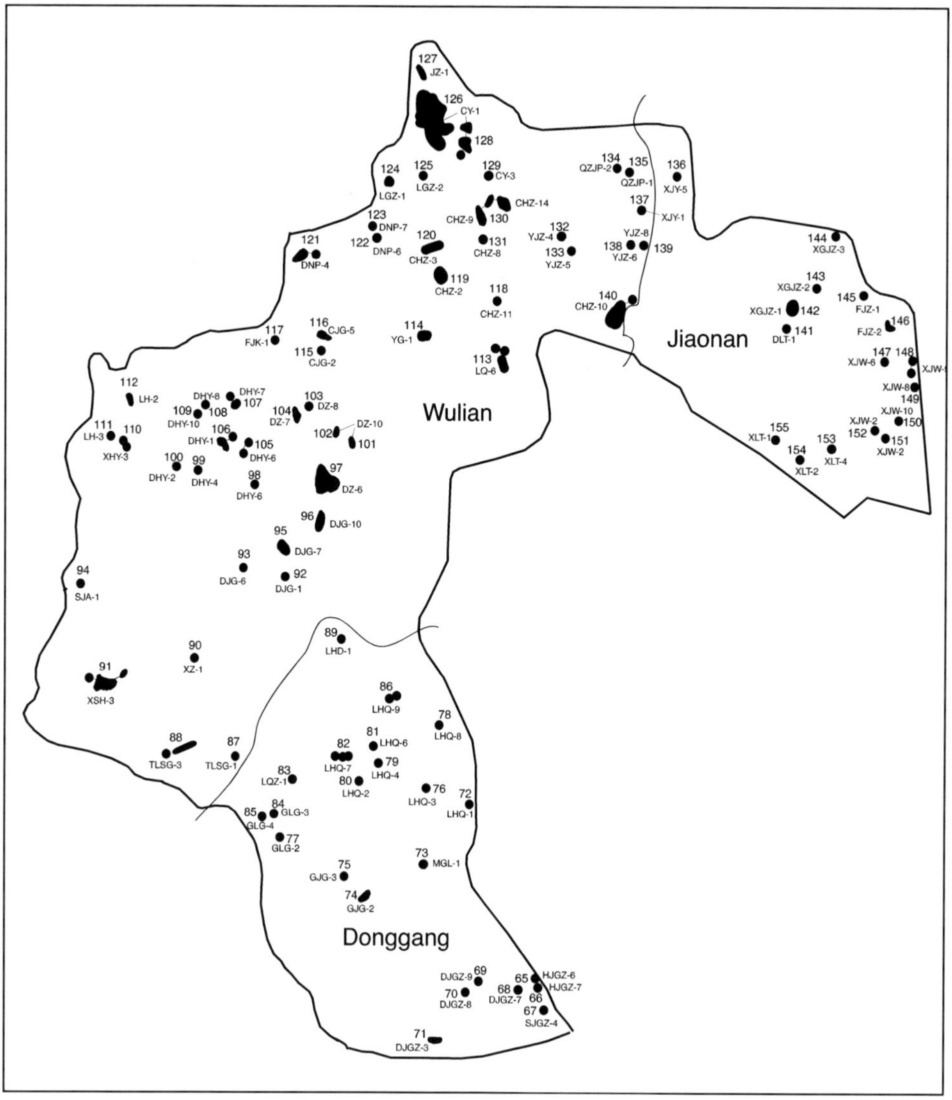

Figure 2.8. Zhou period sites found in the Donggang, Wulian, and Jiaonan Districts during survey Year 3 (1997–1998).

with Zhou and Han period remains are Baoquanmiao (雹泉庙, JN-BQM-1), Houlan (后岚, JN-HL-1), and Dalan (大岚, JN-DL-1).

By the end of the sixth season we had reached the edge of the urban area of Rizhao City. It was not possible to fully cover the core of the rapidly developing urban district. We decided it would be more productive to ask Zhang Zhibo (张治波), a Rizhao resident and crew member, to survey unoccupied pockets of land from 31 January to 1 March 2001. He found important sites from each major era: the Longshan sites Qianwulihe (前五里河, DG-QWLH-1) and Daxiangdian (大香店, DG-DXD-1); Zhou sites Gaojialing (高家岭, DG-

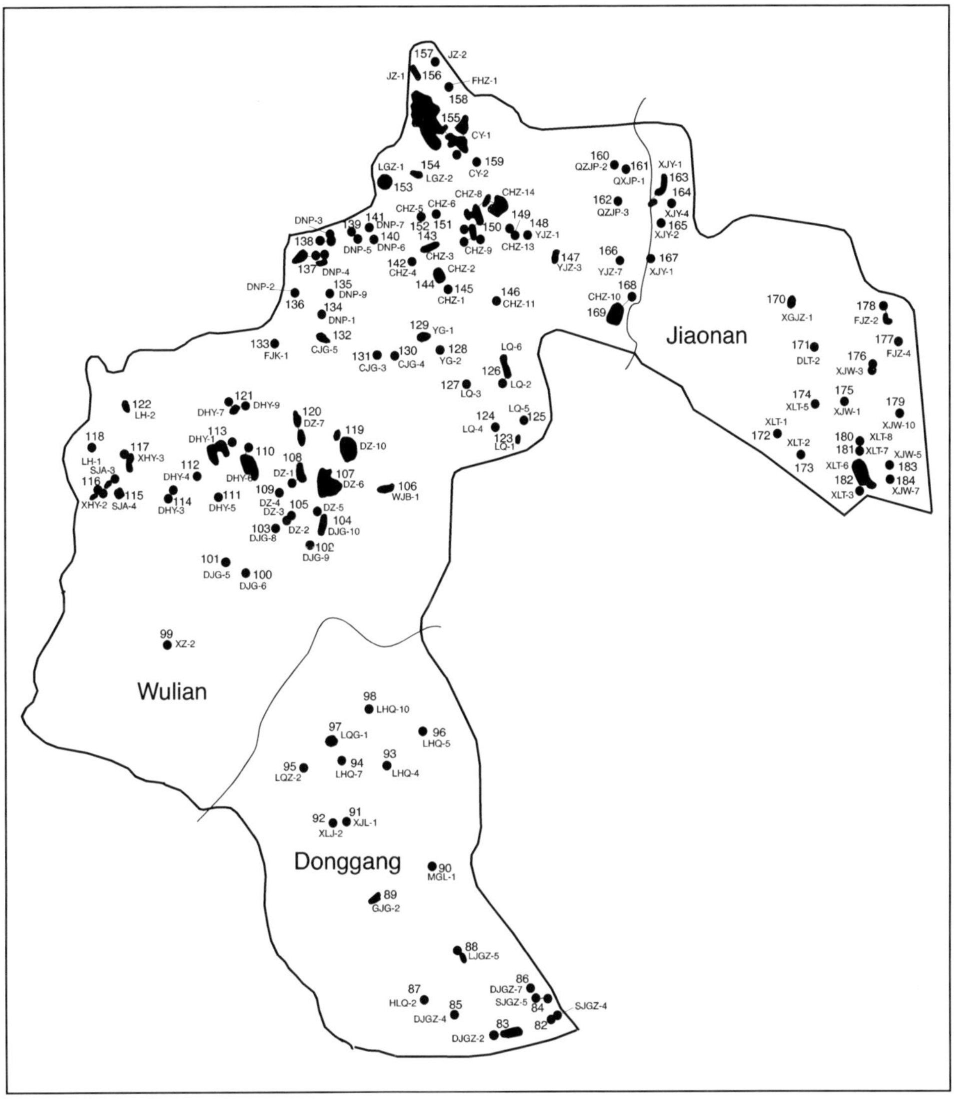

Figure 2.9. Han period sites found in the Donggang, Wulian, and Jiaonan Districts during survey Year 3 (1997–1998).

GaoJL-1), Lijiazhuangzi (厉家庄子, DG-LJZZ-1), and Miaojiacun (苗家村, DG-MJC-1); and Han sites Dongjiatan (董家滩, DG-DJT-1) and Dashiqiaocun (大石桥村, DG-DSQC-5).

Year 7: 10 December 2001–5 January 2002

The seventh season continued in the northern and southern areas. Important Longshan period sites in the southern area along the Futuan River and its branches include Zhengjiadingzi (郑家顶子, DG-ZJDZ-1) and Beidacun (北大村, DG-BDC-4). Two important Zhou period sites we found are Houshanqian (后山前, DG-HSQ-1) and Xishilipu (西十里堡, DG-

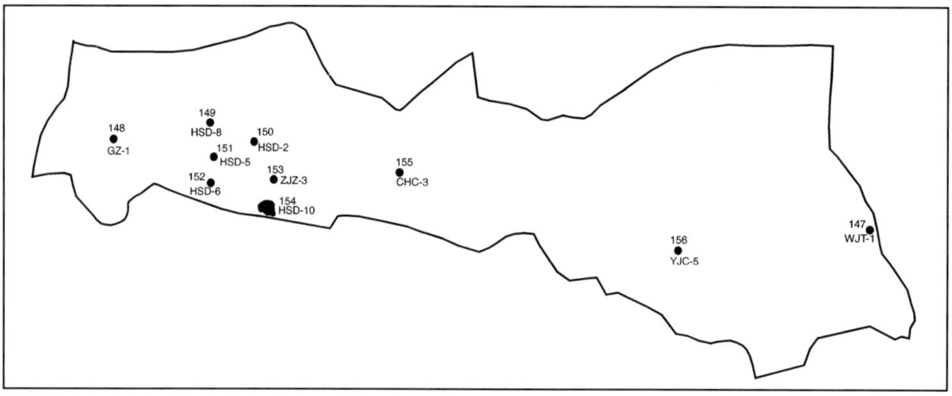

FIGURE 2.10. Longshan period sites found in the Donggang District in the southern survey area of Year 4 (1998).

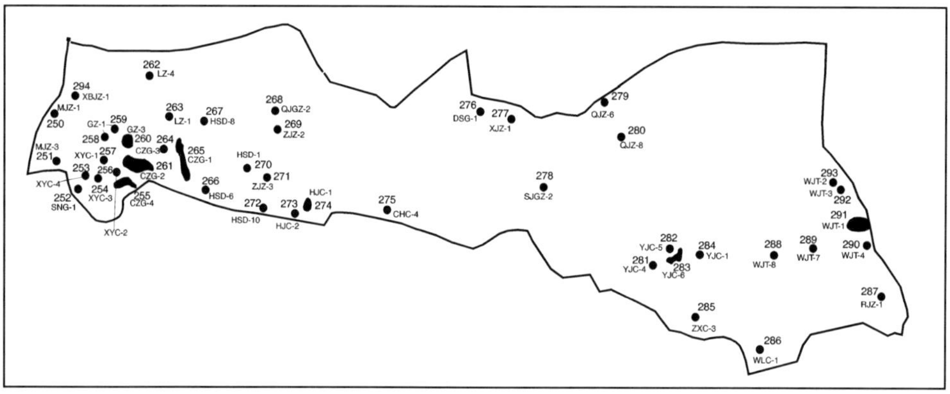

FIGURE 2.11. Zhou period sites found in the Donggang District in the southern survey area of Year 4 (1998).

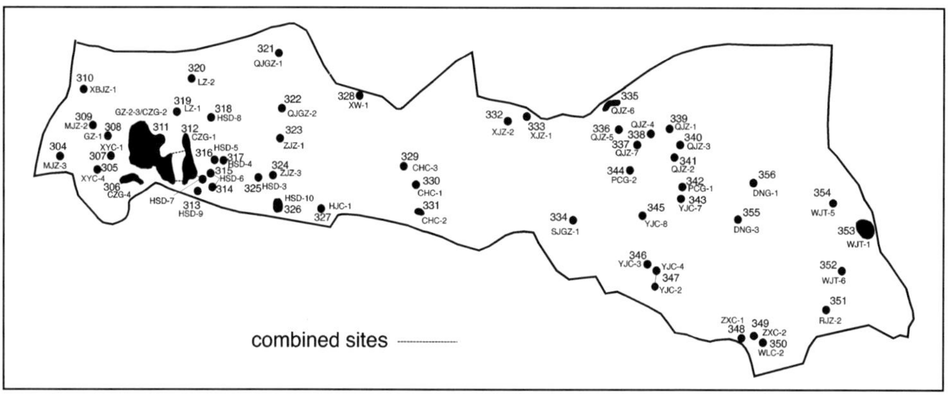

FIGURE 2.12. Han period sites found in the Donggang District in the southern survey area of Year 4 (1998).

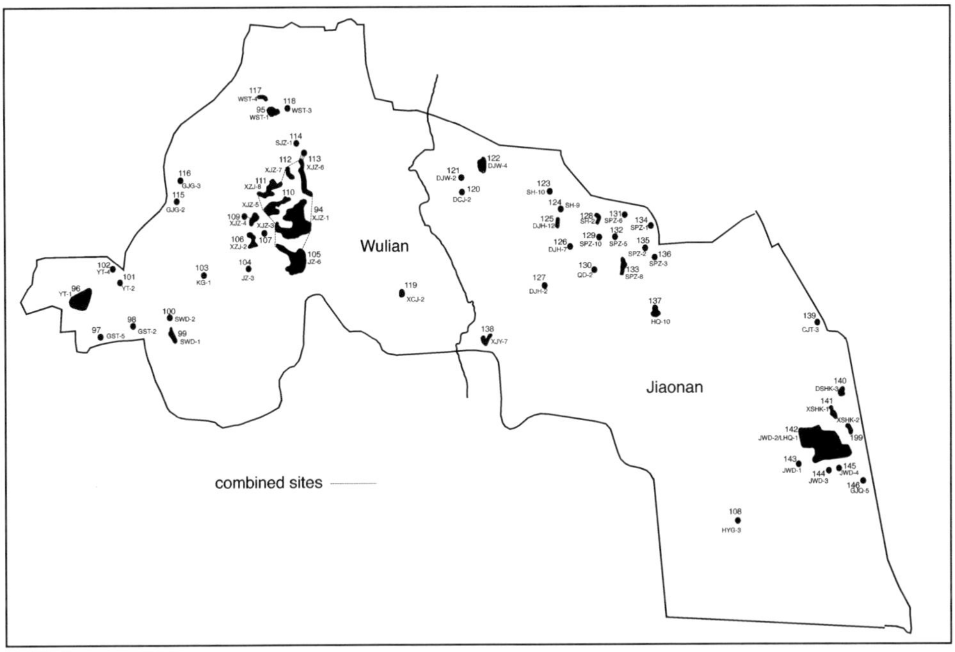

FIGURE 2.13. Longshan period sites found in the Wulian and Jiaonan Districts in the northern survey area of Year 4 (1998).

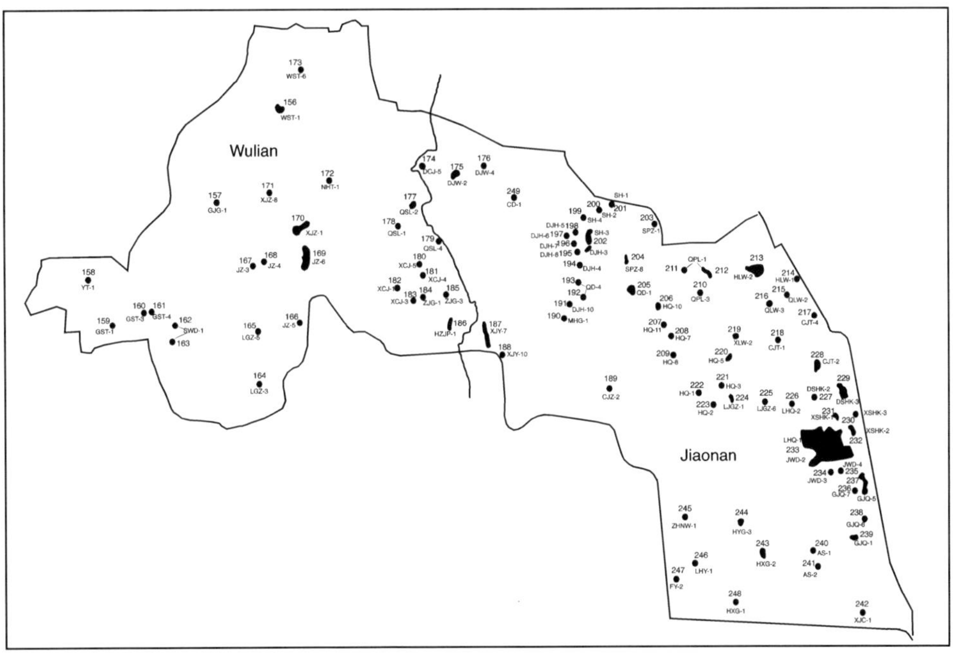

FIGURE 2.14. Zhou period sites found in the Wulian and Jiaonan Districts in the northern survey area of Year 4 (1998).

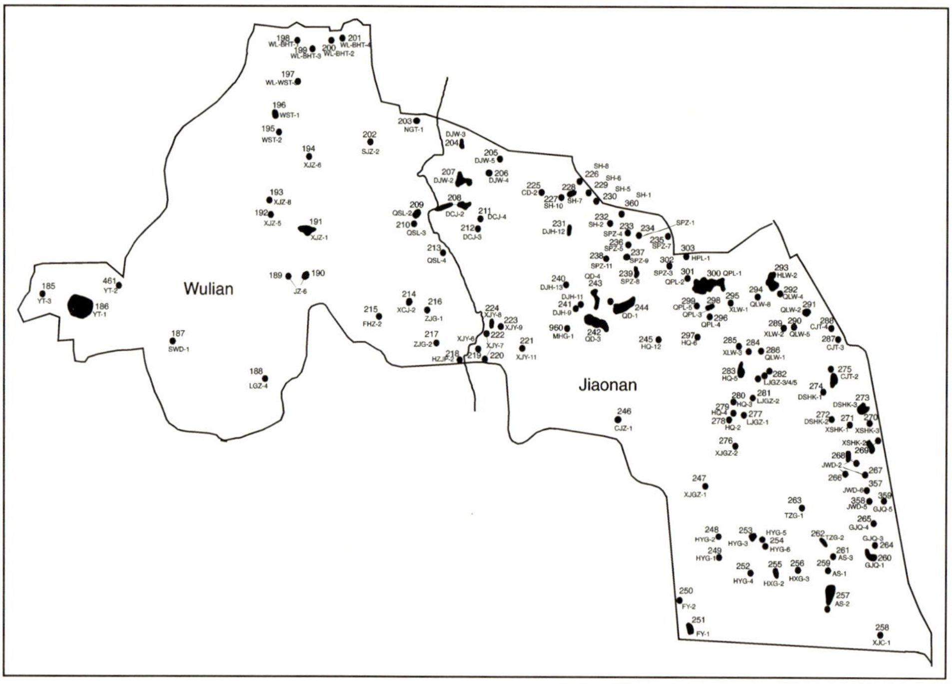

FIGURE 2.15. Han period sites found in the Wulian and Jiaonan Districts in the northern survey area of Year 4 (1998).

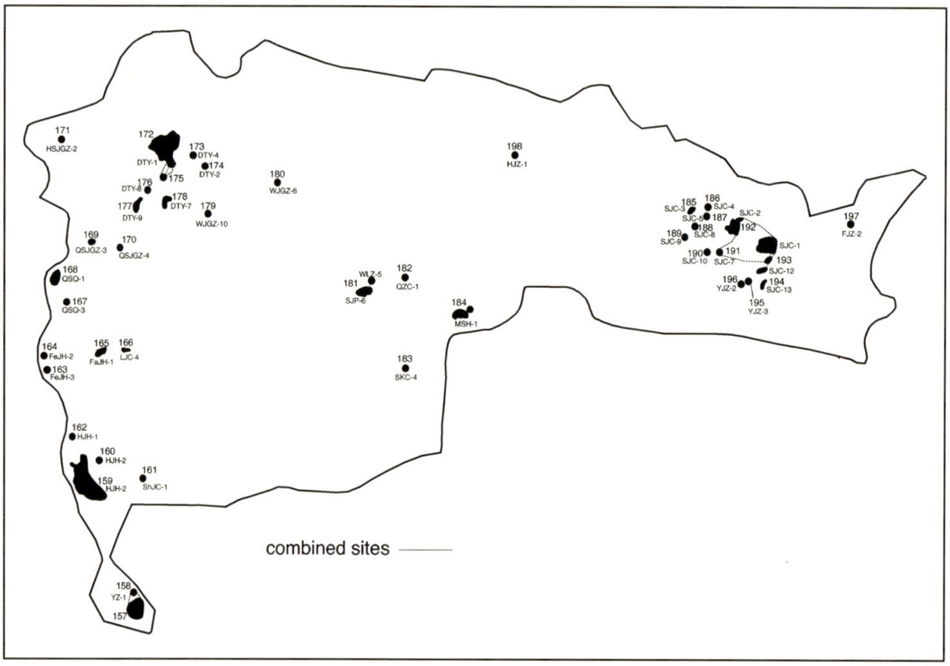

FIGURE 2.16. Longshan period sites found in the Donggang District during survey Year 5 (1999).

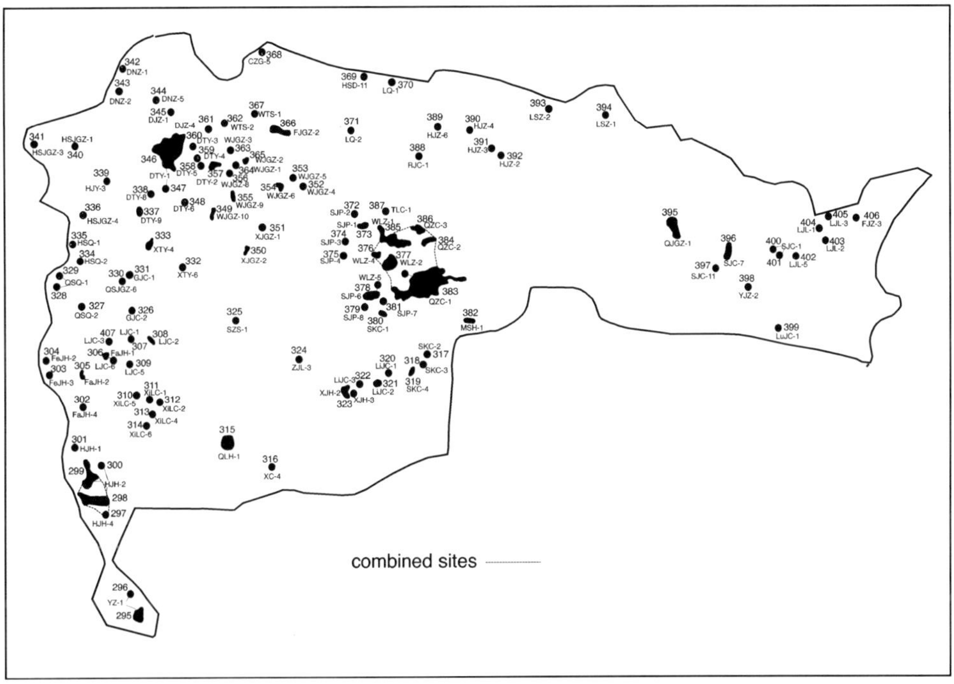

Figure 2.17. Zhou period sites found in the Donggang District during survey Year 5 (1999).

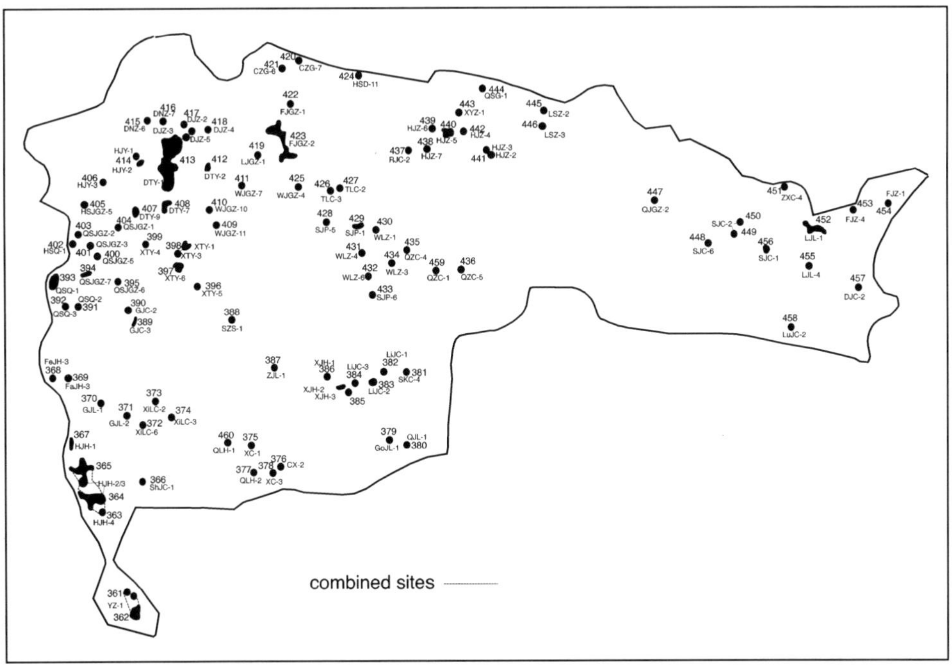

Figure 2.18. Han period sites found in the Donggang District during survey Year 5 (1999).

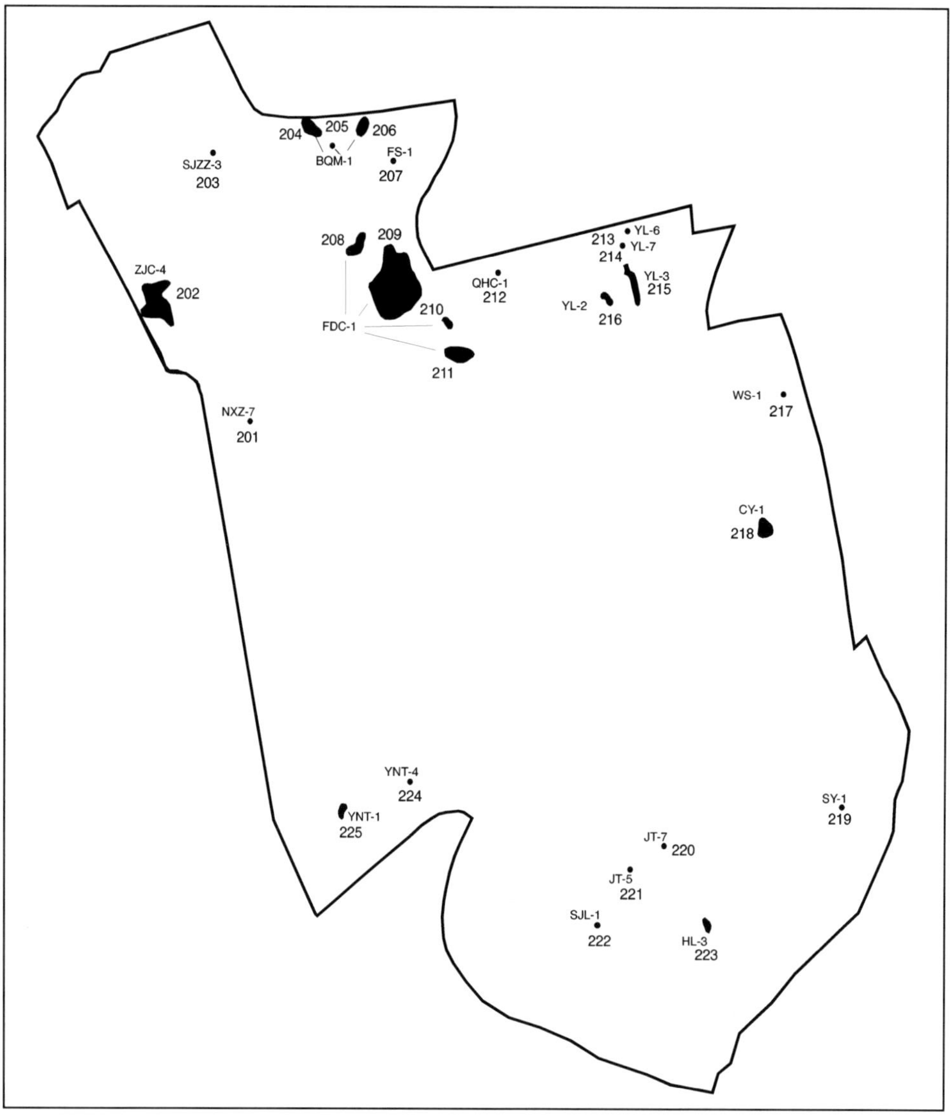

FIGURE 2.19. Longshan period sites found in the Jiaonan District in the northern survey area of Year 6 (2000).

XSLP-2, part of the larger Han period site of Dagucheng, DG-DGC-1/XSLP-2/QEZ-1, 3, 4, 5). Two Han period sites in the southern area are Dagucheng (大古城, DG-DGC-1, above) and Xujialou (徐家楼, DG-XuJL-2). In the north, the main Longshan sites are Zhangjiadazhuang (张家大庄, JN-ZJDZ-3), Dagou (大沟, JN-DG-1, 4), and Xizhuang (西庄, JN-XZ-1). In addition, Tashan (JN-TS-4) has both Dawenkou and Longshan remains. Important new Zhou sites are Nansi (南寺, JN-NS-5, 6, 8), Baozibu (保子埠, JN-BZB-1), Caijiacun (菜家村, JN-CJC-4), and Xizhuang (JN-XZ-1). Major Han sites are Miaohou (庙后, JN-MH-1) and Xiaojiawa (肖家洼, JN-XJWa-14) (Figures 2.25 through 2.30).

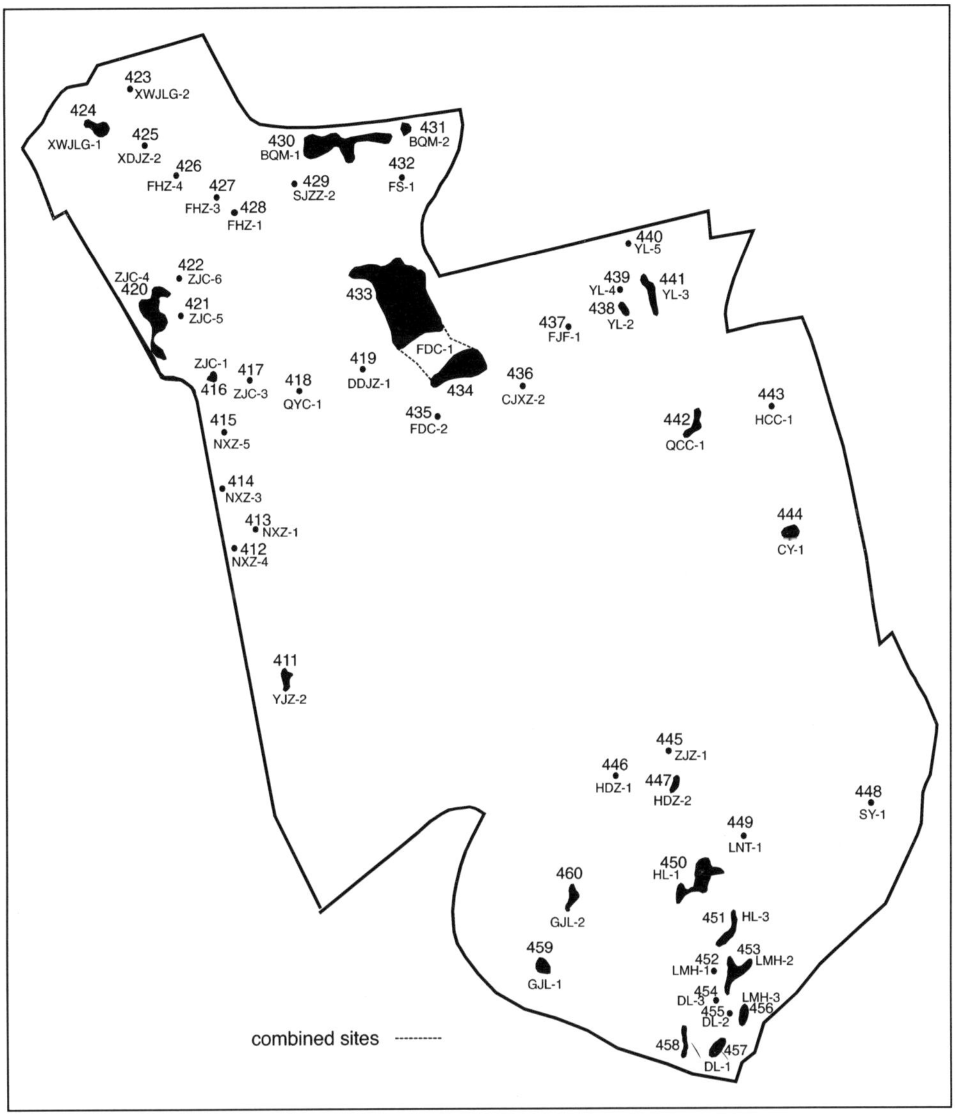

Figure 2.20. Zhou period sites found in the Jiaonan District in the northern survey area of Year 6 (2000).

Year 8: 25 November 2002–18 December 2002

The eighth season of survey took place mainly in the Kui Shan (奎山, Mount Kui) area, the border of the New Technology Development Zone (新技术开发区), and Kuishanzhen (奎山镇) in the watershed of the Guzi River (a branch of the Futuan River). In this southern area we found two sites from the Beixin and early Dawenkou periods for the first time: Nantunling (南屯岭, DG-NTL-4) and Donglianghe (东两河, DG-DLH-1). We also systematically surveyed the previously excavated site of Donghaiyu (东海峪, DG-DHY-1; see Chapter 1). Longshan period sites that we found include Guanjiacun (管家村, DG-

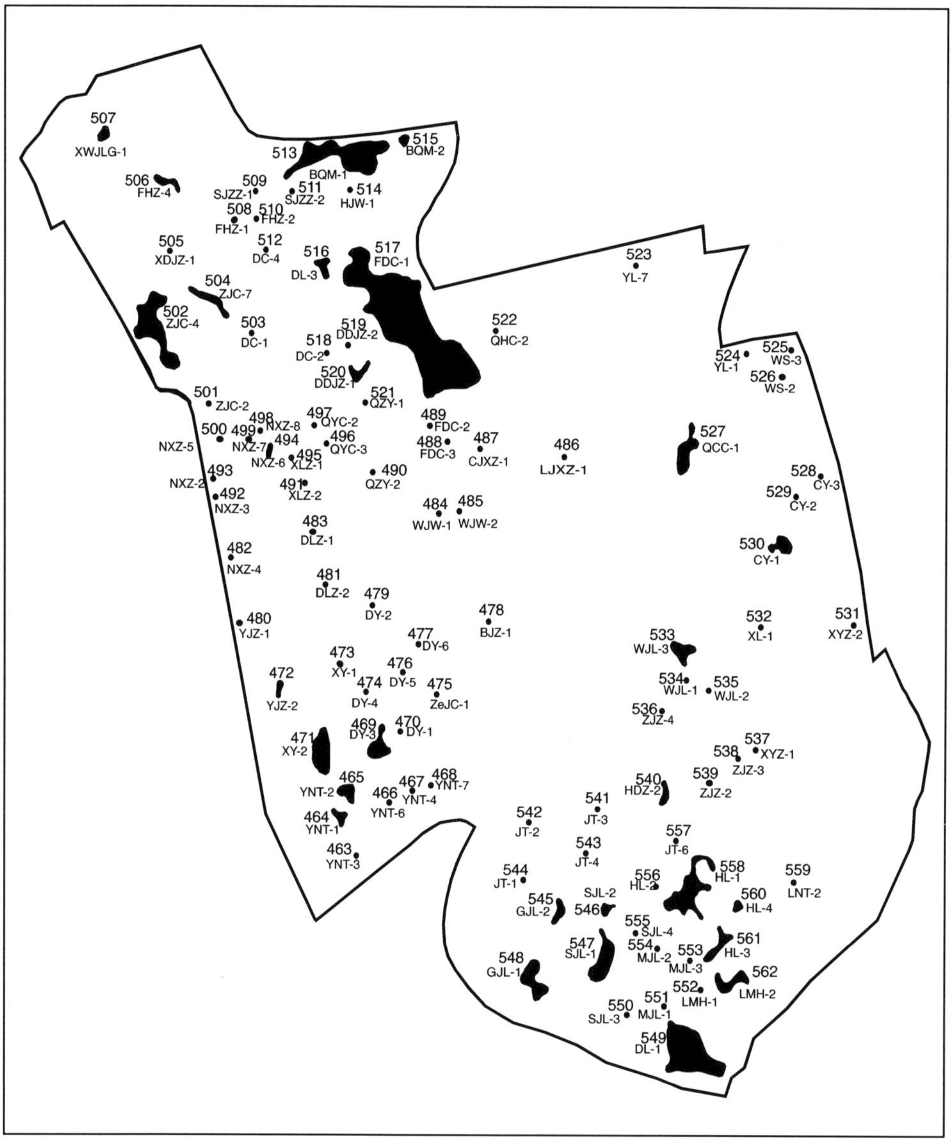

Figure 2.21. Han period sites found in the Jiaonan District in the northern survey area of Year 6 (2000).

GJC-1), Dalingnantou (大岭南头, DG-DLNT-1), Houguzi (后崮子, DG-HGZ-1), and Nanzhangjiacun (南张家村, DG-NZJC-1). Important later sites in the south are Guheya (崮河崖, DG-GHA-2, Zhou period) and Jiaokezhuang (焦柯庄, DG-JKZ-8, 9; Han period). In the northern area, major sites with Longshan and Zhou components are Xisi (西寺, JN-XS-1) and Liuhangdazhuang (柳行大庄, JN-LHDZ-3), and the Han site of Wangzhuang (王庄, JN-WZ-3) (Figures 2.31 through 2.36).

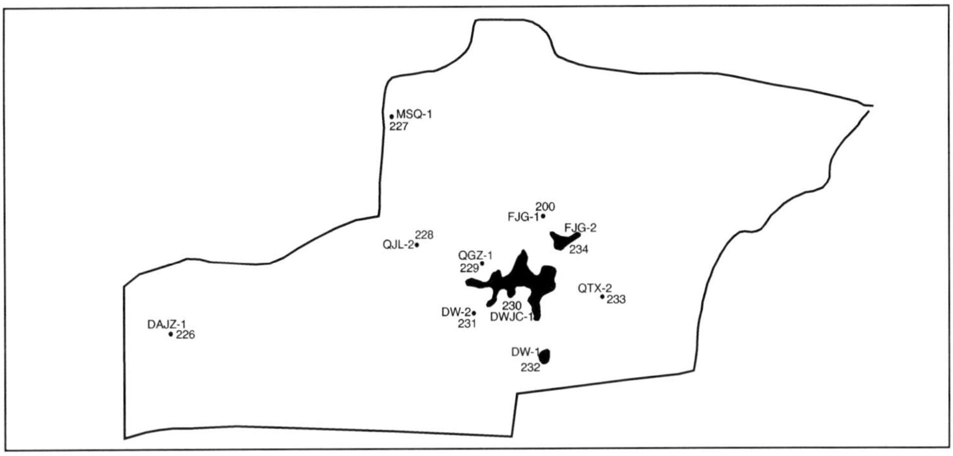

FIGURE 2.22. Longshan period sites found in the Donggang District in the southern survey area of Year 6 (2000).

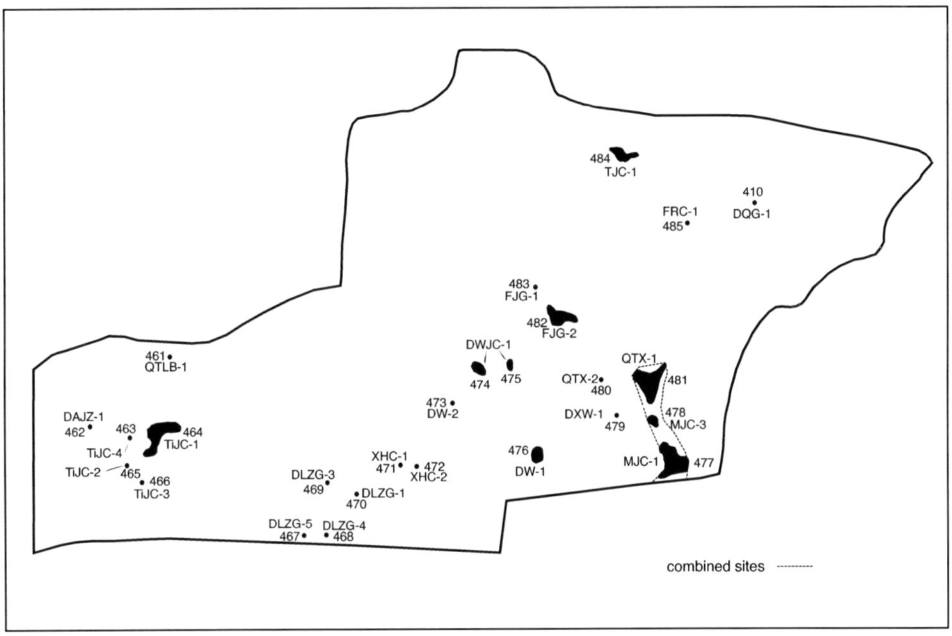

FIGURE 2.23. Zhou period sites found in the Donggang District in the southern survey area of Year 6 (2000).

Year 9: 27 November 2003–21 December 2003

The ninth season focused in the southern area along the southern bank of the Futuan River and covered much of Taoluozhen (涛雒镇) in Donggang and Gaoxingzhen (高兴镇) in the Lanshan (岚山区) District. We systematically surveyed Yaowangcheng, finding that its size for the Longshan period was 300 ha, far larger than the previously estimated size

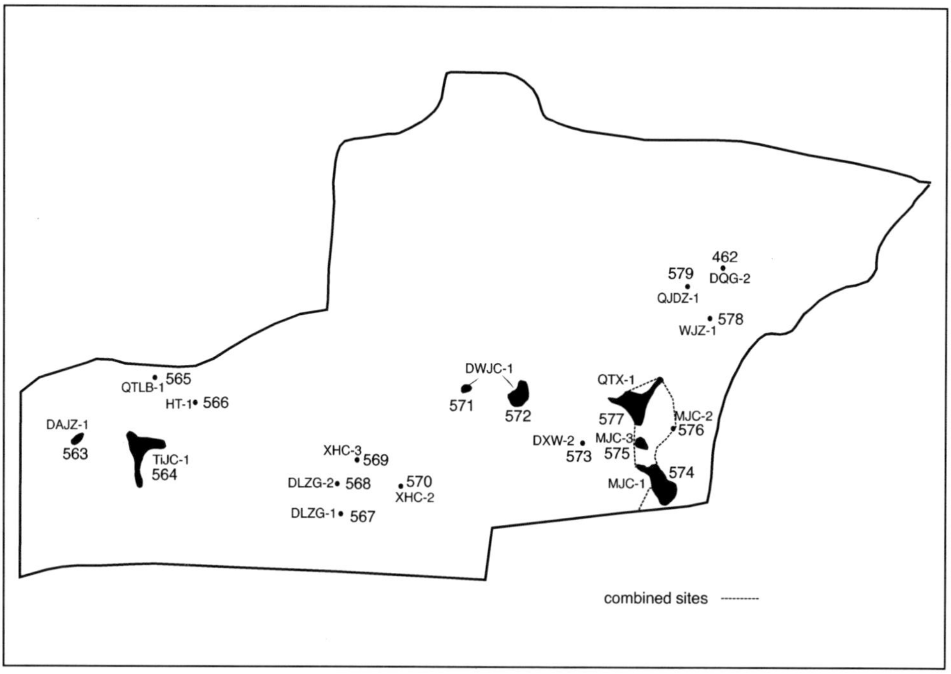

FIGURE 2.24. Han period sites found in the Donggang District in the southern survey area of Year 6 (2000).

of 52 ha (M. Yuan 1955; D. Liu 1958b). Newly discovered sites include Futuan (傅疃, DG-FT-1, Longshan period) and Zhangjiazhuangzi (张家庄子, DG-ZJZZ-1, Longshan period, now considered part of Yaowangcheng [see Chapter 3]) and Zhou sites Qingdun (青墩, DG-QD-5), Chuanzi (川子, DG-CZ-2), and Tianjiayuan (田家园, DG-TJY-1/ZK-1). Important Han period sites were Mujiaxiaozhuang (牟家小庄, DG-MJXZ-1) and Majiacun (马家村, DG-MaJC-1). At the end of this field season we had covered an area of 800 km^2 (Figures 2.37, 2.38, and 2.39).

Year 10: 25 November 2004–25 December 2004

The tenth season of survey took place in the area of the Zhuzi (竹子河), Chuanzi (川子河), and Futuan Rivers in the Lanshan area of Rizhao, including Jufeng (巨峰), Gaoxing (高兴), and Houcun (后村) towns. We focused on areas to the west of Yaowangcheng. We surveyed the previously recognized sites of Jinggou (井沟) and Xiaodaituan (小代疃), and we discovered almost one hundred new prehistoric sites. Included are some large sites dating from the late Dawenkou to the Longshan periods: Matuan (马疃, LS-MT-7), Guojiazhuang (郭家庄, LS-GJZ-3), and Daquhe (大曲河, LS-DQH-5). We also found more sites of the Shang and Zhou periods: Hou'ezhuang (后鹅庄, DG-HEZ-1), Qianjiangshuigou (前浆水沟, DG-QJSG-1), Guojiazhuang (LS-GJZ-1), Baiyun (白云, LS-BY-4), and Qulingnantou (曲岭南头, LS-QLNT-2). Important Han sites were Zhengjiadingzi (郑家顶子, DG-ZJDZ-1) and Xingfang (杏坊, LS-XF-2, 4) (Figures 2.40, 2.41, and 2.42). After ten seasons of survey we had covered nearly 1,000 km^2.

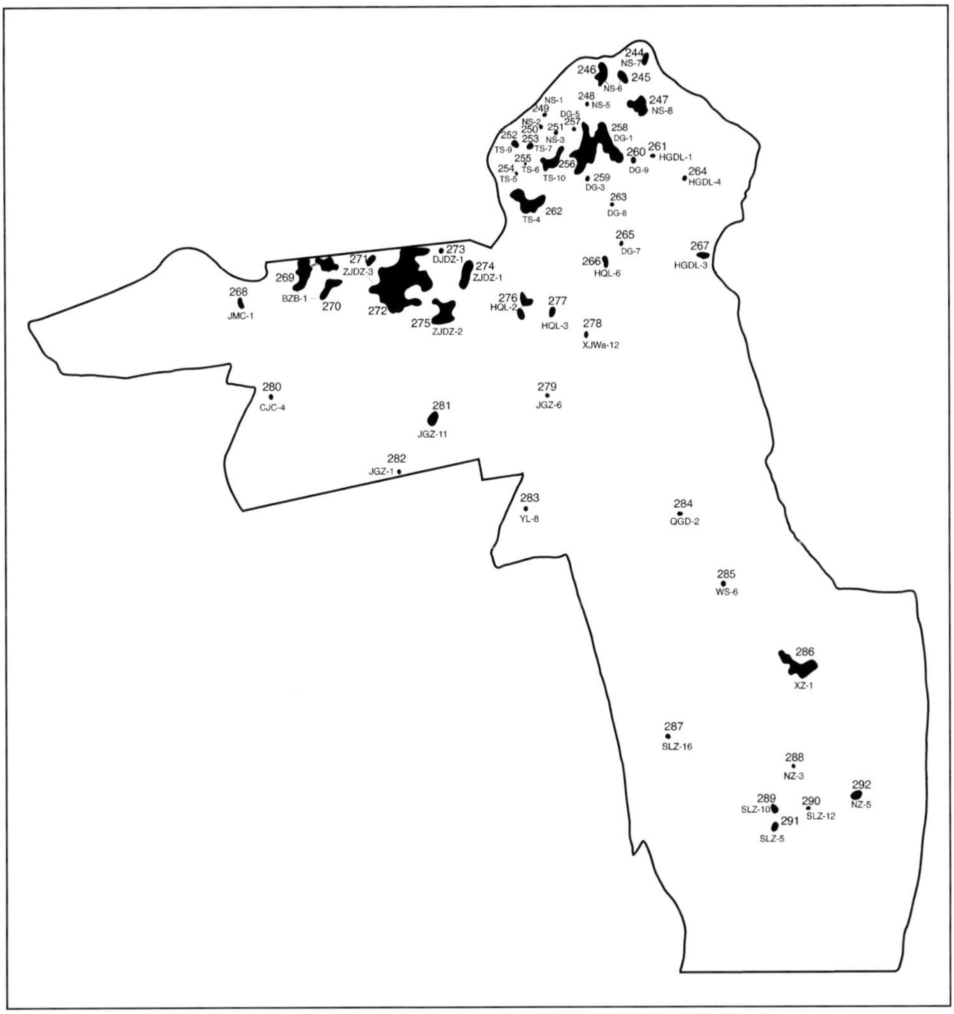

Figure 2.25. Longshan period sites found in the Jiaonan District in the northern survey area of Year 7 (2001).

Year 11: 28 October 2005–2 December 2005

During the eleventh field season we moved south of the boundary from the ninth and tenth seasons at Taoluozhen in Donggang, Jufengzhen, Hushanzhe (虎山镇), and Fenshuizhen (汾水镇) of Lanshan. We had shown from our previous seasons that Yaowangcheng was the largest site in the area during the Dawenkou and Longshan periods, but we wanted to find more information about neighboring areas in the southern Futuan River basin area. We found two important sites about 8 to 12 km in the southwest and southeast of Yaowangcheng: Liujiazhuang (六甲庄, LS-LiuZ-1) and Mengjiaguanzhuang (孟家官庄, LS-MJGZ-3), later judged as a single site and combined (LS-LiuJZ-1/MJGZ-3) and other smaller sites around them. We also found an early Dawenkou site at Xujiacun (徐家村, LS-XJC-2, 3). Important

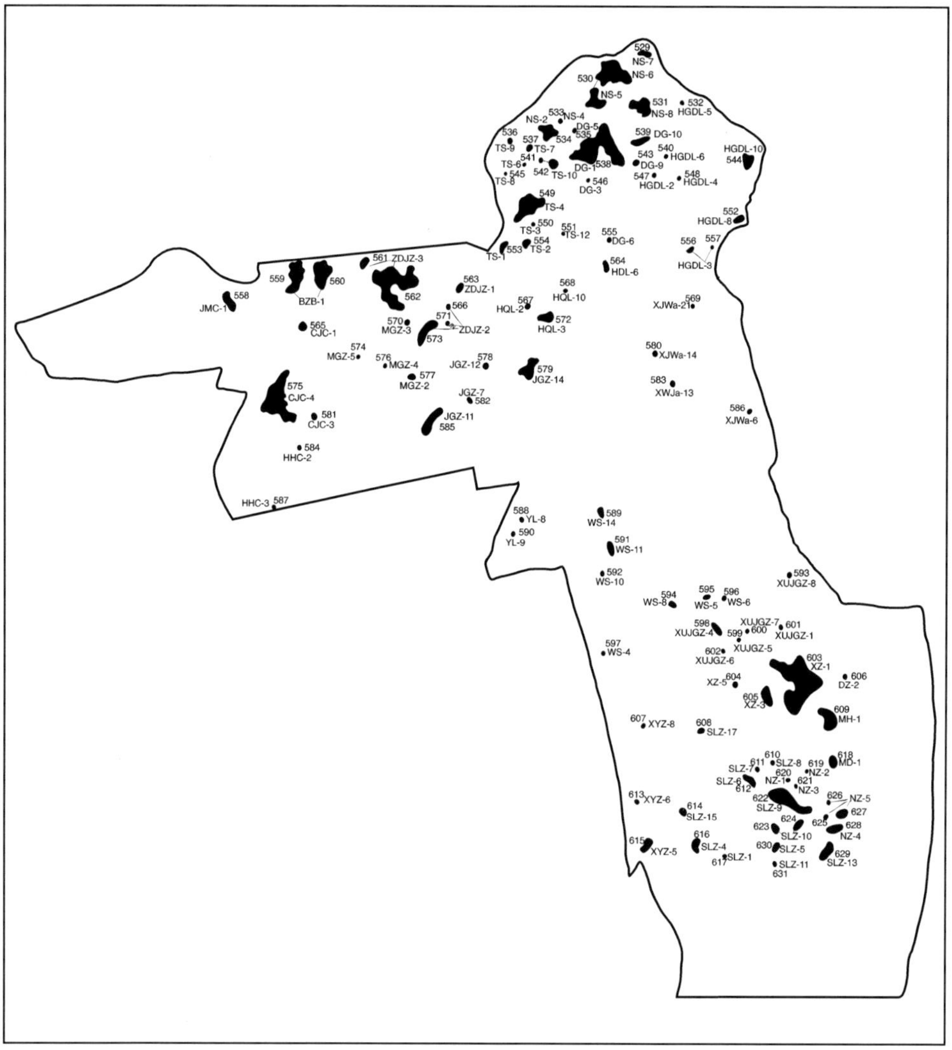

FIGURE 2.26. Zhou period sites found in the Jiaonan District in the northern survey area of Year 7 (2001).

Zhou sites were Donglinzitou (东林子头, DG-DLZT-8), Zhengjiajiezhuang (郑家结庄, LS-ZJJZ-4), and Fenshuizhen (汾水镇, LS-FSZ-1). Important Han sites include Xiaoshanqian (小山前, LS-XSQ-1) and Lingkou (零口, LS-LK-3). By the end of the eleventh season we had surveyed 1,100 m^2 (Fang et al. 2008; Underhill et al. 2008; see Figures 2.43, 2.44, and 2.45).

Year 12: 10 November 2006–13 December 2006

During the twelfth survey season we focused mainly on mountainous areas of the western Lanshan District around the towns of Fenshui, Beikuo (碑廓), Hushan (虎山), and Jufeng (巨峰) in the areas of the Xiuzhen (绣针河), Longwang (龙王河), and Zhuzi (竹子河) Rivers. We surveyed some previously recognized sites, including Qianshuichegou (前水车沟, LS-

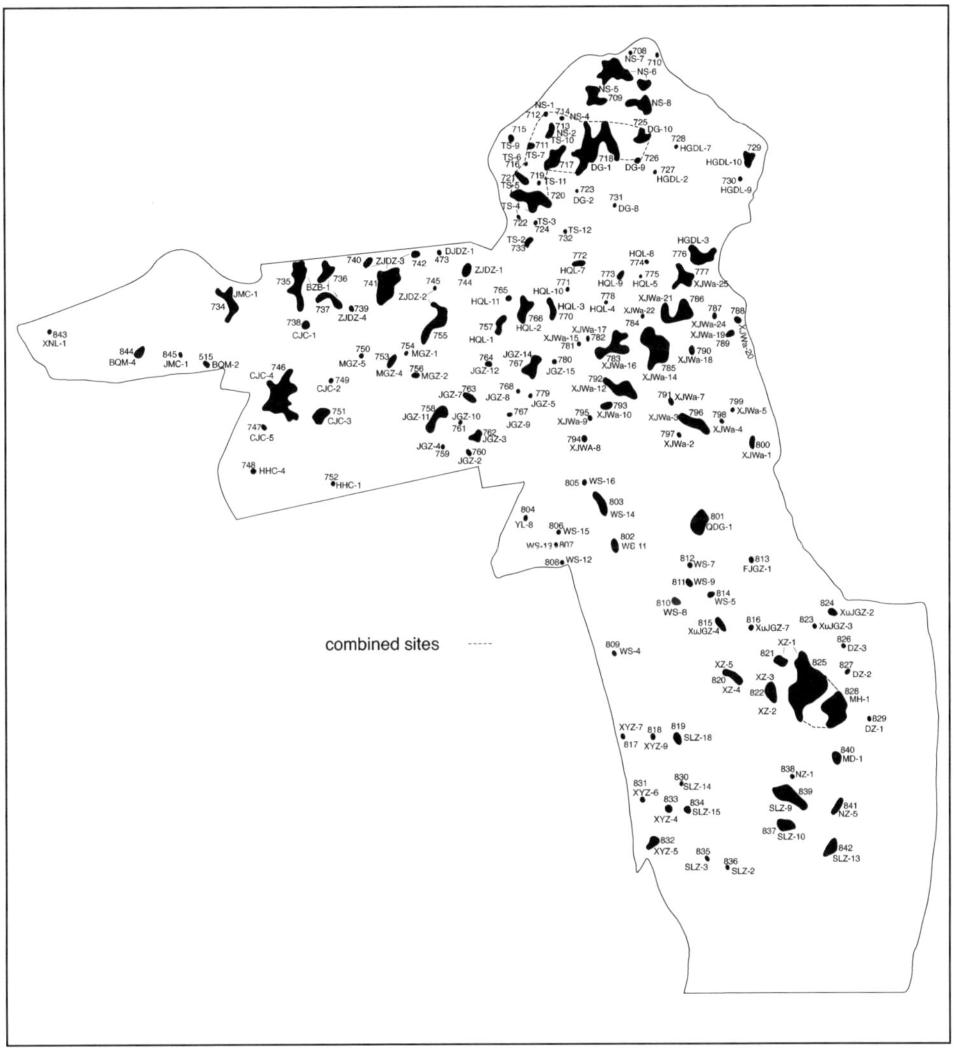

Figure 2.27. Han period sites found in the Jiaonan District in the northern survey area of Year 7 (2001).

QSCG-1, Longshan period) and Xinliu (辛留, LS-XL-1-7, Zhou period). We found more than one hundred new sites dating from the Dawenkou to the Han periods, with cultural layers visible at more than ten sites. These include the Longshan sites of Liujiagou (刘家沟, LS-LJG-4) and Gouwa (沟洼, LS-GW-1). Gouwa also has Yueshi period remains. Important new Zhou sites are Chegou (车沟, former name LS-CG-9; new name LS-DTS-5/CG-9, combined with the Datushan site), Houshaopo (后稍坡, LS-HSP-3), Jijiagou (纪家沟, LS-JJG-4), Dapo (大坡, LS-DP-1), Dabuluo (大卜萝, LS-DBL-1), and Yangjiazhuang (杨家庄, LS-YJZ-1). Datushan (大土山) is an important new Han site (LS-DTS-5/CG-9).

The Longshan sites we found are southeast of Yaowangcheng, including an area where there is a famous serpentine (蛇纹岩) mine at Suoluoshu (梭罗树). It is from the Dawenkou

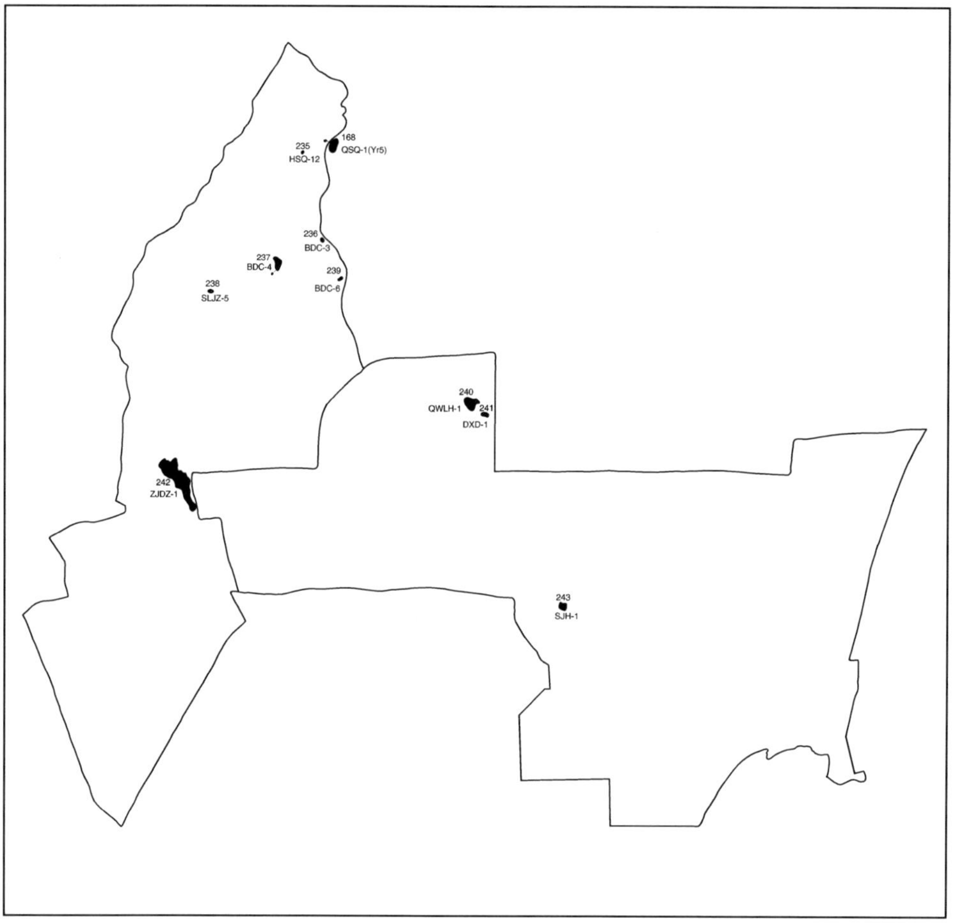

FIGURE 2.28. Longshan period sites found in the Donggang District in the southern survey area of Year 7 (2001).

and Longshan periods and not far from Shuichegou (水车沟), so this resource may have been important at the time. It also may be significant that this region, where we noted serpentine as we surveyed, is near the southeastern part of Yaowangcheng. Another important finding was the relatively large quantity of Yueshi sites in the area. The two sites with Yueshi remains from Year 11, Gouwa (沟洼) and Luochuangou (罗川沟), were located on the south bank of the same (Zhuzi) river. Another important site is Xinliu (辛留) from the Zhou period—it is more than 200 ha in size and may be related to the Quqiuyi (渠丘邑) polity of the Ju state (莒国) as recorded in the text Spring and Autumn Annals (B. Yang 1981, 1:36). The Datushan site of the Han period was at least 300 ha in size, almost as large as Haiqu (海曲), which has been investigated (see He, Zheng, and Cui 2003) by the Shandong Institute of Archaeology. Part of the Datushan area was under the administration of Langya County during the Han dynasty. Our survey results expanded the understanding of the history of the Rizhao area, which had only been known from documents (see Figures 2.46, 2.47, and 2.48).

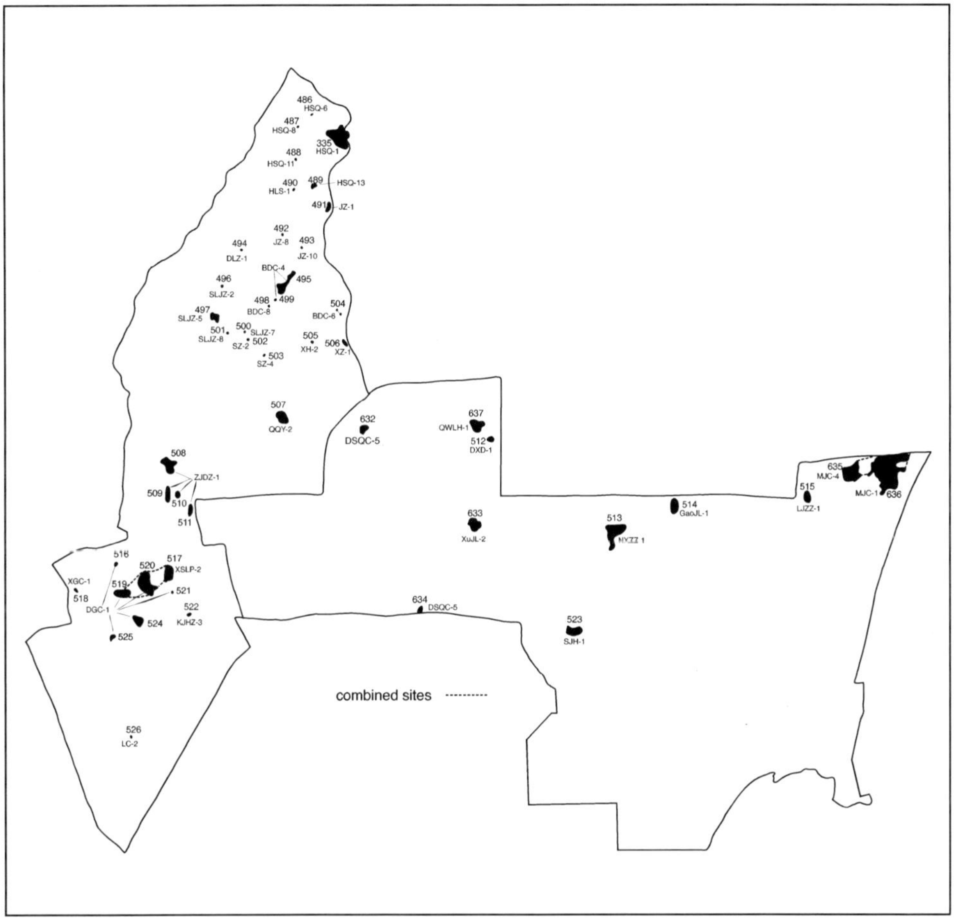

Figure 2.29. Zhou period sites found in the Donggang District in the southern survey area of Year 7 (2001).

Year 13: 1 November 2007–5 December 2007

The thirteenth season of survey took place in five districts: Lanshan and Donggang in the south, Jiaonan and Wulian in the north, and a small part of the southeastern Zhucheng area (see Figures 2.49 through 2.58). The southern area mainly covered terrain along the Futuan River and its branches in Donggang and Lanshan around the towns of Jufeng, Houcun, and Nanhu (南湖). The north area involved the Jili River area and its branches and the Baima River around the towns of Jiaonan at Haiqing, Dachang, Liwuguan (理务关), and Dacun (大村). The southern area was upstream of the Futuan River; we found fewer sites in this hilly area, one of which was the previously known Longshan site of Houmazhuang (后马庄, LS-HMZ-1). A newly found Longshan site is Dahoucun (大后村, LS-DHC-2). Other important Zhou period sites are Lijiawa (李家洼, LS-LJW-3) and Weixingying (卫星营, LS-WXY-1), and there was the Han site of Xihuangshanqian (西黄山前, DG-XHSQ-3). The northern area on the alluvial plain of the Jili and Baima Rivers was flat and fertile, so many

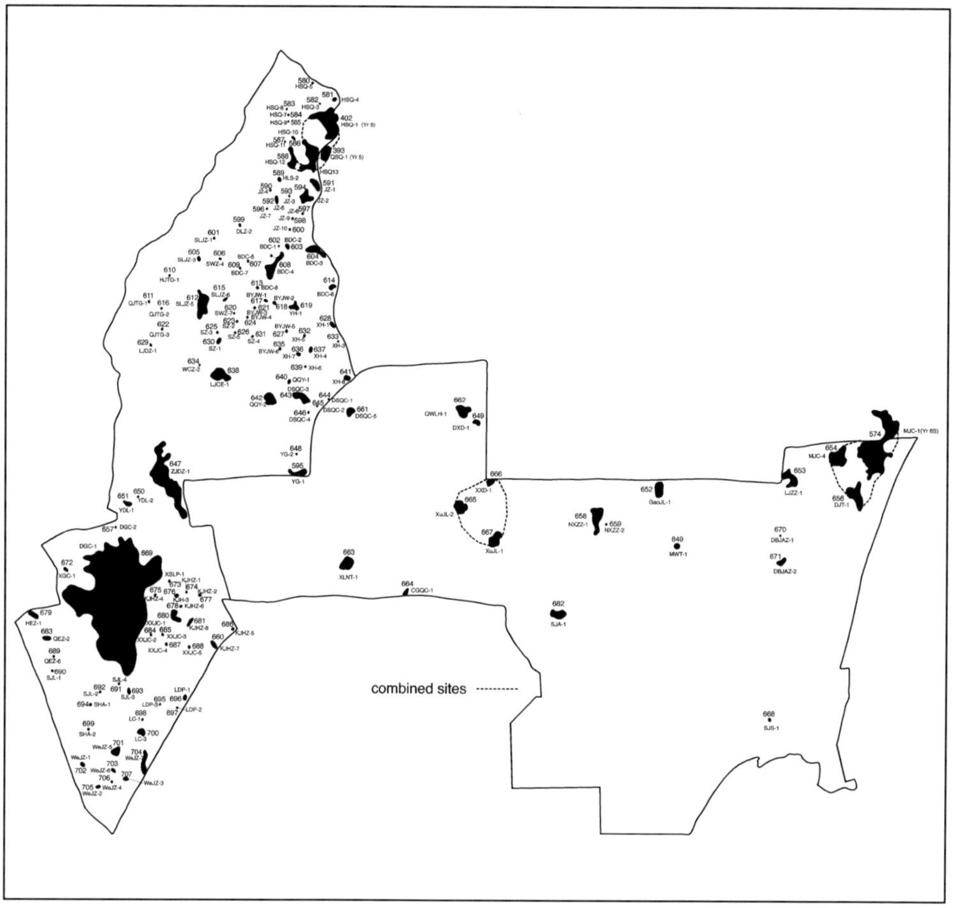

FIGURE 2.30. Han period sites found in the Donggang District in the southern survey area of Year 7 (2001).

new sites were found, including several from the Longshan period: Dingjialiugou (丁家柳沟, JN-DJLG-3), Dingshiqiao (丁石桥, JN-DSQ-2), Shuanghe (双河, JN-SH-11), Tuogou (驼沟, JN-TG-4), Xiejiazhuangzi (解家庄子, ZC-XJZZ-1), and Nanzhangjiazhuang (南张家庄, ZC-NZJZ-1). We also found the Shang period site Xiejiazhuangzi (ZC-XJZZ-1), the Zhou site Nanzhangjiazhuang (ZC-NJJZ-1), and the Han site Xiaocaojiazhuang (小曹家庄, ZC-XCJZ-1, 2, 4). We discovered stone inscriptions on what seems to be a boundary monument between the Jiaonan and Zhucheng Districts, possibly dating to the Han period. By the end of 2007, the area surveyed during the thirteen years was more than 1,440 km^2. We had discovered more than two thousand sites, almost six hundred of which were prehistoric, mainly from the Longshan period.

This book provides a more detailed account of the results from our systematic, full-coverage regional survey between 1995 and 2007 than we have previously published (Cai et al. 1997; Underhill et al. 1998, 2002, 2008; Fang et al. 2002, 2008; Fang 2003a). It complements

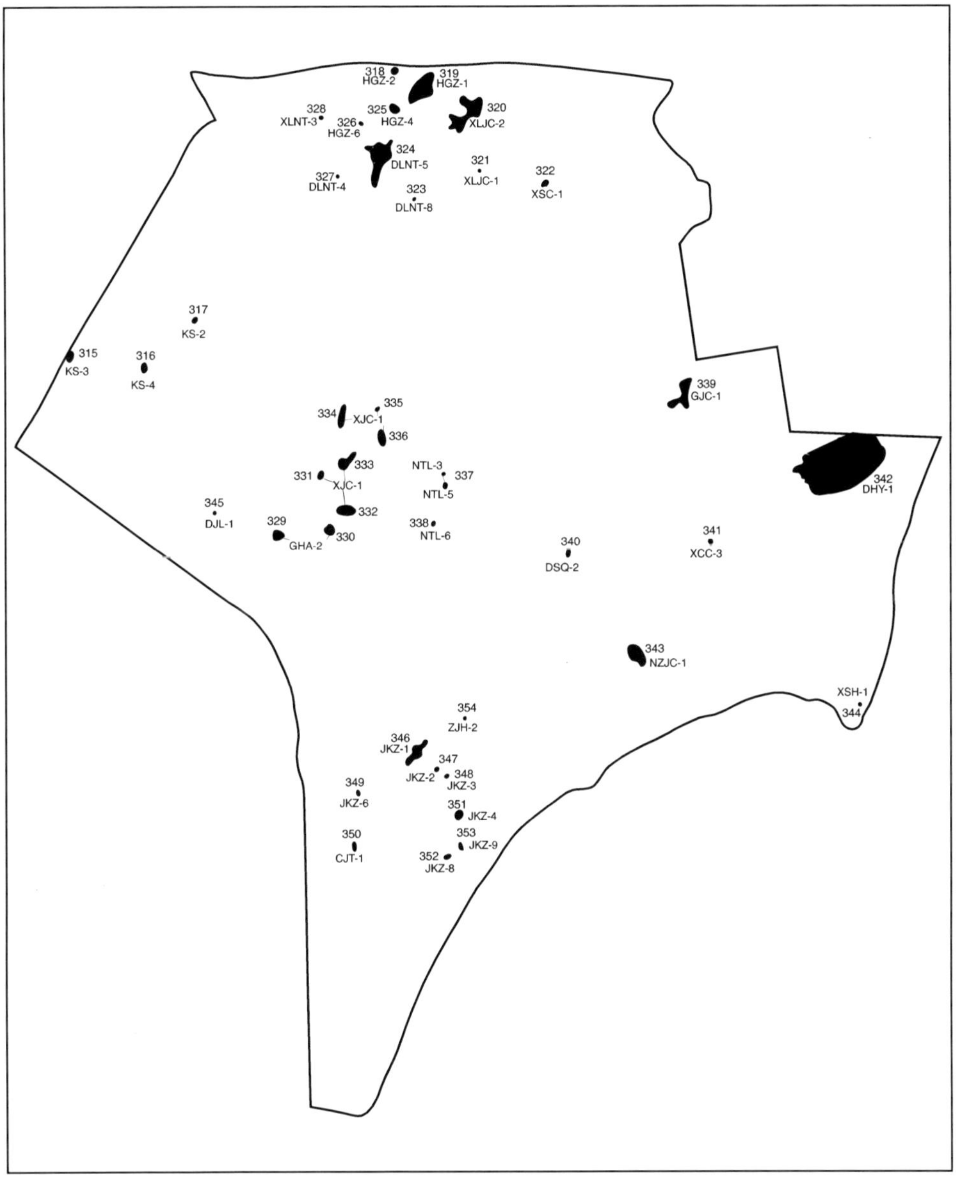

Figure 2.31. Longshan period sites found in the Donggang District in the southern survey area of Year 8 (2002).

the book we published in Chinese (Fang et al. 2012), providing some additional details about methodology and interpretation.

There are other relevant publications that contribute to our understanding of social change in southeastern Shandong. Feinman, Fang, and Nicholas (2019a) completed the systematic regional survey of the northern coastal basin as they expanded survey coverage to the north. Hui (2016) synthesizes data for our 1995–2007 survey and uses geographic information

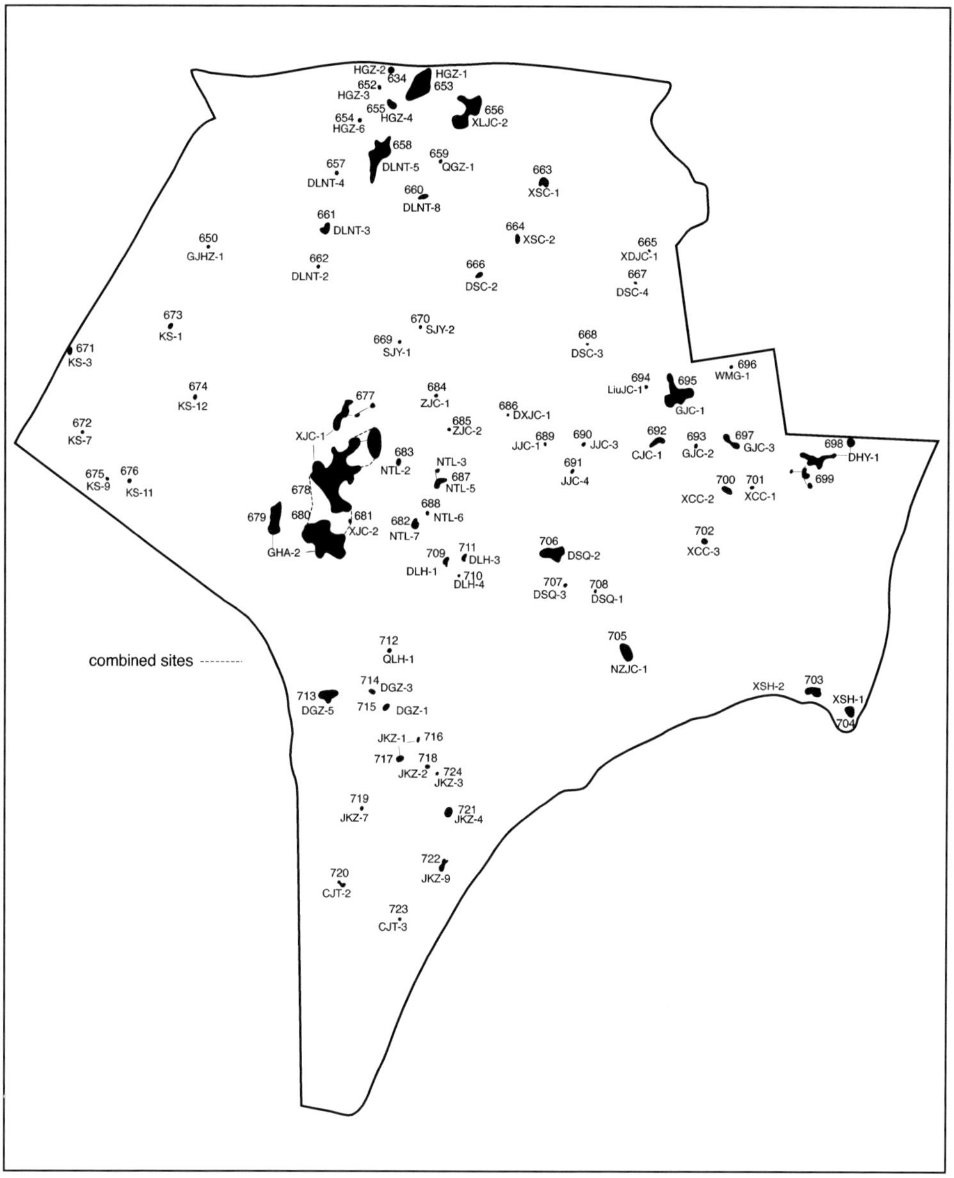

FIGURE 2.32. Zhou period sites found in the Donggang District in the southern survey area of Year 8 (2002).

(GIS) analysis to interpret possible communication routes between settlements. Two other scholars, Bennett (2002, 2007) and Cunnar (2014), evaluate stone tools from Liangchengzhen and other sites in the survey region. Bennett (2004) provides analysis of landscape archaeology in the eastern seaboard region; Chen et al. (2009) report analysis of seeds from some of the survey sites reported here; and Chen et al. (2017) provide new AMS radiocarbon dates for some sites. Fang et al. (2004) provide an initial estimation of demography for the region.

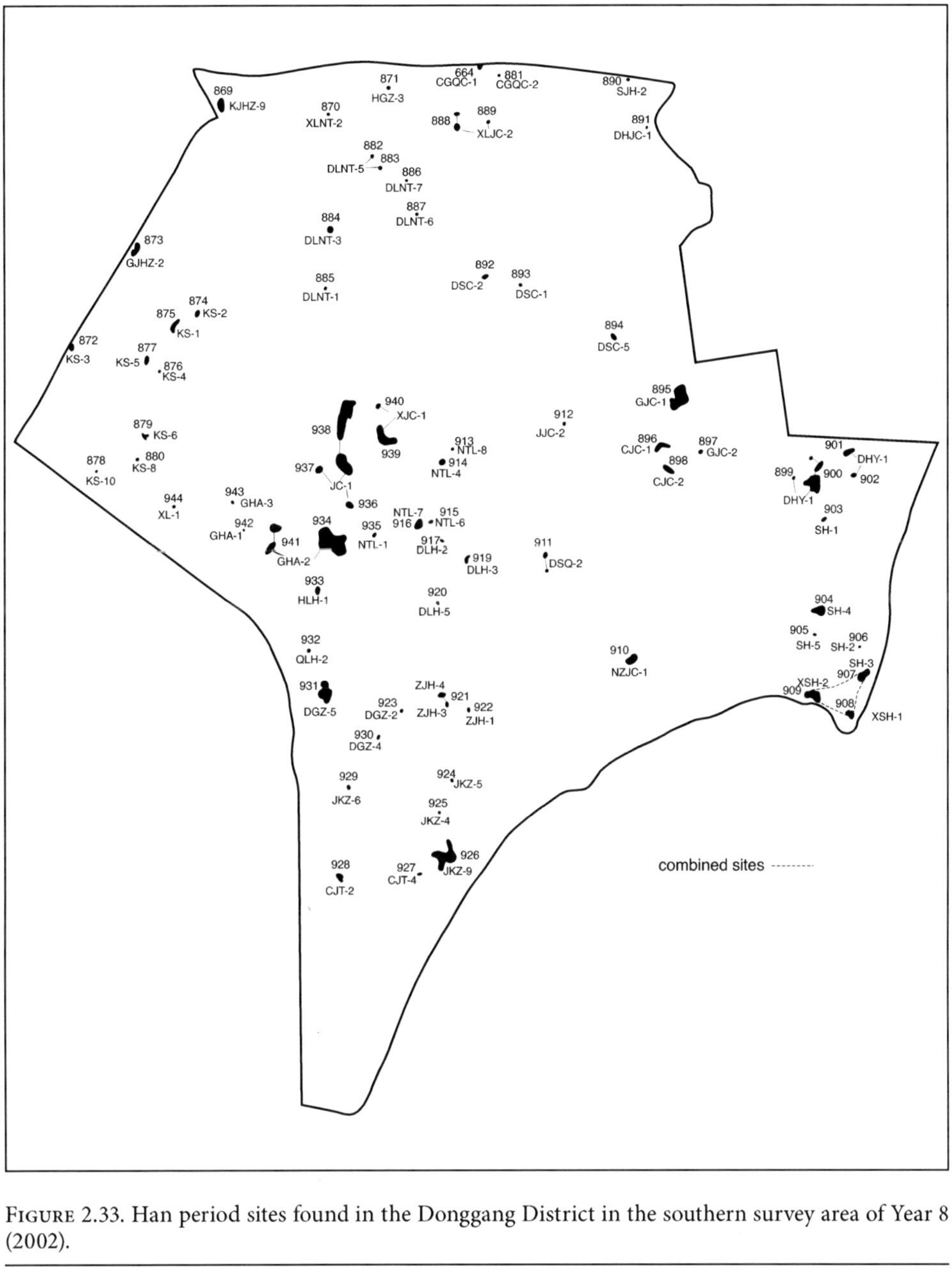

Figure 2.33. Han period sites found in the Donggang District in the southern survey area of Year 8 (2002).

Excavation of Liangchengzhen from 1998 to 2001, the largest Longshan period site in the northern half of our survey region, provided details about major features of the settlement, including moats, traces of walls, and a residential area (Area 1) characterized by abundant evidence for production of stone tools. The excavation report (China–U.S. Cooperative Archaeological Team 2016, 1:19, 3:1, 618) provides a smaller size (about 70 to 80 ha) for the settlement of Liangchengzhen than we refer to here (see Chapters 3 and 4) from the extent

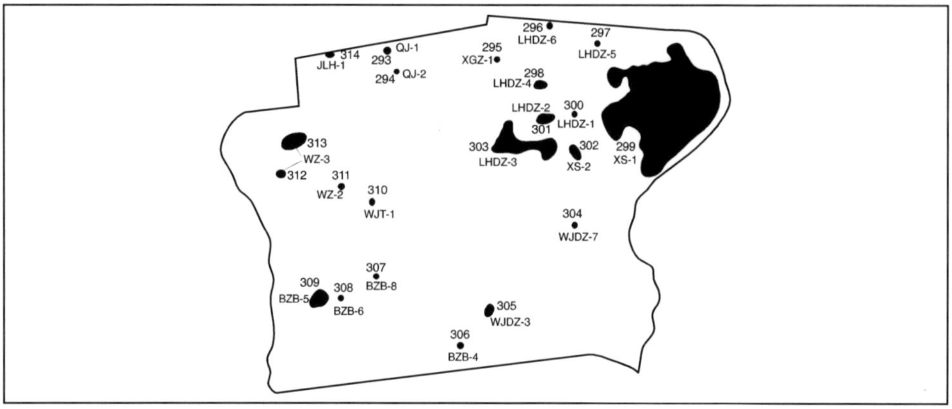

FIGURE 2.34. Longshan period sites found in the Jiaonan District in the northern survey area of Year 8 (2002).

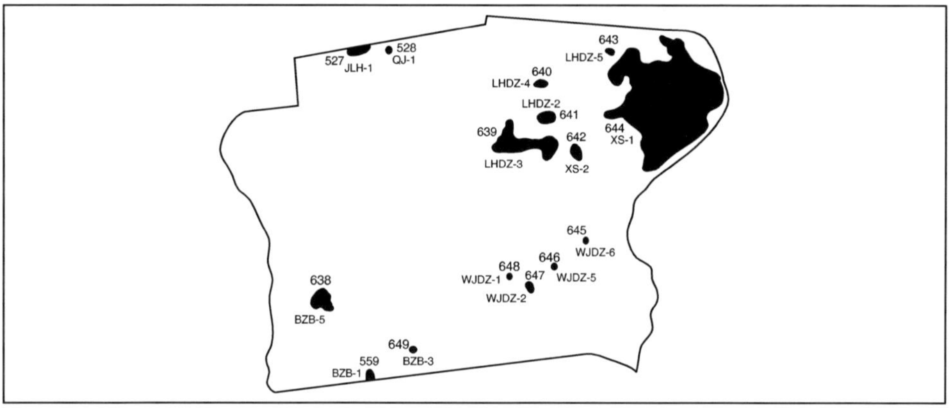

FIGURE 2.35. Zhou period sites found in the Jiaonan District in the northern survey area of Year 8 (2002).

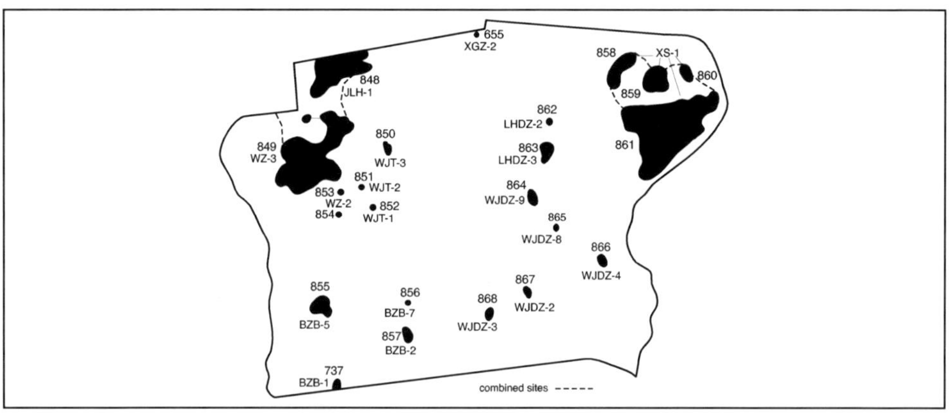

FIGURE 2.36. Han period sites found in the Jiaonan District in the northern survey area of Year 8 (2002).

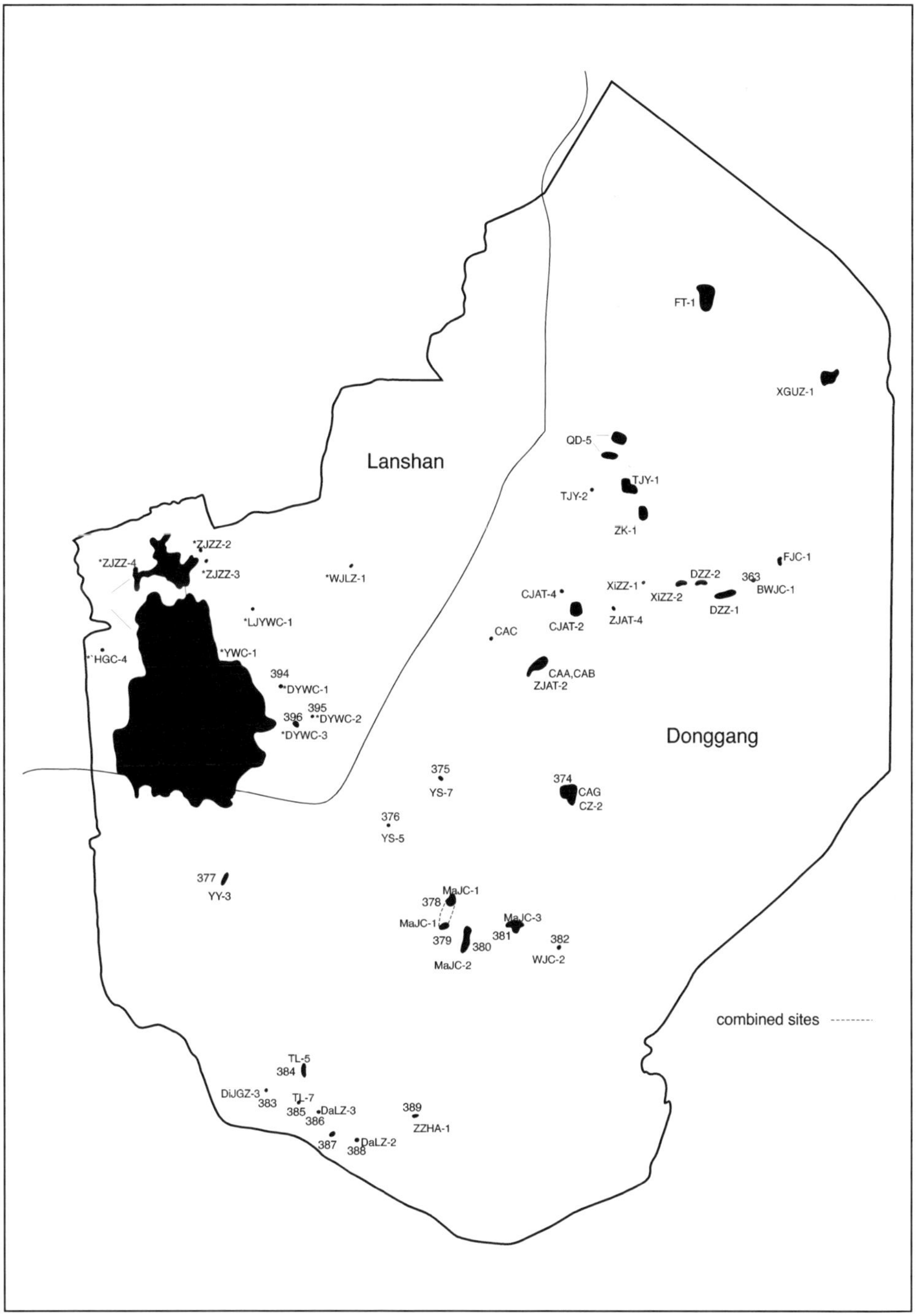

Figure 2.37. Longshan period sites found in the Lanshan and Donggang Districts during survey Year 9 (2003). Because the area was surveyed before the formation of the Lanshan District, all Lanshan sites have a DG prefix.

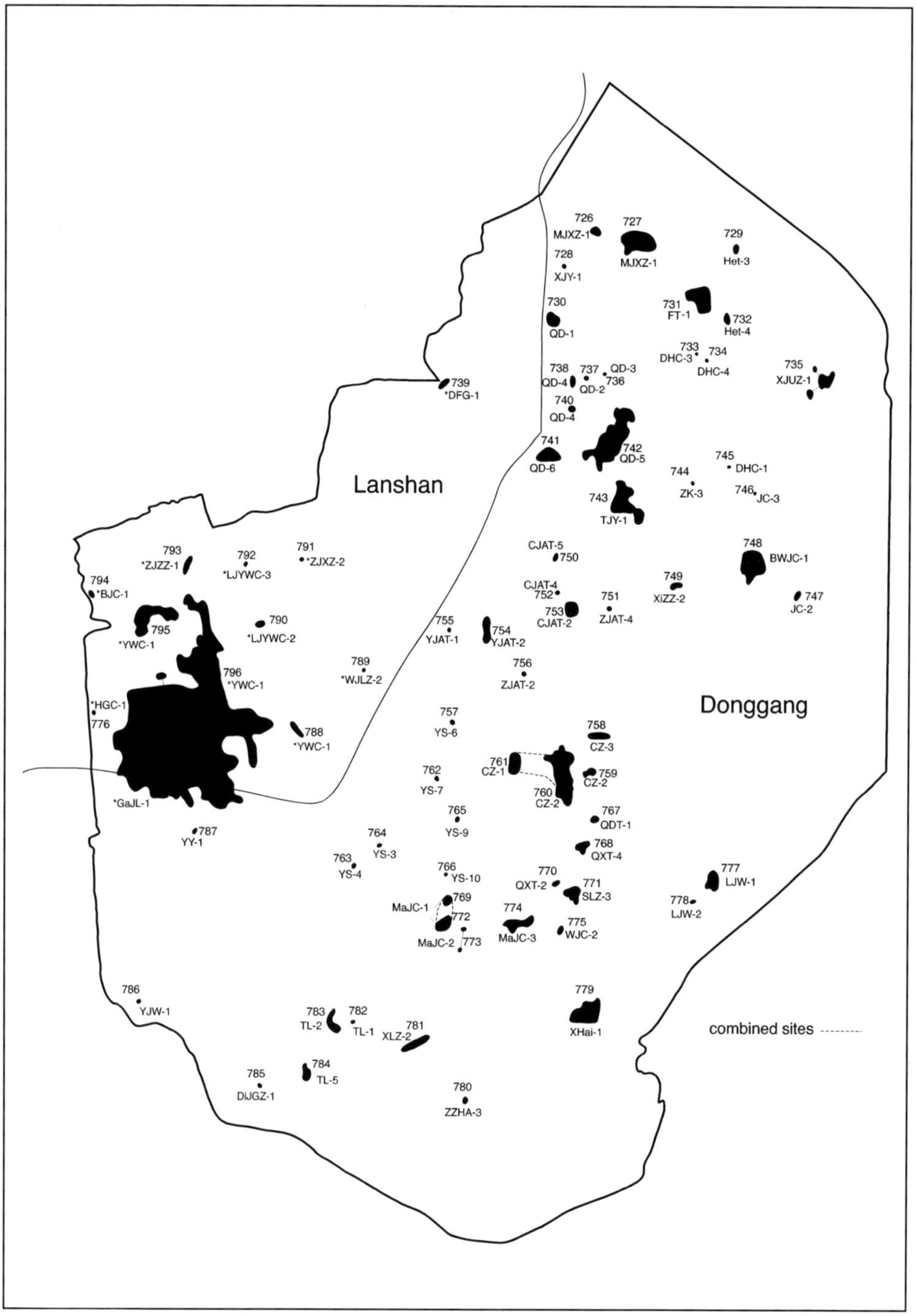

FIGURE 2.38. Zhou period sites found in the Lanshan and Donggang Districts during survey Year 9 (2003). Because the area was surveyed before the formation of the Lanshan District, all Lanshan sites have a DG prefix.

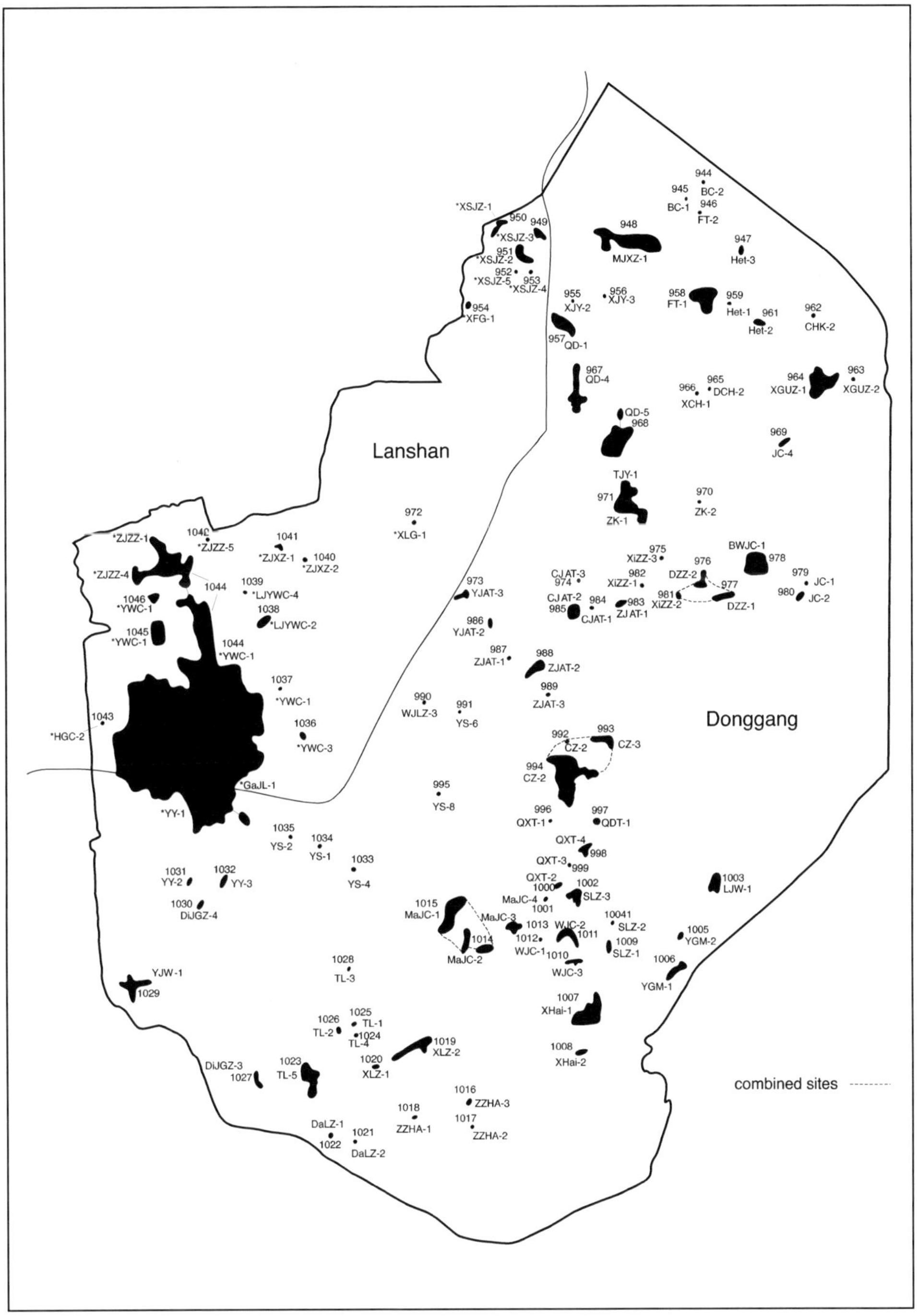

Figure 2.39. Han period sites found in the Lanshan and Donggang Districts during survey Year 9 (2003). Because the area was surveyed before the formation of the Lanshan District, all Lanshan sites have a DG prefix.

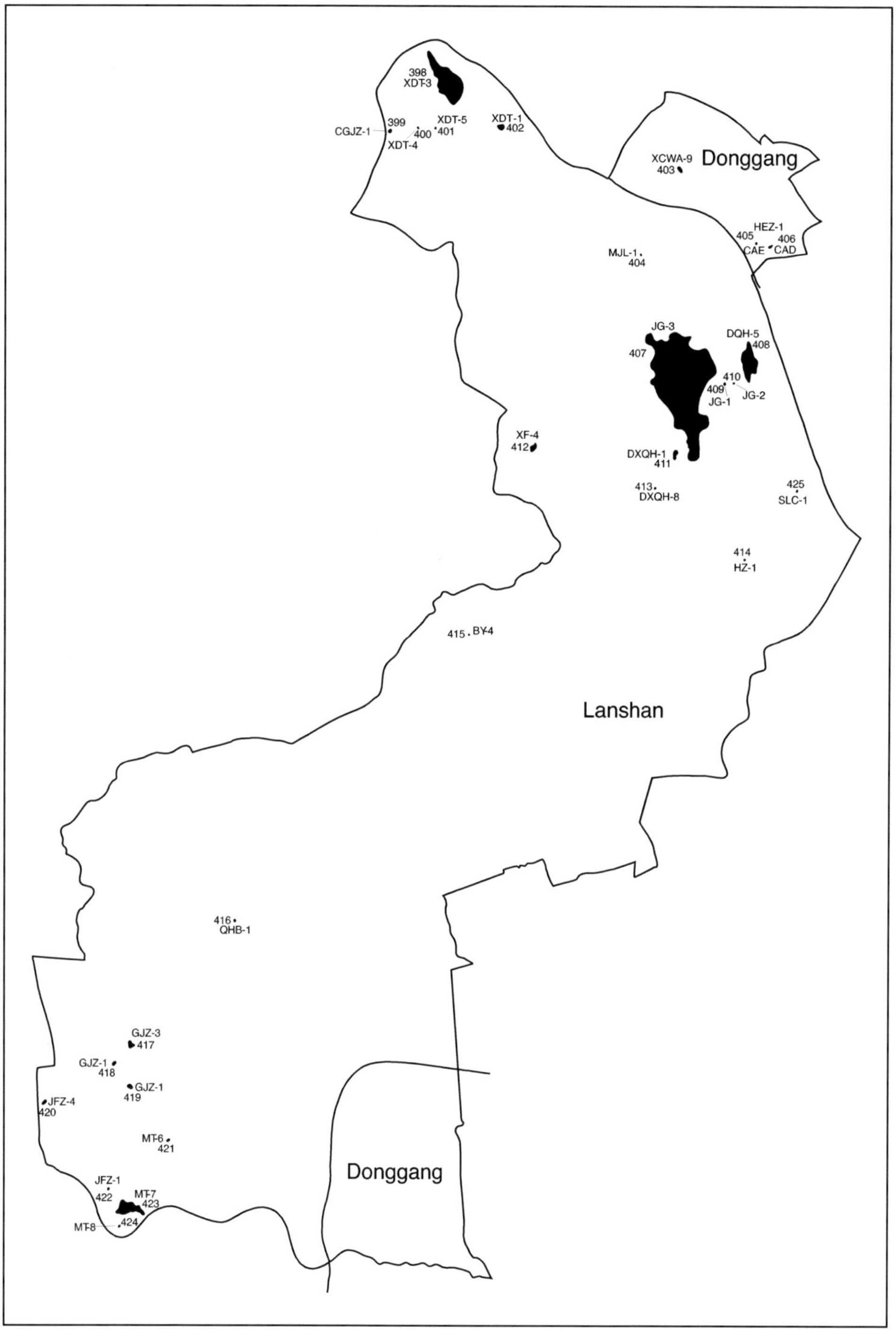

FIGURE 2.40. Longshan period sites found in the Lanshan and Donggang Districts during survey Year 10 (2004).

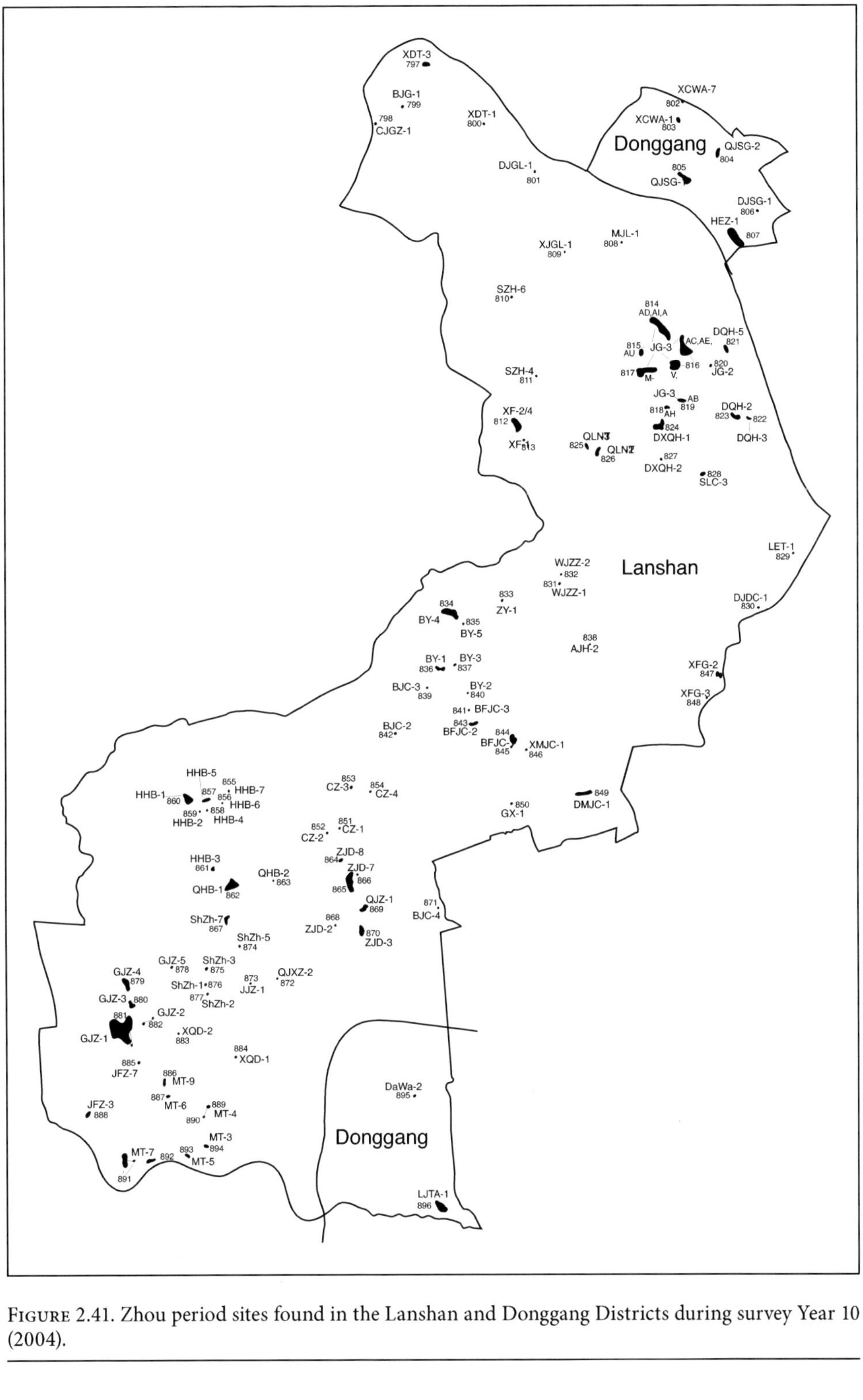

Figure 2.41. Zhou period sites found in the Lanshan and Donggang Districts during survey Year 10 (2004).

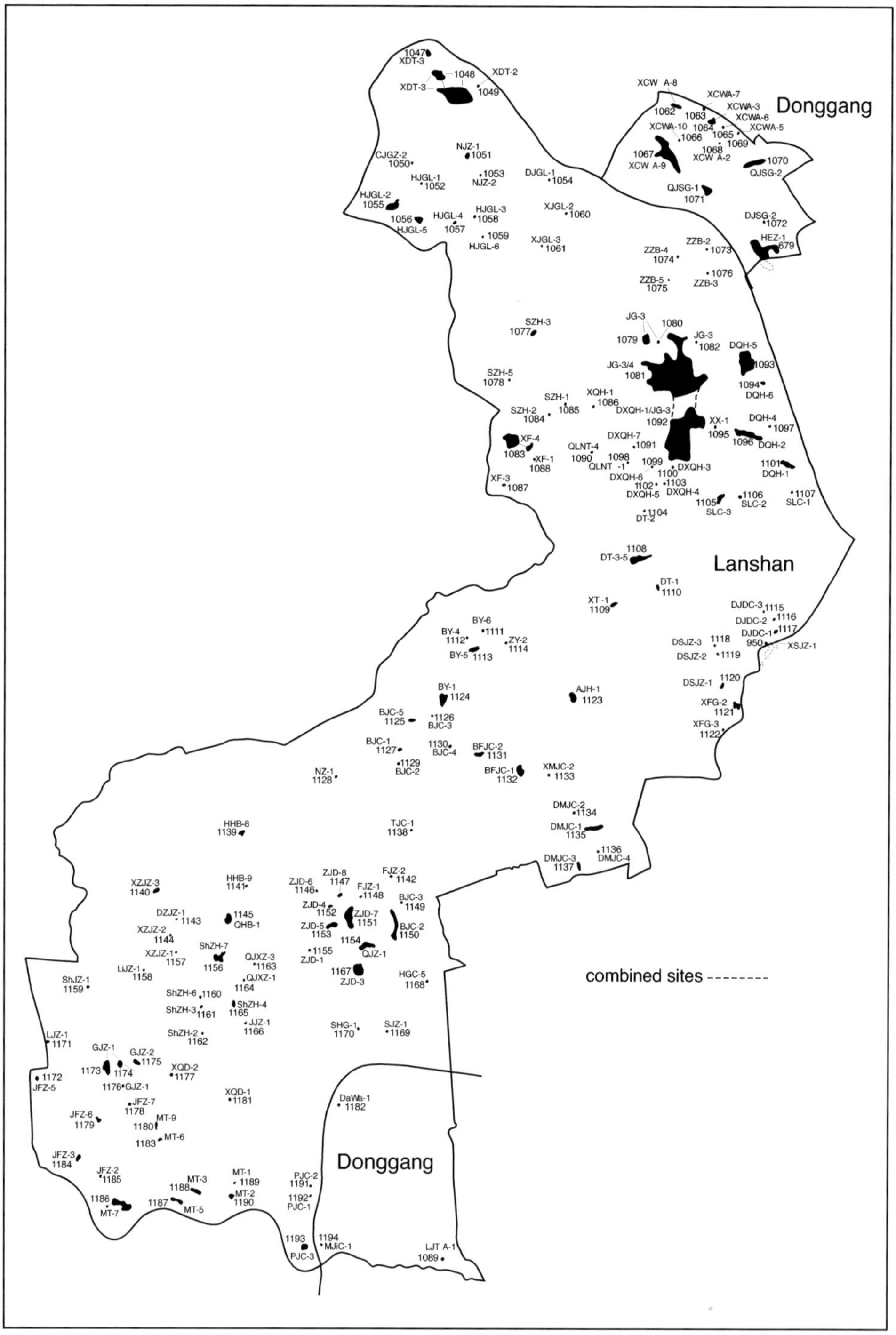

FIGURE 2.42. Han period sites found in the Lanshan and Donggang Districts during survey Year 10 (2004).

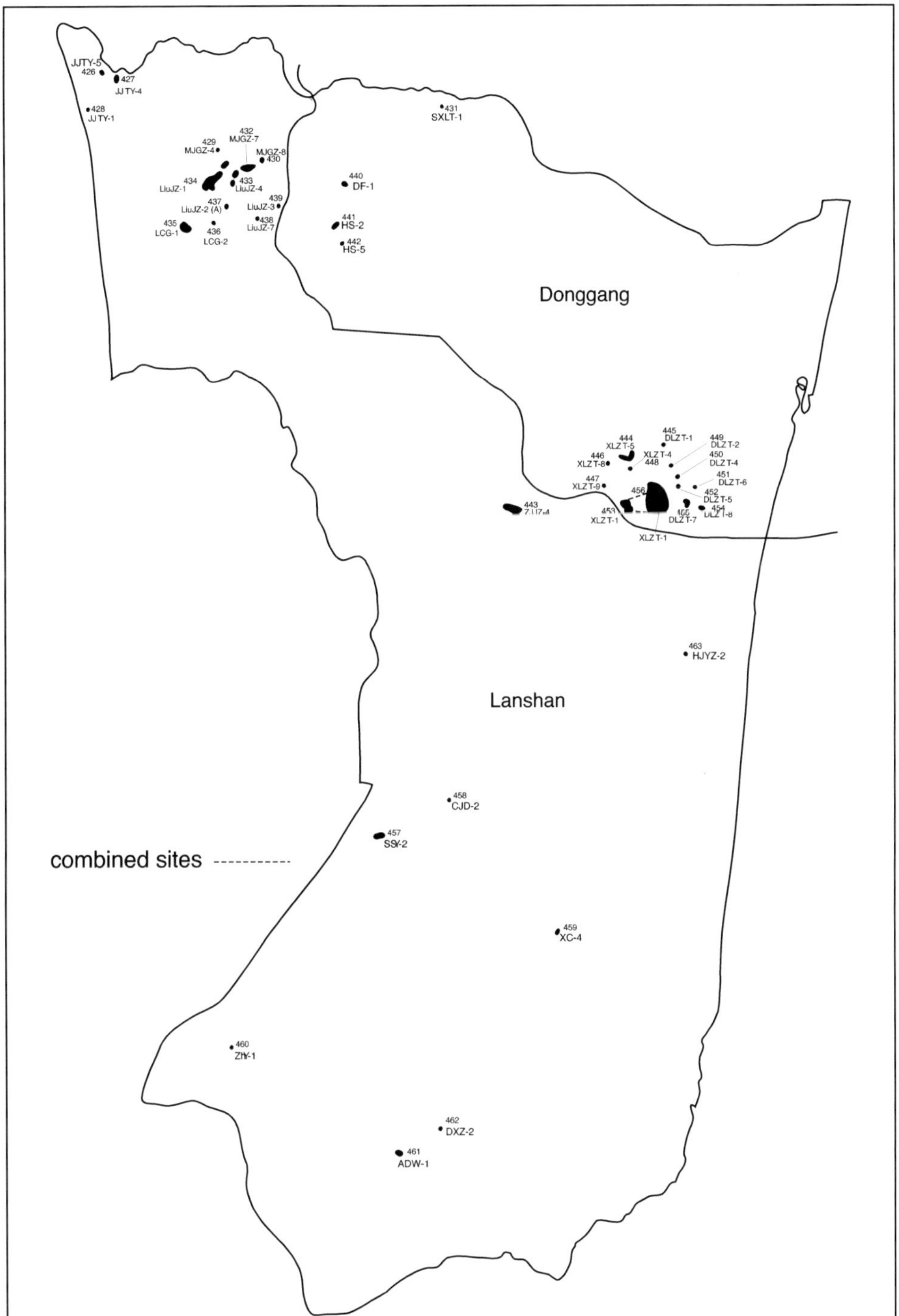

FIGURE 2.43. Longshan period sites found in the Lanshan and Donggang Districts during survey Year 11 (2005).

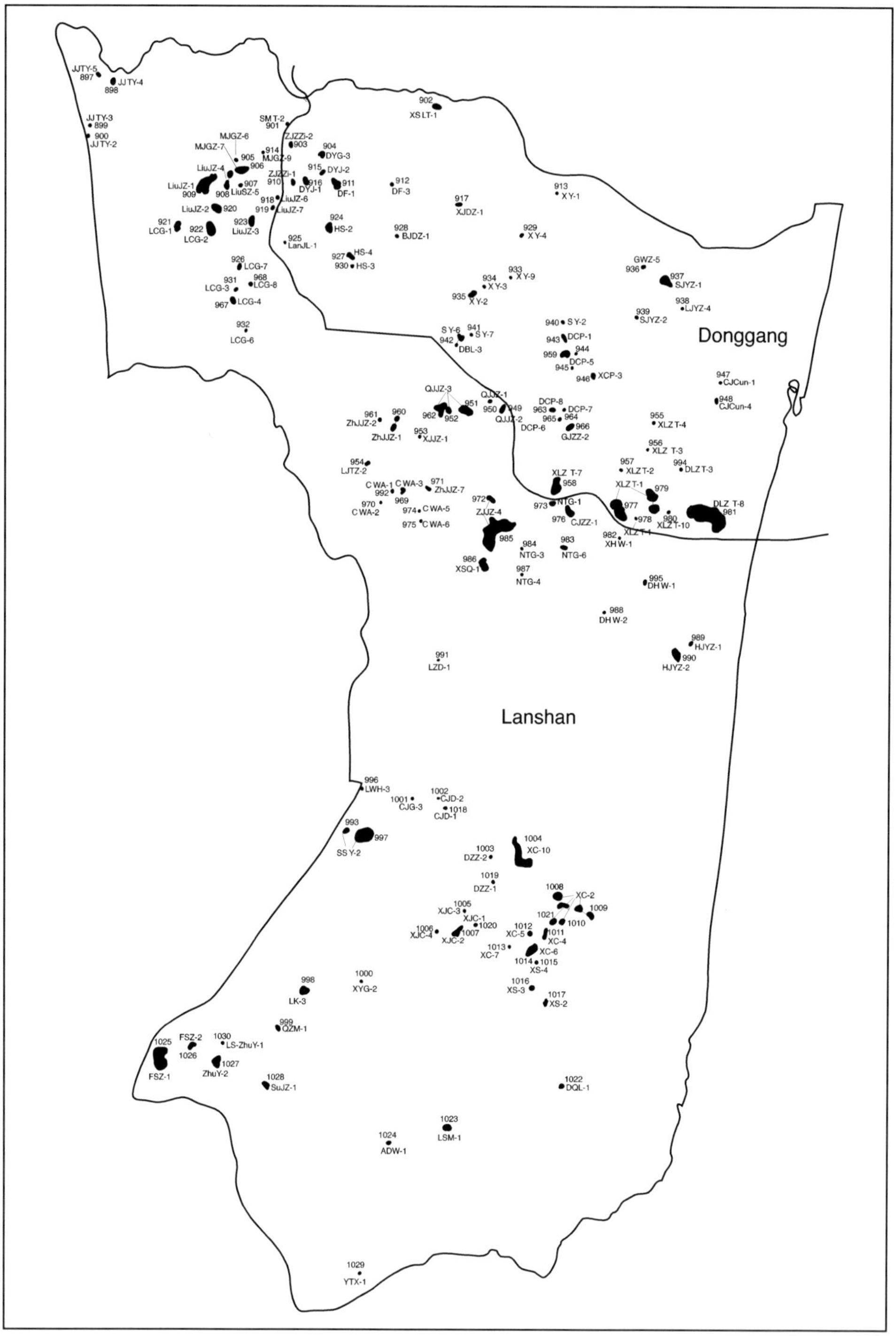

FIGURE 2.44. Zhou period sites found in the Lanshan and Donggang Districts during survey Year 11 (2005).

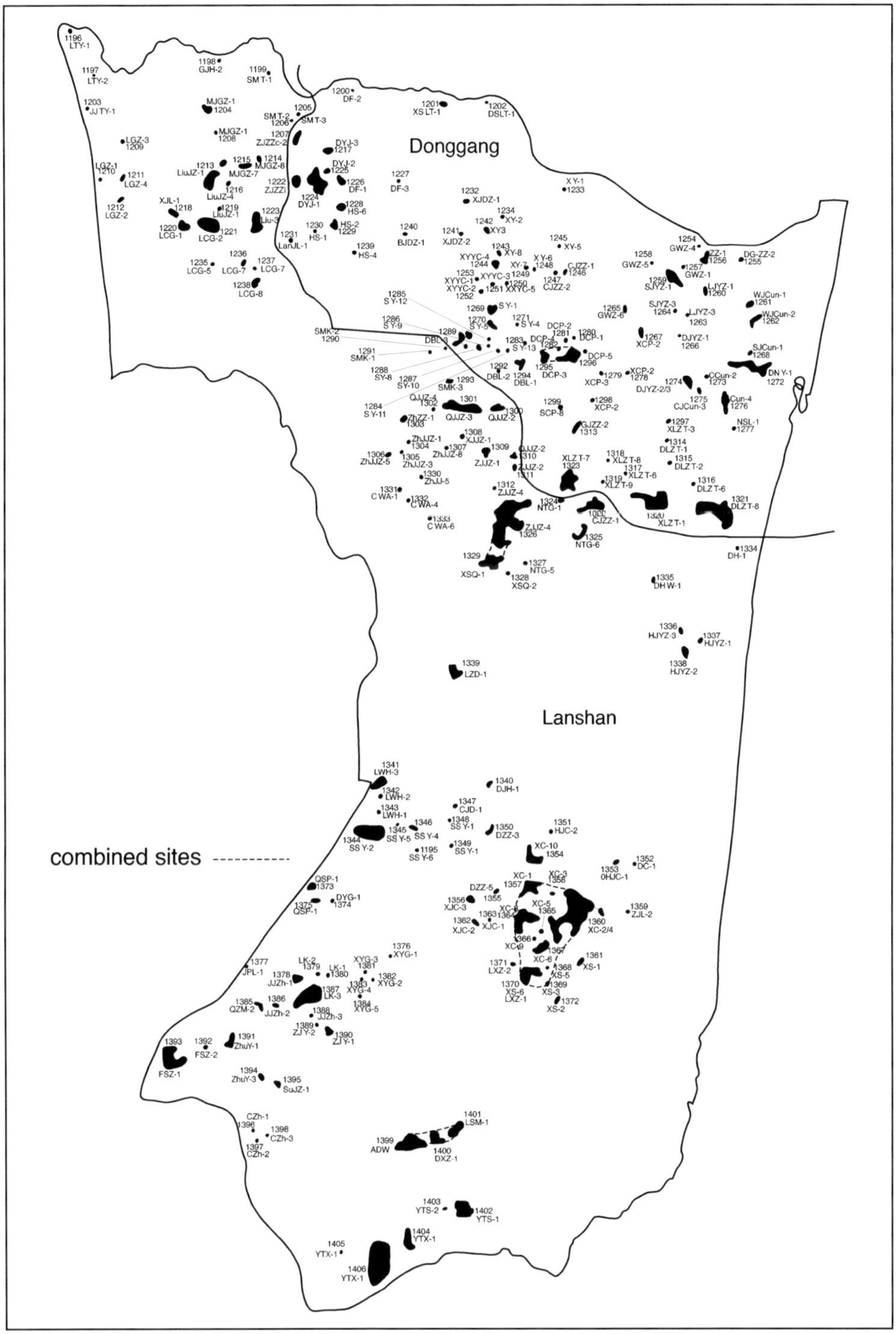

FIGURE 2.45. Han period sites found in the Lanshan and Donggang Districts during survey Year 11 (2005).

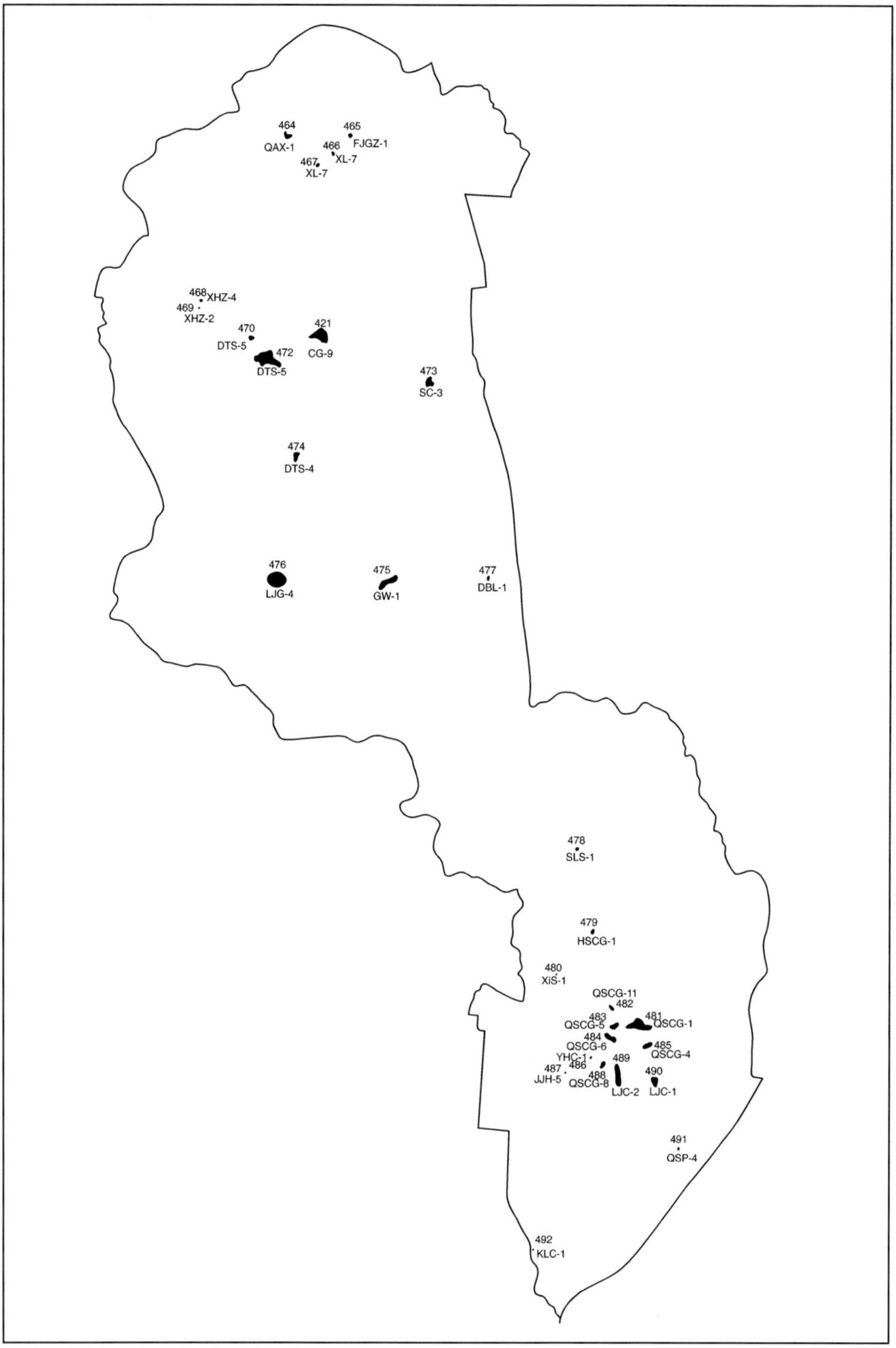

FIGURE 2.46. Longshan period sites found in the Lanshan District during survey Year 12 (2006).

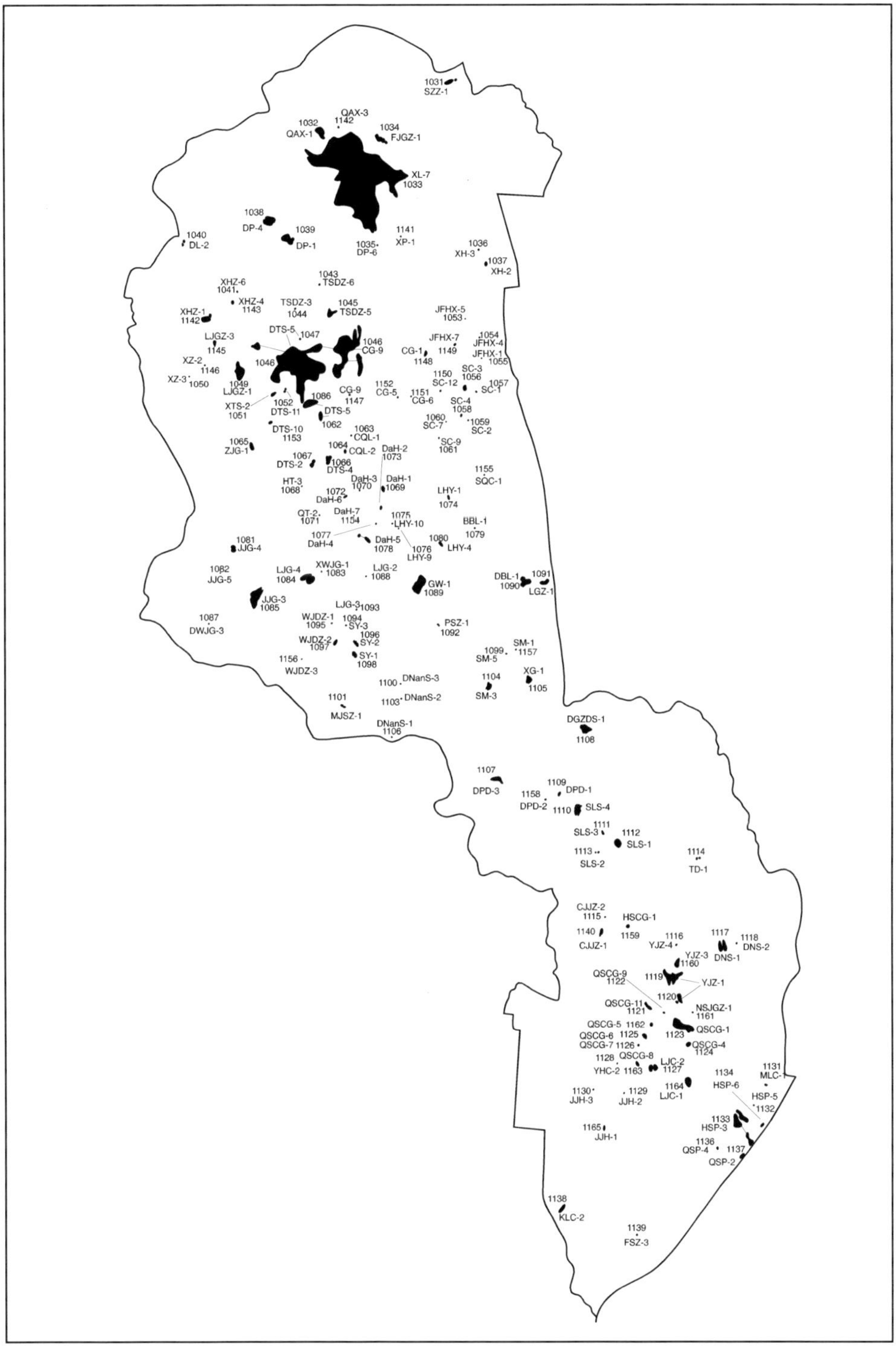

Figure 2.47. Zhou period sites found in the Lanshan District during survey Year 12 (2006).

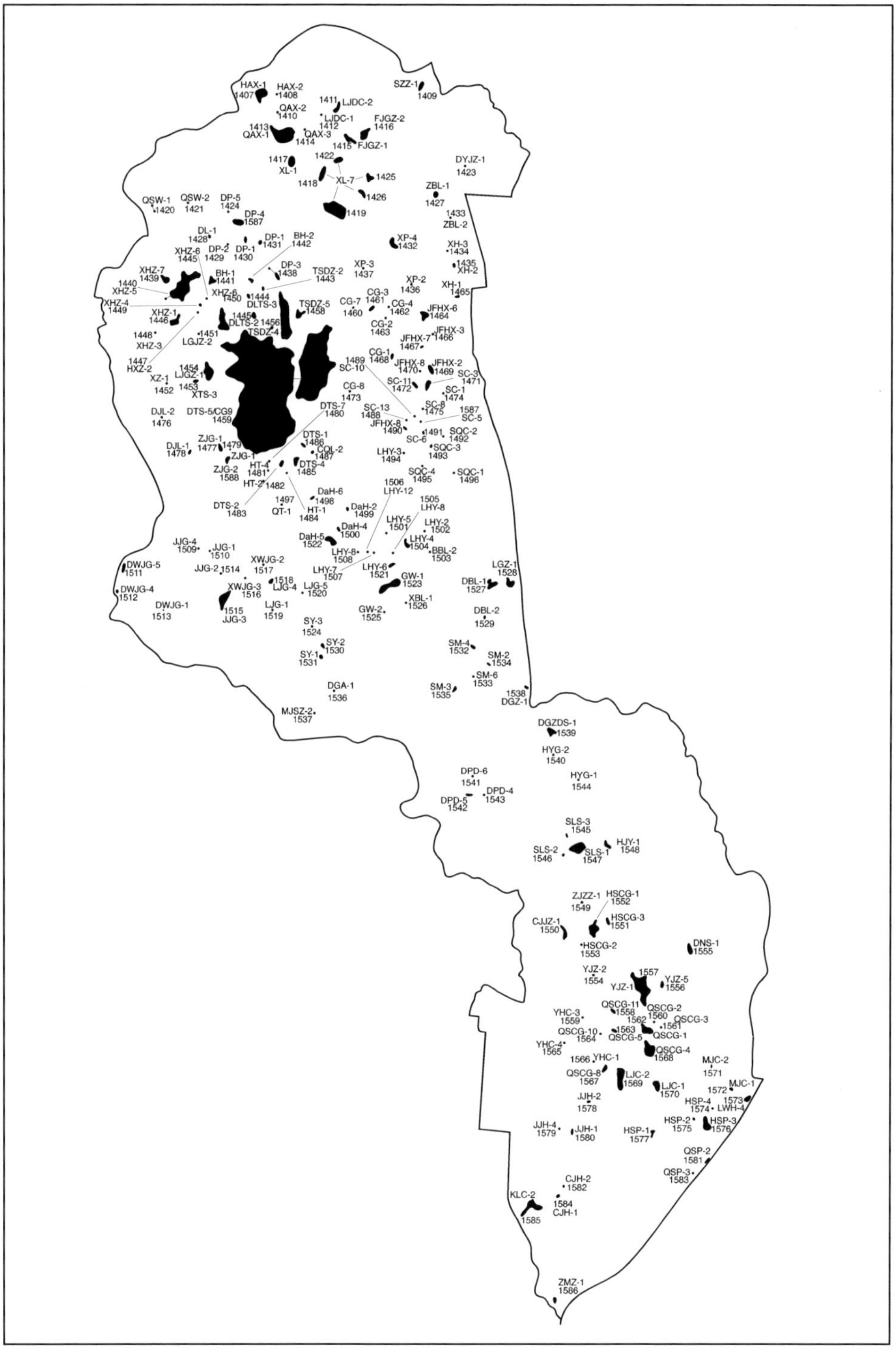

FIGURE 2.48. Han period sites found in the Lanshan District during survey Year 12 (2006).

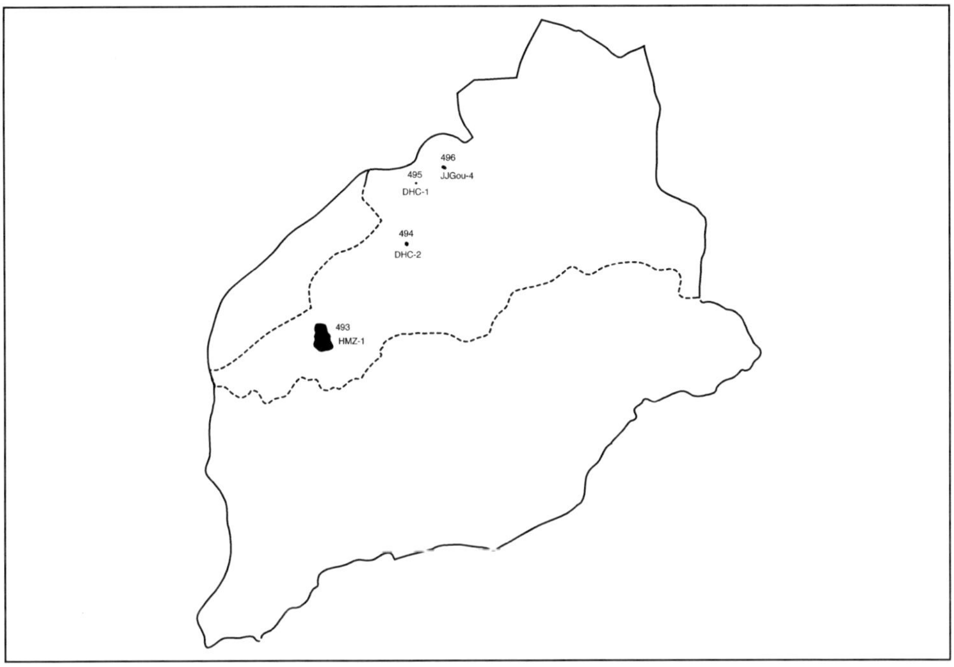

FIGURE 2.49. Longshan period sites found in the Lanshan District during survey Year 13 (2007).

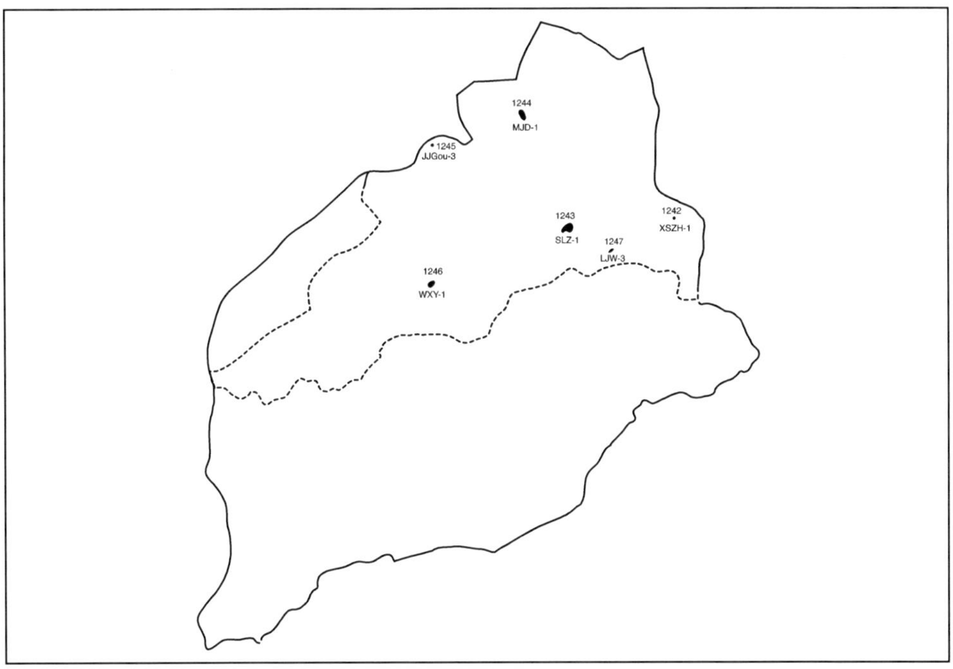

FIGURE 2.50. Zhou period sites found in the Lanshan District during survey Year 13 (2007).

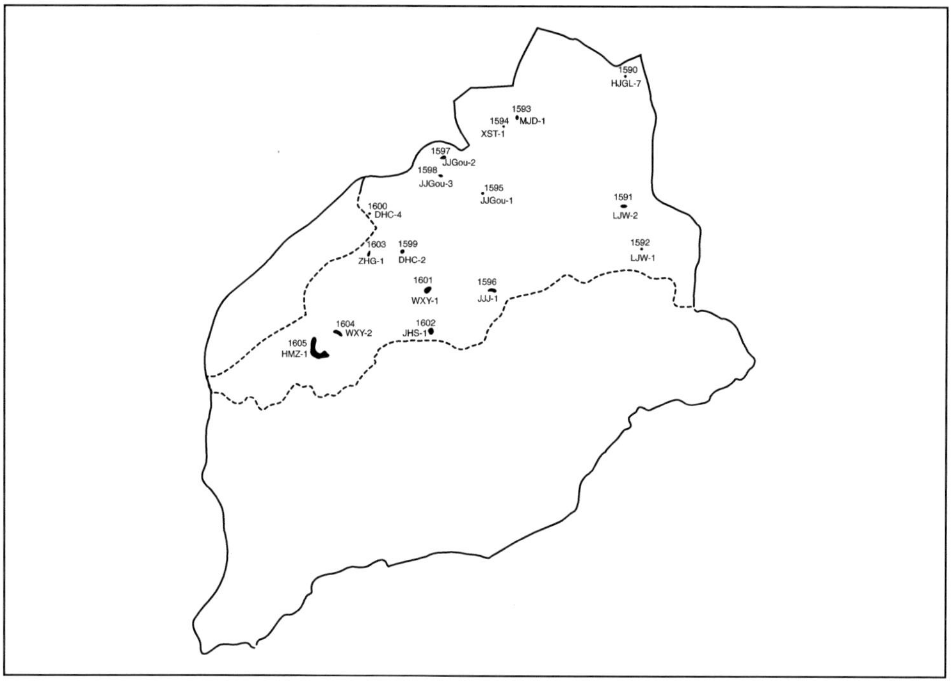

FIGURE 2.51. Han period sites found in the Lanshan District during survey Year 13 (2007).

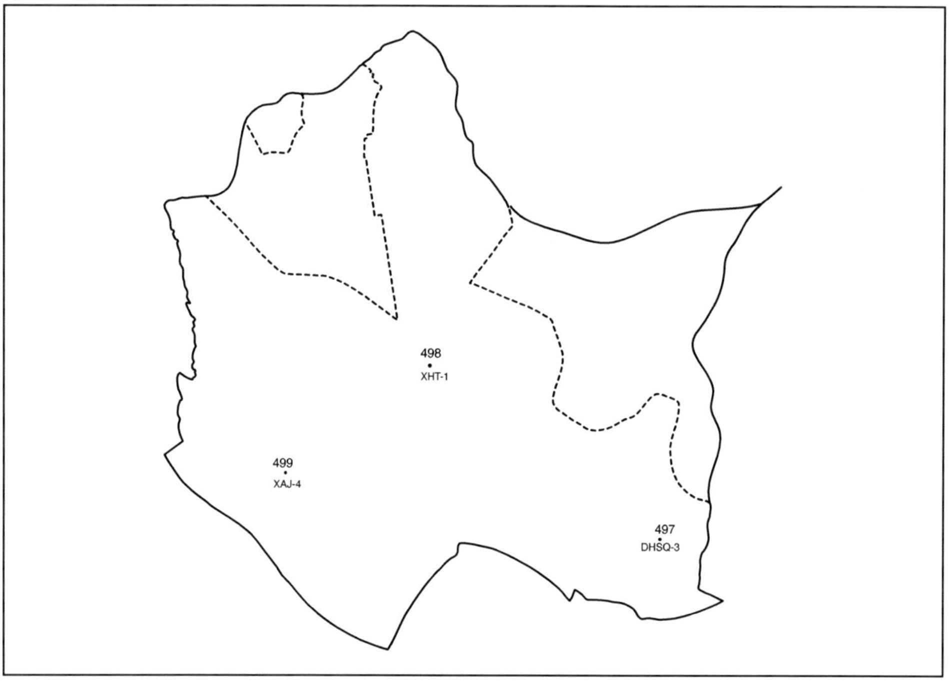

FIGURE 2.52. Longshan period sites found in the Donggang District during survey Year 13 (2007).

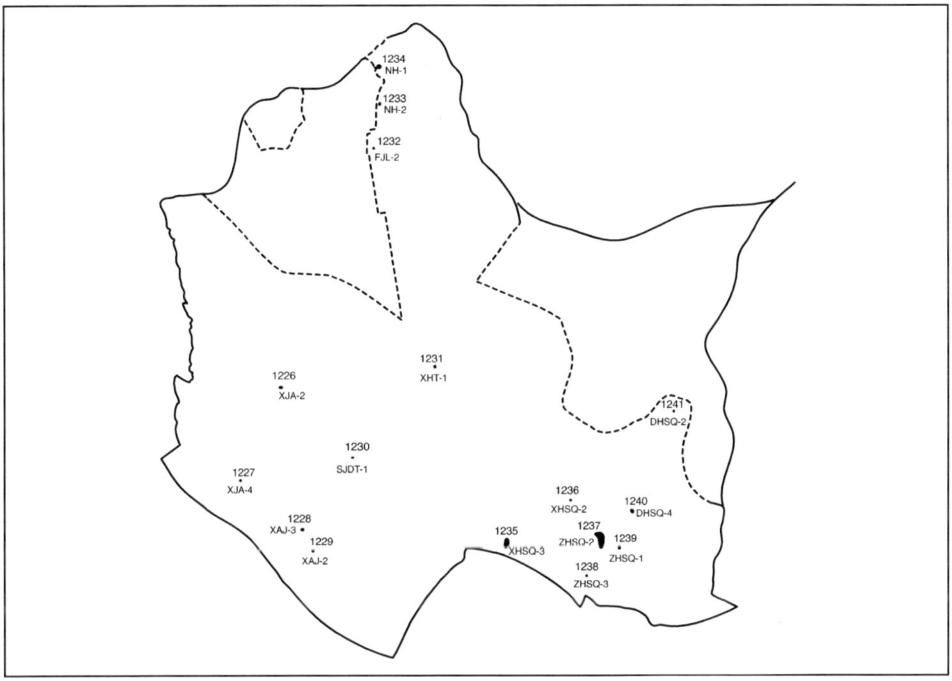

Figure 2.53. Zhou period sites found in the Donggang District during survey Year 13 (2007).

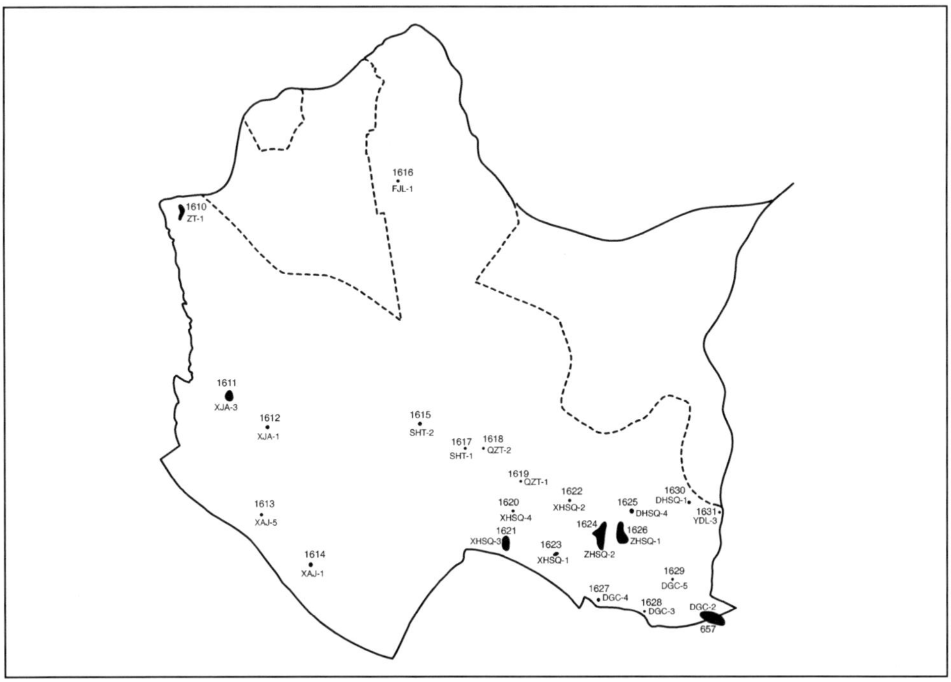

Figure 2.54. Han period sites found in the Donggang District during survey Year 13 (2007).

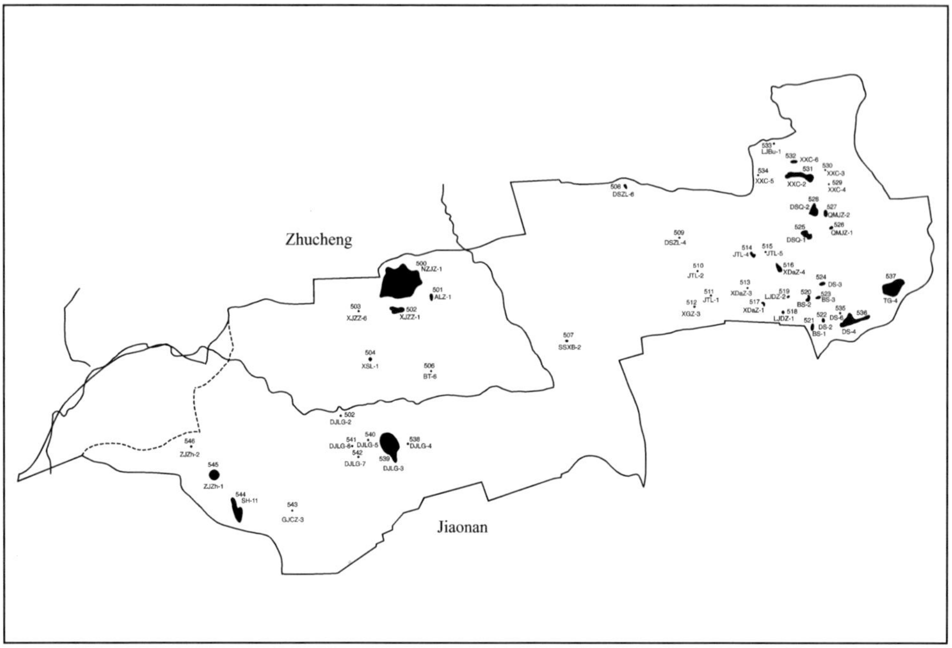

FIGURE 2.55. Longshan period sites found in the Jiaonan and Zhucheng Districts during survey Year 13 (2007).

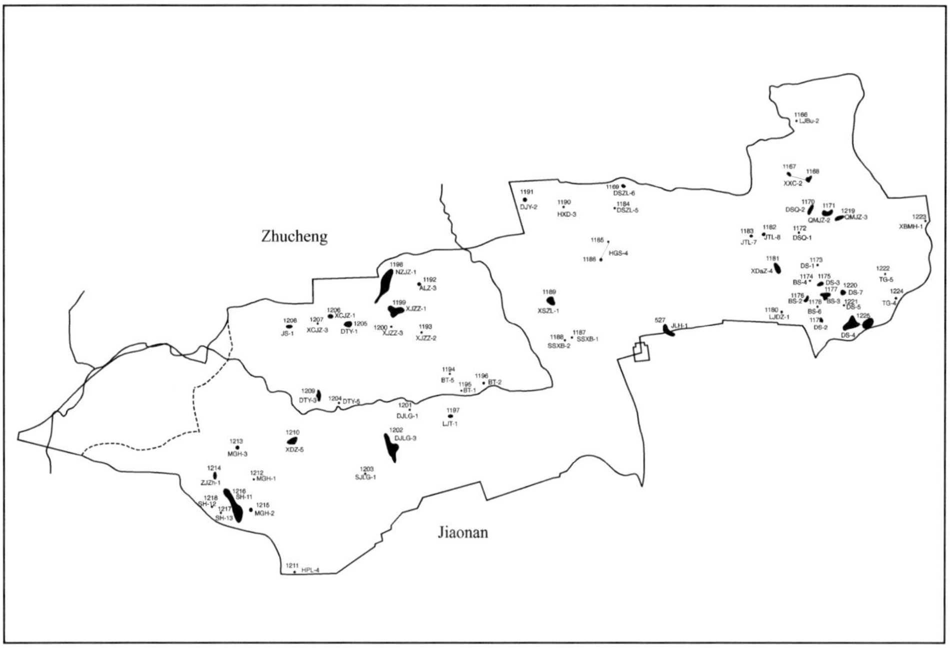

FIGURE 2.56. Zhou period sites found in the Jiaonan and Zhucheng Districts during survey Year 13 (2007).

Figure 2.57. Han period sites found in the Jiaonan and Zhucheng Districts during survey Year 13 (2007).

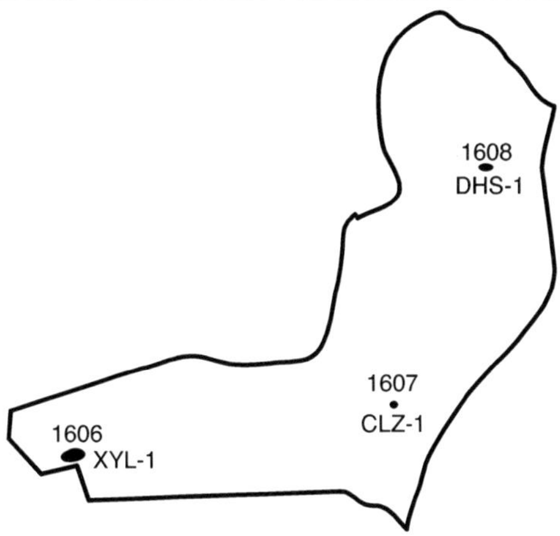

Figure 2.58. Han period sites found in the Wulian District during survey Year 13 (2007).

of the buried cultural deposits that could be identified through probing and excavation, a methodology employed for many other large settlements in China (see Underhill 2017). This relatively conservative approach to interpretation of site size does not consider habitation or use of lands in external areas beyond walls and moats likely to be important for past subsistence activities. Also, walls and moats clearly do not define the limits of all sites in northern

China. No surrounding wall has been identified at Erlitou (IA CASS 2014) or at the late Shang capital of Yinxu at Anyang (Jing et al. 2013).

There is a discrepancy in estimations of settlement size based on surface remains compared with buried features for some other sites in northern China as well, including at Erlitou (see L. Liu et al. [2019] and discussion in Underhill et al. [2021]). It is likely that various post-depositional processes, natural and cultural, affected the distribution of surface remains in parts of our survey region, destroying some early cultural deposits or inflating the sizes of some sites. For example, we learned that in the past farmers had taken soil they judged as more fertile from cultural deposits at Liangchengzhen. In contrast, there is agreement from survey and excavation data about the maximum size of the largest Longshan site (Yaowangcheng; see Chapters 3 and 4) located in the southern half of our survey region. More research is needed to understand post-depositional processes in different areas of northern China that have been continually occupied for millennia. This report provides data for the major sites we identified, including location, environmental context, description at the time of investigation, diagnostic artifacts, and presence of buried cultural layers that permit further investigation by other teams. We used the same methods to assess the size of every site and argue that the resulting tiers of settlement indicating major differences in site size are appropriate and informative for interpreting changes in regional settlement organization over time in the Rizhao area.

Descriptions of Major Sites and Collections

This chapter describes all sites from Late Dawenkou through the Han period that are 10 ha or larger in at least one phase of occupation, or that have cultural layers or other physical remains of ancient features. We also include smaller sites where we found relatively dense scatters or concentrations of sherds on the surface or in cut banks (generally fifty or more sherds) and most of the sites where we collected stone tools. At several sites the only find was one stone tool with no ceramics on the surface, for which no period designation could be given.

These descriptions are intended to highlight the most significant sites in our survey region and to augment the information in site data and ceramic data files (see Fang et al. 2012) that contain details on numbers and types of artifacts collected and specific environmental information. The sites are discussed in five sections, grouped by modern administrative unit: Donggang, Jiaonan, Lanshan, Wulian, and Zhucheng. Sites in each district are listed alphabetically. In Chapter 4 we expand our discussion of the sites from each major cultural period and of the change over time in settlement patterns.

Site Descriptions

Sites are designated by county abbreviations followed by the abbreviation for the nearest town. Site name designations use the following format: the abbreviation of the administrative unit—DG, Donggang (东港) District, JN, Jiaonan (胶南) City, LS, Lanshan (岚山) District, WL, Wulian (五莲) County, and ZC, Zhucheng (诸城) City—then the town or village abbreviation, and lastly the site number (see Chapter 2). In 2004, the Donggang District of the Rizhao City area was divided, with the new administrative center located at Lanshan. Because this change occurred after we had surveyed some areas in Donggang that later became part of Lanshan, all sites in the affected area still have a DG prefix. (In the descriptions below the administrative district is listed correctly as Lanshan.)

In some instances, it was difficult to identify the closest town to a site, given the maps we had available and whether we could find a local villager to ask. When a site spread across administrative boundaries, we chose the county where the town was located. Occasionally, an abbreviation had already been used for another town in the same administrative district; we then either used the first three letters of the town name or inserted additional letters (in lowercase) to make each site name distinctive for analytical purposes. In several cases, what we originally thought were two or more separate sites ended up being one large site by the time we completed surveying an area. For those sites we included all the site names that were given to the site. Some sites at the edge of Rizhao City that were initially surveyed and numbered by crew member Zhang Zhibo (张治波) are noted in the descriptions (see Chapter 2).

For analytical purposes, each site is given a unique number by period, beginning with one and continuing sequentially from one season to the next (see Chapter 2). The sequence of numbers for any one period is independent of the sequence for other periods. For example, the first site listed, DG-ANJ-1, was occupied in three temporal periods: the Longshan number is 28, the Zhou number is 22, and the Han number is 20. In the descriptions of sites below, the period names and numbers in **bold** indicate the period of multicomponent sites that was largest in spatial extent or for which we found the densest concentration of artifacts. Site descriptions also include the name of the town that gives the site its name and the name of the map (and map index number) on which the site is located (see Figure 2.2).

This summary focuses on the major temporal periods for the Rizhao area (see Table 1.1). We identified subdivisions for Dawenkou (Early, Late), Longshan (Early, Middle), Zhou (Western, Eastern), and Han (Western, Eastern) whenever possible.

Donggang District (东港区)

Site: Anjialing DG-ANJ-1 (Year 1, Year 2)

County: Donggang

Town: Anjialing (安家岭)

Map: Anjiacun (安家村) [1-50-24-(18)]

Period and Period Number: **Longshan 28**; **Zhou 22**; Han 20

Cultural Layer: None

Site Description: This site is located on flat terrain in the alluvium, in vegetable gardens and agricultural fields on the west side of the town of Anjialing, at an elevation of 5 m, and on both sides of a tributary of the Chao River (潮河). We made three artifact collections at the site in Year 1 and an additional collection in Year 2. The site was at its largest during the Longshan period, with Early and Middle Longshan sherds dispersed over an area of approximately 10 ha. Although sherd density was greater for the Zhou period (evenly divided between Western and Eastern Zhou), the dispersal of sherds was less, covering only 7 ha. We found only a handful of Han period sherds, also dispersed over an area of approximately 7 ha. We collected one Longshan stone *dao* (石刀) knife at the site.

Site: Anjialing DG-ANJ-4 (Year 2)

County: Donggang

Town: Anjialing (安家岭)

Map: Houxiangou (后显沟) [1-50-24-(10)]

Period and Period Number: Zhou 55

Cultural Layer: None

Site Description: This site is located on flat agricultural terrain in the alluvium 300 m north of the town of Anjialing, at an elevation of 7 m, and 800 m north of a tributary of the Chao River. An area of fish ponds 200 m to the east may follow an ancient water course. Zhou period sherds were dispersed over an area of approximately 2.1 ha. We collected one stone artifact we interpreted as a polishing tool (磨光石器).

Site: Beidacun DG-BDC-4 (Year 7)

County: Donggang

Town: Beidacun (北大村)

Map: Doulingzi (陡岭子) [1-50-23-(39)]

Period and Period Number: Longshan 237, Zhou 495, 499; **Han 608**

Cultural Layer: None

Site Description: This site is located on a slight rise in the piedmont, at an elevation of 40 m. We found sherds to the north and south of the village of Beidacun, and around houses on the west side of the village. It is in fields of winter wheat, vegetable gardens, and some fallow patches. A small stream crosses the southern part of the site. The site is on both sides of a modern channel that crosses the western part of the town. The Han occupation was the largest, covering 6.6 ha. Zhou period sherds were more dispersed, covering 5.2 ha (Zhou 495), with Western Zhou remains in the south and Eastern Zhou in the north. Longshan period pottery (more Early phase than Middle) was found in the southern part of the site, between modern houses, covering an area 3.4 ha. The southern part of site likely extends under these houses. Although we did not observe a cultural layer, the density of Longshan sherds in this part of the site was high.

Site: DG-BDC-6 (Year 7)

County: Donggang

Town: Beidacun (北大村)

Map: Daliancun (大莲村) [1-50-23-(40)]

Period and Period Number: Longshan 239; Zhou 504; Han 614

Cultural Layer: Zhou period

Site Description: This site is located on flat terrain in the alluvium, at an elevation of 27 m, 50 m west of Houlouhe village (后漏河村), and 300 m south of where the Houlouhe River splits into the Linjia River (林家河) and the Feijia River (费家河). It is 400 m east of the town of Beidacun and was in fallow fields at the time of the survey. The site was small in all periods, less than 1 ha. An Eastern Zhou cultural deposit was observed in an area that had been disturbed by modern roadbuilding activities.

Site: DG-BWJC-1 (Year 9)

County: Donggang

Town: Beiwangjiacun (北王家村)

Map: Jiacang (夹仓) [1-50-35-(7)]

Period and Period Number: Longshan 363; **Zhou 748; Han 978**

Cultural Layer: None

Site Description: This site is located on flat alluvial terrain, at an elevation of 3 m, 100 m southeast of the town of Beiwangjiacun, and 150 m south of Feijiacun (费家村). It is 200 m west of a north-flowing tributary of the Nanxin River (南辛河). At the time of the survey, the site area was planted partly in winter wheat and partly as an orchard. The site covered 7.8 ha in Eastern Zhou and 6.8 ha in Han. There was a small scatter of Middle Longshan sherds, less than 0.5 ha, at the southern end of the site on the edge of a shrimp pond.

Site: DG-CZ-1 (Year 9)

County: Donggang

Town: Chuanzi (川子)

Map: Jiacang (夹仓) [1-50-35-(7)]

Period and Period Number: Zhou 761

Cultural Layer: Uncertain

Site Description: The site is located in a shrimp pond, at an elevation of 3 m, with sherds eroding out of the bank of the pond. It is 500 m east of the town of Chuanzi and 500 m south of the Nanxin River. We found sherds from Western and Eastern Zhou, and we estimate the site's size at 3.1 ha. The site was likely part of a larger Zhou community, as two other sites, DG-CZ-2 and CZ-3, were found in shrimp ponds to the east.

Site: Chuanzi DG-CZ-2 (Year 9)

County: Donggang

Town: Chuanzi (川子)

Map: Jiacang (夹仓) [1-50-35-(7)]

Period and Period Number: Longshan 374; **Zhou** 759, **760; Han** 992, **994**

Cultural Layer: None

Site Description: This site is located on flat terrain in the alluvium, at an elevation of only 2 to 3 m, 1,500 m east of the town of Chuanzi, and less than 100 m north of Lijiacun (李家村). The site was in fallow fields at the time of the survey, and the entire area was surrounded by shrimp ponds. Many small water channels cross the site. Han and Zhou period sherds were found throughout the site. We conclude that this site was largest during the Han (Han 994, at 17 ha) and Zhou periods (Zhou 760, twice as large in Eastern Zhou as in Western Zhou, at 14.4 ha). There was a small area of Middle Longshan sherds at the southern end of the site. Given the lack of visibility in shrimp ponds, the site could have been larger in the Zhou and Han periods. The site area may have been part of a larger community that included DG-CZ-1 and CZ-3, which are both found along the sides of shrimp ponds.

Site: DG-CZ-3 (Year 9)

County: Donggang

Town: Chuanzi (川子)

Map: Jiacang (夹仓) [1-50-35-(7)]

Period and Period Number: Zhou 758; Han 993

Cultural Layer: Zhou and Han periods

Site Description: The site is located in shrimp ponds with sherds eroding out of the banks of the ponds, at an elevation of 3 m, 500 m east of the town of Chuanzi, 400 m south of the village of Nanxinhe (南辛河村), and 350 m west of a large saltpan. There was a cultural layer visible in the bank of one pond (we did not find chronologically diagnostic sherds). The site has both Eastern Zhou and Han period remains. It was not possible to measure the size of the whole site, but the area we could check covered 1.5 to 2.5 ha. The site was likely part of a larger Zhou community, as two other sites, DG-CZ-2 and CZ-1, were found in shrimp ponds to the west.

Site: Chengzigou DG-CZG-1/HSD-7 (Year 4)

County: Donggang

Town: Chengzigou (程子沟) and Heshandian (河山店)

Map: Chengzigou (程子沟) [1-50-23-(32)]

Period and Period Number: Shang 13; Zhou 265; **Han 312**

Cultural Layer: Shang, Zhou, and Han periods

Site Description: The site is located on a slight rise in the low piedmont on the west side of a small nearby stream, at an elevation of 35 m, approximately 200 m east of the town of Chengzigou, and 250 m west of Heshandian. The site was mostly in fallow fields at the time of the survey, with some winter wheat and mulberry trees. It was largest during the Han period; we found Han sherds in five of six collection areas, dispersed over 11 ha. Eastern Zhou sherds were sparsely dispersed across four collection areas, covering 5.7 ha on the east side of the site. Shang and Western Zhou sherds were found in only two small areas near the north end of the site, both covering less than 0.5 ha. Two cultural layers were present. The exposed Shang and Zhou cultural layer was dark gray on top of sterile soil in a ditch that cuts into the site. We observed two Han cultural layers (one yellow, one gray), both also at the north end of the site (Figure 3.1). The site may have been part of a larger Han community that also included DG-CZG-2/GZ-2, 3 and CZG-4.

Site: Chengzigou DG-CZG-2/GZ-2, 3 (Year 4)

County: Donggang

Town: Chengzigou (程子沟) and Guozhuang (郭庄)

Map: Chengzigou (程子沟) [1-50-23-(32)]

Period and Period Number: Zhou 260, 261; **Han 311**

Cultural Layer: Han period

Site Description: This site is located on flat terrain in the low piedmont, at an elevation of 35 m, on the north side of the town of Chengzigou. It extends to the north all the way to Guozhuang village and to the west almost to Xiangyang village. Small streams on the north and south define the edges of the site. At the time of the survey most of the site area was planted with winter wheat and the rest was fallow. It likely extends under both Chengzigou and Guozhuang.

FIGURE 3.1. Profile of exposed cultural layer with Han period ceramics at Chengzigou (DG-CZG-1/HSD-7).

The site was largest in the Han period and Han sherds were present in all ten collection areas at the site. At approximately 40.4 ha (including areas under both modern communities), it is one of the larger Han sites in the survey region. We found two large roof tiles at the southern edge of the site, just north of the small stream, that probably were from a relatively large Han period building. The site was smaller in the Zhou period, covering about 9 ha on the north side of Chengzigou (Zhou 261), with a smaller concentration just south of Guozhuang (Zhou 260). Just on the north side of Chengzigou there is a 20 to 40 cm thick gray-black cultural layer that had been exposed by soil removal and downcutting for agriculture. A possible pit and a post-Han coffin also were exposed in the same area. We conclude that the site was part of a larger Han community that also included DG-CZG-1 and CZG-4.

Site: DG-DCP-3 (Year 11)

County: Donggang

Town: Dacaopo (大草坡)

Map: Gaowangzhuang (高旺庄) [1-50-35-(22)]

Period and Period Number: Han 1295

Cultural Layer: Han period

Site Description: The site is located on a slight slope in the alluvium at an elevation of 19 m, 150 m northwest of the town of Dacaopo, and 50 m west and south of a bend in a small stream. It is in fields of winter wheat, some of which are terraced. Recent plowing had exposed a cultural layer of dark sediment, and we collected a fair number of sherds there. The site is entirely Han, covering 2.1 ha. Most likely it was part of a larger Han community that included DG-DCP-4 and DCP-5, less than 150 m to the east. DG-DCP-4 is associated with an adjacent bend in the same small stream.

Site: DG-DCP-5 (Year 11)

County: Donggang

Town: Dacaopo (大草坡)

Map: Gaowangzhuang (高旺庄) [1-50-35-(22)]

Period and Period Number: Zhou 944, 945, 959; **Han 1296**

Cultural Layer: Han period

Site Description: The site is located in the alluvium and edge of a lower slope of a piedmont spur, at an elevation of 14.3 m, and 100 m north of the town of Dacaopo. The piedmont ridge descends from Fenghuang (Phoenix) Mountain (凤凰山), which is about 700 m north of the site. Most of the site was planted in winter wheat. The richest section is between two small stream channels on the north side of the town. In one field we observed a dark patch associated with Han period sherds that appeared to be an exposed cultural layer. We estimated the area where we found Han sherds to be 5 ha, but the small ponds and reservoirs there made it difficult to check the entire area well. Most likely the site was larger in the past. We expect the Han component was part of a larger Han community that included DG-DCP-3 and DCP-4. The site was much smaller in the Zhou period and entirely in the eastern section, where Western Zhou sherds were found in a 1.2 ha area and Eastern Zhou sherds in two small areas smaller than 0.2 ha each.

Site: Dagucheng DG-DGC-1/XSLP-2/QEZ-1, 3, 4, 5 (Year 7)

County: Donggang

Town: Dagucheng (大古城), Xishilipu (西十里铺), and Qiane'zhuang (前鹅庄)

Map: Shilipu (十里铺) [1-50-23-(47)] and Guojiahuzi (郭家湖子) [91-50-23-(55)]

Period and Period Number: Shang 22; Zhou 516, 517, 519, 520, 521, 524, 525; **Han 669**

Cultural Layer: Han period (with slag)

Site Description: This is a very large Han site (265 ha) located on a series of low piedmont ridges, at elevations between 20 to 50 m. It stretches on the north from just east of Xiaogucheng and 250 m south of Dagucheng ("big old town"), to within 100 m of Xishilipu on the east. To the south the site extends all the way to Shijialing and is bordered on the west by Houe'zhuang (后鹅庄) and Qiane'zhuang. The site overlooks the Futuan River (傅疃河) 1,000 m to the west. Several small streams cross the site. Most of the site was fallow at the time of the survey, with some areas planted in winter wheat or covered with greenhouses near Xishilipu. The site was historically the administrative or county seat of Haiqu (海曲) County during the Han period (see Chapters 1 and 4), and there were sections of earthen city walls still intact in the northern and eastern parts of the site.

On the highest part of the piedmont rise just south of the expressway S313 are six tombs or platforms, two of which are known as Da Wang Fen (大王坟, "big king tomb") and Er Wang Fen (二王坟, "second king tomb") (Figure 3.2). Approximately 1,000 m farther

FIGURE 3.2. View of Dagucheng (DG-DGC-1/XSLP-2/QEZ-1, 3, 4, 5) on the rise with visible Han period tombs and platforms.

south on the same piedmont ridge are three additional tombs/platforms (initially labeled DG-QEZ-5 for the nearest town). The largest structure has a platform in front of the tomb that may have supported a Han period building. Just south of this feature we observed many Han bricks decorated with a diamond pattern. There also was a large, flattened stone with a surface indentation that may have held a door pivot pole. The southernmost of these three tombs and platforms had a wall extension running to the south. This remnant may have been part of a wall that surrounded the complex of tombs. A farmer told us that there once was a gate south of these three tombs. This wall segment is on the eastern side of the site. It is possible that it originally connected with the Han period wall.

The densest artifact collections were taken from the northern section of the site, north of the expressway, between two separate north–south wall segments. Although most of this area was occupied during the Han period, there were several scatters of Eastern Zhou sherds just west of Xishilipu, covering 9.9 ha (Zhou 520), 4.8 ha (Zhou 517), and 4.2 ha (Zhou 519). The scatter just west of Xishilipu (Zhou 517) also contained a small area (less than 1 ha) with both Shang-like and Western Zhou sherds (Figure 3.3). Around the two large tombs south of the expressway there also were some Eastern Zhou sherds (Zhou 524). The other scatters of Zhou were all in areas less than 1 ha in size.

Although ceramic densities were sparser south of the expressway, the only cultural layer we observed was Han, a gray layer 100 m south of the expressway and 350 m west of the Da Wang Fen tomb. It also contained some slag that appears to be debris from iron production.

In the 1970s, iron objects, an iron-smelting workshop, and tons of slag were discovered southwest of Dagucheng (大古城) (Yang and Wang 2005). In May 1987, archaeologists

FIGURE 3.3. Shang period *li* (鬲) tripod foot (*left*) and Shang *guan* (罐) jar rim (*right*) from Dagucheng (DG-DGC-1/XSLP-2[CAF]/QEZ-1, 3, 4, 5).

from the Rizhao Museum excavated three Han period tombs east of Dagucheng village and discovered many delicate bronzes, iron objects, glazed pottery, and lacquered items. The excavators believe that these tombs belong to the Wang family graveyard based on two seals dating to late Western Han (Rizhao Museum 2006). In spring 2002, during construction of the Tongjiang–Sanya Expressway (同三高速公路), the Shandong Institute of Cultural Relics and Archaeology excavated more than ninety Han period tombs around the main tomb complex. The project yielded many important artifacts and information. It was named one of the "Top Ten Archaeological Discoveries of 2002" by the national government (D. He, Zheng, and Cui 2003; Zheng and Cui 2003).

Site: DG-DGZ-5 (Year 8)

County: Donggang

Town: Daguzhen (大古镇)

Map: Lujiagou (路家沟) [1-50-23-(64)]

Period and Period Number: Yueshi 14; **Zhou 713**; **Han 931**

Cultural Layer: None

Site Description: The site is located on a low rise in the alluvium, at an elevation of 5 m, 100 m northwest of the town of Daguzhen, and approximately 50 m east of the eastern levee of the Futuan River (Figure 3.4). A modern water channel and road cross the north of the site. It was in mostly fallow fields, with some winter wheat, cornstalks, and cabbage, at the time of the survey. The site was largest during Western Zhou, covering 3.2 ha, and in the Han period, covering 2.8 ha. Yueshi period sherds were found only in the center of the site, in an area of 1.4 ha.

FIGURE 3.4. View of DG-DGZ-5 on the rise.

Site: Donghaiyu DG-DHY-1 (Year 8)

County: Donggang

Town: Donghaiyu (东海峪)

Map: Shanhou (山后) [1-50-24-(57)]

Period and Period Number: Dawenkou 11, 12, 13; **Longshan 342**; Zhou 698, 699; Han 899, 900, 901, 902

Cultural Layer: Dawenkou and Longshan periods

Site Description: The site is located on flat alluvial terrain, at an elevation of 5 m, in and around the town of Donghaiyu (Figure 3.5). The densest deposits are in a raised area on the west side of town and east of the railroad, but we found sherds in all the open areas in town that we could check, including the southeastern edge of Balizhuang (八里庄) on the west side of the railroad. The site is situated between two water channels on the north and south sides of Donghaiyu. Much of the site clearly was covered by the modern town. The ancient settlement extended east to within 500 m of the coast. Most of the site was in fallow fields or winter wheat at the time of the survey; however, we also found some sherds in an orchard in the northwestern part of the site. We made twelve artifact collections. The Longshan occupation was clearly dominant, covering at least 50 ha. This estimate is a minimum and the site could have been at least 75 ha. There are several exposed cultural layers in the western part of the site, representing Late Dawenkou and Longshan (more Early than Middle Longshan) (Figures 3.6 and 3.7). Late Dawenkou pottery was especially prevalent on the rise on the western side of the town, covering 4.2 ha (Dawenkou 11). Zhou (larger for Western Zhou than Eastern Zhou) and Han sherds were dispersed in several small scatters, with the largest scatters for both covering around 4 ha. There were only twenty-five Han period

Figure 3.5. View of the western part of Donghaiyu (DG-DHY-1) from the southwest looking toward the northeast.

Figure 3.6. Exposed Late Dawenkou and Longshan cultural layers at Donghaiyu (DG-DHY-1).

FIGURE 3.7. Late Dawenkou *ding* (鼎) tripod rim (*top row, center*) and Early Longshan period sherds (*top left*: *guan* jar rim, top right: *ding* tripod foot; *bottom row, left to right*: *ding* tripod foot, unfinished *fanglun* [纺轮] spindle whorl, *qigai* [器盖] lid, stem of *dou* [豆] stemmed dish) from Donghaiyu (DG-DHY-1[CABB]).

sherds in an area of little more than 4 ha. The five stone tools we collected are likely from the Dawenkou and Longshan periods (Figure 3.8). During the 1970s, both the Shandong Provincial Museum and Shandong University excavated at Donghaiyu and found houses and burials dating to Late Dawenkou and Early Longshan (Donghaiyu Excavation Team 1976; see Chapter 1).

Site: DG-DJP-2 (Year 1)

County: Donggang

Town: Dajiepai (大界牌)

Map: Lianhecun (联合村) [1-50-24-(17)]

Period and Period Number: **Longshan 5**; Zhou 3; Han 7

Cultural Layer: None

Site Description: This site is located on the top of the slope of a low piedmont ridge, at an elevation of 25 to 40 m, at the southwestern edge of the town of Dajiepai (Figure 3.9). A small stream crosses the west side of the site; a tributary of the Beixiao River (北小河) is 350 m west of the westernmost part of the site, where there is a Han period tomb, just over 300 m west of the town. The site was in winter wheat and fallow fields at the time of the survey. The site was largest during the Longshan period, with sherds scattered over approximately 23.5 ha. Middle Longhan is the best represented, although some Early and Late Longshan ceramics also were collected. Eastern Zhou sherds were found in a smaller area (9.8 ha) along the east side, while Han sherds were found in the northern part of the site, covering

Figure 3.8. Stone *dao* (刀) knife from Donghaiyu (DG-DHY-1[CABB]).

Figure 3.9. Luan Fengshi and Linda Nicholas surveying at DG-DJP-2.

approximately 16.5 ha. We collected five stone tools at the site—four *fu* (斧) axes and one *moshi* (磨石) grinding stone—judged as Longshan, but it also is possible that they date to the Han period.

Site: Dongjiatan DG-DJT-1 (Year 7)

County: Donggang

Town: Dongjiatan (董家滩)

Map: Dawa (大洼) [1-50-24-(41)]

Period and Period Number: Han 656

Cultural Layer: None

Site Description: This site is located on flat alluvium, at an elevation of 4 m, on the southwestern side of the village of Dongjiatan, and 150 m east of a series of shrimp ponds in an agricultural area. Han sherds were dispersed over 7.7 ha. This site was initially surveyed by Zhang Zhibo (Zhang 4; see Chapter 2). Later we checked the site ourselves to add it on our maps. We found sherds as far as the south side of the village. Han sherds on the north side of town were designated DG-MJC-4. The village likely covers what really was one larger Han community that included DG-MJC 1, MJC-3, MJC-4, and QTX-1.

Researchers have discovered bronze ritual vessels at this site, including a *li* (鬲) tripod and a *yi* (匜) pouring vessel dating to Eastern Zhou (early to middle Spring and Autumn period) (Yang, Hu, and Xu 1990). Because we did not find any Zhou period artifacts, it is possible that Zhou remains are covered by the modern village.

Site: Dingjiazhuang DG-DJZ-1 (Year 5)

County: Donggang

Town: Dingjiazhuang (丁家庄)

Map: Chengzigou (程子沟) [1-50-23-(32)]

Period and Period Number: Zhou 345

Cultural Layer: None

Site Description: The site is located on a low rise in the piedmont, at an elevation of 80 m, 100 m west of a small stream, and 350 m west of the town of Dingjiazhuang. We found only a handful of Zhou sherds and one stone tool, in an area of approximately 0.5 ha.

Site: Donglianghe DG-DLH-1 (Year 8, Year 11)

County: Donggang

Town: Donglianghe (东两河)

Map: Lujiagou (路家沟) [1-50-23-(64)]

Period and Period Number: **Beixin 1**; Zhou 709

Cultural Layer: Beixin period

Site Description: This site is located on a piedmont slope on the west side of a hill, Kui Shan (奎山, Mount Kui), on the west side of a large reservoir, at an elevation of 34 m, and 200 m northeast of the town of Donglianghe. Part of the site was fallow at the time of the survey and part was in an orchard (Figure 3.10). We revisited the site in Year 11 and observed several newly exposed cultural layers. Soil samples collected for flotation contained millet (X. Chen 2007). Although the site is only about 0.5 ha in size, we found a dense concentration of Early and Middle Beixin pottery (Figure 3.11). In the same area we collected from a sparse scatter of Eastern Zhou sherds. This is one of the two earliest sites we recorded in the entire survey region; the other is DG-NTL-4, 1,150 m to the north, also on the piedmont slope of Kui Shan.

Site: Dalingnantou DG-DLNT-1 (Year 8)

County: Donggang

Town: Dalingnantou (大岭南头)

Map: Dalingnantou (大岭南头) [1-50-23-(56)]

Period and Period Number: **Longshan 324; Zhou 658**; Han 882, 883

Cultural Layer: None

Site Description: The site is located on the top and north-facing slope of a low piedmont ridge, at an elevation of 15 to 22 m, 150 m southeast of the Guzi River (崮子河), and 400 m north of the town of Dalingnantou. Construction of the railroad across the top of the piedmont ridge destroyed part of the site. The site is mostly Early Longshan (8.8 ha) and Eastern Zhou (6.6 ha); it may have been larger during both periods. Only two small scatters of Han period sherds were found, both less than 0.5 ha.

Site: Donglinzitou DG-DLZT-8 (Year 11)

County: Donggang

Town: Donglinzitou (东林子头)

Map: Donghusancun (东湖三村) [1-50-35-(31)]

Period and Period Number: Longshan 454; **Zhou 981**; **Han 1321**

Cultural Layer: Zhou and Han periods

Site Description: The site is located in the alluvium, at an elevation of 5.5 m, 350 m northwest of Donghu (东湖村) village, 200 m south of the town of Donglinzitou, and 300 m north of Donghusancun. The western part of the site, west of a road and shrimp ponds, was in fields of winter wheat and fallow fields. The eastern part of the site was on sand dunes partially covered with pine trees and modern graves, with shrimp ponds on either side, 200 m west of a new highway and 600 m west of the coast. An artificial channel that had been recently cut through the dunes had exposed a rich cultural deposit of mostly Han period remains. We found another exposed cultural layer just south of this channel on the west side of buildings. Almost the entire site dates to the Zhou (Western and Eastern) and Han periods, covering 15 ha. We found a very small scatter of Longshan sherds west of the road, in the northwestern corner of the site.

Site: DG-DNY-1 (Year 11)

County: Donggang

Town: Dongnanying (东南营)

FIGURE 3.10. Crew members searching for diagnostic sherds in an exposed cultural layer at Donglianghe (DG-DLH-1).

FIGURE 3.11. Early Beixin period pottery sherds from Donglianghe (DG-DLH [CAA]). *Top row:* fine paste possible *qigai* lid, body sherd with fingernail impression, *pen* (盆) basin rim; *middle row:* two *fu* (釜) stove sherds, two *guan* jars with handles; *bottom row:* four *bo* (钵) bowl rims.

Map: Zhanzi (栈子) [1-50-35-(23)]

Period and Period Number: Han 1272

Cultural Layer: None

Site Description: The site is located on flat alluvium, at an elevation of 4 m, in an area of winter wheat fields and shrimp ponds on the north side of the town of Dongnanying and south of a large water channel. We found sherds to within 50 m of the coastal highway (滨海公路). The site dates entirely to the Han period. We estimated the site at 7.1 ha, but because of areas covered by ponds that we could not check adequately, the site could easily be twice as large.

Site: DG-DNZ-2 (Year 5)

County: Donggang

Town: Danuanzhang (大暖嶂)

Map: Chengzigou (程子沟) [1-50-23-(32)]

Period and Period Number: Zhou 343

Cultural Layer: None

Site Description: This site is located on the tip of a low piedmont ridge, just above and west of a small reservoir, at an elevation of 125 m, and 400 m southwest of the town of Danuanzhang. It was terraced for contemporary agriculture but was fallow at the time of the survey (Figure 3.12). The ridge is flat. We found a heavy density of Zhou sherds (both Western and Eastern) in a defensive location common for Zhou sites. The site was less than 1 ha. We also found one stone tool.

Site: DG-DNZ-5 (Year 5)

County: Donggang

Town: Danuanzhang (大暖嶂)

Map: Chengzigou (程子沟) [1-50-23-(32)]

Period and Period Number: Zhou 344

Cultural Layer: None

Site Description: The site is located on a low rise in the piedmont, at an elevation of 90 m, 50 m south of the school in Danuanzhang, and just east of the road. The nearest water source is a small stream that is 150 m away, at the south end of the village. The site was planted in winter wheat. The area of Eastern Zhou sherds was less than 0.5 ha. We also found one stone tool.

Site: DG-DSQ-2 (Year 8)

County: Donggang

Town: Dongshanqian (东山前)

Map: Lujiagou (路家沟) [1-50-23-(64)]

Period and Period Number: Longshan 340; **Zhou 706**; Han 911

Cultural Layer: Zhou period

FIGURE 3.12. View of DG-DNZ-2 on the top and sides of a piedmont spur above a small reservoir.

Site Description: The site is located on a moderate piedmont slope on the south side of Kui Shan, just at the base of the steep slope of the mountain, at an elevation of 65 m. Most of the site is situated on two piedmont ridges on the north and east sides of a small reservoir, 300 m northeast of Xishanqian (西山前), and 550 m north of the town of Dongshanqian (Figure 3.13). There were other new buildings at the southeastern edge. Most of the site was in fallow fields at the time of the survey, but some collections were made in an orchard and in a field of cornstalks. The site was largest in the Zhou period (both Western and Eastern), covering 3.5 ha. One collection area above the northwestern edge of the reservoir included a Zhou cultural layer with dense quantities of Zhou sherds. Han sherds were found just north of the reservoir and also just inside the levee of the reservoir, indicating that most of the Han portion of the site was under water. We estimate the Han occupation area at 2 ha.

Site: Dashiqiaocun DG-DSQC-5 (Year 7)

County: Donggang

Town: Dashiqiaocun (大石桥村)

Map: Rizhaoshi (日照市) [1-50-23-(48)]

Period and Period Number: Zhou 632; **Han 661**

Cultural Layer: None

Site Description: The site is located on flat alluvium, in a peach orchard encircled by houses in Dashiqiaocun village, at an elevation of 24 m, and 350 m southwest of the Houlou River

Figure 3.13. View of DG-DSQ-2 on piedmont ridges near a modern reservoir.

(后漏河). The full size of the site is not known, because much of it is under homes and streets. The area we could observe was 2.2 ha; the site could be considerably larger, since we found ceramics right up to all the buildings. Han period sherd density was greater than that for either Western or Eastern Zhou. The site was initially surveyed by Zhang Zhibo (Zhang 6); we resurveyed site to place it on our maps.

Site: Dataoyaun DG-DTY-1/DJZ-3, 5 (Year 5)

County: Donggang

Town: Dataoyuan (大桃园) and Dingjiazhuang (丁家庄)

Map: Chengzigou (程子沟) [1-50-23-(32)]

Period and Period Number: Longshan 172, 175; Zhou 346, 347; Han 413

Cultural Layer: Longshan period

Site Description: The site is located on a low rise in the alluvium and the base of a low hill to the west, at an elevation of 65 m, on the north and west side of the town of Dataoyuan ("big peach orchard"), and on both sides of the Linjia tributary (林家河) of the Houlou River that runs on the east side of the town (Figure 3.14). It is likely that the site extends under the modern town. Most of the site was fallow at the time of the survey, although some fields were planted in winter wheat. It was large in all three periods (Longshan 172, Zhou 346, and Han 413), covering 20 to 27 ha. The site was much larger in Middle Longshan (20 ha) than in Early (8.1 ha) or Late Longshan (3.4 ha). Few sites in the Rizhao area have remains from Late Long-

FIGURE 3.14. View of Dataoyuan (DG-DTY-1/DJZ-3, 5) in fields on the west side of the village.

shan (see Chapter 4). The site also was slightly larger in Western Zhou (21 ha) than in Eastern Zhou (16.8 ha). An exposed Longshan period burial outlined by two rows of perpendicular stones was part of a 0.5-m thick black cultural layer just west of the river near the northern and richest part of the site (Figure 3.15). In addition to sherds, four stone tools were collected (Figures 3.16 and 3.17). At the southern end of the site, just west of the town in an area of mostly Han period sherds, were small separate concentrations of Middle Longshan sherds (Longshan 175) and Western Zhou sherds (Zhou 347), both less than 1 ha.

The site was investigated by the local Cultural Relics Bureau, which delineated the site area as 3.5 ha (see also Chapter 1). Dataoyuan has been designated a county-level protected site (Rizhao City Library and Linyi District Committee 1986; China Cultural Heritage Bureau 2007:272–273).

Site: Dongwangjiacun DG-DWJC-1 (Year 6)

County: Donggang

Town: Dongwangjiacun (东王家村)

Map: Dawa (大洼) [1-50-24-(41)]

Period and Period Number: **Longshan 230**; Zhou 474, 475; Han 571, 572

Cultural Layer: None

Site Description: This large site is located on a low to middle piedmont ridge, at an elevation of 30 to 42 m, just north of the towns of Dongwangjiacun and Dawacun. The site extends

Figure 3.15. Exposed Longshan period burial outlined by two rows of stones at Dataoyuan (DG-DTY-1/DJZ-3, 5), which is likely a coffin burial.

downslope to the west to within 100 m of a tributary of the Guzi River. A small modern ditch crosses the western part of the site near the base of the ridge. Most of site is west of the Qingdaolu (青岛路) highway, although we did find sherds right up to the edge of modern houses on the north and west sides of the town of Dongjiacun. The site was in fallow fields, winter wheat, and an apple orchard at the time of the survey, and it extended under the norhwestern part of the town (Dongwangjiacun). There was a modern quarry just to the north. The entire site occupation period is Longshan, extending over 46 ha (larger for Middle Longshan than Early Longshan), and it is one of the larger Longshan sites in our survey region. We collected twelve stone tools, most of which clearly date to the Longshan period. We found Zhou (Western and Eastern) and Han sherds in several, much smaller discrete areas, mostly on the slopes. The site may be larger than mapped because of the expansion of the two towns in this area just a short time before our survey; it also may have been part of a larger Longshan community that included DG-FJG-2, located on lower slopes just north of a quarry.

Site: Daxiangdian DG-DXD-1 (Year 7)

County: Donggang

Town: Dashiqiaocun (大石桥村)

Map: Rizhaoshi (日照市) [1-50-23-(48)]

Period and Period Number: Longshan 214; Zhou 512; Han 649

Cultural Layer: None

Figure 3.16. Longshan period artifacts (*top*: white *gui* [鬶] tripod body sherd and *guan* jar large handle; *bottom*: stone tool fragment, white *gui* tripod body sherd, white *gui* tripod foot) from Dataoyuan (DG-DTY-1[CAA]/DJZ-3, 5).

Figure 3.17. Longshan period white pottery body sherds collected from Dataoyuan (DG-DTY-1[CAA]/DJZ-3, 5).

Site Description: The site is located on a low piedmont rise, at an elevation of 18 m, 450 m east of the Xiangdian River (香店河), and just west of Daxiangdian village (大香店村). It was in a fallow field. The area where we found sherds was just under 1 ha, but the site may continue to the east under the modern village of Daxiangdian. The Eastern Zhou and Han periods were better represented than Longshan or Western Zhou. The site was originally surveyed by Zhang Zhibo (Zhang 11); we resurveyed the site to place it on our maps. Because of the modern buildings in the area, the site could be part of a larger site with DG-QWLH-1, located 150 m to the northwest.

Site: DG-DYJ-1 (Year 11)

County: Donggang

Town: Dayangjuan (大羊圈)

Map: Jufengzhen (巨峰镇) [1-50-35-(13)]

Period and Period Number: Zhou 916; **Han 1224**

Cultural Layer: Zhou and Han periods

Site Description: The site is located on a slight slope at the piedmont–alluvium boundary at an elevation of 15 m, on the south side of the town of Dayangjuan. It extends 75 m south of the road to Liujiazhuang (六甲庄). Two small streams cut through the site. The site was in fields of winter wheat and mulberry. The entire site has Han period remains, covering 7.8 ha. We found a small area, smaller than 1 ha, of Western Zhou material on the western side of the site. The Han component may be part of a larger Han component with DG-ZJZZi-1, just over 100 m to the west.

Site: DG-DZZ-1 (Year 9)

County: Donggang

Town: Dongzaozi (东灶子)

Map: Jiacang (夹仓) [1-50-35-(7)]

Period and Period Number: Longshan 364; Han 977

Cultural Layer: Several

Site Description: The site is located among several shrimp ponds in the alluvium, at an elevation of 2 m, and 350 m south of the town of Dongzaozi. We collected Middle Longshan and Han sherds and observed several cultural layers in the banks of the ponds. The measurable area of the site in both periods was 1.4 ha, but this is a minimal estimate. The site was likely part of larger Longshan and Han communities with at least two other sites, DG-DZZ-2 and XiZZ-2, found nearby to the west among other shrimp ponds. At both of those sites we also found Longshan and Han sherds on the banks and sides of the ponds.

Site: Fanjiahe DG-FaJH-1/LJC-6 (Year 5)

County: Donggang

Town: Fanjiahe (范家河) and Linjiacun (林家村)

Map: Daliancun (大莲村) [1-50-23-(40)]

Period and Period Number: **Longshan 165;** Zhou 306

Cultural Layer: Longshan and Zhou periods

Site Description: The site is located on a low rise in the alluvium, at an elevation of 35 m, on the northeast side of Fanjiahe village, and 50 m northwest of the Linjia tributary (林家河) of the Houlou River. The area was planted in winter wheat or was fallow at the time of the survey (Figure 3.18). The site was not large, covering about 1.9 ha in the Longshan period, but a cultural layer was visible in a cut at the site. The Zhou component (both Western and Eastern) was smaller, covering 1.2 ha. This site is part of a cluster of small Zhou period sites in the area.

Site: Fengjiagou DG-FJG-2 (Year 6)

County: Donggang

Town: Fengjiagou (冯家沟)

Map: Dawa (大洼) [1-50-24-(41)]

Period and Period Number: Dawenkou 5, 7; **Longshan 234; Zhou 482**

Cultural Layer: Dawenkou, Longshan, and Zhou periods

Site Description: Most of the site is located on a low piedmont rise, with some parts stretching into the adjacent alluvium to the northeast, at an elevation of 20 to 25 m. It is just south of Fengjiagou and mostly south of the small stream on the south side of town. Most of the site was planted in winter wheat or vegetables at the time of the survey, but some fields were fallow. The Longshan period (twice as large in Early as in Middle Longshan) was well represented, covering 6.5 ha, as was the Zhou period (Western and Eastern), covering 5.5 ha. There also were two small, discrete areas of Late Dawenkou pottery, both less than 0.5 ha in extent. Two cultural layers with evidence of burning were exposed in a cut above a stream on the western end of the site (an area with Dawenkou, Longshan, and Zhou pottery). The site was discovered by a local cultural preservation institute and has been placed under the county's preservation protection (Rizhao City Library and Linyi District Committee 1986; China Cultural Heritage Bureau 2007:272–273).

Site: Fanjiaguanzhuang DG-FJGZ-2 (Year 5)

County: Donggang

Town: Fanjiaguanzhuang (范家官庄)

Map: Chengzigou (程子沟) [1-50-23-(32)]

Period and Period Number: Zhou 366; **Han 423**

Cultural Layer: None

Site Description: The site is located on a low rise in the alluvium, at an elevation of 35 m, extending from the southeastern corner of the town of Fanjiaguanzhuang all the way to the east side of Feijiaguanzhuang (费家官庄) and the north side of Cha'an (茶庵). Several small modern canals run through the site. The setting of the site is agricultural and includes winter wheat, apple orchards, and vegetable gardens; some fields were fallow at the time of the survey. The site was largest during the Han period, covering an area just under 10 ha. Eastern Zhou sherds were found in a 3.6-ha area at the northern end of the site, just south of Fanjiaguanzhuang.

Figure 3.18. View of Fanjiahe (DG-FaJH-1/LJC-6) on a low rise in the alluvium.

Site: Futuan DG-FT-1 (Year 9)

County: Donggang

Town: Futuan (傅疃)

Map: Futuan (傅疃) [1-50-23-(63)]

Period and Period Number: Longshan 355; Yueshi 15; **Zhou 731**; **Han 958**

Cultural Layer: None

Site Description: The site is located on flat alluvium at an elevation of 7 m, less than 50 m southeast of the town of Futuan and 100 m west of Hetao village (河套村). The site was in vegetable gardens and a fruit orchard south of the road between the two communities. A small stream 380 m to the southwest is the nearest water source. Zhou and Han sherds were well represented on the surface, with Zhou (slightly larger in Eastern Zhou than in Western Zhou) covering 6.1 ha and Han covering 7 ha. There were lighter scatters of Longshan pottery (Middle Longshan only, covering 4.6 ha) and Yueshi period pottery (2.3 ha). This site was known to the Rizhao Museum before we conducted our survey.

Site: Gaojialing DG-GaoJL-1 (Year 7)

County: Donggang

Town: Gaojialing (高家岭)

Map: Dawa (大洼) [1-50-24-(41)]

Period and Period Number: Zhou 514; Han 652

Cultural Layer: Possible

Site Description: The site is located on top of a piedmont ridge, at an elevation of 35 m, 1,000 m east of a tributary of the Guzi River, within the boundaries of Rizhao City, just east of Beijng Road, and south of Shandong Road. There is a small stream 100 m to the south, and the site is adjacent to a modern pond in the northwest. It was in fallow fields at the time of the survey. Eastern Zhou and Han sherds were found in a 4-ha area, and a possible thin cultural layer was observed on the northeastern edge of the site. We found Western Zhou sherds in an area less than 0.5 ha in the northeastern part of the site. The site was initially surveyed by Zhang Zhibo (Zhang 5); we resurveyed the site to place it on our maps.

Site: Guheya DG-GHA-2 (Year 8)

County: Donggang

Town: Guheya (崮河崖)

Map: Lujiagou (路家沟) [1-50-23-(64)], Futuan (傅疃) [1-50-23-(63)]

Period and Period Number: Longshan 329, 330; **Zhou** 679, **680**; **Han 934**, 941

Cultural Layer: None

Site Description: The site is located on the top and northern slopes of a low piedmont ridge, between elevations of 10 to 20 m, and 200 m east of the Guzi River. It is 200 m north of Houlianghe village (后两河村), 250 m south of Xujia village (徐家村), and 200 m west of the road between Houlianghe and Xujia. There is a small stream on the north side of the site. The piedmont slope was terraced, many fields were fallow, and others were planted with winter wheat. We gave the same site number to sherd concentrations that we found just west of the river, on a slight rise in the alluvium between the east side of Guhe'ai and the levee on the west side of Guhe'ai. This part of the site most likely was larger in the past. The collections we made there were mostly in fields that were fallow at the time of the survey; however, there was some winter wheat, mulberry trees, and vegetable gardens. The two parts of the site were separated by the floodplain on either side of the river. It is not clear whether both were part of the same larger community in the past. The Zhou (Zhou 680) and Han (Han 934) components on the east side of the river were larger. The Zhou component (larger for Eastern than for Western) covered 15.8 ha (Figure 3.19), whereas the Han component covered 8.4 ha. Small areas of Longshan materials, both about 1.4 ha, were found on both sides of the river. The Zhou period component was part of a larger community that included DG-XJC-1, less than 150 m to the north.

The Rizhao Museum excavated burials from the Zhou period at this site. The site is famous for bronzes of Lai Bo (莱伯, Count Lai) dated between Western and Eastern Zhou (see Chapter 2; S. Yang 1984; F. Li 2006; F. Li and Liang 2018).

Site: Guanjiacun DG-GJC-1 (Year 8)

County: Donggang

Town: Guanjiacun (管家村)

Map: Lujiagou (路家沟) [1-50-23-(64)], Dalingnantou (大岭南头) [1-50-23(56)]

Period and Period Number: Longshan 339; Zhou 695; Han 895

Cultural Layer: Longshan and Zhou periods; two Longshan pits

Site Description: The site is located on a low piedmont rise, at an elevation of 35 m, just north of Guanjia village, and extends north to the railroad. The closest water source is a small

Figure 3.19. Eastern Zhou period small *dian* (掂) weight (*left*) and Western Zhou period body sherd with *shengwen* (绳文) cordmarking (*right*) from Guheya (DG-GHA-2[CAG]).

stream 150 m to the southwest. The site was mostly fallow at the time of survey (Figure 3.20); however, some of the collections were taken from an orchard. At the north end of the town we found a deep, exposed cultural layer with Zhou sherds above Longshan sherds that ran for at least 50 m. The layer had been damaged by modern construction and clearly continued below modern houses. We also found two Longshan period pits nearby. It is likely that the town covers part of the site, especially the Longshan component. We estimated the Longshan component at 5.7 ha, larger in Middle than in Early Longshan. Zhou sherds were found over a 4.8 ha area, with a larger area for Eastern than for Western Zhou. We estimate the Han period site at 4.9 ha.

Site: Gaojiagou DG-GJG-2 (Year 3)

County: Donggang

Town: Gaojiagou (高家沟)

Map: Gaojiagou (高家沟) [1-50-23-(24)]

Period and Period Number: **Longshan 82**; Zhou 74; Han 89

Cultural Layer: None

Site Description: The site is located on a slight slope at the base of a low piedmont ridge on the southeastern side of the town of Gaojiagou, at an elevation of 65 m (Figure 3.21). There are two small streams, less than 50 m away, to the north and south of this low ridge. The site was in fields of winter wheat, with a large reservoir 100 m to the southwest. We found a dense scatter of Middle Longshan sherds covering 1.2 ha; the density of Han and Zhou (Eastern Zhou only) sherds was much less.

Site: DG-GJL-1 (Year 5)

County: Donggang

FIGURE 3.20. View of Guanjiacun (DG-GJC-1) from the east looking toward the west.

FIGURE 3.21. View of Gaojiagou (DG-GJG-2) on the base of a low piedmont ridge.

Town: Gaojialing (高家岭)

Map: Daliancun (大莲村) [1-50-23-(40)]

Period and Period Number: Han 370

Cultural Layer: None

Site Description: The site is located on a flat ridgetop in the low piedmont, at an elevation of 41 m, 250 m northwest of the town of Gaojialing, and 350 m southeast of the Linjia River, a tributary of the Houlou River. The site was in an orchard and surrounded by winter wheat at the time of the survey. We found a high density of Han period sherds in an area smaller than 1 ha.

Site: DG-GWZ-5 (Year 11)

County: Donggang

Town: Gaowangzhuang (高旺庄)

Map: Gaowangzhuang (高旺庄) [1-50-35-(22)]

Period and Period Number: Zhou 936; Han 1258

Cultural Layer: Possible

Site Description: The site is located on flat alluvium, at an elevation of 6 m, 250 m east of the town of Gaowangzhuang, and 200 m south of a large water channel. The area was planted in winter wheat. Most of the sherds were found in an exposed bank in an area smaller than 0.5 ha. We found more Western and Eastern Zhou sherds than Han sherds. The site likely was buried by alluvium and could be part of the same site as DG-SJYZ-1, 250 m to the east.

Site: DG-GZ-1 (Year 4)

County: Donggang

Town: Guozhuang (郭庄)

Map: Chengzigou (程子沟) [1-50-23-(32)]

Period and Period Number: **Longshan 148**; Zhou 258, 259; Han 308

Cultural Layer: Longshan period

Site Description: The site is located on a slight rise in the low piedmont, 200 m west of the town of Guozhuang, at an elevation of 50 m, and just north of a small stream. It was in fallow fields and winter wheat at the time of survey. The site was largest during the Longshan period, covering just over 1 ha. The Longshan portion of the site is on a rise that drops to an old river channel; in this cut we observed a 20 cm thick Longshan cultural layer. Zhou and Han sherds were very sparse, each covering an area smaller than 0.5 ha.

Site: Hou'ezhuang DG-HEZ-1 (Year 7, Year 10)

County: Donggang

Town: Hou'ezhuang (后鹅庄)

Map: Guojiahuzi (郭家湖子) [1-50-23-(55)]

Period and Period Number: Longshan 405, 406; Zhou 807; Han 679

Cultural Layer: Longshan period

FIGURE 3.22. The large, flat stone in a house lot at Houguzi (DG-HGZ-1).

Site Description: The site is located on flat alluvium at an elevation of 12.4 m, 200 m east of the Futuan River, and 700 m east of the town of Houe'zhuang. The first collection at this site was during Year 7 and five more were made during Year 10. The collection areas were in a rice paddy, fallow field, winter wheat, vegetable garden, among poplar trees, and near a modern greenhouse. Han period sherds were found on the entire site, covering 9.3 ha. Zhou sherds (all Eastern Zhou) were found in the western part of the site, covering 5 ha. Longshan sherds were dispersed in two very small areas, the easternmost of which (406, Early Longshan) was found in a cultural layer of black and gray sediment that was exposed 5 cm below the surface during the digging of a rice paddy.

Site: Houguzi DG-HGZ-1 (Year 8)

County: Donggang

Town: Houguzi (后崮子)

Map: Dalingnantou (大岭南头) [1-50-23-(56)]

Period and Period Number: Longshan 319; Zhou 653

Cultural Layer: Longshan and Zhou periods (and a raised platform)

Site Description: This site is located on flat alluvial terrain, at an elevation of 10 m, and mostly under the modern town of Houguzi. We found sherds in vegetable gardens between the southern edge of the town and the north side of the Guzi River. There was a cultural layer on the north side of the town, just south of the railroad. The cultural layer had been badly disturbed by construction of the railroad. There is a raised earthen platform in the west–central part of the town that the local people called Guzi (崮子). There were many Longshan sherds, even in the mudbrick walls of houses. We also observed a large flat stone deeply buried in the ground (Figure 3.22). Villagers told us that some black pottery and burials had been found in the area. The large flat stone could have religious significance. We have estimated the extent of both the Longshan (Middle Longshan only) and Zhou (larger in Eastern than Western) components at 6.6 ha. Given the location of the town in a bend in the Guzi River (with areas we could not check) and the presence of DG-XLJC-2 just south of this bend on the other side of the river, these estimates are most likely too low.

Site: Huangjiahe DG-HJH-2, 3 (Year 5)

County: Donggang

Town: Huangjiahe (黄家河)

Map: Rizhaoshi (日照市) [1-50-23-(48)] and Daliancun (大莲村) [1-50-23-(40)]

Period and Period Number: **Longshan 159**, 160; Zhou 298, 299, 300; Han 364, 365

Cultural Layer: Longshan and Zhou periods

Site Description: The site is located on a low rise in the alluvium and at the base of a low piedmont ridge, at an elevation of 25 to 35 m. It is on the eastern side of the Houlou River, on the southern and western sides of Huangjiahe village, and extended several hundreds of meters to the north. The site was in fallow fields and winter wheat at the time of the survey (Figure 3.23), with some areas in vegetable gardens and an orchard. The densest occupation was Longshan (Longshan 159), covering just over 21 ha (larger in Early than in Middle Longshan). A 1 m thick Longshan cultural layer was found in a cut just above the river on the western side of the site. Zhou (Western and Eastern) and Han remains were more dispersed, found in two separate scatters, one in the northern part of the site (Zhou 299, Han 365) and another in the south (Zhou 298, Han 364), in what was still an open area just south of the town. These components ranged approximately 6 to 8 ha in size. A whole Westerm Zhou pottery *guan* (罐) jar was found in a cut in the southern Zhou component. Also, six stone tools were collected from this site. A new road was being built across the western edge of the site at the time of the survey. Given that we found Zhou and Han sherds in an enclosed compound in the southeastern section of town (DG-HJH-4), we conclude the town covers part of the site and that the site was larger in the past, as large as 30 ha in the Han period and 20 ha in Zhou.

Site: DG-HJH-4 (Year 5)

County: Donggang

Town: Huangjiahe (黄家河)

Map: Rizhaoshi (日照市) [1-50-23-(48)]

Period and Period Number: Zhou 297; Han 363

Cultural Layer: None

Site Description: We found a small concentration of Western Zhou and Han sherds within a walled compound at the southern edge of Huangjiahe village, just north of the highway, at an elevation 30 m, and 350 m east of the Houlou River. The visible site was smaller than 0.5 ha. These components are part of the larger Zhou and Han site we mapped at DG-HJH-2, 3.

Site: DG-HQC-5 (Year 1)

County: Donggang

Town: Heiqicun (黑七村)

Map: Anjiacun (安家村) [1-50-24-(18)]

Period and Period Number: Longshan 33

Cultural Layer: None

Site Description: This site is located on flat terrain on the lower slope of a low piedmont ridge between the villages of Heiqicun and Quanzigou (泉子沟) (approximately 300 m east of Quanzigou), at an elevation of 15 m, and 50 m south of a small stream that flows north to the Chao River (Figure 3.24). The area was plowed for farming and part of the site was in an apple orchard. This single component Longshan site is very small (smaller than 0.5 ha); we collected one stone tool, a *chan* (铲) shovel.

Site: DG-HS-2 (Year 11)

County: Donggang

Town: Huashan (华山)

Map: Daguanzhuang (大官庄) [1-50-35-(21)]

Period and Period Number: Longshan 441; Zhou 924; Han 1229

Cultural Layer: Burnt earth, possible burial

FIGURE 3.23. Gary Feinman surveying at Huangjiahe (DG-HJH-2, 3), situated on a low rise in the alluvium.

FIGURE 3.24. Cai Fengshu, Linda Nicholas, and Luan Fengshi surveying the small Longshan site DG-HQC-5.

Site Description: This site is located on the tip of a low piedmont ridge and the alluvium below it, at an elevation of 27 m, on the northeastern side of the town of Huashan, and on the west side of a small water channel. It was in vegetable gardens and winter wheat at the time of the survey. The site may be larger than the 1.2 ha we were able to survey for the Zhou (Western and Eastern) and Han periods. We found evidence of the Longshan period only on the northern, higher part of the site. A farmer told us she had dug up a few whole vessels several years before, possibly from a burial. We did not see the vessels, so it was not possible to determine the period(s) represented. We also found a few chunks of burnt earth, similar to other clumps that we have observed at other habitation sites.

Site: DG-HSD-5 (Year 4)

County: Donggang

Town: Heshandian (河山店)

Map: Chengzigou (程子沟) [1-50-23-(32)]

Period and Period Number: Longshan 151; Han 316

Cultural Layer: None

Site Description: This small site is located on a slight slope in the piedmont, approximately 300 m northwest of the town of Heshandian, at an elevation of 42 m, and 300 m east of a small stream. The site was fallow at the time of the survey. It is smaller than 0.5 ha for the Longshan and Han periods. We found one small stone tool. The site is near several modern quarries.

Site: Heshandian DG-HSD-10 (Year 4)

County: Donggang

Town: Heshandian (河山店)

Map: Qianshagou (前沙沟) [1-50-24-(25)]

Period and Period Number: **Longshan 154**; Zhou 272; Han 326

Cultural Layer: Longshan period

Site Description: The site is located on flat alluvium on the east side of the town of Heshandian, on the east side of the main highway 204, at an elevation of 26 m. It is just north of a modern channel that comes off the Jinyin River (金银河)and is surrounded by modern buildings. The site probably was larger in the past. It is now covered by modern construction. At the time of the survey the site was planted with vegetables and winter wheat. It was largest during the Longshan period, covering an area over 4 ha. We found three stone tools and a Longshan cultural layer that was exposed in a modern ditch. There were Han period sherds on the western side of the site, covering an area of approximately 2.4 ha. The Zhou component (Western Zhou only) was very small, just over 0.5 ha.

Site: Houshanqian DG-HSQ-1 (Year 5, Year 7)

County: Donggang

Town: Houshanqian (后山前)

Map: Daliancun (大莲村) [1-50-23-(40)]

Period and Period Number: Zhou 335; **Han 402**

Cultural Layer: None

Site Description: The site is located on the tip of a low piedmont spur and surrounding alluvium on the east side of the town of Houshanqian, at elevations between 45 and 55 m. It is on the west side of a small bend in the Feijia River. The densest areas of ceramics were between two small streams east of the town. We often saw this kind of setting for sites, learning that it was a preferred location for settlements. Parts of the site were in an orchard and planted with winter wheat at the time of the survey, and some fields were fallow. The site was larger in the Han period, covering 16.3 ha. It was smaller in the Zhou period, covering 12 ha (twice as large in Eastern as in Western Zhou). The Han site most likely extends to the west and south under the modern town. South of the town we later found another large concentration of Han pottery (DG-HSQ-13/QSQ-1 and HSQ-12) that was part of the same larger community.

Site: DG-HSQ-12 (Year 7)

County: Donggang

Town: Houshanqian (后山前)

Map: Daliancun (大莲村) [1-50-23-(40)]

Period and Period Number: Longshan 235; **Han 588**

Cultural Layer: None

Site Description: The site is located in the low piedmont, at an elevation of 50 m, just north of a small stream, 400 m west of the Feijia River, and 400 m southwest of the town of Houshanqian. It is in a series of terraced fields, some of which were fallow and some were planted in winter wheat at the time of the survey. The site is mostly from the Han period, covering 3.6 ha. There was one small scatter of Longshan pottery smaller than 0.5 ha. The Han component was part of a larger Han community that included DG-HSQ-1 and HSQ-13.

Site: Houshanqian DG-HSQ-13/QSQ-1 (Year 7)

County: Donggang

Town: Houshanqian (后山前)

Map: Daliancun (大莲村) [1-50-23-(40)]

Period and Period Number: Zhou 489; **Han 393**

Cultural Layer: None

Site Description: The site is located on a slight slope that begins in the alluvium and stretches to the low piedmont, at elevations of 40 to 50 m, just south of the town of Houshanqian, and just west of a bend in the Feijia River. The Han component includes a small area that was found on the east side of the river on the west side of Qianshanqian (前山前) in Year 5 (DG-QSQ-1). The site is in an area that had both winter wheat and fallow fields at the time of the survey. Some fields were terraced and a portion of the site was in an orchard. Part of the site is likely covered by the town to the north. Including the area on the east side of the river, the Han occupation covers 14 ha. We found one small scatter of Eastern Zhou sherds at the southern edge of the site, covering less than 1 ha. The Han component was part of a larger community (50 ha at minimum) that included DG-HSQ-12 to the west and HSQ-1 on the north side of the town.

FIGURE 3.25. Eastern Zhou period ceramic fishing weight from Jiaokezhuang (DG-JKZ-8, 9[CAC]).

Site: Jiaokezhuang DG-JKZ-8, 9 (Year 8)

County: Donggang

Town: Jiaokezhuang (焦柯庄)

Map: Caijiatan (蔡家滩) [1-50-35-(8,16)]

Period and Period Number: Longshan 352, 353; Zhou 726; **Han 926**

Cultural Layer: None

Site Description: The site is located on a low rise in the alluvium, at an elevation of 5 m, just northwest of several buildings on the coastal highway (Yanhai Highway, 沿海公路), and 500 m southeast of the town of Jiaokezhuang. It is 350 m northwest of the coast. The closest water source is a small stream 700 m to the northeast. Sherds were found in fallow fields, winter wheat, and a vineyard. The entire site was occupied during the Han period, covering 4.9 ha. There was one small scatter of Eastern Zhou sherds (Figure 3.25) and two of Longshan sherds, each smaller than 1 ha.

Site: Liangchengzhen DG-LCZ-1 (Year 1, Year 6)

County: Donggang

Town: Liangchengzhen (两城镇)

Map: Lianhecun (联合村) [1-50-24-(17)]; also Anjiacun (安家村), Houxiangou (后显沟), and Dantucun (丹土村)

Period and Period Number: **Longshan 12**; Yueshi 6; Shang 1, 2; Zhou 6, 7; Han 11

Cultural Layer: Multiple

Site Description: This well-known Longshan period site was first discovered in 1934 (Fang 2009:358–368) and excavated in 1936 (see Chapter 1). It is one of the earliest Longshan sites to be excavated. The site is under the modern town of Liangchengzhen and in adjacent agricul-

FIGURE 3.26. The rammed earth layers at an exposed Han period tomb at Liangchengzhen (DG-LCZ-1[CAAA]).

tural fields to the north and west. It extends from flat alluvium on the west side of the Chao River near the confluence of the Beixiao River to the top of low piedmont ridges to the north and west of Liangchengzhen. Elevation ranges from about 7 to 30 m. Much of the site was in winter wheat and fallow at the time of the survey, with some areas in apple orchards and vegetable gardens. We resurveyed the site in Year 6 to recheck and confirm its boundaries.

We made dozens of collections of ceramics (and stone tools) to map the size of the site in different periods. The site was occupied from Early Longshan through the Han period. The Longshan occupation, estimated from surface sherds, was the largest (approximately 272 ha), and most of the ceramics and stone tools we collected date to this period. We recovered thirty-one stone tools, including *fu* (斧) axes, *ben* (锛) adzes, *dao* (刀) knives, *chui* (锤) hammers, *lian* (镰) sickles, and *zu* (镞) points. The site was largest in Early and Middle Longshan, with limited representation of Late Longshan. Although the Zhou (both Western and Eastern) and Han occupations were smaller and more dispersed, the site was still large in those periods (approximately 241 ha in the Zhou period [Zhou 6, especially during Eastern Zhou] and 236 ha in the Han period). Five Han tombs are still visible on the piedmont slopes north of Liangchengzhen; one raised area of rammed earth (*hangtu* [夯土]) on the western side of town, part of a burial, was visible when we surveyed the site (Figure 3.26). Many cultural layers, mostly pertaining to the Longshan occupation, are visible across the site, but especially in lower areas near the town. Yueshi period ceramics were recovered in only one collection area in the northwestern part of the site (in Year 6), while Shang period ceramics were recovered in two collection areas, one near the large Han tomb (Dagudui [大堌堆]) northwest of town and the other southwest of town.

As an important Longshan site, for decades various teams of researchers have investigated Liangchengzhen through survey and excavation (Chapter 1). For results of the collaborative excavation between 1998 and 2001, see Luan et al. (2004), Luan (2009), and China–U.S. Cooperative Archaeological Team (2016); see also Crawford et al. (2004, 2005), Jin et al. (2004), McGovern, Fang et al. (2005), McGovern, Underhill et al. (2005), Yu (2005), Cunnar (2007, 2013), Underhill, Wang, and Luan (2017), Druc et al. (2018), and Underhill et al. (2021).

Yang, Hu, and Xu (1990) report discovery of a bronze *ge* (戈) dagger-axe, *mao* (矛) spear, and *zu* (镞) arrowhead dating to the Eastern Zhou (Warring States, 475–221 BC; see Table 1.1) period at Liangchengzhen. The site now has national cultural preservation status in China. Shandong University conducted another excavation at Liangchengzhen in 2018, directed by Song Yanbo (Shandong University and Shandong Provincial Institute of Archaeology 2021).

Site: DG-LCZ-2, 3 (Year 1)

County: Donggang

Town: Liangchengzhen (两城镇)

Map: Anjiacun (安家村) [1-50-24-(18)]

Period and Period Number: Dawenkou 1; **Longshan 25**; Zhou 12, 13, 14; Han 16

Cultural Layer: Multiple periods

Site Description: The site is located in low, flat alluvium between the southern edge of Liangchengzhen and the northern bank of the Jinying River, at an elevation of 8 m. Today the area is used for agriculture, with parts of the site at the time of the survey in winter wheat, fallow, and a pear orchard. Very light sherd density was observed in most parts of the site. We made seven artifact collections. The dominant occupation was Longshan, covering approximately 43 ha. Middle Longshan is the best represented, with Early Longshan less so; only one sherd was clearly Late Longshan. Han period sherds were recovered from an area of 30 ha. Zhou period sherds (only Eastern) were very dispersed, covering a total area of just over 15 ha, with the largest component (Zhou 14) covering 12.2 ha. Dawenkou period ceramics were found in one collection area along the northern side of the river, in an area of approximately 3.8 ha. Most of the stone tools recovered date to the Longshan period, including a *dao* (刀) knife, a *ben* (锛) adze, and two *fu* (斧) axes. A cultural layer containing charcoal, sherds (Dawenkou, Longshan, Zhou, and Han), and burnt clay was observed in the north bank of the river.

Site: DG-LCZ-6 (Year 1)

County: Donggang

Town: Liangchengzhen (两城镇)

Map: Anjiacun (安家村) [1-50-24-(18)]

Period and Period Number: **Longshan 19**; Zhou 11

Cultural Layer: None

Site Description: The site is situated on flat alluvium, at an elevation of 7.4 m, and in agricultural fields at the southern edge of the town of Liangchengzhen near the modern highway 204. It is near DG-LCZ-2, 3, but because of modern construction it is unclear whether the two areas were once part of the same site. The site is 800 m north of the Jinyin River, in fields of winter wheat. Longshan (Middle Longshan only) is the dominant period, covering 3.2 ha. The Zhou occupation (Eastern Zhou only) is much smaller at less than 1 ha. One Longshan period stone tool, a *chan* (铲) shovel, was collected.

Site: Luohuaqian DG-LHQ-4 (Year 3)

County: Donggang

Town: Luohuaqian (萝花前)

Map: Gaojiagou (高家沟) [1-50-23-(24)]

Period and Period Number: **Longshan 83**; Zhou 79; Han 93

Cultural Layer: None

Site Description: The site is located on a low rise in the alluvium about 250 m west of the town of Luohuaqian and approximately 50 m north of a small tributary of the Beixiao River, at an elevation of 40 m. The site was mostly in fallow fields and winter wheat at the time of the survey. A relatively dense scatter of Longshan sherds (Early and Middle) was found in a 4.3 ha area. Sparse scatters of Zhou (Eastern Zhou only) and Han sherds each covered approximately 0.5 ha.

Site: DG-LHQ-10 (Year 3)

County: Donggang

Town: Luohuaqian (萝花前)

Map: Dujiahe (杜家河) [1-50-23-(16)]

Period and Period Number: Han 98

Cultural Layer: Han period tomb

Site Description: The site is located on the east slope of a low piedmont ridge, above a small gully, at an elevation of 68 m, and 750 m northwest of the town of Luohuaqian. The area was an orchard at the time of the survey. There is impermanent water in a gully 100 m to the east. The site consists only of a largely destroyed Han tomb; the top was mostly plowed flat and visible in a cut of the slope. No cover was present and there was nothing inside. The tomb was 2.4 m long and 1.2 m wide, with its outlines defined by ceramic tiles around the perimeter.

Site: DG-LJTA-1 (Year 10)

County: Donggang

Town: Lijiatan'ai (李家潭崖)

Map: Yayue (亚月) [1-50-35-(14)]

Period and Period Number: **Zhou 896**; Han 1098

Cultural Layer: Zhou period

Site Description: The site is located on a slight rise in the alluvium at an elevation of 7.8 m, 100 m north of the Zhuzi River (竹子河), and 250 m east of the town of Lijiatan'ai. Although only sparse sherds were found in fields of winter wheat and rice, while digging a storage pit a farmer had exposed a cultural layer with gray sediment and several large Eastern Zhou sherds. The site covered 2.5 ha in Eastern Zhou. A few Han sherds were collected in an area smaller than 0.5 ha. The area is prone to flooding, so the site may have been larger.

Site: Lijiazhuangzi DG-LJZZ-1 (Year 7)

County: Donggang

Town: Lijiazhuangzi (厉家庄子)

Map: Dawa (大洼) [1-50-24-(41)]

Period and Period Number: Zhou 515; **Han 653**

Cultural Layer: None

Site Description: The site is located on a low rise at the piedmont–alluvium boundary, at an elevation of 10 m, just east of the town of Lijiazhuangzi and the highway (Wendeng Road), and 350 m east of a series of shrimp ponds. It is between two small streams that flow to the shrimp ponds. Part of the site was fallow and part was planted with trees at the time of the survey. The site was mostly Han, covering 5.4 ha. It was half that size in Western Zhou. The site may extend to the west under the modern town. It was originally identified and surveyed by Zhang Zhibo (Zhang 12); we surveyed it again to place it on our maps.

Site: DG-LSZ-1 (Year 5)

County: Donggang

Town: Liangshuizhuang (凉水汪)

Map: Qianshagou (前沙沟) [1-50-24-(25)]

Period and Period Number: Zhou 394

Cultural Layer: None

Site Description: This small site is located on the tip of a low piedmont ridge, at an elevation of 55 m, 10 m southwest of a small stream that flows to a small reservoir, just south of an abandoned village, and 500 m southeast of Liangshuiwang village. The site was fallow at the time of the survey. We found a small amount of Zhou period sherds in an area smaller than 0.5 ha, along with one stone tool.

Site: Majiacun DG-MaJC-1 (Year 9)

County: Donggang

Town: Majiacun (马家村)

Map: Liujiawan (刘家湾) [1-50-35-(15)]

Period and Period Number: Longshan 378, 379; Yueshi 16; Shang 128; Zhou 769, 772; Han 1015

Cultural Layer: Multiple

Site Description: The site is located near several shrimp ponds on flat alluvial land, at an elevation of 2 m, 300 m northwest of the town of Majiacun, and just north of a channel that flows south to the Nanxin River (Figure 3.27). Rich cultural deposits containing Longshan, Yueshi, Shang, Zhou, and Han sherds were found eroding out of the side of a drained shrimp pond. Han, Zhou, and Longshan sherds also were found in a broader area (Figure 3.28).

Figure 3.27. View of multicomponent site Majiacun near modern shrimp ponds (DG-MaJC-1).

Figure 3.28. Yueshi period *yan* (甗) steamer waist (*top row*); Western Zhou period *li* tripod foot (*bottom row, left*), Shang period *jia* (架) support (*bottom row, middle*), and Shang period *li* tripod foot (*bottom row, right*) from Majiacun (DG-MaJC-1[CAB]).

It was difficult to estimate the size of this site in different periods. The area with Yueshi and Shang sherds was smaller than 1 ha. Han sherds were found throughout a 7.6 ha area. Zhou and Longshan sherds were each found in two separate clusters; each Longshan cluster (Early and Middle) was approximately 1.4 ha and the Zhou clusters (Western and Eastern) were between 1.7 and 2.8 ha. In the Longshan, Zhou, and Han periods the site was part of larger communities that included DG-MaJC-2 150 m to the east (also found in shrimp ponds on the western side of Majiacun). The entire area between these two sites is covered with fish ponds. We also found Han sherds on the south side of the town, indicating that the Han component also continued to the east under the town. Even combining these separate sherd scatters may still be an underestimation of the size of this site, as shrimp ponds are extensive in this area. The entire community would have been largest during the Han period.

Site: Miaojiacun DG-MJC-1 (Year 6, Year 7)

County: Donggang

Town: Miaojiacun (苗家村)

Map: Qiaojiadunzi (乔家墩子) [1-50-24-(42)]

Period and Period Number: Zhou 477, 636; Han 574

Cultural Layer: Present, with Han period tombs

Site Description: The site is located on flat alluvial land in an area with a high water table, at an elevation of 4 m, and just east of the town of Miaojiacun. It extends 600 to 700 m to the east toward the coastal highway (沿海公路) just west of the coast, and then to the north to the top of a low rise with an elevation of 10 m. A modern water channel cuts across the center of the site. The site was mostly in fallow fields and winter wheat at the time of the survey. It has both Zhou (Western and Eastern) and Han components. In the Han period it extended over 40.5 ha. Although we gave them separate phase numbers at the time of the survey, the Zhou components are part of the same site in Eastern Zhou. The southern component (Zhou 636, covering 31.2 ha) was occupied during both Western and Eastern Zhou, but it was larger in Eastern Zhou. The northern component (Zhou 477, covering 10.8 ha) was only occupied during Eastern Zhou. Therefore, the site was as large in Eastern Zhou as in the Han period.

The northern part of the site, on the low rise, was disturbed by the construction of new houses at the time of the survey. The workers exposed a cultural layer that brought many sherds to the surface while we were there (Figure 3.29). There were two Han tombs on the top of this low rise. The easternmost one, about 100 m west of the coastal highway, was already largely destroyed. The second was about 300 m farther northwest along the top of the rise. That tomb was on top of a low rectangular platform. The workers told us that they had unearthed a Han burial nearby. A geological marker was placed on the tomb; later a looter's trench was dug into it. This site also was included in Zhang Zhibo's survey (Zhang 2). During both the Zhou and Han periods the site was part of a larger community that included DG-MJC-3, MJC-4, and QTX-1. The Han community also included DG-DJT-1. This site was probably a secondary center in the Zhou period and a primary center in the Han (see Chapter 4). This coastal area has seen much recent development that has destroyed much of this site. Given its location, it may have been even larger during the Han period than we have estimated.

FIGURE 3.29. Western Zhou sherds (*top row*: two *li* tripod rims; *bottom row*: two *li* tripod feet) from the cultural layer at Miaojiacun (DG-MJC-1[CAJ]).

Site: DG-MJC-4 (Year 7)

County: Donggang

Town: Miaojiacun (苗家村)

Map: Dawa (大洼) [1-50-24-(41)]

Period and Period Number: Zhou 635; Han 654

Cultural Layer: None

Site Description: The site is located on a slight rise in the alluvium, at an elevation of 5 m, between the town of Miaojiacun to the north and Dongjiatan (董家滩) village to the south. It extends from a large body of water on the west to a good road on the east. The site area was fallow at the time of survey or planted in winter wheat. Zhou (Western and Eastern) and Han sherds covered an area of 9.9 ha. Bounded by modern towns, water, and roads, this site clearly was larger in the past. The Zhou and Han components were both part of a larger community that included DG-MJC-1, MJC-3, and QTX-1. The Han part of this larger community also extended south to include DG-DJT-1.

Site: Mujiaxiaozhuang DG-MJXZ-1 (Year 9)

County: Donggang

Town: Mujiaxiaozhuang (牟家小庄)

Map: Futuan (傅疃) [1-50-23-(63)]

Period and Period Number: Zhou 726, 727; Han 948

Cultural Layer: None

Site Description: The site is located on a low rise that extends into the alluvium, at an elevation of 9 m, and 100 m south of the town of Mujiaxiaozhuang. A small stream that flows to the Nanxin River curves around the east and north sides of this low rise. Most of the site is in a fruit orchard on this rise. Han sherds were found on the entire site, covering 13.9 m. Zhou sherds were found in two discrete scatters, with the larger (Zhou 727) in the orchard, covering 8.3 ha; a smaller cluster of Zhou sherds was found west of the road.

Site: Majiazhuang DG-MJZ-3 (Year 4)

County: Donggang

Town: Majiazhuang (马家庄)

Map: Chengzigou (程子沟) [1-50-23-(32)]

Period and Period Number: Zhou 251; Han 304

Cultural Layer: Zhou period

Site Description: This is a small site located on the flat top of a piedmont spur that overlooks a natural river channel and a modern reservoir, less than 200 m southwest of the town of Majiazhuang, at an elevation of 68 m (Figure 3.30). The site was clearly defensively located, and the top of the hill was obviously artificially flattened. The site was planted in winter wheat at the time of the survey. In the Zhou period (both Western and Eastern) the site covered about 0.5 ha. There is an exposed cultural layer 2 m long on the north side of the site, with burnt clay inside. The site was even smaller in the Han period, with sherds only found on the west side of the site. There are several other defensively located Zhou period sites nearby (such as DG-SNG-1).

Site: DG-MSH-1 (Year 5)

County: Donggang

Town: Miaoshanhou (庙山后)

Map: Shankoucun (山口村) [1-50-24-(33)]

Period and Period Number: **Longshan 184**; Zhou 382

Cultural Layer: None

Site Description: This site is located on a low piedmont slope, at an elevation of 85 m, just south of a modern reservoir and small stream, and 100 m south of the town of Miaoshanhou. The site area was in vegetable gardens, an orchard, and winter wheat (Figure 3.31). The densest occupation was the Longshan component (both Early and Middle), covering 4 ha. There was a strip of a Western Zhou component at the southern, higher edge of the site, covering 1.2 ha. Two stone tools were found at the site.

Figure 3.30. View of Majiazhuang (DG-MJZ-3) on terraced piedmont spur above a modern reservoir.

Figure 3.31. View of the Longshan and Zhou site DG-MSH-1 located on a low piedmont slope above a modern reservoir.

Site: DG-MWT-1 (Year 6)

County: Donggang

Town: Mingwangtai (明王台)

Map: Dawa (大洼) [1-50-24-(41)]

Period and Period Number: Han 847

Cultural Layer: Han period tomb

Site Description: At the time of our survey, this site consisted of one Han period tomb located in an area of recent quarrying just north of the office of the Public Security Bureau, on top of a low piedmont ridge, and at an elevation of 55 m. The tomb had been almost completely destroyed when we recorded it. We observed some packed earth in the cut wall of the tomb and collected a few large Han sherds that likely date to Eastern Han.

Site: Nantunling DG-NTL-4 (Year 8, Year 11)

County: Donggang

Town: Nantunling (南屯岭)

Map: Lujiagou (路家沟) [1-50-23-(64)]

Period and Period Number: Beixin 2; Dawenkou 14; Han 914

Cultural Layer: Beixin and Dawenkou periods

Site Description: The site is located on top of a long, flat piedmont ridge on the west side of Kui Shan, at an elevation of 34 m. It is just north of a large reservoir, 600 m northeast of the town of Nantunling. The site was in fallow fields and winter wheat at the time of the survey (Figure 3.32). When we revisited this site in Year 11, soil was being removed from this long ridge for construction elsewhere in the area, and Rizhao officials had just stopped this quarrying for soil within meters of the western edge of the site. It had been selected for preservation because of the Late Beixin–Early Dawenkou pottery and cultural layers we had found there (Figure 3.33). The site is not large, smaller than 1 ha. We also collected soil samples from a cultural layer for flotation and recovered plant remains (Chen 2007). A few Han sherds were also found at the site.

Site: DG-NXZZ-1 (Year 7)

County: Donggang

Town: Nanxiaozhuangzi (南小庄子)

Map: Dawa (大洼) [1-50-24-(41)]

Period and Period Number: Zhou 513; Han 658

Cultural Layer: None

Site Description: The site is located on flat terrain at the piedmont–alluvium boundary, at an elevation of 18 m, on both sides of the Rizhao Middle School in the town of Nanxiaozhuangzi, and 300 m east of a tributary of the Guzi River. The site was in fallow fields at the time of the survey. A small water channel crosses the southern part of the site. Eastern Zhou sherds, covering 4.7 ha, and Han sherds, covering 7.6 ha, were found only west of the school. Western Zhou sherds were found on both sides of the school.

FIGURE 3.32. Fang Hui and Linda Nicholas surveying Nantunling (DG-NTL-4).

FIGURE 3.33. Five Beixin or Dawenkou period *ding* tripod feet (*top row, left to second from right*), Early Dawenkou period *ding* tripod foot (*bottom left*), Early Dawenkou period gray *bo* bowl (*second from left, bottom row*), Late Beixin period *hu* (壶) jar handle (*second from right, bottom row*), and two Late Beixin period body sherds with fingernail impressions (*far right, top and bottom rows*) from Nantunling (DG-NTL-4).

Site: Nanzhangjiacun DG-NZJC-1 (Year 8)

County: Donggang

Town: Nanzhangjiacun (南张家村)

Map: Lujiagou (路家沟) [1-50-23-(64)]

Period and Period Number: **Longshan 343**; Yueshi 13; Zhou 705; Han 910

Cultural Layer: None

Site Description: The site is located on the top and slope of a long, low piedmont ridge at an elevation of 20 m, 300 m north of the town of Nanzhangjiacun, and on the west side of the road to Dongshanqian (东山前) village. The site is within 50 m of a small stream on the east, a possible water source for this site. It was in mostly fallow fields at the time of the survey, but there also was some winter wheat. Although the site is not large, only 3.7 ha in the Longshan period (larger in Early than in Middle), the density of sherds was quite high. The Longshan period was the predominant occupation here, with 136 sherds recovered in an area of almost 4 ha. We found light scatters of Yueshi, Eastern Zhou, and Han sherds. Of the five stone tools we collected at the site, two were Yueshi period *fangkong shi chu* (方孔石锄; a *chu* hoe with a square hole).

Site: Qianbianzhuang DG-QBZ-2 (Year 2)

County: Donggang

Town: Qianbianzhuang (前卞庄)

Map: Dantucun (丹土村) [1-50-24-(9)]

Period and Period Number: Zhou 33; **Han 59**

Cultural Layer: None

Site Description: The site is located on flat alluvium between the three modern villages of Houbianzhuang (后卞庄), Qianbianzhuang, and Miaowangzhuang (苗王庄), 100 m northwest of a small bend in the Beixiao River, and at an elevation of 25 m. A small tributary of the river crosses the northern edge of the site. The area was planted in winter wheat and some fields were fallow at the time of the survey. The site was largest during the Han period, covering just over 26 ha; Zhou sherds were found in only one small part of the site, covering 4.1 ha.

Site: DG-QD-1 (Year 9)

County: Donggang

Town: Qingdun (青墩)

Map: Futuan (傅疃) [1-50-23-(63)]

Period and Period Number: Zhou 730; Han 957

Cultural Layer: None

Site Description: The site is located on a low natural rise in the alluvium, at an elevation of 11 m, 600 m northwest of the main part of the town of Qingdun, and 350 m southwest of Xujiayuan (徐家园) village. It is north of the road and a small settlement of houses on a rise. There is a small water channel 200 m west of the site. Most of the area was fallow at the time of survey, but some fields had winter wheat. Most of the surface pottery was Han and the site was largest in that period, covering 5 ha. Eastern Zhou sherds were present only in the western part of the site.

Site: DG-QD-4 (Year 9)
County: Donggang
Town: Qingdun (青墩)
Map: Futuan (傅疃) [1-50-23-(63)]
Period and Period Number: Zhou 738, 740; **Han 967**
Cultural Layer: None
Site Description: The site is located on a low rise in the alluvium, at an elevation of 7 m, on the west side of the town of Qingdun. The low rise is an extension of the rise where DG-QD-1 is located, 300 m to the north. It extends to both sides of the road. A small stream 450 m to the west is the nearest natural water source. The site was planted in winter wheat at the time of the survey, some fields were fallow, and others were planted with fruit trees. Han sherds were well represented on the surface, covering 6 ha. Two small discrete scatters of Eastern Zhou pottery were found, one south of the road and one to the north.

Site: Qingdun DG-QD-5 (Year 9)
County: Donggang
Town: Qingdun (青墩)
Map: Jiacang (夹仓) [1-50-35-(7)]
Period and Period Number: Longshan 357, 358; **Zhou 742**; Han 968
Cultural Layer: None
Site Description: The site is situated on a low rise in the alluvium, at an elevation of 5 m, less than 100 m southeast of the town of Qingdun, and just west of highway 204. The site stretches to the south almost to Tianjiayuan. It is 600 m east of a small stream. The northern part of the site is in a tree nursery. At the time of the survey the rest of the site was partly in winter wheat and partly in fallow fields. There was a fairly high density of Zhou pottery on the surface, covering 18.6 ha (the site was slightly larger in Eastern Zhou than in Western Zhou). Many fewer Longshan sherds were recovered from a comparatively small area of just over 6 ha; Han sherds were more dispersed, found in an area of 10.5 ha in the center of the site. There also were two smaller scatters of Longshan sherds, one Middle Longshan and one Early Longshan. A farmer told us that on the west side of the site he had pulled out from about a meter below the surface a nearly complete "bowl with ring foot" (possibly a Western Zhou *gui* [簋] food bowl) and a bronze knife coin dating to Eastern Zhou.

Site: DG-QDT-1 (Year 9)
County: Donggang
Town: Qiaodongtou (桥东头)
Map: Liujiawan (刘家湾) [1-50-35-(15)]

Period and Period Number: Zhou 762; Han 997

Cultural Layer: Zhou period

Site Description: The site was found in the bank of a shrimp pond in the alluvium, at an elevation of 2 m, where sherds were eroding out of a destroyed cultural layer. The site is 150 m east of Lijiacun and 150 m northeast of the town of Qiaodongtou. The cultural layer contains remains from the Zhou period, both Eastern and Western, but we also collected a few Han sherds. The area of the exposed cultural layer was approximately 0.5 ha. The site could have been larger in the past, but the area today was too modified by shrimp ponds to be able to determine the complete size of the site.

Site: DG-QGG-1 (Year 1)

County: Donggang

Town: Qingganggou (青岗沟)

Map: Lianhecun (联合村) [1-50-24-(17)]

Period and Period Number: Longshan 21; Han 1

Cultural Layer: None

Site Description: The site is located on a low piedmont ridge 150 m west of highway 204 and approximately 700 m northeast of the town of Qingganggou, at an elevation of 20 m. It is 550 m northwest of the Jinyin River (金银河) and its confluence with a small stream (300 m south of the site). The site was in winter wheat and fallow fields at the time of the survey. The scatter of Longshan (Middle Longshan only) sherds extended over 5.7 ha, with the Han period scatter only slightly smaller at around 5.4 ha. We collected one Longshan stone tool that we conclude was used for polishing.

Site: Qinjiaguanzhuang DG-QJGZ-1 (Year 5)

County: Donggang

Town: Qinjiaguanzhuang (秦家官庄)

Map: Sujiacun (苏家村) [1-50-24-(34)]

Period and Period Number: Yueshi 4; Shang 17; Zhou 395

Cultural Layer: Multiple

Site Description: The site is located on a low ridge in the piedmont, at an elevation of 25 m, between the junction of two streams, and 300 m southeast of the town of Qinjiaguanzhuang. Part of the site was planted in winter wheat, but much of it had been destroyed by modern brickmaking (Figure 3.34). Several cultural layers were observed in banks exposed by the digging for clay. The densest occupation was Zhou (mostly Western Zhou, with a small area of Eastern Zhou at the south end of the site), covering 4.6 ha. The cultural layers also included some Yueshi and Shang pottery; those occupations each covered 1.5 ha. We also collected eight stone tools at the site.

Site: Qianjiangshuigou DG-QJSG-1 (Year 10)

County: Donggang

Figure 3.34. View of a partially destroyed Han tomb at Qinjiaguanzhuang (DG-QJGZ-1).

Town: Qianjiangshuigou (前浆水沟)

Map: Shengjiadaituan (盛家代疃) [1-50-23-(46)]

Period and Period Number: Zhou 805; Han 1071

Cultural Layer: None

Site Description: The site is located on flat alluvial terrain, at an elevation of 17.6 m, 120 m west of the town of Qianjiangshuigou, and north of a small road that is north of a bamboo grove on the north side of the Futuan River. The Futuan River is 300 m south of the site; the nearest water source is a small stream that cuts through the western part of the site. The site was for the most part on fallow and plowed fields, but a small portion was in vegetable gardens. We mostly collected Eastern and Western Zhou sherds in a 2 ha area. There was a lower density of Han sherds, and we saw a Han brick. The Han area was 1.4 ha.

Site: Qianlianghe DG-QLH-1 (Year 5)

County: Donggang

Town: Qianlianghe (前两河)

Map: Daliancun (大莲村) [1-50-23-(40)]

Period and Period Number: **Zhou 315**; Han 460

Cultural Layer: Zhou period

Site Description: The site is located on a low rise in the alluvium at the base of a low ridge, at an elevation of 20 m, just east of the Xiangdian River, and 250 m northeast of Qianlianghe village. It was mostly in fallow fields and winter wheat at the time of survey. The site is mostly from the Zhou period, covering 4.5 ha in Western Zhou and about half that for the Eastern Zhou occupation. The construction of a new road exposed thick black cultural layers and some burnt clay in the center of the site (Figure 3.35). There also was a very small Han occupation smaller than 0.5 ha.

Site: DG-QSQ-1 (Year 5)

County: Donggang

Town: Qianshanqian (前山前)

Map: Daliancun (大莲村) [1-50-23-(40)]

Period and Period Number: **Longshan 168**; Zhou 328, 329; Han 393

Cultural Layer: Longshan period

Site Description: The site is located on a low rise in the alluvium, at an elevation of 45 m, on the west side of the town of Qianshanqian, and just east of a small bend in the Feijia River. The town covers the eastern part of the site. Most of the site was in vegetable gardens, fallow fields, and winter wheat at the time of the survey, and some portions were terraced or in orchards. The dominant occupation was Longhshan (slightly larger in Middle Longshan than in Early Longshan), covering 4 ha. A Longshan cultural layer was observed in a 1 m wide segment of a terrace cut. Zhou sherds were observed in two small discrete scatters (both Western Zhou), one to the north (Zhou 329) and one to the south (Zhou 328); both areas are smaller than 1 ha. We found Han sherds in the same area, but during Year 7, when we surveyed west of the river, we found a much larger Han site of which this Han occupation was a part (see DG-HSQ-13/QSQ-1 for a description of the Han component). We also found a small scatter of Longshan pottery on the west side of the river (part of DG-HSQ-13) in Year 7 that is part of the same site.

Site: DG-QTX-1 (Year 6)

County: Donggang

Town: Qiantanxi (前滩西)

Map: Qiaojiadunzi (乔家墩子) [1-50-24-(42)]

Period and Period Number: Zhou 481; Han 577

Cultural Layer: None

Site Description: The site is located on a slight rise in the alluvium, at an elevation of 5 m, in and south of a series of shrimp ponds, and 200 m southwest of the town of Qiantanxi. Most of the site was in fallow fields at the time of the survey, but some fields were planted in winter wheat. The Han period was the best represented, covering 13.6 ha, but Zhou materials (Eastern only) were found in a 10.4 ha area. Parts of the site most likely were destroyed when the shrimp ponds were constructed. The Zhou and Han components are part of a larger community that included DG-MJC-1 and MJC-4. This site would have been a Tier I Han site located very near the coast (see Chapter 4).

Figure 3.35. Surveying an exposed cultural layer in the center of Qianlianghe (DG-QLH-1).

Site: Qianwulihe DG-QWLH-1 (Year 7)

County: Donggang

Town: Qianwulihe (前五里河)

Map: Rizhaoshi (日照市) [1-50-23-(48)]

Period and Period Number: Longshan 240; Zhou 637; Han 662

Cultural Layer: Multiple

Site Description: The site is located on a low rise in the alluvium, at an elevation of 15 m, on the west side of the town of Qianwulihe (south of the road and north of a mental hospital), and just west of the Xiangdian River. Most of the site was on fallow land at the time of the survey, with some remaining cornstalks in a few fields. We found Han, Longshan (Early), and Zhou sherds dispersed over a 5 ha area (Figure 3.36). In a cut near the road we observed several cultural layers and an ancient pit (Figure 3.37). Local people claim to have found whole *guan* (罐) pots during construction of new housing on this site two years before our survey. The site clearly was larger in the past, with the modern town of Qianwulihe now covering part of it. The site was surveyed by Zhang Zhibo (Zhang 11). It also probably included Longshan, Zhou, and Han components found at DG-DXD-1, 150 m to the southeast. This site also most likely extends under a modern village (Daxiangdian) to the east; we could see sherds in an area just smaller than 1 ha. The whole site may have been at least 10 ha.

FIGURE 3.36. Early Longshan period sherds (*left*: *yi* [匜] spouted basin rim; *center and right*: two *ding* tripod feet) from Qianwulihe (DG-QWLH-1).

FIGURE 3.37. An ancient pit exposed at Qianwulihe (DG-QWLH-1).

Site: Qianzhucun DG-QZC-1/WLZ-2 (Year 5)

County: Donggang

Town: Qianzhucun (前竹村) and Woluozi (窝落子)

Map: Shankoucun (山口村) [1-50-24-(33)]

Period and Period Number: Longshan 182; Shang 15, 16; Yueshi 3; **Zhou 383**; Han 459

Cultural Layer: Zhou period

Site Description: The site is located on a series of low piedmont ridges and alluvial terraces, at elevations of 50 to 70 m, on both sides of a stream that flows into the Jinyin River (possibly the headwaters), just south of the town of Qianzhucun. It lies in a variety of agricultural settings, including winter wheat, fallow fields at the time of survey, some orchards, and areas being prepared for the construction of greenhouses. The site was largest in the Zhou period (especially in Western Zhou), when it covered 32.6 ha (13.3 ha in Eastern Zhou). Several Zhou cultural layers, one of which showed evidence of burnt soil, were revealed by modern terracing just north of the river. All other occupations were much smaller. The 2.6 ha area for the Yueshi period was the largest of these other occupations. The Zhou component was part of a larger Zhou community (largest in Western Zhou) that included sites around Qianzhucun and Woluozi (DG-QZC-1–3, WLZ-1–5, SJP-6– 8), all situated on a series of low piedmont ridges separated by several villages. The combined site was at least 100 ha, making it one of the two largest Western Zhou sites in our region (Figure 3.38). The site was called Songzhucun (松竹村). Spring and Autumn period (771–476 BC) burials with pottery and bronze weapons were found during earlier archaeological investigations (Yang, Hu, and Xu 1990).

Site: DG-SHT-1 (Year 13)

County: Donggang

Town: Sanhetuan (三合疃)

Map: Shengjiadaituan (盛家代疃) [1-50-23-(46)]

Period and Period Number: Han 1617

Cultural Layer: Han period

Site Description: The site is located on a slight slope, in the alluvium, approximately 250 m east of the town of Sanhetuan, at an elevation of 35m, and 200 m east of a small stream. The area was fallow at the time of survey. A terrace cut exposed a Han cultural deposit with many Han tiles, 25 to 30 cm below the surface. The area of the cut was small, less than 0.25 ha, but the site was probably larger.

Site: Sujiacun DG-SJC-1, 12 (Year 5)

County: Donggang

Town: Sujiacun (苏家村)

Map: Sujiacun (苏家村) [1-50-24-(34)]

Period and Period Number: **Longshan 193**; Zhou 400, 401; Han 456

Cultural Layer: None

FIGURE 3.38. View of Qianzhucun (DG-QZC-1/WLZ-2) located on low piedmont ridges and alluvial terraces.

Site Description: The site is located in the alluvium, at an elevation of 10 m, on the east side of the town of Sujiacun, and on both sides of a small river that flows directly to the coast. It was mostly fallow and in winter wheat at the time of the survey, although some greenhouses were present as well. The site was largest in the Longshan period, covering 11 ha, and may extend beneath the modern town. It was mostly Early Longshan, with just a small Middle Longshan occupation on the west side. Seven stone tools were collected. There were very small scatters of Zhou (Eastern) and Han sherds, each 1 ha or smaller. The Longshan component was part of a larger Longshan community, especially with DG-SJC-2 on the northwest side of Sujiacun and DG-SJC-7 on the west.

The site was discovered by the local Cultural Preservation Bureau and now has provincial-level cultural preservation protection (Rizhao City Library and Linyi District Committee 1986; China Cultural Heritage Bureau 2007:272–273). Excavations in 2019 by Shandong University were directed by Song Yanbo and Dong Yu. See also Shandong University (2013) for results of coring at the site and X. Chen et al. (2017) for radiocarbon and isotopic analysis of seeds at this and other sites.

Site: DG-SJC-2 (Year 5)
County: Donggang
Town: Sujiacun (苏家村)
Map: Sujiacun (苏家村) [1-50-24-(34)]

Period and Period Number: **Longshan 192**; Han 449, 450

Cultural Layer: Longshan period

Site Description: The site is located on a broad low rise in the alluvium, at an elevation of 25 m, on the northwest side of the town of Sujiacun, and 450 m north of small river that flows directly to the coast. The site was in fallow fields and winter wheat at the time of the survey. The largest component of the site is Longshan (Early only), covering 5.4 ha; many sherds were found in a cut bank at the northern edge of the site. Han sherds were found in two very small discrete scatters, each smaller than 0.5 ha. The Longshan component was part of a larger Longshan community, especially with DG-SJC-1 on the east side of Sujiacun and DG-SJC-7 and SJC-10 on the west. These and the other sites in the Sujiacun area have been disturbed by modern villages and brick factories.

Site: DG-SJC-7 (Year 5)

County: Donggang

Town: Sujiacun (苏家村)

Map: Sujiacun (苏家村) [1-50-24-(34)]

Period and Period Number: Longshan 161; **Zhou 396**

Cultural Layer: Eastern Zhou period tomb

Site Description: The site is located on a low rise in the alluvium, at an elevation of 20 m, on the west side of the town of Sujiacun, and just north of a small river that flows directly to the coast. The site was in a fallow area and in an orchard at the time of the survey. It was largest in the Zhou period (Eastern only), covering 3 ha. There is an Eastern Zhou tomb at the site, and a farmer gave us a ceramic bowl that he said came from the tomb. We found only a trace of Longshan in the southern part of the site just across the river from the Longshan component at DG-SJC-10. This component may have been part of a larger Longshan community, especially with DG-SJC-1 on the east side of Sujiacun, DG-SJC-2 on the northwest, and DG-SJC-10 just south of the river. DG-SJC-7 and other Sujiacun area sites have been disturbed by modern villages and brick factories. A bronze *ge* (戈) dagger-axe inscribed with "*zuo*" (左) from the Spring and Autumn period, which was collected by the local Cultural Preservation Bureau many years ago, may have originated from here (Yang, Hu, and Xu 1990).

Site: Suijiaguanzhuang DG-SJGZ-1 (Year 2)

County: Donggang

Town: Suijiaguanzhuang (隋家官庄)

Map: Lianhecun (联合村) [1-50-24-(17)]

Period and Period Number: Longshan 71

Cultural Layer: None

Site Description: The site is located on the top of a low piedmont ridge, 200 m north of the town of Suijiaguanzhuang, at an elevation of 45 m, and 350 m east of a tributary of the Jinyin River. The site was in winter wheat and fallow fields at the time of the survey (Figure 3.39). Longshan (Early only) sherds were dispersed over an area of 3.4 ha, and one stone tool, a *dao* (刀) knife, was collected (Figure 3.40).

FIGURE 3.39. Surveying at the Longshan site Suijiaguanzhuang (DG-SJGZ-1) on the top of a low piedmont ridge.

FIGURE 3.40. Early Longshan period white *gui* tripod foot (*top left*), stone *dao* knife (*top right*), white body sherd (*lower left*), quartz crystal (*center*), and *guan* jar base (*lower right*) from Suijiaguanzhuang (DG-SJGZ-1).

Site: DG-SJP-6/WLZ-5 (Year 5)

County: Donggang

Town: Shenjiapo (申家坡/) and Woluozi (窝落子)

Map: Shankoucun (山口村) [1-50-24-(33)]

Period and Period Number: **Longshan 181**; Zhou 378; Han 433

Cultural Layer: Longshan period

Site Description: The site is located on a very low piedmont rise, at an elevation of 45 m, just north of a string of reservoirs, 850 m southeast of the town of Shenjiapo, and 500 m southwest of the town of Woluozi. The site was mostly in an apple orchard and a few nearby fallow fields at the time of the survey (Figure 3.41). Both Longshan (Early and Middle) and Zhou (more Eastern than Western) sherds were found in a 3.8 ha area. Trenching in the apple orchard had exposed several Longshan cultural layers and ashy deposits (Figure 3.42). One stone tool was found as well. A few Han sherds were found in an area smaller than 0.5 ha. The Zhou component was part of a larger Zhou community (the largest is Western Zhou) that included sites around Qianzhucun and Woluozi (DG-QZC-1–3, WLZ-1–5, SJP-6–8). The combined site may have been as large as 125 to 150 ha, making it the third or fourth largest Western Zhou site in the Shandong region.

Site: DG-SJYZ-3 (Year 11)

County: Donggang

Town: Sunjiayingzi (孙家营子)

Map: Gaowangzhuang (高旺庄) [1-50-35-(22)]

Period and Period Number: Han 1264

Cultural Layer: Han period tomb

Site Description: The site is located in the alluvium, in a field of winter wheat and cornstalks, at elevation of 5 m, and 150 m southeast of the town of Sunjiayingzi. The site is in an area surrounded by many small ponds. It consists of a very low rise that may be a Han tomb; we found a small fragment of a decorated brick near it.

Site: DG-SKC-1 (Year 5)

County: Donggang

Town: Shankoucun (山口村)

Map: Shankoucun (山口村) [1-50-24-(33)]

Period and Period Number: Zhou 380

Cultural Layer: Zhou period

Site Description: The site is located on a long, low piedmont ridge, at an elevation of 45 m, just east of a small stream, and 400 m northwest of the town of Shankoucun. It was completely within an apple orchard (Figure 3.43). Although we found Zhou sherds (Eastern only) in only a small area (1 ha), trenching in the orchard had exposed a gray, ashy cultural layer.

FIGURE 3.41. View of DG-SJP-6/WLZ-5 located on a low piedmont rise.

FIGURE 3.42. Gary Feinman collecting sherds in a Longshan period cultural layer exposed at DG-SJP-6/WLZ-5.

Figure 3.43. View of the small Zhou site DG-SKC-1 located completely within an apple orchard.

Site: DG-SKC-4 (Year 5)

County: Donggang

Town: Shankoucun (山口村)

Map: Shankoucun (山口村) [1-50-24-(33)]

Period and Period Number: Longshan 183; **Zhou 319**; Han 381

Cultural Layer: None

Site Description: The site is located on a low piedmont rise, at an elevation of 50 m, just east of a small stream in the southeastern corner of the town of Shankoucun. The entire site was in an orchard on a terraced slope. It was not large, but there was a fairly high density of Zhou sherds (Western only) in an area of approximately 1 ha. There were fewer Longshan and Han sherds. The Zhou component probably was part of larger Zhou site (Western) that extended farther up the ridge (with DG-SKC-2 and SKC-3).

Site: DG-SLJZ-5 (Year 7)

County: Donggang

Town: Shanglijiazhuang (上李家庄村)

Map: Doulingzi (陡岭子) [1-50-23-(39)]

Period and Period Number: Longshan 238; Zhou 497; **Han 612**

Cultural Layer: None

Site Description: This site is located in the low piedmont, between 50 and 60 m in elevation, at the base of ridges that grade down to a small tributary of the Guzi River. It is less than 50 m south of the town of Shanglijiazhuang, and 250 m east of the town of Xiejialing (谢家岭). The site is bordered on the east by the small tributary, on the west by the road, and on the north and south by small streams. Most of the site was planted in winter wheat at the time of the survey, but some parts were fallow and others were planted with tea. Four collections were made (CAA, CAB, CAC, and CAD). The site was largest during the Han period, covering 7.9 ha. Zhou and Longshan sherds were found only in the north of the site. The Zhou site (Western only) was 2.4 ha. Although the Longshan occupation covered an area smaller than 1 ha, we did find a dense concentration of Longshan sherds in the cut of a gully wall, on the west side of the site near the road.

Site: DG-SNG-1 (Year 4)

County: Donggang

Town: Saniugou (撒牛沟)

Map: Chengzigou (程子沟) [1-50-23-(32)]

Period and Period Number: Zhou 252

Cultural Layer: None

Site Description: This is a small site located on the flat top of a piedmont spur that overlooks two natural stream channels, 200 m northwest of the town of Saniugou, and at an elevation of 75 m. It has only Western Zhou remains and clearly was situated for defense. The site was planted in winter wheat and part was fallow at the time of the survey (Figure 3.44). It is smaller than 1 ha. There are several other defensively located Zhou sites nearby (such as DG-MJZ-3).

Site: Tianjiacun DG-TiJC-1 (Year 6)

County: Donggang

Town: Tianjiacun (田家村)

Map: Rizhaoshi (日照市) [1-50-23-(48)]

Period and Period Number: Zhou 464; Han 564

Cultural Layer: None

Site Description: The site is located on the eastern slopes of a low piedmont ridge, at an elevation of 35 m, and 100 to 150 m west and northwest of the town of Tianjiacun. A small stream 375 m to the northeast is the nearest water. The low piedmont rise just above alluvial land is an ideal setting for a site. It was mostly on fallow land at the time of the survey. There were several quarries 300 m to the north. The Han occupation (Western Han), covering 12.5 ha, was just slightly larger than the Zhou occupation (Eastern and Western), which covered 9.4 ha.

Site: Taojiacun DG-TJC-1 (Year 6)

County: Donggang

Town: Taojiacun (陶家村)

Map: Sujiacun (苏家村) [1-50-24-(34)]

Figure 3.44. View of DG-SNG-1 on a low piedmont spur above a modern reservoir.

Period and Period Number: Zhou 484

Cultural Layer: None

Site Description: The site is located on two low rises in the middle piedmont, at an elevation of 50 m, and 400 m north of the town of Taojiacun. Both rises likely were artificially flattened (Figure 3.45). The site is just north of a small stream. The area was fallow at the time of the survey, and there are many modern quarries there today. The entire site has only a Zhou component and was larger in Western Zhou (3.1 ha) than in Eastern Zhou (1.3 ha). We collected four stone tools on the site.

Over the years, people have found bronze ritual vessels such as *ding* (鼎) tripods, *li* (鬲) tripods, and *hu* (壶) jars, as well as bronze tools such as *ben* (锛) adzes. These bronzes date to the early Spring and Autumn period (771–475 BC).

Site: Tianjiayuan DG-TJY-1/ZK-1 (Year 9)

County: Donggang

Town: Tianjiayuan (田家园) and Zhaike (宅科)

Map: Jiacang (夹仓) [1-50-35(7)]

Period and Period Number: Longshan 360; **Zhou 743**; **Han 971**

Cultural Layer: None

Site Description: The site is located on a very low rise in the alluvium, at an elevation of 5 m between the towns of Zhaike and Tianjiayuan. A small channel crosses the southern part of the site. This southern portion, northwest of Zhaike, was planted in winter wheat and

FIGURE 3.45. Zhou period site Taojiacun (DG-TJC-1) located on two low rises at the base of a low mountain.

vegetables, and some fields were fallow at the time of the survey. The northern part of the site, southeast of Tianjiayuan, also included a fruit orchard. Han and Eastern Zhou sherds were found in all collection areas, covering 9.5 ha. Western Zhou and Longshan (Early and Middle) sherds were in two discrete areas, one in the north of the site and the other in the south; each scatter was approximately 2 ha.

Site: DG-TL-5 (Year 9)

County: Donggang

Town: Taoluo (涛雒)

Map: Yayue (亚月) [1-50-35-(14)]

Period and Period Number: Longshan 384; Zhou 784; **Han 1023**

Cultural Layer: Han period

Site Description: The site is located in several abandoned shrimp ponds on a slight rise in the alluvium, at an elevation of 4.5 m. It is just north of the north branch of the Zhuzi River and 900 m southwest of the town of Taoluo. Many sherds were found in the old shrimp ponds. A gray cultural layer with Han sherds was found just south of the ponds, on the north bank of a very small stream channel (Figure 3.46). This layer was 50 cm thick and was exposed for 5 m. The Han occupation covered 5.6 ha. Large quantities of Zhou sherds (Western and Eastern)

Figure 3.46. Survey crew members examine the exposed Han period cultural layer at DG-TL-5.

were recovered from within the ponds, in an area of approximately 1.6 ha. A few Longshan sherds were collected from the west side of the pond area. Given the density of Zhou and Han sherds, the original construction of the ponds likely disturbed a site that is deeply buried, so our estimates of the site areas are minimums.

Site: Wujiatai DG-WJT-1 (Year 4)

County: Donggang

Town: Wujiatai (吴家台)

Map: Yujiacun (于家村) [1-50-24-(26)]

Period and Period Number: Longshan 147; **Zhou 291**; **Han 353**

Cultural Layer: Probable Longshan period

Site Description: The site is located on a slight slope, on the first low alluvial terrace above of the sea at an elevation of 8 m, on the east side of the town of Wujiatai. The nearest water source is a series of low ponds 100 m to the south. The site was planted in winter wheat and some fields were fallow at the time of the survey (Figure 3.47). It was largest in the Zhou period (especially in Eastern Zhou), covering 6 ha. Han sherds were found in a 3.9 ha area. There was a badly damaged earthen Han tomb. Several partial stone tools were collected nearby. Longshan sherds were found only in a small area (less than 0.5 ha) in the southeastern part of the site, where there was a 20 cm thick cultural layer.

FIGURE 3.47. View of Wujiatai (DG-WJT-1) on a low alluvial terrace above the sea.

Site: DG-WLZ-1 (Year 5)

County: Donggang

Town: Woluozi (窝落子)

Map: Shankoucun (山口村) [1-50-24-(33)]

Period and Period Number: **Zhou 385;** Han 430

Cultural Layer: None

Site Description: The site is located on a low ridge in the piedmont, at an elevation of 40 to 60 m, 150 m north of the town of Woluozi, and just north of a series of small reservoirs. The Beijing north highway (北京北路)crosses the east side of the site. The site was mostly in fallow fields and winter wheat at the time of the survey. It was largest in the Zhou period, covering 8.83 ha. The Western Zhou component, on the east side of the site, was almost three times as large as the Eastern Zhou component on the west. A few Han sherds, covering less than 1 ha, were found in the northwestern part of the site. The Zhou component was part of a larger Zhou community (largest in Western Zhou) that included sites around Qianzhucun (前竹村) and Woluozi (DG-QZC-1–3, WLZ-1–5, SJP-6–8). The combined site may have been as large as 125 to 150 ha, making it the third or fourth largest Western Zhou site in the Shandong region.

Site: DG-WLZ-3 (Year 5)

County: Donggang

Town: Woluozi (窝落子)

Map: Shankoucun (山口村) [1-50-24-(33)]

Period and Period Number: **Zhou 377**; Han 433

Cultural Layer: None

Site Description: The site is located on a low ridge in the piedmont, at an elevation of 45 m, on the west side of the town of Woluozi and the highway (北京北路). There are small streams north and south of the rise. The site was mostly in fallow fields and winter wheat at the time of the survey, and part of the site was in an orchard. The site was largest in the Zhou period (both Western and Eastern), covering 5.2 ha. Two stone tools were collected. A small amount of Han material, covering less than 1 ha, was found near the town. The Zhou component was part of a larger Zhou community (largest in Western Zhou) that included sites around Qianzhucun and Woluozi (DG-QZC-1–3, WLZ-1–5, SJP-6–8). The combined site may have been as large as 125 to 150 ha, making it the third or fourth largest Western Zhou site in our region.

Site: DG-XBJZ-1 (Year 4)

County: Donggang

Town: Xiaobianjiazhuang (小卞家庄)

Map: Chengzigou (程子沟) [1-50-23-(32)]

Period and Period Number: Zhou 294; **Han 310**

Cultural Layer: Han period burial

Site Description: This is a small site located on a moderate rise in the middle piedmont, 400 m west of the town of Xiaobianjiazhuang, at an elevation of 69 m, and 25 m north of a small stream. The area is used for agriculture. A farmer took us to where he found a Han period *pen* (盆) basin when he was terracing his field. The site was small in the Han period (less than 0.5 ha). It may have been a Han burial area. We also recorded a trace of Western Zhou sherds (also in an area smaller than 0.5 ha).

Site: DG-XCP-3 (Year 11)

County: Donggang

Town: Xiaocaopo (小草坡)

Map: Gaowangzhuang (高旺庄) [1-50-35-(22)]

Period and Period Number: Zhou 946; Han 1279

Cultural Layer: Possible

Site Description: The site is located on flat alluvial terrain, at an elevation of 9 m, on the east side of a small water channel, and 400 m east of the town of Xiaocaopo. It was in an area of fallow fields and dried ponds. Eastern and Western Zhou and Han sherds were found in an area smaller than 0.5 ha, including sherds eroding out of the bank of the stream. The site almost definitely was larger in the past and now is buried in part by alluvium. It is just 300 m southeast of the rich DG-DCP-5 site.

Site: DG-XCWA-9 (Year 10)

County: Donggang

Town: Xiaochangwang'ai (小长汪崖)

Map: Shengjiadaituan (盛家代疃) [1-50-23-(46)]

Period and Period Number: Longshan 403; **Han 1067**

Cultural Layer: None

Site Description: The site is located on a low rise in the alluvium, at an elevation of 18 m, 250 m southwest of the town of Xiaochangwang'ai, and 300 m south of Dachangwang'ai (大长汪崖). The site is 500 to 700 m north of the Futuan River and a small water channel runs through it (Figure 3.48). Part of the site was planted in winter wheat at the time of the survey; part had been exposed by the construction of new houses. We collected large Han sherds that were brought to the surface by the construction. Han sherds were found in an 8.5 ha area. A trace of a Longshan occupation was observed at the very southern end of the site.

Site: DG-XGuZ-1 (Year 9)

County: Donggang

Town: Xiaoguzhen (小古镇)

Map: Futuan (傅疃) [1-50-23-(63)]

Period and Period Number: Longshan 356; Zhou 735; **Han 964**

Cultural Layer: None

Site Description: The site is located in flat alluvium, at an elevation of 3.5 m, on the west side of the town of Xiaoguzhen, and mostly south of the road on the north side of the town. The part of the site just east of the town was in an apple orchard, while other parts of the site were in vegetable gardens and a pine forest. We found a very light scatter of Han sherds in an 8.8 ha area. Zhou sherds (more Eastern than Western) were found in an area half that size (4.4 ha), mostly in the eastern and southern parts of the site.

Site: DG-XHai-1 (Year 9)

County: Donggang

Town: Xiaohai (小海)

Map: Liujiawan (刘家湾) [1-50-35-(15)]

Period and Period Number: Zhou 779; Han 1007

Cultural Layer: None

Site Description: The site is located in low sandy alluvial terrain, at an elevation of 3 m, on the north side of the town of Xiaohai, on the west side of Xiaohaimatou pier (小海码头), and less than 100 m southeast of Wangjiacun (王家村). The site is 400 m northeast of the Zhuzi River. Most of the site was planted in winter wheat at the time of the survey, but there were some fallow patches. Han and Eastern Zhou sherds were found in a 9 ha area. This is a minimal size estimate; the site most likely continues to the east under the Xiaohaimatou pier and to the south under Xiaohai.

Figure 3.48. Gary Feinman collecting sherds from an exposed cultural layer at DG-XCWA-9 located on a low rise in the alluvium above a modern reservoir.

Site: Xujiacun DG-XJC-1 (Year 8)

County: Donggang

Town: Xujiacun (徐家村)

Map: Lujiagou (路家沟) [1-50-23-(64)]

Period and Period Number: Yueshi 12; Longshan 331, 332, 333, 334, 335, 336; **Zhou** 677, **678**; Han 936, 937, 938, 939, 940

Cultural Layer: None

Site Description: The site is located on the top and western slopes of a low piedmont ridge, with its elevation ranging from 25 m at the top of the ridge to 10 m at the base of the lower slope, just north of the towns of Xujiacun and Nantunling (南屯岭). The top of the ridge had been completely quarried, which destroyed that part of the site. The site extends to the south under Xujiacun. We also found sherd scatters near the southeastern corner of the town. The southernmost part of the site is 50 m north of a tributary of the Guzi River. Much of the site was fallow at the time of the survey, although we found sherds in gardens, in winter wheat, in mulberries, and in town. The site was largest in the Zhou period (Zhou 678, larger in Eastern than Western), covering 30 ha at a minimum. Han sherds were dispersed in several places, with the largest scatter (Han 938) covering 9.4 ha along the northwestern part of the site. All the Longshan concentrations were smaller than 2.5 ha. Yueshi period pottery was found in one small collection area (smaller than 0.5 ha) in the northwestern portion of the site. The Zhou component was part of a larger community with DG-GHA-2 to the south, which was as large as 60 ha in Eastern Zhou (half that size in Western Zhou).

Site: Xiangjiagou DG-XJG-1 (Year 1)

County: Donggang

Town: Xiangjiagou (相家沟) (abandoned)

Map: Anjiacun (安家村) [1-50-24-(18)]

Period and Period Number: **Longshan 29**; **Zhou 25**; Han 23, 24

Cultural Layer: None

Site Description: The site is located on a moderate slope on the north side of a low piedmont ridge called Zhuziling, just north of the abandoned village of Xiangjiagou on the lower slope. Although several gullies on the site occasionally have water, the nearest permanent water source is the Jinyin River 400 m to the north. The elevation ranges from 10 to 40 m. The site was covered with winter wheat and in fallow fields at the time of the survey (Figure 3.49). Longshan (mostly Middle Longshan, but also some Early and Late) and Zhou (more Eastern than Western) sherds were found in all four collections made at the site; both components together covered approximately 21.3 ha. The Han occupation was smaller, covering just less than 10 ha (in two collection areas).

Site: DG-XLJC-2 (Year 8)

County: Donggang

Town: Xiaolijiacun (小李家村)

Map: Dalingnantou (大岭南头) [1-50-23-(56)]

Period and Period Number: **Longshan 320**; **Zhou 656;** Han 888, 889

Cultural Layer: None

Site Description: The site is located on the top and slopes of a low piedmont ridge, at an elevation of 20 m, on the northwest corner of Biejiacun, 200 m north of the town of Xiaolijiacun, and 100 m northeast of Qianguzi (前崮子). The site extends down to the alluvium in an outside bend of the Guzi River, both outside and inside the bend. Most of the site was planted in winter wheat or was fallow. It was largest in the Longshan period (larger in Early than in Middle), covering 8.1 ha, and in the Zhou period (larger in Eastern than Western), covering 8.4 ha. Several small scatters of Han sherds were found, all smaller than 1 ha. We could not check the western side of the bend in the Guzi River, an area covered by the town of Houguzi, but given the location of DG-HGZ-1 on the western edge of the town, on the other side of the river just west of this bend, both sites may have been part of a larger community in both the Longshan and Zhou periods.

Site: DG-XLNT-1 (Year 7)

County: Donggang

Figure 3.49. View of crew surveying Xiangjiagou (DG-XJG-1) located on a low piedmont slope.

Town: Xiaolingnantou (小岭南头)

Map: Rizhaoshi (日照市) [1-50-23-(48)]

Period and Period Number: Han 663

Cultural Layer: None

Site Description: The site is located on the eastern slope of a piedmont ridge overlooking the alluvium, at an elevation of 20 m, 1,300 m west of the Guzi River. The area we were able to survey was entirely enclosed by a gated compound that was planted with trees. The site definitely is larger than the 5.3 ha we could survey. It was entirely in the Han period. It was originally surveyed by Zhang Zhibo (Zhang 15).

Site: DG-XLZ-2 (Year 9)

County: Donggang

Town: Xiaoliuzhuang (小刘庄)

Map: Yayue (亚月) [1-50-35-(14)]

Period and Period Number: Zhou 781; **Han 1019**

Cultural Layer: Han period tomb

Site Description: The site is located on low alluvial terrain, at an elevation of 3 m, 25 to 150 m south of the Zhuzi River, and just north of the town of Xiaoliuzhuang. It was mostly planted in winter wheat. Han was the dominant occupation, covering 4.5 ha. There was a remnant of a low raised linear mound that likely was a Han tomb. We observed a cultural layer in this feature, including some ash and burnt soil, and the corner of a Han brick also was exposed. There was a very light scatter of Eastern Zhou sherds in a 2 ha area in the part of the site closest to the river. More of the site could be buried under the alluvial soil.

Site: Xilinzitou DG-XLZT-1 (Year 11)

County: Donggang

Town: Xilinzitou (西林子头)

Map: Hushanpu (虎山铺) [1-50-35-(30)]

Period and Period Number: Dawenkou 26; **Longshan** 453, **456**; Zhou 977, 978, 979; Han 1320

Cultural Layer: Multiple

Site Description: The site is located on a low rise in the alluvium, at an elevation of 5 m, 100 m south of the town of Xilinzitou (south of a water tower and several ponds). The densest part of the site is between two small roads, 250 m northeast of a small tributary of the Longwang River (龙王河), which curves around the base of the piedmont rise to the south. The area west of these roads is lower and likely was leveled in the past. However, we did find sparse scatters of sherds up to 500 m farther west and to within 50 m of the northeastern corner of Chenjiazhuang (陈家庄村) that may be part of the Longshan site. A larger tributary of the Zhuzi River is 650 m to the north, so this is a very nice location for a site. Most of the site was in winter wheat fields, but some areas were fallow, often with cornstalks (Figure 3.50). The soil of the site was very gray and we observed several cultural layers. The site was largest in the Longshan period (Longshan 456, Early and Middle), covering 17.9 ha (Figure 3.51). We found a smaller concentration of Early Longshan sherds 250 m farther west. Given the possible soil removal between the two areas, the site easily could have been at least 50% larger, or around 25 ha. We collected many Late Dawenkou sherds from the densest concentration at the site, in the north, in a 4.6 ha area. Eastern and Western Zhou sherds were dispersed in three separate concentrations in the southern part of the site; the largest two scatters (Zhou 977, 979) were both around 5 ha. There was a light scatter of Han sherds in the southern part of the site, covering 11.4 ha. We collected more than ten stone tools (Figure 3.52); some mostly likely in process, indicating stone tool production at the site. We also found a broken, polished yellow ornament made of fine stone resembling jade.

The site was discovered by scholars at the Institute of History and Philology of the Academia Sinica in the 1930s (S. Liang 1959). A local Cultural Relics Bureau later resurveyed it (Rizhao City Library and Linyi District Committee 1986).

Site: DG-XLZT-7 (Year 11)

County: Donggang

Town: Xilinzitou (西林子头)

Map: Hushanpu (虎山铺) [1-50-35-(30)]

Period and Period Number: Zhou 958; **Han 1323**

Cultural Layer: Zhou and Han periods

Site Description: The site is located on a slight rise in the alluvium, at an elevation of 12 m, 400 m north of Nitiangou, 50 m east of the highway, and 900 m west of the town of

Figure 3.50. Crew surveying Xilinzitou (DG-XLZT-1).

Figure 3.51. Late Dawenkou period *dakouzun* (大口樽) large-mouthed jar (*top row, left*), Early Longshan period *ding* tripod foot and *yan* steamer foot (*top, second and third from left*), Late Longshan *ding* tripod foot (*top right*); Middle Longshan period *guan* jar rim (*bottom left*), and *ding* tripod foot (*bottom right*) from Xilinzitou (DG-XLZT-1[CAA]).

FIGURE 3.52. Longshan period stone tools (*top row, left to right*: two *ben* adzes, *dao* knife, *fu* [斧] axe; *bottom row, left to right*: two *chui* [锤] hammerstones, round piece-unfinished tool) from Xilinzitou (DG-XLZT-1[CAA]).

Xilinzitou. It is on the northwestern side of a tributary of the Zhuzi River. The collection areas are in fallow and winter wheat fields, vegetable gardens, and orchards. The construction of a new road across the northern part of the site exposed a cultural layer where we collected many very large sherds. Han sherds were found throughout the site, covering 6.2 ha. The Zhou component (Western and Eastern) was more concentrated in the western part of the site, in a 2.5 ha area.

Site: DG-XSH-1 (Year 8)

County: Donggang

Town: Xiaoshanhou (小山后)

Map: Shanhou (山后) [1-50-24-(57)]

Period and Period Number: Longshan 344; Zhou 704; Han 908

Cultural Layer: Han period

Site Description: The site is located on a low piedmont spur that comes right down to the coast, at an elevation of 10 m, just south of the town of Xiaoshanhou and the highway. The closest water is a small stream 400 m to the west. The site was in fallow fields at the time of the survey, adjacent to buildings on the eastern side. Han sherds were densely scattered in a 1 ha area, and we observed a thin cultural layer of Han sherds at the southernmost tip of the piedmont spur. We also collected a few Eastern Zhou and Longshan sherds. This site easily could be much larger, especially in the Han period, as it connects with DG-XSH-2 between the highway and the southwestern side of the town and with DG-XSH-2 and XSH-3 to the north on the east side of the town and the highway.

Site: Xujialou DG-XuJL-2 (Year 7)

County: Donggang

Town: Xujialou (徐家楼)

Map: Rizhaoshi (日照市) [1-50-23-(48)]

Period and Period Number: Zhou 633; Han 665

Cultural Layer: Possible post-Han period

Site Description: The site is located on a low piedmont rise, at an elevation of 21 m, just east of the Guzi River, and approximately 300 m south of the confluence of the Houlou River and the Xiangdian River. We found the site in an open area on the west side of the town of Xujialou. It extends under the town to at least the east. The site was in plowed, fallow fields at the time of survey. Part of it was near a quarry. The site is near the Kailai Hotel (凯莱大酒店). We found both Han and Zhou (Eastern only) sherds in a 4.5 ha area. A cultural layer was exposed in a cut, but it may represent a time period later than Han. Given the setting of this site on a low piedmont ridge above a confluence, and the fact that we found two other Han concentrations on this same ridge that is now almost completely covered with modern construction, it seems highly likely that all the Han remains were part of one much larger community (DG-XuJL-1, 2; XXD-1).

Site: DG-XXD-1 (Year 7)

County: Donggang

Town: Xiaoxiangdian (小香店)

Map: Rizhaoshi (日照市) [1-50-23-(48)]

Period and Period Number: Han 666

Cultural Layer: Han period

Site Description: The site is located on top of a low piedmont ridge, at an elevation of 38 m, 600 m east and above the junction of the Houlou and Xiangdian Rivers with the Guzi River, and surrounded by the modern town of Xiaoxiangdian. Recent bulldozer cuts from construction activities revealed large quantities of sherds and many roof tiles, including a round decorated end tile (Figure 3.53). Given the size and quantity of tiles, they are likely the remains of a large and elaborate building.

In other bulldozer cuts there were slightly darker sediments, also loaded with sherds. The area we could map was smaller than 2 ha, but the exact size of the site is not known because of the construction; it most likely extends at least to the south and west. The setting of the site, on top of a low piedmont rise above the junction of the rivers, may be the key factor in the location of this site. It likely was part of a much larger Han community with DG-XuJL-1 and XuJL-2, also mapped in other open areas on this piedmont ridge. It is hard to estimate the size of this combined area, but, given the ideal location of these three sites on a low piedmont ridge near a large river, it is possible that the Han community was as large as 60 ha.

FIGURE 3.53. A ceramic roof tile collected from Han period site DG-XXD-1.

Site: Xinzhuangzi DG-XZZ-1 (Year 5)

County: Donggang

Town: Xinzhuangzi (辛庄子)

Map: Daliancun (大莲村) [1-50-23-(40)]

Period and Period Number: Yueshi 2; Shang 14

Cultural Layer: None

Site Description: This is a small site on flat alluvial terrain, at an elevation of 45 m, on the north side of the town of Xinzhuangzi, and just east of the Linjia River. It was planted in winter wheat and vegetables at the time of the survey. The site was only 1.7 ha, but it was in a nice location, with a good density of sherds. Although we did not find any diagnostic sherds, the collected sherds are most likely Shang (including many vessel bodies in local Shang style); at least one sherd may be from the Yueshi period. The thick reddish-brown sherds with sandy paste that we collected date to the early Neolithic. We recommend more research at this site.

Site: DG-YJAT-2 (Year 9)

County: Donggang

Town: Yinjia'aotou (尹家鳌头)

Map: Jiacang (夹仓) [1-50-35-(7)]

Period and Period Number: Longshan 372; Zhou 754; Han 986

Cultural Layer: Longshan and Zhou periods

Site Description: The site is located on a slight rise in the alluvium, at an elevation of 4 m, 100 m south of the town of Yinjia'aotou and 80 m north of the Chuanzi River (川子河). The

FIGURE 3.54. Survey crew members examining an exposed cultural layer at DG-YJAT-2 situated on a low rise in the alluvium.

site is on the west side of the road, in winter wheat and vegetables; some areas were fallow (Figure 3.54). A black cultural layer was exposed in a field at the southern end of the site. The only Longshan sherds (Early and Middle) were found in this small area, in less than 0.5 ha. Zhou sherds were found over the entire site, covering 1.8 ha (larger in Western than in Eastern Zhou), while Han sherds were only found in the northern part, in an area smaller than 1 ha. Today Yinjia'aotou is a location for making salt, and this may have been an important activity in the past too.

Site: DG-YJAT-2 (Year 9)

County: Donggang

Town: Yinjia'aotou (尹家鳌头)

Map: Jiacang (夹仓) [1-50-35-(7)]

Period and Period Number: Longshan 373; Zhou 756; Han 988

Cultural Layer: None

Site Description: The site is located on flat alluvial terrain, at an elevation of 3.5 m, in several shrimp ponds between the Chuanzi River and a small channel to the north, and 500 m southwest of Zhangjia'aotou (张家鳌头). We picked up sherds in the earthern walls of the ponds, mostly Longshan and Han, in a 2.3 ha area. A few Eastern Zhou sherds were found in a very small area next to the levee of the river.

Site: DG-YJC-6 (Year 4)

County: Donggang

Town: Yujiacun (于家村)

Map: Yujiacun (于家村) [1-50-24-(26)]

Period and Period Number: Zhou 283

Cultural Layer: Tomb

Site Description: The site is located on a low piedmont ridge just north of a small reservoir, 400 m south of the town of Yujiacun, and at an elevation of 30 m. Much of the site was in an orchard at the time of the survey. It has both Western and Eastern Zhou remains covering about 2.3 ha. A farmer generously allowed us to photograph an Eastern Zhou bronze sword he said he had found in a tomb that had been exposed in a stream cut at the north end of the site (Figure 3.55).

Site: DG-YS-6 (Year 9)

County: Donggang

Town: Yousuo (右所)

Map: Jiacang (夹仓) [1-50-35-(7)]

Period and Period Number: Zhou 757; Han 991

Cultural Layer: Zhou period

Site Description: The site is located in shrimp ponds on low alluvial terrain, at an elevation of 3 m, on both sides of the Nanxin River, 100 m west of the highway, 300 m north of Chuanzi, and 1,100 m northeast of the town of Yousuo. Han sherds were found north of the river in an area smaller than 0.5 ha. Many Western and Eastern Zhou sherds were eroding out of a 1 m thick dark cultural layer that was visible for about 10 m in the bank of a pond on the south side of the river. Initial construction of a shrimp pond likely disturbed a buried Zhou site that probably is larger than the small area (less than 0.5 ha) where we observed sherds.

Site: Yingzi DG-YZ-1 (Year 5)

County: Donggang

Town: Yingzi (营子)

Map: Rizhaoshi (日照市) [1-50-23-(48)]

Period and Period Number: Longshan 157, 158; Zhou 295, 296; Han 361, 362

Cultural Layer: Multiple

Site Description: The site is located on flat alluvial terrain, at an elevation of 18 m, on the south side of the Houlou River in what were several open fields north of the town of Yingzi and west of Rizhao City High School. According to Yang Shenfu (杨深富), a researcher at the Rizhao Museum, the site used to be larger and extends under modern homes, especially to the south. A pit near modern houses revealed a cultural layer. The site was in fallow fields, winter wheat, and vegetables at the time of the survey. Zhou (Western only) and Longshan sherds were well represented, with a bit lesser density of Han material. All three components were found in a 4.3 ha area between houses (Longshan 157, Zhou 295, Han 362). Additional smaller, discrete

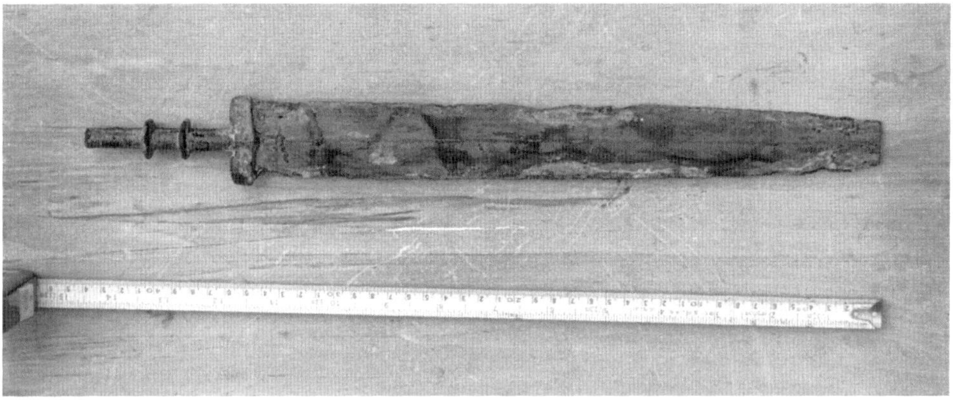

FIGURE 3.55. An Eastern Zhou period bronze sword found by a farmer from a tomb at DG-YJC-6.

sherd scatters were found to the north along the river channel; we gave them separate site numbers. However, given the modern development and that part of the site is under modern houses, a more realistic size estimate (including all components for each period) is between at least 7.5 and 10 ha.

The site was discovered by a local Cultural Relics Bureau and now has county preservation status (China Cultural Heritage Bureau 2007:272–273).

Site: Zhengjiadingzi DG-ZJDZ-1 (Year 7)

County: Donggang

Town: Zhengjiadingzi (郑家顶子)

Map: Shilipu (十里铺) [1-50-23-(47)]

Period and Period Number: **Longshan 242**; Zhou 508, 509, 510, 511; **Han 647**

Cultural Layer: Present, but periods(s) unclear

Site Description: The site is located mostly on two piedmont ridges that extend from the base of the mountains down into the alluvium, ranging from 40 to 75 m in elevation, and on the west side of a small stream that flows on the west side of the towns of Zhengjiadingzi and Xiangjiazhuang (相家庄). The flatter alluvial areas of the site were in vegetable gardens or fallow at the time of the survey; there also were some abandoned greenhouses (Figure 3.56). The sloping piedmont areas were mostly fallow or planted in winter wheat. The site was largest in the Han period (33.5 ha), covering all but the very highest part of the site. This site is less than 1,000 m north of the Dagucheng (大古城) site and may have functioned with that large site to guard entry into the area.

The Longshan component, covering 27.5 ha, included all the alluvial areas of the site and the lower piedmont slopes. The site was twice as large in Middle Longshan as it was in Early Longshan. Western Zhou pottery was found in four discrete, separate locations. One concentration (Zhou 511, 1.5 ha) was in the alluvial part of the site (along with Longshan and Han materials), where a black cultural layer was found on the west side of the stream near the northwest corner of the abandoned village of Xiangjiagou. The other three Zhou scatters were

FIGURE 3.56. View of Zhengjiadingzi (DG-ZJDZ-1) on the piedmont slopes at the base of the mountain.

on the piedmont slope. The largest of these (Zhou 508, 5.1 ha) was at the very highest part of the site on an artificially flattened spur just below a small modern reservoir. This setting is common for Western Zhou sites in our area. It is the only part of the site where we recovered any Eastern Zhou pottery, covering less than 2 ha. Earlier investigators found bronze weapons, including a sword of the Spring and Autumn period, at the site (Yang, Hu, and Xu 1990).

Site: DG-ZuJY-1 (Year 1)

County: Donggang

Town: Zhujiayao (朱家窑)

Map: Lianhecun (联合村) [1-50-24-(17)]

Period and Period Number: Han 81

Cultural Layer: None

Site Description: The site consists of one Han period tomb situated on top of a low piedmont rise 200 m north of the town of Zhujiayao, at an elevation of 56.6 m, and approximately 300 m from three different modern reservoirs (to the north, east, and west). The tomb has been largely destroyed and was being used at the time of the survey for storing sweet potatoes. A small Ming period (AD 1368–1644) tomb is approximately 100 m to the northeast.

Jiaonan City (胶南市)

Site: Baoquanmiao JN-BQM-1 (Year 6)

County: Jiaonan

Town: Baoquanmiao (雹泉庙)

Map: Jinggezhuang (井戈庄) [1-50-12-(59)]

Period and Period Number: Longshan 204, 205, 206; Zhou 430; **Han 513**

Cultural Layer: None

Site Description: The site is located on the top and south-facing slope of a flat-topped low piedmont rise, at elevations between 20 and 25 m, just south of the town of Baoquanmiao, and about 800 m west of the Jili River (吉利河). The site was waterlogged, possibly because of an underground spring. The area was mostly fallow at the time of the survey, but winter wheat and cabbage also were present. There is a small quarry within the site limits. The site was largest and best represented for the Han period, covering 26.2 ha. It was slightly smaller in the Zhou period (Eastern only), extending over 16.2 ha closer to the town and to the north and west. We found Longshan pottery in three small discrete scatters. Two on the west were Early Longshan, the largest at 3.1 ha. The scatter just south of town was Middle Longshan, in a 2.2 ha area.

Site: Baozibu JN-BZB-1 (Year 7)

County: Jiaonan

Town: Baozibu (保子埠)

Map: Jinggezhuang (井戈庄) [1-50-12-(59)]

Period and Period Number: Longshan 269, 270; Zhou 559, 560; Han 735, 736, 737

Cultural Layer: Zhou period

Site Description: The site is located on flat alluvial terrain, at an elevation of 10 m, 200 m east of the Jili River, and just south of the town of Baozibu. The site is mostly in plowed fields; the western part of the site was partially planted in mulberries at the time of the survey. Han, Zhou, and Longshan sherds were found on both sides of the road all the way to the levee of the river to the west, and to the south within 400 m of Caijia village (蔡家村). Although we found sherds in an area approximately 700 m east–west and 600 m north–south, sherd scatters for each period were more discrete, so that no one discrete temporal component was larger than 8 ha (Longshan 269). The largest Han component covered 6.8 ha, and both Zhou components were around 5 ha (both were larger in Western Zhou than in Eastern). A Zhou cultural layer was exposed in a plowed field in the northeastern part of the site (Zhou 560). Most of the separate components for each period were just over 100 m apart, so it is possible that all were part of one larger community during all three periods.

Site: JN-BZB-5 (Year 8)

County: Jiaonan

Town: Baozibu (保子埠)

Map: Jinggezhuang (井戈庄) [1-50-12-(59)]

Period and Period Number: Longshan 309; Zhou 638; Han 855

Cultural Layer: Present, but period(s) unclear

Site Description: The site is located on a slight rise in the alluvium, at an elevation of 14 m, and 350 m northwest of the town of Baozibu. The main channel of the Jili River is 250 m to the west. Most of the site was in fallow fields. A gray cultural layer was visible in a cabbage pit. We found Longshan, Eastern and Western Zhou, and Han sherds. The site was slightly larger in the Han and Zhou periods (1.7 ha) than in the Longshan period (1.2 ha).

Site: Caijiacun JN-CJC-4 (Year 7)

County: Jiaonan

Town: Caijiacun (蔡家村)

Map: Jinggezhuang (井戈庄) [1-50-12-(59)]

Period and Period Number: Longshan 280; **Zhou 575**; **Han 746**

Cultural Layer: None

Site Description: The site is located on flat alluvial terrain, at an elevation of 12 m, 100 m east of the Jili River, and less than 50 m south of the town of Caijiacun. The site is in mulberries, plowed fields, and a small area of trees. We found sherds on the southeast corner of the town and all the way to the levee. The site was largest in the Han period, covering 12.9 ha, and just slightly smaller in the Zhou period, covering 11.2 ha. The site was much larger in Eastern Zhou than Western Zhou. We found Longshan pottery in just one small (less than 0.5 ha) collection area on the west side of the site, near the levee.

Site: Caiyuan JN-CY-1 (Year 6)

County: Jiaonan

Town: Caiyuan (菜园)

Map: Weijiawan (魏家湾) [1-50-24-(3)]

Period and Period Number: Longshan 218; Zhou 444; **Han 530**

Cultural Layer: Present, likely more than one period

Site Description: Most of the site is located on the top and slopes of a low rise in the low piedmont, at an elevation of 8 m, 150 m south of Caiyuan, and just north of a small channel that flows west to the Baima River (白马河). Most of the site was within an apple orchard on the low rise, although part of the site extended to the west across the road. Terracing for the orchard exposed a cultural layer on the eastern slope of the rise that was very close to the surface. Although the site is not large, the density of sherds was high (Figure 3.57). Han sherds were found in a 4 ha area, Longshan sherds in a 3.2 ha area; there were only a few Zhou sherds. Additionally, two stone tools were found.

Site: Dagou JN-DG-1, 4 (Year 7)

County: Jiaonan

Town: Dagou (大沟)

Map: Tashandianzi (塔山店子) [1-50-12-(52)]

Figure 3.57. Early Longshan period sherds (*top row, left to right*: body sherd with *lanwen* [篮文]/basket design, *ding* foot, *pen* basin rim, two *guan* jar rims; *bottom row, left to right*: three *ding* tripod feet, *yan* steamer foot, *qigai* lid, *ding* tripod foot) from Caiyuan (JN-CY-1[CAA]).

Period and Period Number: Longshan 258; Zhou 538; Han 718

Cultural Layer: Han period platforms and tombs

Site Description: The site is located on the top and slopes of a low piedmont ridge that overlooks the alluvium, with a top elevation of 61 m. It is 400 m north of the town of Dagou, and 650 m southeast of the confluence of the Baima River and a small tributary at Xisi village (西寺村). The site was planted in winter wheat and parts were fallow at the time of the survey. Longshan (Early and Middle), Zhou (larger in Western than Eastern Zhou), and Han materials were found over most of the site, all in areas ranging between approximately 13 and 16 ha. We also collected one Longshan stone tool. The site clearly was most important in the Han period; we mapped ten low earthen platforms at the site, ranging between 1 and 3 m high. Three platforms were clustered on the eastern ridgetop in an area with sparse sherds. The other seven platforms were clustered on the southern extension of the western ridgetop. The platforms have been damaged by farming. Cuts in the platforms reveal rammed earth construction and occasional sherds (several were Zhou sherds). These platforms do not appear to be tombs. They might have been used for some special purpose. The tombs must belong to the Han period, but it is not clear whether any were in use earlier (Figure 3.58).

This whole piedmont ridge system is above a bend in the Baima River. We found many other Longshan, Zhou, and Han sites nearby. The concentration of Han sites is especially high, with almost a dozen smaller sherd concentrations (JN-DG-9, DG-10, NS-1, NS-2, NS-4–7, TS-10, TS-11), including a site 450 m to the southwest that had a Han tomb (JN-TS-4), all clustered together. This dense concentration of Han materials covers at a minimum 95 ha. This piedmont ridge system also had large populations in the Longshan, Zhou, and Han periods. Clearly, there was a large concentration of people in this area from Longshan through Han, but especially in Han, when the combined site area of JN-DG-1, 4, and XS-1 would have been almost 150 ha. It was the major Han center in this part of our survey region.

FIGURE 3.58. View of Han period tombs on top of piedmont slope at Dagou (JN-DG-1, 4).

Site: JN-DJLG-3 (Year 13)

County: Jiaonan

Town: Dingjialiugou (丁家柳沟)

Map: Houpolou (后坡楼) [1-50-12-(58)]

Period and Period Number: **Longshan 539**; Zhou 1202; Han 1661

Cultural Layer: Longshan period

Site Description: The site is located on a slightly raised area in the alluvium, at an elevation of 35 m, on the southeast side of the town of Dingjialiugou. It is on both sides of a recently paved road and extended approximately 500 m from the southern edge of town. The site was in a mix of cabbage, wheat, and fallow fields, with some areas in poplar trees. The nearest water is a small stream to the south that crosses part of the site.

A Longshan cultural layer was found in an exposed profile by the side of the paved road (Figure 3.59). A pit with Longshan sherds was found in the profile. Also found in the profile was a groundstone tool and a hard earth surface, *ying tu mian* (硬土面), interpreted as an activity area. There was a high density of Longshan sherds on the surface, as well as many stone tools, including two *zu* (镞) points, a *dao* (刀) knife, and two other groundstone tools. The richest part of the site was on the east side of the road. The density on the west side of the road was lower. We measured the Longshan area at 13.9 ha (larger in Early than in Middle), but it most likely was somewhat larger in the past and may have extended under the southern part of the town. We found some Zhou pottery on the east side of the road (more Eastern than Western), covering approximately 8.1 ha. Sparse remains of the Han period were found in the center of the site, on both sides of the road.

Figure 3.59. A Longshan period cultural layer exposed at JN-DJLG-3.

Site: Dongjiawa JN-DJW-4 (Year 4)

County: Jiaonan

Town: Dongjiawa (董家洼)

Map: Dongjiawa (董家洼) [1-50-12-(57)]

Period and Period Number: **Longshan 122**; Zhou 176; Han 206

Cultural Layer: Longshan period

Site Description: The site is located on flat terrain in the low piedmont, at an elevation of 69 m, just south of the town of Dongjiawa between two small stream channels that flow south into the Dijia River Reservoir (狄家河水库). The site was dispersed across several terraced wheat and fallow fields at the time of the survey (Figure 3.60). Chicken coops covered part of the site. The site was largest in the Longshan period (Early and Middle), covering approximately 3.9 ha. A thin Longshan cultural layer was revealed in a cabbage pit, and black and gray cultural layers were exposed in two terrace cuts on the site. Burnt clay was noted and one stone tool was recovered. The site was smaller in the Zhou (Eastern only) and Han periods, covering less than 1 ha along the west side of the site.

Site: Dalan JN-DL-1 (Year 6)

County: Jiaonan

FIGURE 3.60. Crew surveying Dongjiawa (JN-DJW-4) near village.

Town: Dalan (大岚)

Map: Shaojilan (邵家岚) [1-50-24-(11)]

Period and Period Number: Zhou 457, 458; **Han 549**

Cultural Layer: None

Site Description: The site is located on two low piedmont rises (and the area between them) that extend into the alluvium within 500 m of the coast south of the town of Dalan, at an elevation of 6 to 10 m. The site is on the west and south sides of Dalan and extends south to coastal shrimp ponds. Part of the site is covered by the town. The surrounding area was mostly cleared for farming, with some areas quarried. A small stream 300 m to the west is the nearest water source. The Han occupation spanned 26 ha. Zhou sherds (all Eastern Zhou) were found in two discrete, smaller scatters on either side of the town, both at around 2 ha.

Site: JN-DLT-2 (Year 4)

County: Jiaonan

Town: Dalutuan (大芦疃)

Map: Dongchaohe (东潮河) [1-50-24-(1)]

Period and Period Number: Han 1171

Cultural Layer: Han period tomb

Site Description: This is a small site located on top of a low piedmont rise, 1,100 m west of Dalutuan village, between Dalutuan and the villages of Xujiawa (徐家洼) and Fanjiazhuang

Figure 3.61. View of JN-DS-4 located on an alluvial terrace.

(范家庄), on the west side of the road, and at an elevation of 53 m. The nearest natural water course is a small stream 400 m to the west. Fields were fallow at the time of the survey. Sparse sherds were found with a Han tomb that is partially destroyed. The site is smaller than 0.5 ha.

Site: JN-DS-4 (Year 13)

County: Jiaonan

Town: Dongsi (东寺)

Map: Tashandianzi (塔山店子) [1-50-12-(52)]

Period and Period Number: Longshan 536; Zhou 1225; Han 1710

Cultural Layer: None

Site Description: The site is located on a slight slope, on an alluvial terrace stretching 700 m between the towns of Dongsi and Tuogou, and at an elevation of 19 to 24 m. It is 40 m north of a tributary of the Baima River; this tributary joins the Baima River 700 m to the west. At the time of survey most of the site was fallow, with some cabbage and some trees (Figure 3.61). Longshan, Zhou (Eastern and Western), and Han sherds were collected throughout the site. Han sherds were found more on the south of the site, covering 5.7 ha. Eastern Zhou was more in the east, covering 3.9 ha, while we found Western Zhou sherds in the west, in a 3.6 ha area. Longshan material was more in the north, covering 6.1 ha.

FIGURE 3.62. Remnant of a Han period tomb at Dongsi (JN-DS-11).

This site (also called Tuogou [驼沟]) was discovered by a local Cultural Relics Bureau, which estimated the area at 6 ha, an estimate close to ours. The site is now designated a Jiaonan City preservation site (China Cultural Heritage Bureau 2007:150–151).

Site: JN-DS-11 (Year 13)

County: Jiaonan

Town: Dongsi (东寺)

Map: Tashandianzi (塔山店子) [1-50-12-(52)]

Period and Period Number: Han 1715

Cultural Layer: Han period tombs

Site Description: The site is located just northwest of the top of a low piedmont ridge, at an elevation of 33 m, approximately 900 m northeast of the town of Dongsi, 650 m northwest of Tuogou, and 450 m south of the Baima River. The site was in a fallow field (Figure 3.62). It consists of two Han tombs, both of which have been plowed to less than 50% of their original height. These mounded earthern features are made of fine, rammed earth. The site is part of a concentration of Han tombs with JN-TG-1 and JN-TG-6. These three Han tomb sites are on three different slopes of the same low piedmont ridge, forming a triangle that is 350 m on each side.

Figure 3.63. Dawenkou period *ding* tripod feet (*top row*) and Early Longshan period sherds (*bottom: left to right*: rim of unknown form, two *ding* feet) from JN-DSHK-3[CAA].

Site: JN-DSHK-3 (Year 4)

County: Jiaonan

Town: Dashihekou (大石河口)

Map: Liujiaguanzhuang (刘家官庄) [1-50-24-(2)]

Period and Period Number: Dawenkou 2; Longshan 140; **Zhou 229**; Han 273

Cultural Layer: None

Site Description: The site is located mostly on two very slight natural rises in the alluvium at an elevation of 29 m, and at the northeastern edge of the reservoir south of Dashihekou village. It extends north to within 150 m of the southeastern corner of the village and south to the stream channel on the east side of the reservoir. The site was mostly in winter wheat and fallow fields at the time of the survey. It was largest in the Zhou period (covering 3.5 ha in Eastern Zhou and 3.1 ha in Western Zhou) and was slightly smaller in the Longshan (2.3 ha) and Han (2.7 ha) periods. Burnt soil and burnt slag had been exposed by recent plowing at the site. We also found several Dawenkou sherds in an area smaller than 0.5 ha (Figure 3.63).

Site: JN-DSQ-2 (Year 13)

County: Jiaonan

Town: Dingshiqiao (丁石桥)

Map: Huagenshan (花根山) [1-50-12-(51)]

Period and Period Number: Longshan 528; Zhou 1170

Cultural Layer: Longshan period

Site Description: The site is located on flat terrain in the alluvium, at an elevation of 20 m, on the southeastern side of the town of Dingshiqiao. Sherds were found next to the wall of the easternmost house and the town clearly covers part of the site. The sherd scatter extends southeast 200 m and 200 m east to a small modern water channel. The site is 650 m north of the Baima River. It was in fallow fields and winter wheat at the time of the survey. In one field very gray soil seemed to be a disturbed Longshan cultural deposit. We also found a Longshan stone tool there. The entire site was from the Longshan period (Early and Middle), covering 3.1 ha. We found Eastern Zhou sherds on the western part of the site, closer to town, covering 1.4 ha.

Site: JN-DSZL-7 (Year 13)

County: Jiaonan

Town: Dongshizilu (东十字路)

Map: Huagenshan (花根山) [1-50-12-(51)]

Period and Period Number: Han 1696

Cultural Layer: Han period tombs

Site Description: The site is located on the top of a low piedmont ridge, at an elevation of 72 m, approximately 400 m northeast of the town of Dongshizilu, and 400 m north of the highway (Yuanda Lu, 袁大路). The site consists of four earthen Han tombs or mounds in an area approximately 75 by 75 m. Although no sherds were found at this site, the tombs are likely from the Han period, because Han sherds were collected from several similar tombs in the area and there is a large Han tomb (JN-JTL-7) lower on the same ridge. One of the tombs has been plowed almost completely, while the three others are partially destroyed. All four are lower than 2 m.

Site: Fengduncun JN-FDC-1 (Year 6)

County: Jiaonan

Town: Fengduncun (凤墩村)

Map: Jinggezhuang (井戈庄) [1-50-12-(59)]

Period and Period Number: Longshan 208, 209, 210, 211; Zhou 433, 434; **Han 517**

Cultural Layer: Han period

Site Description: This very large site is located mostly in flat alluvium, at an elevation of 8 to 9 m, on the north, east, and south sides of the town of Fengduncun, and on the west side of the Jili River (Figure 3.64). The site extends north to within 100 m of Houjiawa and west to Dongdingjiazhuang (东丁家庄). In some areas the soil was wet because of a high water table. Modern uses of the site include as vegetable gardens, an orchard, and fields for cabbage and winter wheat, although some fields were fallow at the time of the survey. Part of the site was covered by the modern town. The site was largest in the Han period, covering 94.5 ha. At

FIGURE 3.64. View of the large, multicomponent site Fengduncun (JN-FDC-1).

the southern end, between the town and the river, there is a low platform (1 m high) on the east side of town. The town's name, Fengduncun (凤墩村), translated as "Phoenix Mound Village," probably comes from this platform. Farther south, about 100 m north of Wangdong, we found a dark Han cultural layer about 0.3 m below the modern surface. The Eastern Zhou occupation may not have been as large and is less dense with sherds on the surface. We initially divided this occupation into two separate components, larger on the north side of town (Zhou 433, 54.2 ha) than on the south (Zhou 434, 15.4 ha). They likely were one larger community. The Western Zhou component was much smaller. The Longshan occupation also may have been smaller, with the larger component (Longshan 209, larger in Early than in Middle) located on the north side of the town, covering 32.6 ha. Smaller Longshan scatters (5 ha or less) were found farther north and south of town.

Site: JN-GJL-1 (Year 6)

County: Jiaonan

Town: Gengjialan (耿家岚)

Map: Shaojialan (邵家岚) [1-50-24-(11)]

Period and Period Number: Zhou 459; **Han 548**

Cultural Layer: None

Site Description: The site is located on a moderate rise in the alluvium, at an elevation of 10 m, on the west side of Gengjialan, and 300 m northeast of the Baima River. Part of it is on a rocky outcrop with sandy soil. The surrounding area was mostly cleared for farming, with a chicken farm adjacent to the site. This site extends to the west and to the south to shrimp ponds. It was largest in the Han period (larger in Eastern Han than Western Han), covering 7.4 ha. It was much smaller in the Zhou period (Eastern only), less than 2 ha in the center of the site.

Site: JN-GJQ-5 (Year 4)

County: Jiaonan

Town: Guojiaqiao (郭家桥)

Map: Liujiaguanzhuang (刘家官庄) [1-50-24-(2)]

Period and Period Number: Longshan 146; **Zhou 237**; **Han 359**

Cultural Layer: Han period tomb

Site Description: The site is located on a low rise in the alluvium, at an elevation of 9 m, 500 m northeast of the town of Guojiaqiao, 400 m southeast of Jiawangdun, and 150 m west of a modern water channel. The area was used for agriculture. The site was largest in Eastern Zhou, covering 3.8 ha. In the center of the site, at the highest point on the rise, there is a Han period tomb; we also found a handful of Longshan sherds near the tomb. The site was smaller than 1 ha in both the Longshan and Han periods.

Site: JN-HGDL-3 (Year 7)

County: Jiaonan

Town: Huanggudunling (皇姑墩岭)

Map: Xiaojiawa (肖家洼) [1-50-12(60)]

Period and Period Number: **Longshan 267;** Zhou 556, 557; **Han 776**

Cultural Layer: Longshan and Han periods

Site Description: The site is located on alluvial terrain at the north edge of a modern reservoir, at the base of a low piedmont slope, at an elevation of 40 m, and between several streams and gullies that flow to the reservoir. It is 350 m south of the town of Huanggudunling. An area of the site was planted in winter wheat and part was fallow at the time of the survey (Figure 3.65). Part of the site, including several cultural layers, was exposed because of low water in the reservoir. The site easily could be larger and covered by the remaining water in the reservoir. Although we found Longshan sherds in an area that was no larger than 1 ha (Figure 3.66), two cultural layers contained Longshan material (more Early than Middle). We found Han sherds dispersed over 5 ha and one Han cultural layer near the reservoir. The Han layer was directly above the Longshan layer. Zhou period material was found in two very small discrete scatters on the north end of the site, neither larger than 0.5 ha.

Site: Houlan JN-HL-1 (Year 6)

County: Jiaonan

Town: Houlan (后岚)

Map: Shaojialan (邵家岚) [1-50-24-(11)]

FIGURE 3.65. Survey crew checking exposed cultural layers at Huanggudunling (JN-HGDL-3) situated at the base of a low piedmont slope at the north edge of a modern reservoir.

FIGURE 3.66. Early Longshan period sherds (*top row*: three *yi* spouted basin rims; *bottom row*: five *ding* tripod feet) from JN-HGDL-3[CAA].

Period and Period Number: Zhou 450; **Han 558**

Cultural Layer: None

Site Description: The site is located on a low piedmont ridge that extends into the alluvium close to the coast, at an elevation of 45 m, and 50 m north of the town of Houlan. There is a small stream on the east side of the site. Some of the site was planted with winter wheat. It was largest in the Han period (larger in Western Han than in Eastern Han), at 15.6 ha. Sparsely distributed Eastern Zhou ceramics extended over a 9.9 ha area.

Site: Houlaowo JN-HLW-2 (Year 4)

County: Jiaonan

Town: Houlaowo (后老窝)

Map: Houpolou (后坡楼) [1-50-12-(58)]

Period and Period Number: Zhou 213; Han 293

Cultural Layer: None

Site Description: The site is located on low rise in the low piedmont, at an elevation of 50 m, and on the west side of Houlaowo village. A small water channel cuts across the northwestern edge of the site. It was in fallow fields and winter wheat at the time of the survey. It was occupied in the Zhou and Han periods, but was slightly larger in Eastern Zhou, covering 6.2 ha, than in the Han period at 4.9 ha. The site was very small in Western Zhou, covering less than 1 ha at the northeast corner of the village.

Site: JN-HQ-3 (Year 4)

County: Jiaonan

Town: Haiqing (海青)

Map: Liujiaguanzhuang (刘家官庄) [1-50-24-(2)]

Period and Period Number: Zhou 221; **Han 280**

Cultural Layer: Han period tomb

Site Description: The site is located on a low rise in the alluvium, at an elevation of 31 m, 700 m southeast of the town of Haiqing, 25 m east of a small stream, and 300 m south of the reservoir. It was planted in winter wheat at the time of the survey. Based on the heavy density of Han sherds noted in a 0.3 ha area, the site may have had a tomb, although no stone or brick was found to confirm this. A few Eastern Zhou sherds also were collected.

Site: JN-HQ-10 (Year 4)

County: Jiaonan

Town: Haiqing (海青)

Map: Houpolou (后坡楼) [1-50-12-(58)]

Period and Period Number: **Longshan 137**; Zhou 206

Cultural Layer: Longshan period

Site Description: The site is on slight rise in the alluvium, at an elevation of 25 m, 800 m east of the town of Haiqing, and just west of the modern water channel that flows south to the

Figure 3.67. View of JN-HQ-10 in area cleared for apple orchards.

Chao River. The site was in land cleared for apple orchards at the time of the survey (Figure 3.67). Longhan pottery (Early and Middle) was abundant, covering an area of 2.8 ha. Gray and black Longshan cultural layers had been exposed in pits dug for cabbage storage and one polished stone tool was found. Some possible metal slag was collected as well. A small amount of Eastern Zhou material was observed in an area of approximately 1.4 ha.

Site: JN-JGZ-11 (Year 7)

County: Jiaonan

Town: Jinggezhuang (井戈庄)

Map: Jinggezhuang (井戈庄) [1-50-12-(59)]

Period and Period Number: Longshan 281; Zhou 585; Han 758

Cultural Layer: None

Site Description: The site is located in flat alluvium, at an elevation of 10 m, abutting the levee on the east side of the Baima River, and 100 m west of the town of Jinggezhuang. The area around the site was mostly fallow at the time of the survey, with some winter wheat and chicken farms (Figure 3.68). Although the site was not large, the sherd density was high for all three periods. The site was largest in the Han period, covering 3.5 ha, and next largest in the Zhou period (Eastern and Western), covering 3 ha. Longshan pottery (Early and Middle) was observed only in the southern part of the site, covering 1.5 ha. We collected one Longshan stone tool. The site was discovered by a local Cultural Relic Bureau and reported to have an area of 0.25 ha, a much smaller size than our survey results (China Cultural Heritage Bureau 2007:150–151).

FIGURE 3.68. Survey crew and visitors at JN-JGZ-11.

Site: JN-JJC-1 (Year 2)

County: Jiaonan

Town: Jiangjiacun (姜家村)

Map: Houxiangou (后显沟) [1-50-24-(10)]

Period and Period Number: Longshan 78; Zhou 49; **Han 48**

Cultural Layer: None

Site Description: The site is located on top of a low rise in the alluvium, at an elevation of 20 m, 400 m southwest of the town of Jiangjiacun, and 1,400 m northeast of a tributary of the Chao River. Fields at the site were fallow at the time of the survey. The site was largest in the Han period, covering 2.3 ha, and includes a Han tomb (locally called Huigudui, 灰堌堆) in the eastern part of the site (Figure 3.69). Sparse scatters of Longshan (1.2 ha) and Zhou (smaller than 0.5 ha) sherds were found only in the western part of the site.

Site: JN-JLH-1 (Year 8, Year 13)

County: Jiaonan

Town: Jilihe (吉利河)

Map: Huagenshan (花根山) [1-50-12-(51)]

Period and Period Number: Longshan 314; Zhou 527; **Han 848**

Cultural Layer: None

FIGURE 3.69. Survey crew members at the Han period tomb at JN-JJC-1.

Site Description: The site is located on the lower slopes of a very broad low piedmont ridge that grades gradually upward to the north to a much higher piedmont ridge between the Jili and Baima Rivers. The elevation is 20 to 25 m. The site is 100 m east of the town of Jilihe and extends to the north side of the paved highway. It is 800 m east of the main channel of the Jili River. The site was in fallow fields, winter wheat, and groves of mulberry and poplar trees at the time of the survey. It was largest in the Han period, covering 12.8 ha. Eastern Zhou sherds were found in a 4.5 ha area on the north edge of the site. The Longshan area was smaller than 0.5 ha and on the west side of the site.

The Han component of JN-JLH-1 was part of a Han larger community that includes JN-WZ-3, just over 100 m to the south and close to the southeast edge of Jilihe. The site may also continue under the modern town, as we found more Han pottery on the northwestern side of Jilihe in Year 13. There are several Han tombs (JN-JLH-4, 5, 6, 8) associated with this site just north on a low piedmont ridge system.

Site: Jilihe JN-JLH-4, 5, 6, 8 (Year 13)

County: Jiaonan

Town: Jilihe (吉利河)

Map: Huagenshan (花根山) [1-50-12-(51)]

Period and Period Number: Han 1730, 1729, 1732, 1731

Cultural Layer: Han period tombs

Site Description: In Year 13 we mapped five Han tombs dispersed on a piedmont slope north of Jilihe on a higher area of this low piedmont slope (between 30 and 35 m of elevation); three tombs to the south (JN-JLH-4, 5, 6) and two to the north at JN-JLH-8. Villagers told us there had been nine tombs there but that several had been plowed. Most of those we could see were very reduced (Figure 3.70). There is a site marker on one (JN-JLH-5). At another we found several Han bricks. A farmer showed us two large carved rectangular stone blocks with a net design. These blocks were being used by farmers as a makeshift bridge south of Jilicun village. The farmer said that these stones had come from one of the tombs. The tombs likely were associated with the Han site at Jilihe (JN-JLH-1). There are additional Han tombs on this piedmont ridge system, including four tombs or platforms (JN-DSZL-7) on the high ridge northwest of Dongshizilu and four other tombs at JN-JTL-3, 6, 7.

Site: JN-JMC-1 (Year 7)

County: Jiaonan

Town: Jimeicun (吉湄村)

Map: Jinggezhuang (井戈庄) [1-50-12-(59)]

Period and Period Number: Longshan 268; Zhou 558; Han 734

Cultural Layer: None

Site Description: The site is located on a low rise in the alluvium, at an elevation of 15 m, on the south, east, and north sides of the town of Jimeicun, and 150 m south of the Shengshui River (盛水河). It is 400 m southwest of the junction of the Shengshui River with the Jili River. The site was in fallow fields at the time of the survey. Han sherds were dispersed over a 4.2 ha area, and the site probably extends under the modern town. Zhou sherds (more Eastern than Western) were found in a 1.8 ha area. Longshan pottery was found only in one small collection area smaller than 1 ha, but we collected two stone tools that can be dated to the Longshan period.

Site: Jintouling JN-JTL-3, 6, 7 (Year 13)

County: Jiaonan

Town: Jintouling (金头岭)

Map: Huagenshan (花根山) [1-50-12-(51)]

Period and Period Number: Han 1728, 1727, 1724

Cultural Layer: Han period tombs

Site Description: These sites are located on low piedmont ridges, at elevations of 35 to 50 m, north and northwest of the town of Jintouling. The largest tomb is at JN-JTL-7, just south of the new road, and 600 m west of a modern water channel. This tomb measures 25 by 25 m at the base. There is another possible tomb 200 m farther down the slope to the east. At JN-JTL-3, there is a relatively intact Han period tomb positioned on the very tip of a piedmont rise 500 m northwest of Jintouling. At JN-JTL-6, two possible Han tombs were located north-east of Jintouling. We collected some Han sherds just north of these features. These tombs may be part of a much larger grouping of Han tombs in this area, including JN-DSZL-1 to the north, the JN-JLH tombs to the west, and the JN-DS and JN-TG tombs to the east (all found in Year 13), as well as the JN-DG-1, 4, and QGD-1 tombs on piedmont ridges on the other side of the Baima River (from Year 7).

FIGURE 3.70. Remnants of Han period tombs at Jilihe (JN-JLH-4, 5, 6, 8).

Site: Jiawangdun JN-JWD-2/LHQ-1 (Year 4)

County: Jiaonan

Town: Jiawangdun (贾王墩) and Lianhuaqian (莲花前)

Map: Liujiaguanzhuang (刘家官庄) [1-50-24-(2)]

Period and Period Number: **Longshan 142; Zhou 233**; Han 266, 267, 268

Cultural Layer: Longshan and Zhou periods

Site Description: The site is located on two slightly raised areas and the area between them on the alluvium, at an elevation of 25 m, beginning at the northern edge of the town of Jiawangdun and extending to within 150 m of Xiaoshihekou village (小石河口村) to the north, and 300 m of Lianhuaqian on the northwest. A small water channel crosses the middle of the site north–south. The site was partly fallow and partly planted in winter wheat at the time of the survey. It was largest in the Longshan period (especially in Early Longshan, it was much smaller in Middle Longshan), covering 52 ha, and the Zhou period (both Western and Eastern), covering 56 ha. There are two Han tombs at the site (Han 267 and Han 268), although Han sherds were sparse (Figure 3.71). One of the tombs (Han 268) is on a possible earthern platform cut by modern farming, with an earlier cultural layer exposed in several pits and cuts. The Han residential components are mostly on the eastern side of the site and belong to

FIGURE 3.71. One of the Han period tombs at Jiawangdun (JN-JWD-2/LHQ-1).

the same community with JN-GJQ-5, JWD-5, JWD-6, and XSHK-2. The site was recorded by a local Cultural Relics Bureau (China Cultural Heritage Bureau 2007:150–151).

Site: JN-JWD-5 (Year 4)

County: Jiaonan

Town: Jiawangdun (贾王墩)

Map: Liujiaguanzhuang (刘家官庄) [1-50-24-(2)]

Period and Period Number: Han 358

Cultural Layer: Han period tomb

Site Description: The site is located on top of a low rise in the alluvium, at an elevation of 11 m, 400 m southeast of the town of Jiawangdun, and between two north–south stream channels. The area was planted in winter wheat, with some fields fallow, at the time of the survey. The site consists of only one small Han tomb. It is 200 m south of another lone Han tomb at JN-JWD-6. The site is part of a cluster of sites with Han tombs that includes JN-JWD-2, GJQ-5, JWD-5, JWD-6, and XSHK-2.

Site: JN-JWD-6 (Year 4)

County: Jiaonan

Figure 3.72. Longshan period sherds (*left to right*: Middle Longshan *guan* jar rim and *ding* tripod foot; Early Longshan *ding* tripod foot and *yan* steamer foot) from Liuhangdazhuang (JN-LHDZ-3[CAA]).

Town: Jiawangdun (贾王墩) and Lianhuaqian (莲花前)

Map: Liujiaguanzhuang (刘家官庄) [1-50-24-(2)]

Period and Period Number: Han 357

Cultural Layer: Han period tomb

Site Description: The site is located on a slight rise in the alluvium, at an elevation of 16 m, 150 m southeast of the town of Jiawangdun, and between two north–south stream channels. The fields were fallow at the time of the survey. The site consists of only one small Han tomb, now largely destroyed. It is 200 m north of another lone Han tomb at JN-JWD-5. The site is part of a cluster of sites with Han tombs that include JN-JWD-2, GJQ-5, JWD-5, JWD-6, and XSHK-2.

Site: Liuhangdazhuang JN-LHDZ-3 (Year 8)

County: Jiaonan

Town: Liuhangdazhuang (柳行大庄)

Map: Huagenshan (花根山) [1-50-12-(51)]

Period and Period Number: **Longshan 303**; Yueshi 7; **Zhou 639**; Han 863

Cultural Layer: None

Site Description: The site is located on alluvial terrain, at an elevation of 15 m, and 500 m south of the town of Liuhangdazhuang. The site is 700 m northwest of a bend in the Baima River. Sherds were found in a mixed area of winter wheat, cabbage, and fallow fields. The site was largest in the Longshan (larger in Early than in Middle Longshan) and Zhou (Eastern and Western) periods, covering 5.7 ha in both (Figure 3.72). Yueshi pottery was collected from a small scatter on the western part of the site and Han sherds from a small scatter on the eastern side. The site is only 400 m west of the large Longshan site at Xisi and may have been part of that larger community.

Site: JN-LJLC-1 (Year 2)

County: Jiaonan

Town: Liangjialuochuan (梁家罗川)

Map: Dantucun (丹土村) [1-50-24-(9)]

Period and Period Number: **Longshan 50**; Zhou 43, 44, 45; Han 42

Cultural Layer: None

Site Description: The site is located on flat alluvium just west of the Beixiao River, 100 m south of the town of Liangjialuochuan, approximately 200 m north of DG-LCZ-1, and at an elevation of 15 m. The surrounding area was mostly planted in winter wheat. Longhshan (Early and Middle) was the dominant occupation, covering 21 ha. The site was about half that size in the Han period (9.7 ha). Zhou (only Western) ceramics were very dispersed, covering no more than 0.5 ha.

Site: Miaoho JN-MH-1 (Year 7)

County: Jiaonan

Town: Miaohou (庙后)

Map: Shalingzi (沙岭子) [1-50-24-(4)]

Period and Period Number: Zhou 609; **Han 828**

Cultural Layer: None

Site Description: The site is located on flat alluvial terrain, at an elevation of 8 m, west and north of the town of Miaohou, and on the south, west, and north sides of Yaxiashangzhuang (崖下上庄). The site is less than 100 m north of a small stream. Part of the site was planted in winter wheat and part was in fallow fields at the time of the survey. The Han site probably extends under both towns and is at least 8.5 ha. The Zhou component (Eastern and Western) was smaller, covering 3.5 ha, and mostly on the west side of the town. The Han component was part of a much larger Han community that includes JN-XZ-1 north of the highway.

Site: JN-MHG-1 (Year 4)

County: Jiaonan

Town: Mahugou (玛琥沟)

Map: Dongjiawa (董家洼) [1-50-12-(57)]

Period and Period Number: Zhou 190; Han 960

Cultural Layer: Han period tomb

Site Description: The site is located on a low rise in the alluvium, at an elevation of 41 m, less than 100 m north of the town of Mahugou, and 200 m southwest of the tributary from the Dijia River Reservoir. The site was planted in winter wheat at the time of the survey. It consists of a small scatter of Western Zhou sherds, covering approximately 0.5 ha just north of the village, and a Han tomb approximately 100 m to the northwest. A small stream channel divides these two parts of the site.

Site: Nansi JN-NS-5, 6, 8 (Year 7)

County: Jiaonan

Town: Nansi (南寺)

Map: Tashandianzi (塔山店子) [1-50-12-(52)]

Period and Period Number: Longshan 245, 246, 247, 248; Zhou 530, 531; **Han 709**

Cultural Layer: Han period

Site Description: The site is located on two low piedmont rises that extend down into the alluvium, at elevations ranging between 25 to 45 m, and about 20 m south of a tributary of the Baima River. The southern part of the site abuts a deep gully. It was on fallow land and planted in winter wheat at the time of the survey, but some of the site near the river was planted with cabbage. We initially gave the three main concentrations of sherds three separate site numbers, but after ceramic analysis it seemed more likely that, at least during the Han period, the three were part of one large site. The Han occupation extends over 16.4 ha. In the northern part of the site, near the river, modern cabbage storage trenches revealed a higher density of Han sherds, including a large Eastern Han brick. The Zhou occupation was more dispersed, in two separate scatters—the largest one to the north covered 10.5 ha and was much larger in Eastern Zhou than in Western Zhou. The other Zhou occupation was slightly smaller (3.2 ha) and only Western Zhou. Longshan period remains were even more dispersed, in four separate scatters, the largest of which was only 3.2 ha.

Site: JN-NXZ-2 (Year 6)

County: Jiaonan

Town: Nanxinzhuang (南辛庄)

Map: Liujiaguanzhuang (刘家官庄) [1-50-24-(2)]

Period and Period Number: Han 493

Cultural Layer: Han period tomb

Site Description: This small site is located on a low piedmont rise overlooking a large patch of alluvium to the east, at an elevation of 14 m, 300 m west of the town of Nanxinzhuang, and just east of a modern water channel that flows south to the coast. The area was planted in winter wheat at the time of the survey. The site consists of one Han tomb that was leveled for farming.

Site: JN-NXZ-4 (Year 6)

County: Jiaonan

Town: Nanxinzhuang (南辛庄)

Map: Liujiaguanzhuang (刘家官庄) [1-50-24-(2)]

Period and Period Number: Zhou 412; Han 482

Cultural Layer: Han period tomb

Site Description: This small site is located on a low piedmont spur overlooking a large patch of alluvium to the east, at an elevation of 14 m, 700 m southwest of Nanxinzhuang, and just east of a modern water channel that flows south to the coast. The area was fallow at the time of the survey. The site consists of one Western Han tomb that had been leveled for farming. The tomb was oriented east–west. We also collected a few Eastern Zhou sherds.

Site: JN-QCC-1 (Year 6)

County: Jiaonan

Town: Qiancaochang (前曹场)

Map: Weijiawan (魏家湾) [1-50-24-(3)]

Period and Period Number: Zhou 442; **Han 527**

Cultural Layer: None

Site Description: The site is located on a small low piedmont rise surrounded by alluvium on all sides, at an elevation of 12 m, 150 m east of the Baima River, and 300 m west of the town of Qiancaochang. It is in a very favorable location. The area was fallow at the time of the survey. The site was largest in the Han period, covering 7.4 ha. We collected some Eastern Zhou material in the northern half of the site, covering 3 ha.

Site: JN-QD-1 (Year 4)

County: Jiaonan

Town: Qingdun (青墩)

Map: Dongjiawa (董家洼) [1-50-12-(57)]

Period and Period Number: Zhou 205; **Han 244**

Cultural Layer: None

Site Description: The site is located on a moderate slope on the top and sides of a low ridge in the piedmont, at an elevation of 50 m, and 300 m north of the town of Qingdun. The site is located between four small streams. It was mostly in fallow fields, with some winter wheat at the time of the survey. It was largest in the Han period, covering 6.5 ha. The site was much smaller in the Zhou period (Eastern Zhou only), covering only 1.8 ha on the eastern side. It was probably part of a larger Han community along with JN-QD-3 and QD-4.

Site: JN-QD-3 (Year 4)

County: Jiaonan

Town: Qingdun (青墩)

Map: Dongjiawa (董家洼) [1-50-12-(57)]

Period and Period Number: Han 242

Cultural Layer: None

Site Description: The site is located on a low rise in the piedmont, at an elevation of 36 m, and on the northwestern side of the town of Qingdun. The east side of site had been disturbed by a modern brick kiln and factory. The site extends 400 m to the west to a small channel and is 125 m north of a stream that feeds into the Dijia River Reservoir. Both watercourses should have been natural water resource for the site. The site was in fallow fields and winter wheat at

Figure 3.73. View of the Han period tombs on top of the piedmont ridge at JN-QGD-1.

the time of the survey. A light Han sherd scatter covered approximately 7.7 ha. The site was probably part of a larger Han community along with JN-QD-1 and QD-4.

Site: JN-QGD-1 (Year 7)

County: Jiaonan

Town: Qigudun (七古墩)

Map: Xiaojiawa (肖家洼) [1-50-12(60)]

Period and Period Number: Han 801

Cultural Layer: Han period with tombs

Site Description: The site is located on the very top of a ridge in the low piedmont that is known locally as Qigudun ("seven ancient mounds"), at an elevation of 68 m. This ridgetop is 1,100 m south of Xiaojiawa, 1,150 m west of Fengjiaguanzhuang, and 1,200 m northeast of Wangshan. The site consists of seven Han period tombs clustered on the top of the ridge (Figure 3.73). One was largely destroyed and many others had been partially destroyed by villagers through looting and the removal of earth for farming and construction. Several tombs were over 3 m high. A gray cultural layer with a high density of sherds was exposed in a cut in an orchard just north of the tombs. The site was not large, only 4.5 ha. The Han cultural layer in JN-WS-7 on the lower slope of Qigudun could be an indication of a larger Han community associated with this tomb complex, but sherds were hard to find in the eroded slopes of the ridge.

Site: JN-QLW-2 (Year 4)

County: Jiaonan

Town: Qianlaowo (前老窝)

Map: Houpolou (后坡楼) [1-50-12-(58)]

Period and Period Number: Zhou 215; **Han 291**

Cultural Layer: None

Site Description: The site is located on top of a low rise in the piedmont that has been quarried for rock, at an elevation of 69 m. It is 400 m east of the town of Qianlaowo, and 350 east of a small stream that flows into a modern reservoir, which is the closest water source for this site. The area was fallow at the time of the survey. A light density of Han sherds was found in a 1.4 ha area, likely exposed by quarrying activities. Zhou pottery (Eastern only) was much less well represented, covering an area smaller than 0.5 ha.

Site: JN-QLW-5 (Year 4)

County: Jiaonan

Town: Qianlaowo (前老窝)

Map: Houpolou (后坡楼) [1-50-12-(58)]

Period and Period Number: Han 290

Cultural Layer: Han period tomb

Site Description: The site is located on top of a low rise in the piedmont, at an elevation of 76 m, and 800 m south of the town of Qianlaowo. The nearest water is a small reservoir 400 m to the southwest. The only cultural material was a small Han tomb probably associated with JN-QLW-2, QLW-3, and QLW-6.

Site: JN-QMJZ-3 (Year 13)

County: Jiaonan

Town: Qianmaojiazhuang (前毛家庄)

Map: Tashandianzi (塔山店子) [1-50-12(52)]

Period and Period Number: Zhou 1219; Han 1719

Cultural Layer: Han period

Site Description: The site is located on flat terrain in the alluvium, at an elevation of 20 m, and extends 50 m west of the town of Qianmaojiazhuang. It is 600 m north of the Baima River. The site was in a combination of fallow fields, winter wheat, and cabbage at the time of the survey. Many Han sherds were visible in cabbage pits and a ditch that crossed the site, both of which likely cut into Han cultural deposits. There was a high density of Han sherds for a small area covering only 1.4 ha. We found some Eastern Zhou sherds in the southern part of the site, in a 1.2 ha area.

Site: Qianpolou JN-QPL-1 (Year 4)

County: Jiaonan

Town: Qianpolou (前坡楼)

Map: Houpolou (后坡楼) [1-50-12-(58)]

Period and Period Number: Zhou 211, 212; **Han 300**

Cultural Layer: None

Site Description: The site is located on flat alluvium and low rises, at an elevation of 31 m, and 100 m south of the town of Qianpolou. Two small water channels cross the site and another defines its southern boundary. The site is 350 m east of a large modern water channel that feeds into the Chao River. It was on agricultural land, including vegetable gardens, winter wheat, and fallow fields at the time of the survey. Part of the site was terraced. The site was largest in the Han period, covering 12.6 ha. Two separate small concentrations of Zhou pottery (both Eastern Zhou) were found on the east and west ends of the site. Both were around 1 ha.

Site: JN-SH-2 (Year 4)

County: Jiaonan

Town: Shuanghe (双河)

Map: Dongjiawa (董家洼) [1-50-12-(57)]

Period and Period Number: Longshan 128; Zhou 200; Han 232

Cultural Layer: Han period tomb

Site Description: The site is located on a low rise in the low piedmont just above flat alluvium, at an elevation of 44 m, 350 m southwest of the town of Shuanghe, and 300 m south of a modern water channel. The area was terraced for agriculture but fallow at the time of the survey. Several small water channels cross the site. The site was occupied in the Longshan (Early), Zhou (Western), and Han periods, but never was larger than 1 ha. There is a possible Han tomb to the southwest, just upslope from where we found most of the sherds.

Site: JN-SH-11 (Year 13)

County: Jiaonan

Town: Shuanghe (双河)

Map: Dongjiawa (董家洼) [1-50-12 (57)]

Period and Period Number: Longshan 544; Zhou 1216; Han 1635

Cultural Layer: Longshan and Zhou periods

Site Description: The site is located on a long low rise in the alluvium, at an elevation of 40 m, on the east and north sides of the village of Shuanghe, and on the west side of a small channel of the Magou River (马沟河). The site is 100 m south of a larger stream channel. The site continues for 400 m north of the village. Most of the site was in winter wheat and fallow fields (Figure 3.74). The area with the most visible remains was just north of the village, where we observed a rich cultural layer with Longshan and Zhou sherds in the cut edge of a raised field. There were almost no sherds in the lower area to the west. This area clearly was leveled in the past, destroying part of the site. The site most likely was larger and extended farther

FIGURE 3.74. View of JN-SH-11 situated on a long rise in the alluvium.

west than the area that we mapped and where we collected sherds. The site was largest in the Zhou period (slightly larger in Eastern than in Western), covering at a minimum 9.6 ha. The Longshan site (Early and Middle) covered at least 6.5 ha. Han sherds were dispersed over an area of 7.8 ha. We collected two Longshan stone tools.

Site: JN-SJL-1 (Year 6)

County: Jiaonan

Town: Shaojialan (邵家岚)

Map: Shaojialan (邵家岚) [1-50-24-(11)]

Period and Period Number: Longshan 222; **Han 547**

Cultural Layer: Han period tomb

Site Description: The site is located on a low piedmont rise and extends into the alluvium to the southwest, at an elevation of 5 to 15 m, on the west and north sides of the town of Shaojialan, and 800 m northeast of the Baima River. It was in winter wheat and fallow fields at the time of the survey. Part of the site is covered by the western side of the town. The site was largest in Western Han, covering 9.9 ha. There is a mostly destroyed Han tomb on the rise 100 m north of the village, with a large looter's pit in the tallest remaining part of the tomb.

There was a small area of Longshan material (smaller than 0.5 ha) less than 100 m north of the tomb.

Site: Shimiaozicun JN-SMZC-3 (Year 2)

County: Jiaonan and Donggang

Town: Shimiaozicun (石庙子村)

Map: Houxiangou (后显沟) [1-50-24-(10)]

Period and Period Number: Yueshi 5; **Zhou 52**; **Han 54**

Cultural Layer: None

Site Description: The site is located on a slight slope in the alluvium, at an elevation of 9 m, less than 100 m southeast of the town of Shimaozicun and on both sides (but mostly south) of the highway that divides Jiaonan District to the north from Donggang District to the south. The site was named for the nearest town in Jiaonan, even though most of the site is in the Donggang District. It is bordered on the north by a small stream. Part of the site area was in fallow fields and part was planted in winter wheat. Scatters of both Eastern Zhou and Han sherds covered just over 8 ha. The Yueshi period was minimally represented in one collection, with an estimated site size smaller than 0.5 ha.

Site: JN-SPZ-1 (Year 4)

County: Jiaonan

Town: Shuipozi (水泊子)

Map: Houpolou (后坡楼) [1-50-12-(58)]

Period and Period Number: Longshan 134; **Zhou 203**; Han 235

Cultural Layer: Longshan and Zhou periods

Site Description: The site is located on flat alluvium, at an elevation of 33 m, near a bend in a modern water channel, and 100 m east of the town of Shuipozi. The site was in fallow fields, with some areas planted in winter wheat and others used for vegetable gardens at the time of the survey. It was 1 ha or smaller in all periods. The densest material was from the Zhou occupation (more Eastern than Western), although minimal amounts of Han and Longshan material also were collected. A gray ashy cultural layer was exposed in a cabbage pit in an area where we found both Longshan and Zhou sherds.

Site: JN-TG-1, 6 (Year 13)

County: Jiaonan

Town: Tuogou (驼沟)

Map: Tashandianzi (塔山店子) [1-50-12(52)]

Period and Period Number: Han 1712, 1714

Cultural Layer: Han period tombs

Site Description: These two sites are located on the slopes of the low piedmont ridge north of the town of Tuogou: JN-TG-6 on the eastern slope and JN-TG-1 on the southern slope. Each site consists of one probable Han tomb. We believe these are Han tombs because the earthern mounds have the form of other Han tombs we have found in the area. The two Han tombs are 350 m apart and each is 350 m from the two tombs at JN-DS-11, which are on the northwestern slope of the same piedmont ridge.

Site: JN-TG-4 (Year 13)

County: Jiaonan

Town: Tuogou (驼沟)

Map: Tashandianzi (塔山店子) [1-50-12-(52)]

Period and Period Number: **Longshan 537**; Zhou 1224; Han 1713

Cultural Layer: Probably Longshan period

Site Description: The site is located on the lower slopes of a low piedmont ridge, extends into the alluvium to within 20 m north of a tributary of the Baima River, at an elevation of 32 m, and less than 100 m northeast of the town of Tuogou. The lower parts of the site are on former terraces raised above the river. The piedmont slopes were fallow fields and planted in winter wheat. Alluvial areas were planted with cabbage. In one cabbage pit we saw a black cultural layer. Longshan remains are found over the entire site area (the site is larger in Early than in Middle Longshan), covering 11 ha. On the western part of the site there was a trace of Han and Zhou materials, with Western Zhou sherds in the alluvium and Han sherds on the piedmont slope. The site was most likely part of a larger Longshan community with JN-DS-4 to the west. The sherd concentrations are separated by the town of Tuogou.

Site: JN-TS-4 (Year 7)

County: Jiaonan

Town: Tashan (塔山)

Map: Jinggezhuang (井戈庄) [1-50-12-(59)]

Period and Period Number: Dawenkou 9; **Longshan 262**; **Zhou 549**; **Han 720, 722**

Cultural Layer: Longshan period, with Han period tomb

Site Description: The site is located on a low rise in the alluvium, at an elevation of 12 to 17 m, less than 50 m east of the Baima River, and 250 m north of the town of Tashan. Most of the site is between two small streams that flow west to the Baima River. It was fallow land and planted in winter wheat at the time of the survey. There was a relatively high density of Longshan, Zhou, and Han sherds in the eight collections we made (Figure 3.75). The Longshan occupation (Early and Middle) extended over an area of 7.3 ha, and a dark patch of soil exposed by plowing in the northern part of the site contained many Longshan sherds. We also collected a Longshan stone tool. The Zhou occupation (slightly larger in Eastern than in Western Zhou) covered 7 ha. The Han occupation, covering 6.5 ha, included a mostly destroyed Han tomb eroding out of the bank of the stream on the north side of the site. We collected one Han brick there. Dawenkou period remains were found in just one collection area.

Site: JN-WS-7 (Year 7)

County: Jiaonan

Town: Wangshan (汪山)

Figure 3.75. Longshan period sherds (*top row*: Early Longshan period *guan* jar rim, Middle Longshan period *guan* jar rim; *bottom row*: Early Longshan period *ding* tripod foot, Early Longshan period *guan* jar rim) from JN-TS-4[CAG].

Map: Xiaojiawa (肖家洼) [1-50-12(60)]

Period and Period Number: Han 812

Cultural Layer: Han period

Site Description: The site is located on a lower piedmont slope descending to the southwest from Qigudun, at an elevation of 45 m, on the west side of a small stream that flows to a small reservoir, and 950 m northeast of the town of Wangshan. A gray-black cultural layer with Han sherds was exposed in the bank of the stream. The site was fallow at the time of the survey. The area with sherds was smaller than 0.5 ha. The location of this Han cultural layer on a lower slope just 400 m from the tombs of JN-QGD-1 may indicate that both were part of a larger Han community. It was hard to find sherds in the eroded slopes of this piedmont ridge. There were several other very small scatters of Han sherds in the vicinity of JN-WS-7.

Site: Wangzhuang JN-WZ-3 (Year 8)

County: Jiaonan

Town: Wangzhuang (王庄)

Map: Huagenshan (花根山) [1-50-12-(51)]

Period and Period Number: Longshan 312, 313; **Han 849**

Cultural Layer: None

Site Description: The site is located at the end of a long, broad, low piedmont ridge that grades off into the alluvium, at an elevation of 22 m. The site is between two towns, less than 100 m north of Wangzhuang and just south of the southeast corner of the Jili River. It is 250 m east of the Jili River. Sherds were found in fallow fields, winter wheat, and cabbages. The site was largest in the Han period, covering 18 ha. There were two small scatters of Longshan sherds on the west side, closest to the river. The site was part of a larger Han community with JN-JLH-1, just over 100 m to the north.

Site: JN-XDZ-3, 5 (Year 13)

County: Jiaonan

Town: Xiaodianzi (小店子)

Map: Houpolou (后坡楼) [1-50-12-(58)]

Period and Period Number: Zhou 1210; Han 1642

Cultural Layer: Boundary marker stones

Site Description: The site is located in the alluvium at the base of a low broad piedmont rise, at an elevation of 44 m, and 150 m northeast of the town of Xiaodianzi. Han sherds were sparsely distributed, mostly on the north side of a modern water channel. On the south side of the channel a cut rock that sticks out above the modern surface may have been a Han period boundary marker (Figure 3.76; we found several Han sherds nearby), like others we have noted in this area (JN-XDZ-6 and ZC-DTY-3). This area is near the modern boundary between the Zhucheng and Jiaonan Districts. The Han component was small, less than 1 ha. There was a slightly larger site area for the Zhou period (Western and Eastern) northwest of the stone.

Site: JN-XDZ-6 (Year 13)

County: Jiaonan

Town: Xiaodianzi (小店子)

Map: Shandongtou (山东头) [1-50-12(49)]

Period and Period Number: Han 1725

Cultural Layer: Boundary marker stones

Site Description: The site is located on top of a low piedmont rise, at an elevation of 31 m, 1,000 m northwest of the town of Xiaodianzi, 1,100 m east of Houhedong, and 500 m west of the Rizhu highway (日诸公路). The site consists of a series of five cut rocks that are unlikely to be natural. Two stones stand higher than the others and another three are lower. They protrude from the ground in a row. One of the taller stones looks like the horse's head of a knight chess piece (Figure 3.77). The stones are in a fallow area. We did not collect any sherds, but from the setting the stones are likely to be Han boundary markers, similar to those at two nearby sites, JN-XDZ-3, 5, and ZC-DTY-3.

Site: JN-XJGZ-2 (Year 4)

County: Jiaonan

Town: Xujiaguanzhuang (徐家官庄)

Figure 3.76. A U-shaped marker stone at JN-XDZ-3, 5.

Figure 3.77. Possible cut stone markers at JN-XDZ-6.

Map: Liujiaguanzhuang (刘家官庄) [1-50-24-(2)]

Period and Period Number: Han 276

Cultural Layer: Han period tomb

Site Description: The site is located on top of a low piedmont ridge, at an elevation of 46 m, 300 m northwest of the town of Xujiaguanzhuang, and 400 m west of a small stream at base of ridge. The fields were fallow at the time of the survey. The site consists of two small earthern Han period tombs.

Site: JN-XJW-1 (Year 3)

County: Jiaonan

Town: Xujiawa (徐家洼)

Map: Dongchaohe (东潮河) [1-50-24-(1)]

Period and Period Number: Han 175

Cultural Layer: Han period tomb

Site Description: The site is located on a slight slope at the edge of a low piedmont ridge, at an elevation of 28 m, 500 m west of the town of Xujiawa, and 100 m east of a modern channel. The only cultural material was a Han period tomb located 400 m east of the Han tomb at JN-XLT-5.

Site: Xujiawa JN-XJW-4 (Year 3)

County: Jiaonan

Town: Xujiawa (徐家洼)

Map: Houxiangou (后显沟) [1-50-24-(10)]

Period and Period Number: Longshan 93

Cultural Layer: Longshan period

Site Description: The site is located on a low rise in the alluvium, 650 m southeast of the town of Xujiawa, and less than 50 m east of a large modern channel. Small ditches cross the site and part of it was flooded at the time of the survey. Some villagers mentioned that the site used to sit on a much higher rise, but that most of the soil had been taken away. The elevation at present is approximately 10 m. The site was located in fields of winter wheat and near a pine forest. A dense concentration of Middle Longshan sherds was found in a 1.1 ha area. There were several pits of gray, non-sandy soil exposed on the surface, and most of the collected sherds came from these features.

Site: JN-XJWa-12 (Year 7)

County: Jiaonan

Town: Xiaojiawa (肖家洼)

Map: Xiaojiawa (肖家洼) [1-50-12(60)]

Period and Period Number: Han 792

Cultural Layer: None

Site Description: The site is located on a slight rise in the alluvium, at an elevation of 19 m, on the west side of the town of Xiaojiawa, and 100 m north of the bend of a tributary of the Baima River. The site was in fallow fields at the time of the survey. We found a high density of Han sherds in a 4.6 ha area. The site may continue to the east under the modern town. Other concentrations of Han sherds were found in and around Xiaojiawa, which is just north of a bend in the tributary. The site may have been part of a larger Han community, especially including JN-XJWa-14 (with tomb) and possibly XJWa-16.

Site: Xiaojiawa JN-XJWa-14 (Year 7)

County: Jiaonan

Town: Xiaojiawa (肖家洼)

Map: Xiaojiawa (肖家洼) [1-50-12(60)]

Period and Period Number: Zhou 580; **Han 785**

Cultural Layer: Han period tomb

Site Description: The site is located mostly on flat alluvial terrain, at an elevation of 25 m, on the north side of the town of Xiaojiawa, and just west of a small stream that flows into a tributary of the Baima River. The site was in fallow fields and planted in winter wheat at the time of the survey. It is predominantly from the Han period, covering 9.4 ha. There is a Han tomb on the higher slope in the northwestern part of the site, just north of a modern ditch. Eastern Zhou pottery was found in one small area of less than 0.5 ha. The site likely continues under Xiaojiawa to the south. It was probably part of a larger Han community with other Han sites that we found in and around the modern town, especially including JN-XJWa-12, and possibly XJWa-16 and XJWa-21.

Site: JN-XJY-7 (Year 4)

County: Jiaonan

Town: Xujiayao (徐家窑)

Map: Dongchaohe (东潮河) [1-50-24-(1)]

Period and Period Number: Longshan 138; **Zhou 187**; Han 220, 222

Cultural Layer: Longshan and Zhou periods

Site Description: The site is located on a slight slope in the piedmont, 100 m north of the town of Xujiayao, and at an elevation of 38 m. A small stream cuts through the north end of the site. Part of the site was in winter wheat, with some areas fallow and others in gardens at the time of the survey (Figure 3.78). The site was largest in the Zhou period (Western and Eastern), covering 3.7 ha. There was a sparse scatter of Early Longshan sherds over an area of 2.7 ha. A thin cultural layer was exposed in the edge of one agricultural terrace on the site. Two small discrete areas of Han sherds were found farther to the west and upslope, neither larger than 1 ha.

Site: JN-XLT-5 (Year 3)

County: Jiaonan

Town: Xiaolutuan (小芦疃)

FIGURE 3.78. JN-XJY-7 located in fields just beyond the row of small trees.

Map: Dongchaohe (东潮河) [1-50-24-(1)]

Period and Period Number: Han 174

Cultural Layer: Han period tomb

Site Description: The site is located on a slight slope at the edge of a low piedmont ridge, at an elevation of 30 m, and 400 m north of the town of Xiaolutuan. The closest water source is a small stream 200 m to the west on the other side of the low ridge. The only cultural material was a Han tomb 400 m west of the Han tomb at JN-XJW-1.

Site: Xiuqiyuan JN-XQY-4 (Year 2)

County: Jiaonan

Town: Xiuqiyuan (修齐园)

Map: Dantucun (丹土村) [1-50-24-(9)]

Period and Period Number: **Longshan 54**; Zhou 46; Han 43

Cultural Layer: None

Site Description: The site is located on flat alluvium, less than 50 m north of the Beixiao River, 150 m north of the town of Xiuqiyuan, and at an elevation of 10 m. The site was in fallow fields and winter wheat, and part of the site was being converted into a greenhouse. Relatively dense scatters of Longshan sherds (Early and Middle) were found in a 5.2 ha area. Han sherds

Figure 3.79. One of the several exposed cultural layers at the multicomponent Xisi site (JN-XS-1).

were found in the eastern part of the site, covering 3.4 ha. A Zhou occupation was much smaller at less than 0.5 ha.

Site: Xisi JN-XS-1 (Year 8)

County: Jiaonan

Town: Xisi (西寺)

Map: Huagenshan (花根山) [1-50-12-(51)]

Period and Period Number: Dawenkou 10; **Longshan 299**; Yueshi 8, 9, 10; Zhou 644; Han 858, 859, 860, 861

Cultural Layer: Several

Site Description: This large site is located on an alluvial rise, at an elevation of 15 m, just west of an inside bend of the Baima River where it joins a tributary from the east. The site extends from the river north and west to Liujiadazhuang. It clearly continues below the modern village of Xisi. The area surrounding the village is mainly agricultural. The fields were fallow in places at the time of the survey, with winter wheat in others. Some areas were planted with cabbage, vegetable gardens, and an apple orchard. There were cultural layers exposed in several locations (Figure 3.79).

FIGURE 3.80. Early Longshan period *yan* steamer foot (*left*) and Longshan period stone *ben* (锛) adze (*right*) from Xisi (JN-XS-1[CACC]).

FIGURE 3.81. Yueshi period *yan* steamer foot and vessel handle with soapstone inclusions from Xisi (JN-XS-1[CAAA]).

Figure 3.82. Longshan period *bei* (杯) cup fragment and *wan* (碗) bowl from Xisi (JN-XS-1).

The site was densely settled for a long time. Dawenkou pottery was found only in a small collection area on the northwestern side of the site. The Longshan occupation covered at least 52 ha and may have been slightly larger in Early Longshan (Figure 3.80). The Zhou occupation covered 50 ha. We found Han sherds in several discrete scatters throughout the site, the largest of which was 25 ha, but collectively the Han occupation was just as large as the Zhou occupation. In addition to the ceramic sherds, there were Han bricks in two of the collections, indicating a locus of Han burials. Yueshi sherds were dispersed in several discrete scatters, the largest at 9 ha (Figure 3.81).

The richest part of the site was the low rise on which the town sits. Most of the cultural layers were observed on the west and north sides of Xisi. Cultural layers were found in five different collection areas: CAC, CAG, CAX, CABB, and CACC. Some layers span approximately 1.5 m. The layers in CAC and CAG were exposed in a cabbage pit. The layers in CAX, CABB, and CACC abut the modern town, and the adobe bricks in the house walls there show gray soil and ancient sherds. These layers are in the raised area on the map. Finally, a farmer from the town showed us a whole Longshan pot (a bowl) and a black ceramic cup base, perhaps from a burial (Figure 3.82).

The Han component clearly was associated with the nearby areas of Han platforms/tombs on a piedmont ridge system just on the other (southeast) side of the river at Dagou (JN-DG-1, 4), serving as the major Han center in this part of our survey region. The site was discovered by the local Cultural Relics Bureau and is now designated a Qingdao City preservation site (China Cultural Heritage Bureau 2007:150–151).

Site: JN-XSHK-2 (Year 4)

County: Jiaonan

Town: Xiaoshihekou (小石河口)

Map: Liujiaguanzhuang (刘家官庄) [1-50-24-(2)]

Period and Period Number: Longshan 199; Zhou 232; Han 269

Cultural Layer: Han period tomb

Site Description: The site is located on flat terrain in the alluvium, at an elevation of 20 m, 550 m southeast of the town of Xiaoshihekou, 500 m northeast of Jiawangdun, and 100 m west of a modern water channel. The site was in fallow fields and planted in winter wheat at the time of the survey. It was occupied in the Longshan, Eastern Zhou, and Han periods, covering approximately 1.8 ha. The Han component includes a small tomb east of the main sherd concentrations. The site is part of a cluster of sites with Han tombs (including JN-JWD-2, GJQ-5, JWD-5, JWD-6).

Site: JN-XWJLG-1 (Year 6)

County: Jiaonan

Town: Xiwangjialiugou (西王家柳沟)

Map: Houpolou (后坡楼) [1-50-12-(58)]

Period and Period Number: **Zhou 424**; Han 507

Cultural Layer: None

Site Description: The site is located on a low rise in the low piedmont, at an elevation of 45 m, 300 m south of the upper headwater of the Shengshui River, and 400 m southeast of the town of Xiwangjialiugou. The fields surrounding the site were fallow at the time of the survey. There was a small quarry on the rise near the site. The site is mostly Zhou (Eastern and Western), covering 3.3 ha. Some Han sherds were collected in the western half of the site.

Site: Xizhuang JN-XZ-1 (Year 7)

County: Jiaonan

Town: Xizhuang (西庄)

Map: Shalingzi (沙岭子) [1-50-24-(4)]

Period and Period Number: Longshan 286; **Zhou 603**; **Han 825**, 821

Cultural Layer: None

Site Description: The site is located on a low piedmont rise and gently sloping alluvial terrain, at elevations of 20 to 25 m, just north of the highway on the north side of the villages of Xizhuang and Miaohou (庙后村). Part of the site abuts a small stream on the west. It was in fallow fields and planted in winter wheat at the time of the survey. Han and Zhou (more Eastern than Western) sherds were dispersed over most of the site, covering 19 ha in the Han period and 18.5 ha in the Zhou period. Early Longshan sherds were found in a much smaller area (5.4 ha) in the center of the site. The Han component (and possibly the Eastern Zhou) was part of a much larger community that includes JN-MH-1 south of the highway. The two sherd concentrations are separated by the modern highway and the two villages.

Site: JN-YJZ-2 (Year 6)

County: Jiaonan

Town: Yinjiazhuang (殷家庄)

Map: Liujiaguanzhuang (刘家官庄) [1-50-24-(2)]

Period and Period Number: Shang 21; Zhou 411; Han 472

Cultural Layer: Unclear

Site Description: The site is located on a very slight rise in the alluvium, at an elevation of 3 m, just east of a small water channel, and 100 m south of the town of Yinjiazhuang. The site was planted in winter wheat and is near rice paddies. We observed a cultural layer 0.3 to 0.5 m below the present surface. The site was approximately 2.4 ha in all three periods (Eastern and Western Zhou, Late Shang, and Western Han).

Site: Zhoujiacun JN-ZJC-4 (Year 6)

County: Jiaonan

Town: Zhoujiacun (周家村)

Map: Houpolou (后坡楼) [1-50-12-(58)]

Period and Period Number: Dawenkou 6; Longshan 202; Zhou 420; **Han 502**

Cultural Layer: Han period

Site Description: This large site is located on a series of low hills in the low piedmont, at elevations between 30 and 55 m, just north of a large patch of alluvial land and just east and upslope of a series of modern reservoirs. The site is 500 m west of the town of Zhoujiacun, and a modern highway cuts through the center of the site. The area was mostly fallow at the time of the survey, with some fields planted in winter wheat. The site is largest in Western Han, covering 19.9 ha on both sides of the highway (a bit of Eastern Han was found south of the highway). There was an exposed Han cultural layer above a small stream channel in the most northeastern part of the site. Most of the Zhou material (Eastern and Western) was found north of the highway, with a small area of Eastern Zhou south of the highway. In total, the Zhou site was 13.2 ha. The Longshan occupation, covering 12.4 ha, was mostly north of the highway, with the Early Longshan component larger than the Middle Longshan. One collection area of approximately 1.5 ha on the east side of the site north of the highway also had some Late Dawenkou pottery.

Site: Zhangjiadazhuang JN-ZJDZ-3 (Year 7)

County: Jiaonan

Town: Zhangjiadazhuang (张家大庄)

Map: Jinggezhuang (井戈庄) [1-50-12-(59)]

Period and Period Number: Dawenkou 8; **Longshan 272**, 271; Zhou 561, 562; Han 740, 741, 742, 745

Cultural Layer: Longshan period

Site Description: The site is located on a series of small low rises and surrounding flat terrain in the alluvium, at an elevation of 12 m, just west of the town of Zhangjiadazhuang, and south of the road from Tashan to Baozibu. It is 400 m west of the levee of the Baima River, and most of the site is between two north–south modern water channels. The site was planted in winter wheat and cabbage, and some fields were fallow at the time of the survey. The core of the site is associated with the highest rise, which had been cut down by agricultural activities, where there were several areas of exposed dark cultural deposits, including two cultural layers (Figure 3.83). The site was largest in the Longshan period (larger in Middle than in Early), covering 30.3 ha. Dispersed Zhou sherds (much more Eastern than Western) were found in a 13 ha area. Han sherds were found in four discrete scatters, the largest of which covered 8.8 ha. One *zao* (凿) chisel and two *dao* (刀) knives that we collected are probably Longshan. Dawenkou pottery was found in one small area (less than 0.5 ha) in the northwestern corner of the site (Figure 3.84). The site was discovered by a local Cultural Relics Bureau and is currently designated a Jiaonan City preservation site (China Cultural Heritage Bureau 2007:150–151).

Site: JN-ZJZh-1 (Year 13)

County: Jiaonan

Town: Zangjiazhuang (臧家庄)

Map: Dongjiawa (董家洼) [1-50-12-(57)]

Period and Period Number: **Longshan 545**; Zhou 1214; Han 1634

Cultural Layer: Longshan period

Site Description: The site is located on a low piedmont rise, above alluvial land to the south, at an elevation of 50 m, just south of the highway and a tea factory on the east side of the town of Zangjiazhuang. The site was in mostly in fallow fields at the time of the survey and planted with some winter wheat and mulberries. An Early Longshan cultural layer with many sherds was exposed on the eastern side, in a terrace bank just above a small modern water channel. There was a sparse distribution of sherds on top of the piedmont rise. The site was mostly Early Longshan, covering an area of 3.2 ha. Sparse scatters of Eastern Zhou and Han sherds were found closer to the top of the rise, both covering less than 1 ha.

Lanshan District (岚山区)

Site: LS-ADW-1 (Year 11)

County: Lanshan

Town: Andongwei (安东卫)

Map: Lanshanzhen (岚山镇) [1-50-35-(46)]

Period and Period Number: Longshan 461; Zhou 1024; **Han 1399**

Cultural Layer: None

Site Description: The site is located on alluvial terrain at an elevation of 10 m, east of a road, and in the remaining open area north of Shijiazhuang (史家庄) and south of Dongxiaozhuang (东小庄). With the rapidly growing local population, there is not much open area left. We found sherds on both sides of a small stream and up to the edges of houses. The area was mostly in vegetable gardens. We found Han sherds throughout a 9.2 ha area where it

FIGURE 3.83. Fang Hui examining an exposed Longshan period cultural layer at Zhangjiadazhuang (JN-ZJDZ-3).

FIGURE 3.84. Dawenkou period and Longshan period sherds (*top row*: Middle Longshan *guan* jar rim and *ding* tripod rim; *bottom row*: Early Longshan period *yi* spouted basin rim, Late Dawenkou period *ding* tripod foot) from Zhangjiadazhuang (JN-ZJDZ-3[CAG]).

was possible to check between houses. There was a small area of Longshan sherds just north of the town of Shijiazhuang and a small area of Eastern Zhou material around some houses on the northwest.

The site was known to the Rizhao Museum, the Lanshan Cultural Relics Bureau, and the Shandong Provincial Institute of Archaeology. It had been heavily damaged by modern development, and we could not check all areas where we were told there had been cultural remains. The site was definitely larger than what we could see and measure. It also was part of a larger Han community with LS-DXZ-1 and LSM-1 farther up a piedmont slope to the east.

Site: LS-AJH-1 (Year 10)

County: Lanshan

Town: Anjiahu (安家湖)

Map: Panjiawa (潘家洼) [1-50-23-(62)]

Period and Period Number: Han 1123

Cultural Layer: None

Site Description: The site is located on the top of a long sloping ridge in the low piedmont, at an elevation of 33 m, 90 m west of the town of Anjiahu, and on the south side of the road. There are two small streams on either side of this north–south trending ridge, both about 250 m from the site. The site was in fallow fields, winter wheat, and an area of haystacks. There was a relatively high density of Han sherds in a 1.5 ha area.

Site: LS-BFJC-2 (Year 10)

County: Lanshan

Town: Gaoxing (高兴镇), formerly Beifanjiacun (北范家村)

Map: Panjiawa (潘家洼) [1-50-23-(62)]

Period and Period Number: Zhou 843; Han 1131

Cultural Layer: Possible

Site Description: The site is located on flat ground in the alluvium, at an elevation of 25.5 m, north of the railroad in the northwestern corner of the town of Beifanjiacun (now called Gaoxing), and 150 m northeast of a small stream. It was in a vegetable garden, winter wheat fields, and fallow fields. The soil was grayish in some areas, which could be an indication of disturbed cultural deposits. We found many Han sherds in an 11 ha area. The railroad and modern houses separate this site from LS-BFJC-1, another Han and Zhou site on the east side of the town; it is possible that both had been part of the same larger community.

Site: LS-BY-1 (Year 10)

County: Lanshan

Town: Baiyun (白云), formerly Kangtou (炕头)

Map: Panjiawa (潘家洼) [1-50-23-(62)]

Period and Period Number: Zhou 836; Han 1124

Cultural Layer: None

Site Description: The site is located on a slight slope in the low piedmont, at an elevation of 40 m, and on the north bank of a small stream 250 m south of of the town of Baiyun (formerly Kangtou). The slight rise of the site is bounded on the east and west by small streams that flow into the reservoir. We found sherds in fields just north of the reservoir as well as in its banks. There was a small area of Han material just south of the reservoir and east of the road. We measured 21 ha for the Han occupation and 1.2 ha for the Eastern Zhou occupation. The site may have been larger in the past but is now partially submerged under the reservoir. The Zhou portion may connect to LS-BY-3, a small area of Eastern Zhou material that we found 150 m to the east.

Site: Baiyun LS-BY-4 (Year 10)

County: Lanshan

Town: Baiyun (白云), formerly Kangtou (炕头)

Map: Panjiawa (潘家洼) [1-50-23-(62)]

Period and Period Number: Longshan 415; Shang 27; **Zhou 834**; Han 1112

Cultural Layer: Longshan period

Site Description: The site is located on a gradual slope in the low piedmont, at elevations of 70 to 85 m, and mostly on the west side of a series of small ponds 100 m northeast of the town of Baiyun (formerly Kangtou). We made two small collections on the east side of the stream and reservoirs. The highest section of the site was planted in tea, while most of the rest of the site was in fallow fields (Figure 3.85). The site was largest in the Zhou period (mostly Western Zhou with only a small area of Eastern Zhou), covering 3.2 ha (all west of the reservoir). We also found Shang sherds in the same area (covering 1.7 ha). This part of the site is situated in a very typical defensive location for Shang and Western Zhou sites in our survey region. The low rise of this part of the site may have been artificially built up. Recent moving of earth in that area had exposed a very high density of Western Zhou sherds. We found very small areas of Han and Longshan sherds on the east side of the stream, including a dark cultural layer about 40 cm thick in a terrace cut just above the stream that contained Middle Longshan sherds. About 100 m farther south (and south of the reservoir) we found another small site (LS-BY-5) on both sides of the stream that probably had been part of the same community in both Western Zhou and Han.

Site: LS-CJH-1 (Year 12)

County: Lanshan

Town: Chenjiahu (陈家湖)

Map: Jiepailing (界牌岭) [1-50-35-(37)]

Period and Period Number: Han 1584

Cultural Layer: Han period tomb

Site Description: This site is located on the southern tip of a very low piedmont rise, at an elevation of 20 m, 75 m southeast of the town of Chenjiahu, 200 m south of the railroad, and 550 m from a tributary of the Xiuzhen River (绣针河). The use of the area is agricultural, planted with winter wheat; some fields were fallow. The site consists of a Han tomb and sparsely distributed sherds. The tomb is roughly 20 by 20 m and 2 m high.

FIGURE 3.85. Survey crew checking for sherds in terraced fields at LS-BY-4.

Site: LS-DGZDS-1 (Year 12)

County: Lanshan

Town: Daguanzhuangdongshan (大官庄东山)

Map: Daguanzhuang (大官庄) [1-50-35-(21)]

Period and Period Number: Zhou 1108; Han 1539

Cultural Layer: None

Site Description: The site is located on the top of a low piedmont ridge, at an elevation of 54 m, 250 m southwest of the town of Daguanzhuangdongshan, and 100 m west of a small reservoir. It seems to have been a preferred location for a settlement. We found cultural remains in winter wheat and fallow fields between two small stream channels. There were Zhou (Western and Eastern) and Han sherds in a 2 ha area. A modern brick factory to the north may have truncated the site. We found one Western Zhou stone tool.

Site: LS-DMJC-1 (Year 10)

County: Lanshan

Town: Dongmujiacun (东牟家村)

Map: Bijiacun (毕家村) [1-50-35-(6)]

Period and Period Number: Zhou 849; Han 1135

Cultural Layer: Possible

Site Description: The site is located on a low rise in alluvial terrain, at an elevation of 12.5 m, on the north side of the town of Dongmujiacun, and on the south side (south of the levee) of the Mujiacun River (牟家村河), a tributary of the Chuanzi River. The site was entirely in vegetable gardens, mostly cabbage. There was a fairly high density of sherds that had been brought to the surface by the digging of cabbage pits that exposed buried cultural deposits. Given its location, the site probably extends to the south under the town; it could be considerably larger than the 1.5 ha area we mapped for the Western Zhou and Han occupations on the north edge of the town.

Site: LS-DNS-1 (Year 12)

County: Lanshan

Town: Dongnanshan (东南山)

Map: Huangjiayu (黄家峪) [1-50-35-(29)]

Period and Period Number: Zhou 1039; Han 1555

Cultural Layer: None

Site Description: The site is located on a low piedmont rise, at an elevation of 31.5 m, 200 m west of the town of Dongnanshan, and 300 m south of Cuijingyang (崔景阳村). The site was in tea fields and bounded on the north and south by two small streams. There was a high density of Zhou (Eastern and Western) and Han sherds in a 1.5 ha area.

Site: Dapo LS-DP-1 (Year 12)

County: Lanshan

Town: Dapo (大坡)

Map: Dapo (大坡) [1-50-35-(4)]

Period and Period Number: **Zhou 1039**; Han 1430, 1431

Cultural Layer: None

Site Description: The site is located on a low piedmont slope, at an elevation of 42 m, on the northwest side of the town of Dapo, and just south of a school. The nearest water source is a small stream 200 m to the northeast; a modern water channel passes through the western part of the site. Most of the site was in fallow fields. Although not large, we found a dense scatter of Zhou sherds (more Eastern than Western) just south of the school. The site was largest in the Zhou period (larger in Eastern than in Western Zhou), covering 3.1 ha. There were two small areas of Han materials, on the east and the west of the water channel.

Site: LS-DP-4 (Year 12)

County: Lanshan

Town: Dapo (大坡)

Map: Dapo (大坡) [1-50-35-(4)]

Period and Period Number: Zhou 1038; Han 1587

Cultural Layer: Present

FIGURE 3.86. View of the small Western Zhou period site LS-DPD-2 situated on a steep-sided low piedmont ridge.

Site Description: The site is located on a low piedmont ridge, at an elevation of 56 m, 350 m northwest of the town of Dapo, and less than 50 m southeast of the railroad. It is bounded on the north by a small stream and on the west by a road. The site was in tea fields and fallow fields. We found a high density of Eastern Zhou sherds and lesser amounts of Western Zhou and Han sherds. A farmer had overturned soil that exposed a cultural deposit with many large sherds. We collected one stone tool. The site was only 2.1 ha.

Site: LS-DPD-2 (Year 12)

County: Lanshan

Town: Dapengding (大棚顶)

Map: Daguanzhuang (大官庄) [1-50-35-(21)]

Period and Period Number: Zhou 1158

Cultural Layer: Western Zhou period

Site Description: The site is located on the tip of a low piedmont ridge, an at elevation of 51 m, less than 50 m south of the town of Dapengding, and 20 to 30 m east of a serpentine quarry. This very small site (less than 0.5 ha) is just north of a small cement aqueduct. The site was in

Figure 3.87. The modern serpentine quarry near LS-DPD-2.

winter wheat, vegetables, and fallow fields (Figure 3.86). We found a Western Zhou cultural layer exposed in a terrace cut. Most of the sherds were collected from this small area. This site may well have been larger before the serpentine quarry was expanded to its present size (Figure 3.87). The location of the site may be related to the serpentine source.

Site: Daquhe LS-DQH-5 (Year 10)

County: Lanshan

Town: Daquhe (大曲河)

Map: Guojiahuzi (郭家湖子) [1-50-23-(55)]

Period and Period Number: **Longshan 408**; Zhou 821; **Han 1093**

Cultural Layer: None

Site Description: The site is located on flat ground in the alluvium at an elevation of 12.4 m, 150 m west of the levee of the Futuan River, and 200 m north of the town of Daquhe. It was in fields of winter wheat, fallow patches, and mulberry trees. It was largest in the Longshan period (larger in Early than in Middle Longshan), covering 10.1 ha. The Han component was not quite as large, covering 7.1 ha. Western Zhou sherds were collected from a small area in the southern section of the site.

FIGURE 3.88. View of the Shang and Zhou period site LS-DQL-1 on top of a long, low, steep-sided piedmont ridge.

Site: LS-DQL-1 (Year 11)

County: Lanshan

Town: Daqianli (大阡里)

Map: Lanshanzhen (岚山镇) [1-50-35-(46)]

Period and Period Number: Shang 29; Zhou 1022

Cultural Layer: None

Site Description: The site is located on the very tip of a long low terraced ridge in the piedmont, at an elevation of 61 m, in one of the few open areas left on the south slope of the high mountain northwest of Lanshan (岚山) and the highway that passes through the saddle to the coast. The location (defensively placed on the end of a flat ridgetop near water) is very typical of Shang and Zhou period sites in our survey region. The site is less than 100 m from new houses in the port city of Lanshan. The nearest water source is a small stream 30 m south of the site. The site was located in winter wheat and plowed fields (Figure 3.88). Most of the sherds were Eastern and Western Zhou with a few Late Shang-like sherds. The site area was smaller than 0.5 ha.

Site: Datushan LS-DTS-5/CG-9 (Year 12)

County: Lanshan

Town: Datushan (大土山) and Chegou (车沟)

Map: Datushan (大土山) [1-50-35-(12)]

Period and Period Number: Longshan 470, 471, 472; Zhou 1046, 1047, 1048, 1062, 1086; **Han 1459**

Cultural Layer: Multiple

Site Description: This very large Han site is located under and north of the town of Datushan; it ranges in elevation from 30 m in alluvial areas to 50 to 60 m on piedmont ridges. This is an ideal setting for a settlement, situated where the upper channel of the Zhuzi River splits into a northern branch and a southern branch. The richest part of the site is on alluvial terrain north of Datushan. The site stretches north to a branch of the Zhuzi River that flows on the south side of Dinglutushan and east across the branch that flows south (on the east side of Datushan), to within 400 m west of the town of Chegou. East of this river channel the site abuts a levee on the north and extends south to the base of a piedmont slope. On the west side of the channel (by Datushan), the site extends to the first piedmont spurs south of the town. On the west, the site continues up a broad piedmont slope to within 200 m of the east side of Liujiaguanzhuang and LS-LJGZ-1, a possible Han cemetery site.

We initially found this site on the east side of the Zhuzi River channel and labeled it LS-CG-9. The southern area of alluvium there was mostly fallow with some fields in winter wheat. We mostly found only Han remains there. The northern part of this area includes a nursery with pine trees. Many sherds dating to the Longshan, Zhou (more Eastern than Western), and Han periods were visible in ditches. Longshan remains (Longshan 471) were found in a small area at the northernmost part of the site, almost entirely among pine trees, covering approximately 5.9 ha. Trenching in several areas there revealed dense concentrations of Early Longshan sherds.

The much larger portion of the site is on the western side of the river channel (LS-DTS-5). This area was planted in winter wheat, with many fields fallow (on alluvium and piedmont slopes), although we did find sherds in vegetable gardens just north of Datushan and in orchards just west of the river channel. We found Han material in all collections there. We also found smaller scatters of Han materials on the lower tips of the piedmont ridges that descend to the east and south sides of the town (LS-DTS-3, DTS-6, DTS-8–11). There was poor visibility of surface remains in several low areas on the west side of town and east of Xitushan, but we still found small scatters of Han sherds there (LS-DTS-9-1, XTS-1, XTS-2). Given the scatters of Han sherds present on all sides of Datushan, we concluded that the modern community sits on top of the ancient site and included the entire area in our estimate of the size of the Han occupation (286.6 ha). The site could be even larger, as we did not include many smaller, isolated clusters of Han sherds (LS-DTS-2, DTS-4, DTS-7, HT-1, HT-2, HT-4) that continue up the piedmont slopes south of Datushan.

There is a raised rectangular area 850 m north of the town of Datushan and 50 m east of the road that is the richest part of the site (Figure 3.89). Approximately 250 by 250 m in size at the time of the survey, this remmant platform, called Bei Chengzi (北城子, "Northern City"), likely is the source of the town's name (大土山, "big earth mountain"). The platform may have been walled. There were several cultural layers with gray soil exposed on the west side of this raised area and many areas of exposed dark soil on top of it; in cultural layers with dark sediments on the south side of this raised area we observed glazed and other decorated Han pottery (Figures 3.90 and 3.91). In a large area around this platform we found Eastern Zhou sherds (with smaller areas of Western Zhou). The area with Zhou pottery (Zhou 1046) con-

FIGURE 3.89. Crew surveying an exposed cultural layer (CAR) on the edge of the raised area in the center of Datushan (LS-DTS-5/CG-9).

nects with the LS-CG-9 section of the site on the east side of the channel, covering a total area of about 75.4 ha. Other discrete scatters of Zhou material across the site were all very small.

We also found Longshan pottery (mostly Early, Middle Longshan pottery was present in only one small collection area) in cultural layers on the west side of the raised area, on top, and around it (Longshan 472). Longshan pottery also was present on the west side of the road, covering a total area of 9.2 ha. One other small area of Early Longshan sherds was found on the west side of the road 350 m south of Dingliuzhoushan village (丁碌磚山村). We collected several stone tools, including two *moshi* (磨石) grinding tools, a *dao* (刀) knife, a *fu* (斧) axe, and a *zao* (凿) chisel (Figures 3.92 and 3.93). A *fanglun* (纺轮) spindle whorl was also found.

The site was discovered by a local Cultural Relics Bureau and is designated a county-level cultural preservation site (China Cultural Heritage Bureau 2007:272–273). The size of this site is similar to the Dagucheng site, which was the administrative or county seat of Haiqu County in the Han period. Thus Datushan could also have been a county town. Historical records indicate that there were fifty-one counties and states in the Langya Jun Commandery (琅琊郡) during the Qin and Han periods, for which the locations of twenty county towns are still unknown (An 1993:121–123; Zhou 2006:238–247). The Datushan site could be one of these county towns that may be associated with Gaoguang County.

Ye Guishou of the Qing Dynasty names the following counties: "There are Gumu County (姑幕县), Lingmen County (灵门县), Qi County (萁县), Pi or Bei County (椑县),

Figure 3.90. Two Han period sherds (*left*) and tile end (*far right*) from Datushan (LS-DTS-5/CG-9[CA1]).

Figure 3.91. Han period glazed rim sherd (*left*) and *qigai* lid (*right*) from Datushan (LS-DTS-5[CAZ]/CG-9).

Xiquan County (析泉县), Gaoxiang County (高乡县), Gaoguang County (高广县), Xinshan County (新山县), and Gaoyang County (高阳县) in Langya Jun of Xuzhou" (Ye 1997:566). The county town of Gaoguang is unknown. The county town of Gaoyang is near Henggoucun (横沟村) of Zhuluxiang (朱芦乡), 30 km northeast of Shizilu Town (十字路镇) in Junan County (莒南县).

FIGURE 3.92. Longshan period sherds (*top left*: Early Longshan *qigai* lid; *bottom, left to right*: Early Longshan *ding* tripod foot, Late Longshan white *gui* tripod handle) and stone *fu* axe (*right*) from Datushan (LS-DTS-5[CAX]/CG-9).

Site: LS-DZZ-5 (Year 11)

County: Lanshan

Town: Dazhuangzi (大庄子)

Map: Qiaonantou (桥南头) [1-50-35-(38)]

Period and Period Number: Han 1355

Cultural Layer: Han period burials

Site Description: The site is located on a gentle slope at the juncture of the alluvium and piedmont at an elevation of 61 m, west of a modern quarry, north of the railroad, and less than 100 m southeast of the town of Dazhuangzi. The nearest water source is a small stream 60 m northwest of the site. Villagers who showed us this site in 2005 told us that burials had been found there within the previous five years; this information was later confirmed by officials at the Rizhao Museum. We saw a large pot protruding from a cut profile (Figure 3.94). We found

FIGURE 3.93. Middle Longshan period white *gui* tripod sherd from Datushan (LS-DTS-5[CAZ]/CG-9).

a few Han sherds in the area and another possible Han period tomb 250 m farther east and 100 m north of the railroad. The site was exposed when the railroad was built.

Site: LS-FJGZ-1 (Year 12)

County: Lanshan

Town: Feijiaguanzhuang (费家官庄)

Map: Dapo (大坡) [1-50-35-(4)]

Period and Period Number: Longshan 465; Zhou 1034; **Han 1415**

Cultural Layer: Bricks from Han period structure or tomb

Site Description: The site is located on a gradual slope on the lower tip of a low piedmont ridge, at an elevation of 40 m, less than 50 m northeast of an upper branch of the Zhuzi River, and 400 m southwest of the town of Feijiaguanzhuang. It was in fallow fields and fields of winter wheat. The site mostly contains Han period materials, covering 2.3 ha. We

FIGURE 3.94. Gary Feinman examining a large Han period sherd protruding from a quarry wall at LS-DZZ-5.

found many Han bricks, indicating a possible Han building or tomb. We also collected a decorated end tile. The sherd density was light. There were lesser amounts of Eastern Zhou and Longshan sherds.

Site: Fenshuizhen LS-FSZ-1 (Year 11)

County: Lanshan

Town: Fenshuizhen (汾水镇)

Map: Mazhan (马站) [1-50-35-(45)]

Period and Period Number: Zhou 1025; Han 1393

Cultural Layer: None

Site Description: The site is located in flat alluvium, at an elevation of 8 m, 150 m south of the town of Fenshuizhen, and 100 m east of the highway (204). It is bounded on the east and west by modern reservoirs and by a new road on the south. It is 450 m north of the Xiuzhen River and 100 m east of a tributary. The site was in fallow fields and fields of winter wheat. Han remains were found over the entire site, covering 8.3 ha. We found Eastern and Western Zhou sherds in the western part of the site, covering 6.7 ha. The site may have been larger in the past. We found sherds right up to some new houses on the northwest corner of the site.

Site: Guojiazhuang LS-GJZ-1 (Year 10)

County: Lanshan

Town: Guojiazhuang (郭家庄)

Map: Shangjiazhuang (尚家庄) [1-50-35-(5)]

Period and Period Number: Longshan 418, 419; Shang 28, **Zhou 881**; Han 1173, 1174, 1176

Cultural Layer: Possible

Site Description: The site is located on flat alluvial terrain surrounding a low rocky outcrop and a low piedmont spur to the east, at an elevation of 21 m, on the south side of the highway, and 300 m southwest of the village of Guojiazhuang. A small tributary of the Zhuzi River runs through the site. The site is in mostly fallow fields, but parts were in winter wheat and a pine tree nursery. We made ten collections at this rich Zhou period site (both Western and Eastern) that covered 12.4 ha. Because of its elevation above the rest of the site, the rocky outcrop, just south of the highway, may have had a special use. We also found half a dozen pieces of burnt orange clay.

Longshan sherds were found in two small discrete scatters: one including the rocky outcrop (Longshan 419) and the other at the southeastern edge of the site. Although most of the Longshan pottery was undiagnostic to further temporal specificity, we did find one Late Longshan sherd near the rocky outcrop. There was a small area of Shang sherds south of the outcrop. Han sherds were found in three discrete areas, the largest of which (Han 1173, 2.5 ha) included the rock outcrop. This settlement may have been part of a larger Zhou community with LS-GJZ-3 and GJZ-4, both on the west side of the village and north of the highway.

Site: Gouwa LS-GW-1 (Year 12)

County: Lanshan

Town: Gouwa (沟洼)

Map: Liujiagou (刘家沟) [1-50-35-(20)]

Period and Period Number: Longshan 475; Yueshi 19; Zhou 1089; Han 1523

Cultural Layer: Thick, with sherds from all periods

Site Description: The site is located on a low rise in the alluvium, at an elevation of 30 m, 500 m north of the town of Gouwa, and 120 m east of the highway. It is on both sides of a tributary of the Zhuzi River. The site was in winter wheat and fallow fields, and part was in vegetable gardens (Figure 3.95). The setting is an ideal location for a settlement. The richest section was on the east side of the river, just above a bend in the river, where we found an exposed cultural layer in the side of the bank. This layer was 2 m thick and gray, with mostly Early Longshan and Yueshi sherds in its lower part (Figure 3.96) and Zhou (mostly Western) and Han sherds in the upper part. We found one Longshan *zao* (凿) chisel and one stone *lian* (镰) sickle. The site was not large in any period: 4 ha in the Longshan (larger in Early than in Middle Longshan) and 4.9 ha in the Zhou (larger in Eastern than in Western) and Han periods. We found several Yueshi sherds in the center of site near the cultural layer, covering about 0.5 ha.

Site: LS-HHB-1 (Year 10)

County: Lanshan

FIGURE 3.95. Gouwa (LS-GW-1) situated on a low rise in the alluvium above a tributary of the Zhuzi River.

FIGURE 3.96. Yueshi period (*top row, left to right*: *qigai* lid rim, *ding* tripod foot) and Longshan period (*bottom, left to right*: Early Longshan *yi* spouted basin rim, Middle Longshan *yi* spouted basin rim), and a stone *zao* (凿) chisel (*at right*) from Gouwa (LS-GW-1[CAA]).

Town: Houhuangbu (后黄埠)

Map: Shangjiazhuang (尚家庄) [1-50-35-(5)]

Period and Period Number: Zhou 860

Cultural Layer: None

Site Description: The site is located on the top a low piedmont spur, at an elevation of 80.8 m, on the west side of a small stream between two reservoirs, and 650 m northwest of the town of Houhuangbu. It was in a terraced tea field about 200 m southwest of a tea factory. The site was entirely from the Zhou period (Western and Eastern), with a relatively high density of sherds over an area of 1.4 ha. The area may have been artificially flattened for terracing. Locations like this, a flat spot above a water source, are common for Western Zhou sites in our survey region. The site may have been part of a larger Zhou community (especially in Western Zhou) with LS-HHB-4 farther south on the same ridge and HHB-5 on the adjacent piedmont slope to the east.

Site: LS-HHB-5 (Year 10)

County: Lanshan

Town: Houhuangbu (后黄埠)

Map: Shangjiazhuang (尚家庄) [1-50-35-(5)]

Period and Period Number: Zhou 857

Cultural Layer: Western Zhou period

Site Description: The site is located on top of a low, broad, sloping piedmont ridge, at an elevation of 75 m, 110 m south of a tea factory (Tianrun [天润]), and 550 m north of the town of Houhuangbu. The nearest water source is a stream 60 m to the west. The site was in tea fields. A thin (4 cm) cultural layer was exposed in a road cut on the west side of the site. The site was entirely Western Zhou, covering less than 1 ha. It may have been part of a larger Zhou community (especially in Western Zhou) with LS-HHB-4, HHB-1, and HHB-2 on the adjacent piedmont slope to the west.

Site: Houshaopo LS-HSP-3 (Year 12)

County: Lanshan

Town: Houshaopo (后稍坡)

Map: Jiepailing (界牌岭) [1-50-35-(37)]

Period and Period Number: Zhou 1133; Han 1576

Cultural Layer: Multiple

Site Description: The site is located on flat terrain in the alluvium at an elevation of 10 m, on the northeast and east sides of the town of Houshaopo, and next to the confluence of two tributaries of the Longwang River. The site stretches along the tributary between the Shenhai Expressway (沈海高速) on the north to the highway on the south. Most of the site was planted in winter wheat; a portion was in a fallow cornfield and part was in a grove of poplars. We saw black and gray cultural deposits in the banks at the confluence in the northeast corner of the town. A farmer told us that whole pots had been found in this area and in the poplar grove to the north. We estimated the Zhou component at 3.5 ha and the Han component at

2.8 ha. But the site, extending west under the modern town, was probably larger in the past; today the area is very disturbed.

Site: LS-HMZ-1 (Year 13)

County: Lanshan

Town: Houmazhuang (后马庄)

Map: Houmazhuang (后马庄) [1-50-23-(61)]

Period and Period Number: **Longshan 493**; Han 1605

Cultural Layer: Longshan period

Site Description: The site is located on the top of a broad, low piedmont spur that stretches into the alluvium, at elevations of 40 to 50 m, 100 m north of the Daqu River (大曲河), 400 m east of the town of Houmazhuang, and 250 m south of the highway. Most of the site was west of the road. This is an ideal location, raised but near water, and less than 500 m west of the confluence of a small stream with the main river. Most of the site was fallow, with some areas planted in winter wheat. We observed two cultural layers on the eastern edge of the site. The site was largest in the Longshan period (larger in Early than in Middle Longshan), covering 10.2 ha. We found Han sherds mostly on the southern and western edges of the site, covering 4 ha.

Site: Jinggou LS-JG-3/DXQH-1 (Year 10)

County: Lanshan

Town: Jinggou (井沟)

Map: Shanzihe (山字河) [1-50-23-(54)]

Period and Period Number: Dawenkou 21, 22; **Longshan 407**, 411; Shang 25; Zhou 814, 815, 816, 817, 818, 819, 824; Han 1081, 1092

Cultural Layer: Multiple, for more than one period

Site Description: This large multicomponent site is centered at the town of Jinggou, but extends over a large area of alluvial terrain and the low piedmont ridge north of the town, and at elevations ranging from 13 m to almost 50 m. The site begins in the alluvium on the east side of Dongxiaoquhe village (东小曲河村), just north of the road, and about 450 m south of the Daqu River (we labeled this area LS-DXQH-1 on our maps; areas north of the river are LS-JG-3). The site stretches north to alluvial terrain on the north side of the Daqu River and south of Jinggou (to within 200 m of the west side of Xinxing village [新兴村]). On the west side of Jinggou the site extends for 500 m to within 350 m of the east side of the Xiaoqu River (小曲河). It continues up the piedmont slope, north of Jinggou along an aqueduct that skirts the ridge all the way to its highest part, covering most of the lower slopes.

We made forty-six collections at the site. Collection areas in the alluvium were in winter wheat fields, mulberry groves, poplar groves, vegetable gardens, and fallow fields. Collection areas in the piedmont were in winter wheat fields, fallow fields, and orchards.

The site was largest in the Longshan period, covering 121 ha on both sides of the river. Dawenkou period sherds were found in two main patches. One was on the north side of Jinggou exposed in cuts made when the aqueduct was built (Dawenkou 21). Just south of the aqueduct and north of Jinggou (adjacent to some houses) was a thick cultural layer about 100 m

Figure 3.97. Burnt soil in a cultural layer at Jinggou (LS-JG-3/DXQH-1).

long. There was a patch of burnt soil in the cultural layer (Figure 3.97). Seven stone tools were found in this area, including two fragments, one unknown tool, a *chui* (锤) hammerstone, a *ben* (锛) adze, a *dao* (刀) knife, and a *fu* (斧) axe. Residents of this area have found pottery, including a partial Late Dawenkou cup (Figure 3.98) and an Early Longshan cup (Figure 3.99), and eight stone tools: a *fu* (斧) axe, three *ben* (锛) adzes, a *zao* (凿) chisel, a *dao* (刀) knife, a *chan* (铲) spade, and a *zu* (镞) projectile point. The cultural layer and Longshan sherds extend to the houses and clearly continue underneath, indicating the ancient site core is under the modern town. The other patch of the Dawenkou component was in the alluvial area south of town and north of the river (Dawenkou 22). One small patch of Shang material was found in this same alluvial terrain north of the river (Figure 3.100). Small scatters of Eastern and Western Zhou sherds were found on both sides of the river, although only Eastern Zhou material was found on the piedmont slopes north of Jinggou.

Han period remains were found on both sides of the river and on the piedmont slope. There were large Han sherds and grayish soil roughly 250 to 275 m south of the river, indicating that a cultural layer had been plowed up. Although we initially gave the two Han segments, separated only by the modern town, two separate phase numbers, they were most likely part of one larger Han community. This site was already known to the Rizhao Museum and is a county-level cultural preservation site (China Cultural Heritage Bureau 2007:272–273).

FIGURE 3.98. A Late Dawenkou period *bei* cup collected from Jinggou (LS-JG-3/DXQH-1).

Figure 3.99. Stone tools and Early Longshan ceramic *bei* cup previously collected by a farmer at Jinggou (LS-JG-3/DXQH-1).

Figure 3.100. Late Dawenkou *yan* steamer foot (*left*), Early Longshan *ding* tripod foot (*center*), and Late Shang *li* tripod foot (*right*) from Jinggou (LS-JG-3[CAG]/DXQH-1).

Site: Jijiagou LS-JJG-4 (Year 12)

County: Lanshan

Town: Jijiagou (纪家沟)

Map: Datushan (大土山) [1-50-35-(12)]

Period and Period Number: **Zhou 1081**; Han 1509

Cultural Layer: Zhou period

Site Description: The site is located on a narrow, terraced spur in the low piedmont, at an elevation of 62 m, and 50 m north of the town of Jijiagou. There is a small stream on the north at the base of this low, raised area. The site was in winter wheat and fallow fields (Figure 3.101). On the north side of the slope, just above the stream, we saw an exposed cultural layer in the side of a terrace. The cultural layer contained many Western Zhou sherds (Figure 3.102), some burnt soil, and tiny flecks of charcoal. The layer had been cut into by plowing. There was also a moderate density of Zhou (Eastern and Western) sherds on the modern surface above this cultural layer. One stone tool was found at this site. The site area was small, less than 1 ha. A trace of Han material was found on the slope just north of the small stream. We also collected soil samples at this site; flotation results were published by X. Chen et al. (2009).

Site: LS-JJH-2 (Year 12)

County: Lanshan

Town: Jiajiahu (贾家湖)

Map: Jiepailing (界牌岭) [1-50-35-(37)]

Period and Period Number: Zhou 1129; Han 1578

Cultural Layer: None

Site Description: This site is located on the south side of a defensible, rounded piedmont knob, at an elevation of 47.8 m, 450 m northeast of a large factory, and 750 m east of the town of Jiajiahu. The nearest water source is a tributary of the Longwang River 900 m to the west. The top of the knob is covered with trees. Just south of the grove was a fallow field with a high density of Han sherds. The site is small, less than 0.5 ha. There was a very small scatter of Eastern Zhou sherds north of the trees.

Site: LS-LCG-1 (Year 11)

County: Lanshan

Town: Luochuangou (罗川沟)

Map: Daguanzhuang (大官庄) [1-50-35-(21)]

Period and Period Number: Longshan 435; Yueshi 17; Zhou 921; Han 1220

Cultural Layer: Multiple

Site Description: The site is located on flat ground in the alluvium at an elevation of 28 m, on the southeast side of a tributary of the Zhuzi River, 150 m northwest of the town of Luochuangou. It was in corn and fallow fields at the time of the survey (Figure 3.103). Dark soil was visible in plowed areas and several cultural layers were visible in the exposed bank above the stream, where large sherds were eroding out. We collected Early Longhsan, Yueshi, East-

FIGURE 3.101. Survey crew collecting sherds from terrace edge at Zhou period site Jijiagou (LS-JJG-4).

FIGURE 3.102. Zhou period sherds (*top row*: Eastern Zhou *pen* basin rim and body sherd with intricate design; *bottom row*: two Western Zhou *li* tripod feet) from Jijiagou (LS-JJG-4[CAA]).

FIGURE 3.103. View of LS-LCG-1 in plowed fields in the alluvium.

ern and Western Zhou, and Han sherds in this area (less than 1 ha). Yueshi and Longshan sherds were especially prevalent (Figure 3.104). Longshan and Han sherds also were found to the east, covering 2.6 ha. We found two stone tools. The site may have been part of a larger Han community with LS-LCG-2, 150 m to the east, where we found dispersed Han sherds on the north and east sides of Luochuangou.

With permission from the Cultural Relics Bureau of China, Shandong University excavated this site in July 2007. The excavation results confirmed the data from the survey for site chronology and the nature of the occupation. Because of the location of the site near Liujiazhuang (六甲庄), the excavation report (Shandong University 2016) designated the site as Liujiazhuang.

Site: Liujiazhuang LS-LiuJZ-1/MJGZ-3 (Year 11)

County: Lanshan

Town: Liujiazhuang (六甲庄) and Mengjiaguanzhuang (孟家官庄)

Map: Jufengzhen (巨峰镇) [1-50-35-(13)]

Period and Period Number: Longshan 434; Zhou 909; Han 1213

Cultural Layer: Longshan period

Site Description: The site is located on flat terrain in the alluvium, at an elevation of 15 m, and on both sides of a small bend in the Xiangjialou River (相家楼河). Most of the site is on the south side of the bend and 50 m north of a brick factory on the west side of the town of

Figure 3.104. Yueshi period sherds (*top row, left to right*: *qigai* lid, rim from *he* [盒] box, and *qigai* lid; *bottom row, left to right*: *qigai* lid knob, decorated body sherd, and perforated *yan* steamer rim) from LS-LCG-1[CAA].

Liujiazhuang. This part of the site was in fallow fields, winter wheat, and mulberry. We found Early Longshan, Eastern Zhou, and Han sherds in this area. In a raised area on the north side of the river, 250 m south of the town of Mengjiaguanzhuang, we found more Han and Longshan sherds on both sides of the modern water channel. Many Longshan sherds were eroding from the bank just above the river. We also collected a stone *zao* (凿) chisel there. The site was between 5 and 6 ha for all three periods. Earlier investigators found a bronze *hu* (壶) jar at this site that dates to the early Spring and Autumn period (Yang, Hu, and Xu 1990).

Site: LS-LiuJZ-2 (Year 11)

County: Lanshan

Town: Liujiazhuang (六甲庄)

Map: Jufengzhen (巨峰镇) [1-50-35-(13)]

Period and Period Number: Longshan 437; Zhou 920; Han 1219

Cultural Layer: Han period burial

Site Description: The site is located in the alluvium, at an elevation of 14 m, on the west side of the town of Liujiazhuang, and on both sides of a school. A small stream passes between the town and the site. The site is in fields of winter wheat. We found Eastern Zhou sherds on the east and west sides of the school and estimate the Zhou component at 1.4 ha. There are a few Early Longshan sherds on the east side of the school. We found a decorated Han brick, probably from a burial, near the southeast corner of the school. Farmers reported finding other bricks nearby.

Site: Liujiagou LS-LJG-4 (Year 12)

County: Lanshan

Town: Liujiagou (刘家沟)

Map: Liujiagou (刘家沟) [1-50-35-(20)]

Period and Period Number: Longshan 476

Cultural Layer: Longshan period

Site Description: The site is located on a low rise in the alluvium, at an elevation of 44 m, on the north side of the town of Liujiagou, and on the south side of a tributary of the Zhuzi River. This was an advantageous location (Figure 3.105). We found sherds right up to the houses, so the site likely was at least twice as large as the area we could survey. The area where we collected was in winter wheat and fallow fields. Two cultural layers were visible in the cut and terraced edge of the rise. One cultural layer had been recently exposed by plowing. The soil was very dark or black and the area had a moderate density of Longshan sherds. This layer runs horizontally for at least 15 m. The other cutural layer is at the easternmost edge of the site and had been recently exposed by plowing. The site was largest in the Longshan period (larger in Early than in Middle Longshan), which we estimate was at least 8.3 ha. We found Late Longshan sherds only in one small area. A small area of Eastern and Western Zhou sherds covered an additional 3.1 ha to the east, and a small area of Han on the west was less than 1 ha.

Site: LS-LJGZ-1 (Year 12)

County: Lanshan

Town: Liujiaguanzhuang (刘家官庄)

Map: Datushan (大土山) [1-50-35-(12)]

Period and Period Number: Zhou 1049; Han 1454

Cultural Layer: Han period cemetery

Site Description: The site is located on the top of a broad low piedmont ridge, at an elevation of 61 m, just over 100 m south of the town of Liujiaguanzhuang, and west of the road from that village to Xitushan (西土山). The nearest water source is a small stream 100 m to the north, at the south edge of the town. The site was mostly fallow, but with some winter wheat. We only found a light scatter of sherds (mostly Han, and a trace of Eastern Zhou) in a 4.8 ha area, but we were told that recent earth moving for agriculture had exposed a Han tomb on this ridge. The Han cemetery supposed to have been in this area likely was associated with LS-DTS-5, the very large Han site just to the east. There may have been a mound on top of the cemetery, which was leveled by plowing in the 1970s.

Site: Lingkou LS-LK-3 (Year 11)

County: Lanshan

Town: Lingkou (零口)

Map: Jiepailing (界牌岭) [1-50-35-(37)]

Period and Period Number: Zhou 998; Han 1387

Cultural Layer: None

Figure 3.105. Gary Feinman collecting sherds at Liujiagou (LS-LJG-4), located on the low rise and extending under the modern village.

Site Description: The site is located on a moderate to gentle slope on a low ridge in the piedmont, at an elevation of 32 m, and stretching from the south side of the town of Lingkou to the east side of Jiangjiazhuang (蒋家庄). There are several small streams near the site. It was in winter wheat and fallow fields. Most of our collections were Han sherds, covering 11.2 ha. There was a small area with Eastern Zhou sherds on the south side of Lingkou.

Site: LS-LJZ-1 (Year 10)

County: Lanshan

Town: Liujiazhuang (六甲庄)

Map: Shangjiazhuang (尚家庄) [1-50-35-(5)]

Period and Period Number: Han 1171

Cultural Layer: Possible

Site Description: The site is located in flat alluvium, at an elevation of 24 m, on the north side of the town of Liujiazhuang, east of the highway, and 250 m east of the Zhuzi River. It was in an orchard and cultivated fields. We found a high density of Han sherds in a small area, less than 1 ha. The site may continue south under the modern town.

Figure 3.106. View of LS-LZD-1 in fields between the water channel and the base of the low piedmont ridge in the distance.

Site: LS-LZD-1 (Year 11)

County: Lanshan

Town: Louzidi (楼子底)

Map: Hushanpu (虎山铺) [1-50-35-(30)]

Period and Period Number: Zhou 991; Han 1339

Cultural Layer: Possible

Site Description: The site is located at the base of a low piedmont slope where it transitions into alluvium, at an elevation of 15 m, mostly on the south side of the town of Louzidi, and 50 m northwest of the new Tongsan Expressway (同三高速). There is a small stream on the west side of the site and a modern water channel on the south (Figure 3.106). The area south of town was all Han, covering 2.4 ha. We found many sherds in an area with many greenhouses. Construction of the greenhouses likely disturbed a buried cultural layer. We found a small area of Eastern Zhou sherds in a vegetable garden on the west side of town.

Site: Matuan LS-MT-7 (Year 10)

County: Lanshan

Figure 3.107. Crew surveying Matuan (LS-MT-7) on top of alluvial terrace.

Town: Matuan (马疃)

Map: Jufengzhen (巨峰镇) [1-50-35-(13)]

Period and Period Number: Dawenkou 23; **Longshan 423**; Zhou 891, 892; Han 1186

Cultural Layer: Dawenkou, Longshan, and Western Zhou periods

Site Description: The site is located on a low rise in the alluvium (the first rise above low-lying land just north of the river), at an elevation of 16 m, and 300 m north of a sharp bend in the Zhuzi River. It is 200 m east of a small water channel that flows into the river and 600 m southwest of the town of Matuan. The site was mostly in winter wheat and fallow fields (Figure 3.107). The setting is an ideal location for a settlement. This flat rise may be at least partially artificial, as we found an exposed rich black cultural layer in the edge of the raised terrace. In this area we found several Late Dawenkou sherds in addition to many Longshan sherds (Figure 3.108). By far the most sherds we collected were Longshan (Early and Middle) when the site covered 7 ha. We also collected five stone tools and observed many stone chunks on the surface, which suggest some stone reduction may have occurred at the site (Figure 3.109). Dozens of Han sherds were collected along the north edge of the site, covering 3 ha. Zhou sherds were found in separate discrete scatters: Eastern Zhou sherds on the western part of the site (Zhou 891, 3.2 ha) and Western Zhou sherds on the east (Zhou 892, 1 ha), where we also saw an exposed cultural layer 10 to 30 cm below the modern surface that ran for 10 m.

FIGURE 3.108. Late Dawenkou period sherds (*top row*: *dakouzun* big-mouthed jar rim, *ding* tripod foot) and Longshan period sherds (*bottom row*: left, Middle Longshan *yi* spouted basin rim; *right*, two Early Longshan *ding* tripod feet) from Matuan (LS-MT-7[CAE]).

FIGURE 3.109. Longshan period stone *dao* knife (*left*) and *fu* axe (*right*) collected from Matuan (LS-MT-7[CAC]).

Site: LS-QAX-1 (Year 12)

County: Lanshan

Town: Qian'aixia (前崖下)

Map: Dapo (大坡) [1-50-35-(4)]

Period and Period Number: Longshan 464; Zhou 1032; **Han 1413**

Cultural Layer: None

Site Description: The site is located on a gradual slope in the alluvium, on the first low rise above a stream channel, at an elevation of 31 m. It is 350 m east and southeast of the town of Qian'aixia, on the east side of a small channel. The site extends east 400 m (across a second small channel) to the north bank of a branch of the Zhuzi River. The site was in fallow fields and winter wheat. It was mostly from the Han period, covering 10.4 ha. We found a smaller area of Eastern Zhou material on the eastern part of the site and a small area of Longshan material in the center, just north of a levee.

Site: LS-QJJZ-3 (Year 11)

County: Lanshan

Town: Qinjiajiezhuang (秦家结庄)

Map: Gaowangzhuang (高旺庄) [1-50-35-(22)]

Period and Period Number: Zhou 951, 952, 962; **Han 1301**

Cultural Layer: Zhou period

Site Description: The site is located on a gradual slope in the alluvium, at an elevation of 28 m, between the north side of the town of Qinjiajiezhuang and the southeast edge of Shimenkou (石门口村). It is on both sides of the small stream that runs through the area. The site is in fields of winter wheat, fallow fields (corn was harvested), and vegetable gardens (Figure 3.110). There was a good number of Han sherds in most of our collections, covering 7.3 ha. The site was more dispersed in the Zhou period (Western and Eastern), although we did find an exposed cultural layer of ashy sediment on the north bank of the small stream about 100 m east of the town. There were many Western and Eastern Zhou sherds in this part of the site (Zhou 951), covering 2 ha (Figure 3.111). We found sherds right up to the edge of houses so the site most likely is larger than we could map it. We also found two Western Zhou stone tools (Figure 3.112).

Site: Qulingnantou LS-QLNT-2 (Year 10)

County: Lanshan

Town: Qulingnantou (曲岭南头)

Map: Shanzihe (山字河) [1-50-23-(54)]

Period and Period Number: Shang 26; **Zhou 826**

Cultural Layer: Probably Zhou period, possibly Shang period

Site Description: The site is located on the west side of low piedmont ridge, at an elevation of 24 m, and just east of small stream channel on the southeast side of the town of Qulingnantou. This stream flows north to the Daqu River, less than 200 m to the north. The site was

FIGURE 3.110. View of site Qinjiajiezhuang (LS-QJJZ-3) on a gradual slope in the alluvium.

FIGURE 3.111. Western Zhou period sherds (*top row*: two *li* tripod feet, two vessel rims; *bottom row*: body sherd with applique decoration, shoulder sherd with *chuoyinwen* [戳印文]/punctured decoration, *guan* jar shoulder sherd with *xianwen* [线文]/incisions around the body and *shengwen*/cordmarking) from LS-QJJZ-3[CAB].

FIGURE 3.112. Two Western Zhou period stone *fu* axes collected from LS-QJJZ-3[CAA].

located in fallow fields, vegetable gardens, winter wheat fields, and a cornfield. Sherds were found all the way down to the stream channel. There were areas of gray soil that may have been a destroyed cultural layer. We found a high density of Zhou sherds (especially Western) and some Late Shang sherds in the same area as the gray soil. The site is very disturbed and cut by the modern stream channel, so it may have been larger in the Zhou period than the 1.6 ha that we could document (Figure 3.113). The Shang period area was very small. We later found an area of Eastern and Western Zhou sherds (LS-QLNT-3) just over 100 m to the west on a low piedmont rise on the other side of the small stream channel, less than 25 m south of the town. Both could have been part of a larger community that is now partially covered by the town. The combined site may have been 5 to 6 ha in Western and Eastern Zhou.

Site: Qianshuichegou LS-QSCG-1 (Year 12)

County: Lanshan

Town: Qianshuichegou (前水车沟)

Map: Huangjiayu (黄家峪) [1-50-35-(29)]

Period and Period Number: Dawenkou 28; Longshan 481; Zhou 1123; Han 1562

Cultural Layer: Several for Longshan and Late Dawenkou periods

Site Description: The site is located on a raised area in the alluvium, at an elevation of 19 m, on the north and northeast sides of the town of Qianshuichegou. It is 120 to 200 m west of the Longwang River and stretches to the Jufen highway (巨汾公路, to the west) along the north edge of the town. We found sherds in fallow fields and winter wheat (Figure 3.114). We do not think the raised area is completely natural, as we found cultural layers in several cut banks of the rise on the northeastern side of town. One of the cultural layers was exposed for at least 30 m. Here we found a good representation of Late Dawenkou sherds in a 2.2 ha area. We found Early and Middle Longshan material in a larger area, including on the north side

FIGURE 3.113. Stone ornament from unidentified period (*top row*), Western Zhou period vessel handle (*bottom row, left*), and Late Shang *li* tripod rim (*bottom row, right*) from Qulingnantou (LS-QLNT-2[CAA]).

FIGURE 3.114. View of Qianshuichegou (LS-QSCG-1) situated on low rise in the alluvium.

of town, covering 5.7 ha (Figure 3.115). There also was some Late Longshan pottery in the site core. We found a Longshan spindle whorl and two stone tools (Figure 3.116). Western and Eastern Zhou sherds were present more on the western part of the site, also covering 5.7 ha. There was a light scatter of Han sherds on the western part as well, covering 3.5 ha. The north part of the site likely was cut by an old river channel, so the site may have been larger than we were able to map. The Han component could have been part of a larger community with LS-QSCG-4, 120 m to the south. This site was known to the Rizhao Museum, with a defined area of 4 ha (China Cultural Heritage Bureau 2007:272–273).

Site: LS-QSP-1 (Year 11)

County: Lanshan

Town: Qianshaopo (前哨坡)

Map: Jiepailing (界牌岭) [1-50-35-(37)]

Period and Period Number: Han 1373

Cultural Layer: None

Site Description: The site is located on a low piedmont spur that extends into the alluvium at an elevation of 12 m, 50 m east of the highway, and 200 m southwest of the town of Qianshaopo. It was mostly in winter wheat and fallow fields. There was a high density of Han sherds, in a 1.3 ha area on top of this flattened rise.

Site: LS-SSY-2 (Year 11)

County: Lanshan

Town: Songshuyuan (松树园)

Map: Jiepailing (界牌岭) [1-50-35-(37)]

Period and Period Number: Longshan 457; Zhou 993, 997; Han 1344

Cultural Layer: None

Site Description: The site is located on flat alluvium at an elevation of 9 m, 200 m west of the town of Songshuyuan, 200 m east of the highway, and between 50 and 100 m south of the Longwang River. Most of the site is in a fruit orchard and planted in winter wheat. The entire site was occupied in the Han period, covering 8.8 ha. We found Eastern Zhou sherds (Zhou 997, 5.6 ha) on the eastern part of the site and a much smaller area of Western Zhou materials on its western edge. There is a small patch of Middle Longshan sherds on the eastern section.

Site: LS-SY-1 (Year 12)

County: Lanshan

Town: Shanyu (山峪)

Map: Liujiagou (刘家沟) [1-50-35-(20)]

Period and Period Number: Zhou 1098; Han 1531

Cultural Layer: Zhou period

FIGURE 3.115. Late Dawenkou period (*left: hu* jar base; *middle: gui* tripod handle) and Early Longshan period (*right: ding* tripod foot) sherds from Qianshuichegou (LS-QSCG-1[CAA]).

Site Description: The site is located on a raised area on a piedmont ridge, at an elevation of 51 m, and 75 m west of the town of Shanyu. The nearest water source is a small stream 100 m north of the site. It was in winter wheat and fallow fields. Recent plowing had exposed a rich deposit of Zhou pottery (more Western than Eastern). There was just a trace of Han period material. The site was small, less than 1 ha. It was most likely part of the same larger site with LS-SY-2, 120 m to the north, where we found another dense concentration of Zhou pottery.

Site: LS-SY-2 (Year 12)

County: Lanshan

Town: Shanyu (山峪)

Map: Liujiagou (刘家沟) [1-50-35-(20)]

Period and Period Number: Zhou 1096; Han 1530

Cultural Layer: Possible

Site Description: The site is located on flat raised area at the tip of a piedmont spur, at an elevation of 48 m, 30 m west of the town of Shanyu. The nearest water source is a small stream 80 m to the west. We found a moderate density of Zhou sherds (Eastern and Western) and a trace of Han material in a deeply plowed fallow field. The plowing most likely disturbed a lower cultural deposit. The site was not large, less than 1 ha. Most likely it was part of the same larger site with LS-SY-1, 120 m to the south, where we found another dense concentration of Zhou pottery.

FIGURE 3.116. A Longshan period stone *zao* chisel from Qianshuichegou (LS-QSCG-1[CAA]).

Site: LS-TSDZ-1 (Year 12)

County: Lanshan

Town: Tushandongzhuang (土山东庄)

Map: Datushan (大土山) [1-50-35-(12)]

Period and Period Number: Han 1457

Cultural Layer: None

Site Description: The site is located on flat terrain in the alluvium at an elevation of 33 m, 75 m east of the town of Tushandongzhuang, and 30 m north of the upper branch of the Zhuzi River. The site was located in fallow fields, winter wheat, tea, and mulberry fields, as well as near greenhouses. We found a sparse scatter of Han sherds in a narrow area (approximately 200 m east–west and 750 m north–south), covering 14.6 ha. The site was probably part of a larger Han community with LS-DTS-5 south of the river.

Site: Xiaocun LS-XC-2, 4 (Year 11)

County: Lanshan

Town: Xiaocun (小村)

Map: Qiaonantou (桥南头) [1-50-35-(38)]

Period and Period Number: Longshan 459; Zhou 1008, 1009, 1010, 1011, 1021; **Han 1360**

Cultural Layer: Longshan period

Site Description: This large site is located on a series of low piedmont ridges and lower alluvial terrain, at elevations ranging from 10 to 20 m, on the south and east sides of the town of Xiaocun, and on the south side of Hanjiacun (韩家村) and Dacun (大村). We found sherds in all open areas between these latter two towns, on both sides of the railroad, so the site clearly continues under the town. This site had been heavily damaged by modern construction, brick factories, and kilns. The piedmont slopes where the site is located are at the base of steep mountains; erosion and runoff have washed away parts of the site. Several streams pass through the site. Most of the piedmont slopes not covered with brick factories were fallow fields and interspersed with fields of winter wheat; in these areas we found many sherds (Figure 3.117). Our collections at the site were dominated by Han sherds, which were in every collection we made. Our minimal estimate for this site is 28.6 ha, but this does not include areas in the modern town where it was not possible to check for sherds. Zhou period sherds (Western and Eastern) were found in several much smaller concentrations throughout the site, none larger than about 2 ha. The only Longshan pottery we found was associated with a cultural layer that was exposed by channel downcutting, approximately 150 m south of Xiaocun. The soil in this cultural layer was gray. Most of the Longshan sherds were found in this cutural layer, in an area smaller than 0.5 ha.

The Han component of the site was part of a much larger Han community on the lower broad piedmont slopes at the base of the mountains by Lanshan that includes LS-XC-1/XC-9 and XS-6. The mapped segments are separated by modern towns, brick factories, reservoirs, or gullied slopes that have destroyed the site. The combined site would have been over 150 ha, thus a Tier I site (see Chapter 4). From the upper slopes, there would have been a commanding view of the flatter alluvial area to the north.

Site: LS-XC-8 (Year 11)

County: Lanshan

Town: Xiaocun (小村)

Map: Qiaonantou (桥南头) [1-50-35-(38)]

Period and Period Number: Han 1364

Cultural Layer: None

Site Description: The site is located on flat piedmont terrain, at an elevation of 20 m, between the old and new sections of the village of Xiaocun, and on the north and west sides of a brickyard. The site is just east of the village of Xiaocun. The nearest water source is a small stream 100 m to the southwest. The collection areas were in winter wheat fields and vegetable gardens. The site is entirely from the Han period. The section we could survey covered 7.7 ha, but the southern part of the site was destroyed by the brick factory. We found sherds right up to the east side of new houses on the west, so the site mostly likely extended farther west. It is part of the larger LS-XC-2, 4 Han period site to the east, from which it is separated by the brickyard. The site was discovered by workers from the local Cultural Relics Bureau, who noted Han burials and other remains (China Cultural Heritage Bureau 2007:272–273).

Figure 3.117. Crew members surveying at Xiaocun (LS-XC-2, 4).

Site: LS-XC-10 (Year 11)

County: Lanshan

Town: Xiaocun (小村)

Map: Qiaonantou (桥南头) [1-50-35-(38)]

Period and Period Number: Zhou 1004; Han 1354

Cultural Layer: Possible Han period burial

Site Description: The site is located on flat terrain in the alluvium, at an elevation of 6 m, and 100 m north of new houses between the towns of Dazhuangzi and Hanjiacun, and on the northeast corner of an area covered with fill for the construction of new houses. The fields of our collection areas were were mostly fallow. Some fields, however, were planted with winter wheat and some had cornstalks from the recent harvest. The nearest water source is a channelized stream that cuts through the west side of the site. We found a Han period brick, indicating a possible burial. The site was not large, only 5 ha in Eastern Zhou and 2.8 ha in the Han period.

Site: Xiaodaituan LS-XDT-3 (Year 10)

County: Lanshan

FIGURE 3.118. View of Xiaodaituan (LS-XDT-3) on alluvial terrain under the modern town and extending up the piedmont slopes in the foreground.

Town: Xiaodaituan (小代疃)

Map: Shengjiadaituan (盛家代疃) [1-50-23-(46)]

Period and Period Number: Dawenkou 20; **Longshan 398**; Zhou 797; Han 1047, 1048

Cultural Layer: Longshan period

Site Description: Part of the site is located on a low piedmont rise above the alluvium at an elevation of 30 m on the west side of the town of Xiaodaituan, while the rest is in the alluvium and under the modern town. The site is on the south bank of the southern branch of the Futuan River. It was in vegetable gardens, terraced fields for wheat, and fallow fields at the time of the survey (Figure 3.118). There are several exposed cultural layers on the west side of town. Many fields had grayish soils, reflecting ancient cultural deposits. The cultural layers and most of the surface pottery pertain to the Longshan period, when we estimate the site covered 21.5 ha (Figure 3.119). Some Late Dawenkou ceramics were collected in a small area (2.8 ha) in the northwest corner of town. No Zhou ceramics were found in the higher portions of the site, but some Eastern Zhou sherds were collected from a low alluvial area north of the main part of the site. A sparse scatter of Han materials was noted on the east and west sides of the town and on the higher slopes west of town, covering approximately 13.9 ha. We also collected five stone tools (Figure 3.120). The site was known to the Rizhao Museum and is a provincial-level cultural preservation site (China Cultural Heritage Bureau 2007:272–273).

FIGURE 3.119. Longshan period sherds (*top row*: Early Longshan *qigai* lid, Middle Longshan *guan* jar rim; *bottom row*: Early Longshan *yan* steamer foot and *ding* tripod foot, Middle Longshan *ding* tripod foot on right) from Xiaodaituan (LS-XDT-3[CAD]).

FIGURE 3.120. Stone tools (*top row*: *lian* [镰] sickle; *bottom row*: *ben* adze) collected from Xiaodaituan (LS-XDT-3[CAD]).

Site: Xingfang LS-XF-2, 4 (Year 10)

County: Lanshan

Town: Xingfang (杏坊)

Map: Shanzihe (山字河) [1-50-23-(54)]

Period and Period Number: Longshan 412; Zhou 812; Han 1083

Cultural Layer: Zhou period

Site Description: The site is located on a broad low piedmont rise, at an elevation of 19 m, less than 100 m south of the Daqu River, and on the north and northeast side of the village of Xingfang. It is in terraced fields of winter wheat and some fallow fields. Han sherds were found just north of town and on the low piedmont rise to the west, covering 5.6 ha. Zhou sherds (Eastern only) were found mostly on the northeast corner of the village. Sherds were eroding from the profile of a raised area that had recently been downcut. This raised area likely was not natural. Zhou sherds also were found on a raised area to the north, covering 2.3 ha in all. Longshan sherds were found only in the raised area next to the northeastern corner of the village, in an area just under 1 ha. The site was known to the Rizhao Museum and is a county-level cultural preservation site (China Cultural Heritage Bureau 2007:272–273).

Site: LS-XHZ-5 (Year 12)

County: Lanshan

Town: Xihezhuang (西合庄)

Map: Dapo (大坡) [1-50-35-(4)]

Period and Period Number: Han 1440

Cultural Layer: None

Site Description: The site is located on a moderate slope on low piedmont ridges at an elevation of 63 m, on the east side of the town of Xihezhuang. It is on both sides of the road, extending south to the reservoir and north across a small stream channel. The site extends east all the way to the railroad. Another stream channel crosses through the middle of the site, on the northeast side of the town. These channels flow to the upper branch of the Zhuzi River. The site was in winter wheat and fallow fields. The density of sherds was not high, but the scatter covered a 14.8 ha area.

Site: LS-XJC-1 (Year 11)

County: Lanshan

Town: Xujiacun (徐家村)

Map: Qiaonantou (桥南头) [1-50-35-(38)]

Period and Period Number: Zhou 1020; Han 1363

Cultural Layer: Western Zhou period

Site Description: The site is located on a low piedmont rise between two channels, at an elevation of 17 m, 250 m east of the town of Xujiacun, and 50 m southwest of new construction on the west side of Xiaocun. The site was in winter wheat fields. There was an exposed cultural layer with many Western Zhou sherds, in a small area of less than 0.5 ha (Figure 3.121). It

Figure 3.121. Western Zhou period sherds (*top row, left to right*: *guan* jar rim, *li* tripod rim; *bottom row*: two *li* tripod feet) from LS-XJC-1[CAA].

had been exposed by the construction of new houses nearby. There was only a trace of Han cultural material at the site.

Site: Xujiacun LS-XJC-2, 3 (Year 11)

County: Lanshan

Town: Xujiacun (徐家村)

Map: Qiaonantou (桥南头) [1-50-35-(38)]

Period and Period Number: Dawenkou 27; Zhou 1005, 1007; Han 1356, 1362

Cultural Layer: Dawenkou period

Site Description: The site is located on mostly flat terrain at the transition from the alluvium to the piedmont, at an elevation of 20 m, and on the east side of the village of Xujiacun. Most of the site is probably under the modern village. It is on both sides of a small stream channel on the east side of Xujiacun. The stream flows north to the Longwang River. The site was found in vegetable gardens, wheat fields, and woods (Figure 3.122). On the east side of the village and the west bank of the stream, in a very low area, were several cultural layers with Early Dawenkou pottery. These cultural layers (exposed by digging and farming) included bone fragments, stone fragments, burnt clay, and sherds. The cultural layers were composed of deep gray-black soil. Fifteen stone tools, including three *moshi* (磨石) grinding tools, a *zao* (凿) chisel, a *chan* (铲) shovel, and a *fu* (斧) axe, were found at the site. Additionally, a

FIGURE 3.122. Survey crew members checking exposed deposits in road cut at Xujiacun (LS-XJC-2, 3).

stamped ceramic *fanglun* (纺轮) spindle whorl was found. The area with the cultural layers was approximately 1 ha, but this is a minimum as the Dawenkou site (and maybe a cemetery) is deeply buried and probably extends under the modern village to the west (Figures 3.123, 3.124, 3.125, 3.126, and 3.127). The setting of this site, on the northwestern side of a large mountain near the coast, is similar to two other early Neolithic sites we found (DG-NTL-4 and DLH-1). Dispersed Zhou (Western and Eastern) and Han sherds were found in vegetable gardens and in fallow and winter wheat fields north and south of the village, all around 1 ha or smaller.

Site: Xinliu LS-XL-1–7 (Year 12)

County: Lanshan

Town: Xinliu (辛留)

Map: Dapo (大坡) [1-50-35-(4)]

Period and Period Number: Longshan 466, 467; **Zhou 1033**; Han 1417, 1418, 1419, 1422, 1425, 1426

Cultural Layer: Multiple

Site Description: The site is located on two low piedmont knobs (more than 1,000 m apart) and the alluvial terrain between them, under and around the town of Xinliu, and just south of a bend in the north branch of the Zhuzi River. The site elevation ranges from 36 m in the

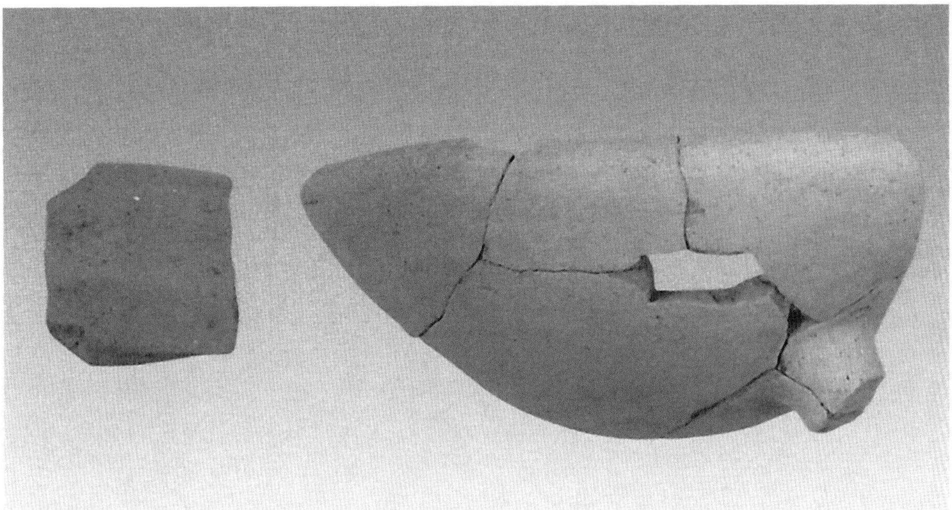

Figure 3.123. Early Dawenkou period sherds (*dou* stemmed dish plate rim with red slip, *bo* footed bowl) from Xujiacun (LS-XJC-2, 3[CAD]).

Figure 3.124. Early Dawenkou period sherds (*top row, left to right*: *bo* bowl rim, *dou* stemmed dish plate rim, *bo* bowl body sherd with white slip and red paint; *bottom row*: *ding* tripod rim, two *bo* bowl rims with red slip) from Xujiacun (LS-XJC-2, 3[CAD]).

FIGURE 3.125. Early Dawenkou period sherds (*top row, left to right*: body sherd with red slip, *hu* jar rim, *ding* tripod body sherd with handle trace, *ding* tripod handle; *bottom row, left to right*: *bo* bowl rim, three *ding* tripod feet) from Xujiacun (LS-XJC-2, 3[CAA]).

FIGURE 3.126. Two Dawenkou period *fanglun* spindle whorls (*left*: possibly Early Dawenkou; *right*: Early Dawenkou) from Xujiacun (LS-XJC-2, 3[CAD]).

Figure 3.127. Early Dawenkou period stone tools (*left to right*: unfinished tool, *zao* chisel, pounder) collected from Xujiacun (LS-XJC-2, 3[CAD]).

alluvium to 58 m in the piedmont. Although the town is completely surrounded by the site, the richest area is on the south and southeastern sides of the town, in areas of vegetable gardens, tea, winter wheat, and fallow fields. The site extends east to a levee on the west side of the river. It stretches to the south to the top of a second low piedmont knob that is 400 m south of the railroad, where we found sherds in fallow fields, winter wheat, and tea fields. The site also extends to the low piedmont ridge on the northwestern side of the town (Figure 3.128). Most of this ridge was fallow, but there were areas of winter wheat and an orchard. This part of the site was defensibly located.

The entire site area has Western and Eastern Zhou remains, covering approximately 138.7 ha (Figures 3.129, 3.130, and 3.131). We saw two Western Zhou cultural layers adjacent to the village (10 cm below the modern surface) on the southeast side of the town, which had recently been exposed by plowing. We collected many *li* (鬲) tripod feet and *guan* (罐) sherds. We found two very small areas of Longshan material: one was Middle Longshan (Longshan 467) on the south side of the town, and the other was Early Longshan (Longshan 466), south of a small water channel 150 m east of the town. We found Han sherds dispersed in many small discrete scatters across the site; the two largest were defensively located on the piedmont ridges (Han 1417, 2.5 ha, to the north and Han 1418, 9.6 ha, to the south).

The site was discovered by a local Cultural Relics Bureau and is a county-level cultural preservation site (China Cultural Heritage Bureau 2007:272–273). Judging by its location and size, the site may be Quqiu Cheng (渠丘城, "the city of Quqiu") mentioned in the "Eighth and the Ninth Year of the Duke Cheng of Lu" section of *Zuozhuan* (左传, *The Commentary of Zuo*), the annotated narrative to the classic chronicle *Chunqiu* (春秋, *Spring and Autumn Annals*) (B. Yang 1981). This possibility warrants further investigation. The English translation of *Zuozhuan* (Durrant, Li, and Schaberg 2016, 2:783) mentions Quqiu as a walled town attacked by the Chu state during a campaign against the Ju state.

FIGURE 3.128. The northwestern part of Xinliu (LS-XL-1–7) on the top and slopes of a low piedmont ridge.

FIGURE 3.129. Zhou period sherds (*top row*: Eastern Zhou *guan* jar rim; *bottom row, left to right*: Western Zhou *li* tripod foot and *li* tripod rim) from Xinliu (LS-XL-1–7[CAJ]).

FIGURE 3.130. Zhou period sherds (*top row*: two Western Zhou *guan* jar rims; *bottom row*: Western Zhou body sherd with applique decoration, Eastern Zhou *li* tripod foot) from Xinliu (LS-XL-1–7[CAL]).

FIGURE 3.131. A broken Western Zhou period stone point (*left*) and *li* tripod foot (*right*) collected from Xinliu (LS-XL-1–7[CAX]).

Site: LS-XS-2 (Year 11)

County: Lanshan

Town: Xiasi (下寺)

Map: Qiaonantou (桥南头) [1-50-35-(38)]

Period and Period Number: Zhou 1017; Han 1370

Cultural Layer: Later Ming or Qing tomb nearby

Site Description: The site is located on a raised area between two gullies in the middle piedmont on the north side of the Lanshan Mountains, at an elevation of 64 m, 200 m south of the town of Xiasi, and just south of an abandoned Ming or Qing period temple that was built on the very tip of a small piedmont ridge. There is a commanding view of the area to the north. The site was mostly in fallow fields, but also in some winter wheat. The area is terraced today. We found Western and Eastern Zhou and Han sherds in a 0.5 ha area.

Site: Xiasi LS-XS-6/LXZ-1 (Year 11)

County: Lanshan

Town: Xiasi (下寺) and Liuxiaozhuang (刘小庄)

Map: Qiaonantou (桥南头) [1-50-35-(38)]

Period and Period Number: Han 1370

Cultural Layer: Han period

Site Description: The site is located on a gradual piedmont slope crossed by two gullies, at an elevation of 55 m, on the northeast side of the town of Liuxiaozhuang, and 200 m west of Xiasi. The southern part of the site was being dug for making bricks when we were surveying. The nearest water source is a stream that runs through the site. We found sherds in both winter wheat and fallow fields. Two cultural layers were exposed in cuts made by the digging. The soil in one layer was very ashy. Many sherds were visible in the other cut profile. The site was entirely from the Han period, covering 7.8 ha. We gave this site its own name because it is separated by modern brickyards from other Han sites to the north. But all these Han concentrations likely were part of a very large Han community on the lower broad piedmont slopes at the base of the Lanshan Mountains. The site had been greatly damaged by brick factories and heavy gullying of runoff from the mountains. We regard it as part of a large Han community.

Site: Xiaoshanqian LS-XSQ-1 (Year 11)

County: Lanshan

Town: Xiaoshanqian (小山前)

Map: Hushanpu (虎山铺) [1-50-35-(30)]

Period and Period Number: Zhou 986; **Han 1329**

Cultural Layer: None

Site Description: The site is located on a long, low flat piedmont ridge, at an elevation of 24 m, 100 m southeast of the town of Xiaoshanqian, and 150 m west of the new Tongsan Expressway (同三高速). Most of the site is between two small streams (and the remains of

Figure 3.132. Survey crew members examining an exposed cultural layer at Yangjiazhuang (LS-YJZ-1).

an abandoned aqueduct). The entire site was from the Han period, covering 5.1 ha. A smaller area in the center had both Western and Eastern Zhou materials. The site is 150 m south of a larger Zhou and Han site to the north (LS-ZJJZ-4). Both were part of a larger community, especially in the Han period.

Site: Yangjiazhuang LS-YJZ-1 (Year 12)

County: Lanshan

Town: Yangjiazhuang (杨家庄)

Map: Huangjiayu (黄家峪) [1-50-35-(29)]

Period and Period Number: Shang 30; **Zhou 1119**, **1120**; **Han 1557**

Cultural Layer: Western Zhou period

Site Description: The site is located on flat terrain in the alluvium, at an elevation of 20.5 m, and 130 m of south of the town of Yangjiazhuang. It extends 700 m to the south to the confluence of a tributary and the Longwang River. The highway crosses the southern part of the site. The area south of the highway was fallow. North of the highway there were groves of poplar, fields of winter wheat, and fallow patches (Figure 3.132). The site was largest in the Han period, covering 10.9 ha on both sides of the highway. Zhou material (both Western and Eastern) was found in two separate, smaller areas: one north of the highway (4 ha) and the other south of the highway (1.4 ha) close to the river. There, at the southern tip of the site just above the river, we found an exposed Western Zhou cultural layer (Zhou 1120). There we also found Late Shang sherds and two stone tools.

Site: LS-YTS-1 (Year 11)

County: Lanshan

Town: Yantaishan (烟台山)

Map: Lanshanzhen (岚山镇) [1-50-35-(46)]

Period and Period Number: Han 1402

Cultural Layer: Han period

Site Description: The site is located on the top of a low piedmont knob called Yantai Mountain (烟台山) on the south side of the Lanshan Mountains, at an elevation of 30 m, and in an area completely surrounded by the houses of the villages of Wangjiazhuang (王家庄) and Yantaixi (烟台西). The nearest water source is 200 m east of the site. The piedmont spur has been quarried, but it has now been partially filled in. There was a light density of Han sherds on the hill. We found a thick Han cultural layer that contained many Han tiles (with nicer than usual designs). The layer is near the top of the knob and was exposed through terracing. From the number and quality of the tiles, it is possible that there had been some sort of Han building there. The location (on the knob) could have been used as an observation point for the coast. The site was in fallow and winter wheat fields, a quarry, trees, gardens, and the modern town.

Site: LS-YTX-1 (Year 11)

County: Lanshan

Town: Yantaixi (烟台西)

Map: Mazhan (马站) [1-50-35-(45)]

Period and Period Number: Zhou 1029; Han 1404, 1405, 1406

Cultural Layer: None

Site Description: The site is located entirely within a modern salt factory, just east of where the Xiuzhen River meets the coast, and south of the expanding Lanshanzhen community. Mostly Han sherds were found in very scattered locations throughout the ponds, and some were found on levee banks in between and bordering the pans. We gave all the components the same site number, but we cannot realistically estimate the size of the site. In one area we found Eastern Zhou pottery. Some of the Han pottery we found may be associated with salt making. In some areas we found porcelains and other modern ceramic vessels for salt making as well.

Site: Yaowangcheng DG-YWC-1/GaJL-1 (Year 9)

County: Lanshan

Town: Yaowangcheng (尧王城) and Gaojialing (高家岭)

Map: Bijiacun (毕家村) [1-50-35-(6)]

FIGURE 3.133. A view of the large Yaowangcheng site (DG-YWC-1/GaJL-1).

Period and Period Number: Dawenkou 15, 16, 17, 18, 19; **Longshan 397**; Zhou 787, 795, 796; Han 1044, 1045, 1046

Cultural Layer: Many, most are Longshan period; two Han period tombs

Site Description: This is a very large, multicomponent site located under and around the modern villages of Anjiayaowangcheng (安家尧王城), Nanxinzhuang (南辛庄), and Zhangjiazhuangzi (张家庄子). The site is in a favorable location centered on a bend in the Nanxin River. It ranges from low alluvial areas near the river, at an elevation of 10 m, to higher piedmont slopes to both the north and south, where the elevation is 30 m. The densest deposits and sherd scatters are just north of the bend in the river, and between and north of Nanxinzhuang and Anjiayaowangcheng. However, we found cultural material in a much larger area. The site extends east to the western edge of Dayaowangcheng village (大尧王城村) and north almost to the top of the low piedmont spur 2 km north of Nanxinzhuang. We found Longshan and Han sherds as far north as 900 m north of the aqueduct. On the west the site extends 750 m west of the river, to a modern north–south ditch. The site extends south of the river for 900 m in the Longshan and Zhou periods, and 1,500 m south in the Han period, all the way to two Han tombs on the northeastern corner of Yayue village (亚月村). On the southwest the site extends to within 250 m of the northeastern corner of the town of Gaojialing (高家岭).

FIGURE 3.134. Rammed earth exposed at Yaowangcheng (DG-YWC-1/GaJL-1).

Most of the area was agricultural. We found cultural materials in a variety of settings, including winter wheat, fallow fields, cabbage pits, and orchards (Figure 3.133). In addition to the rich cultural layers north of Nanxinzhuang, we also found several cultural layers on the south side of the river.

Because we did not know how large the site would be, different sections were initially given different field names. The two largest portions are YWC-1 (north of the river) and GaJL-1 (south of the river), but other large areas also include YY-1 (south), ZJZZ-1, and ZJZZ-4 (north). Although most of the site is now in the Lanshan administrative district, our survey was done before that governmental district was established. Therefore, all the components for this site were given a DG prefix (for Donggang District). Although the district prefix has been changed to Lanshan (LS) in the data files (see Chapter 2), we have kept the DG prefix in the site name here, because that is how all the artifact collection bags stored in the Rizhao City Museum are labeled.

The site was occupied from the Late Dawenkou period through the Han period. We found Dawenkou period remains in five discrete areas: two south of the river, one west of Nanxinzhuang, and two north and northeast of Nanxinzhuang. The largest area with Dawenkou material, on the west, was 5.8 ha. Several others are associated with cultural layers. It seems likely that these scatters were part of two or three larger Dawenkou communities now separated by modern towns.

The highest density of material is from the Longshan period and covers a 367.5 ha area. Most of the cultural layers have Longshan material. In many areas these cultural deposits were at least 0.5 m deep. We recorded many cultural layers on the north side of Nanxinzhuang, where there is a large, raised platform that had been partially destroyed by soil removal. A cut profile on the side of this feature (our CAAA) exposed a raised area, comprising alternating bands of yellow and gray soil (possibly rammed earth layers), that was most likely used as a platform for structures (Figure 3.134). What is likely a sacrificial pit containing four dog skeletons was part of an exposed cultural layer in CAUU, on the south edge of the platform. Just to the east, CABB contained a thick (1.5 to 2 m) eroding cultural layer. Large sherds were found in the cultural layer in CAEE, just to the south of this raised area. Cultural layers were also found in CATT, CAVV, CAWW, CAYY, and CAZZ, all on the north and west side of Nanxinzhuang. Many raised fields just west of the main road (in CAPP, CAQQ, CARR, and CASS) revealed eroding cultural layers. The largest exposed cultural layer ran for 32 m on the south side of Anjiayaowangcheng (in CAII) and may extend farther than was visible at the time of the survey. The cultural layer in CARR, west of the road north of Anjiayaowangcheng, contained what looked like a moat. In addition to sherds, we collected twenty-one stone tools, fifteen of which were diagnostic Longshan tools (Figures 3.135 and 3.136).

Zhou and Han materials were less abundant, but still present throughout large portions of the site. We estimate the Zhou occupation at 226.6 ha and the Han at 309 ha. The Han occupation extended to the south to two Han tombs just north of Yayue.

The site has been surveyed and excavated multiple times (see Chapter 1), most recently in 2019 by the Shandong Team of the Institute of Archaeology of the Chinese Academy of Social Sciences. Bronze weapons of the Zhou period were found (Yang, Hu, and Xu 1990) in addition to Late Dawenkou and Longshan remains. Our estimate for the size of Yaowangcheng is similar to the estimate derived from these excavations (see Shandong Archaeological Team, Shandong Provincial Institute, and Rizhao Bureau 2015; Z. Liang 2016).

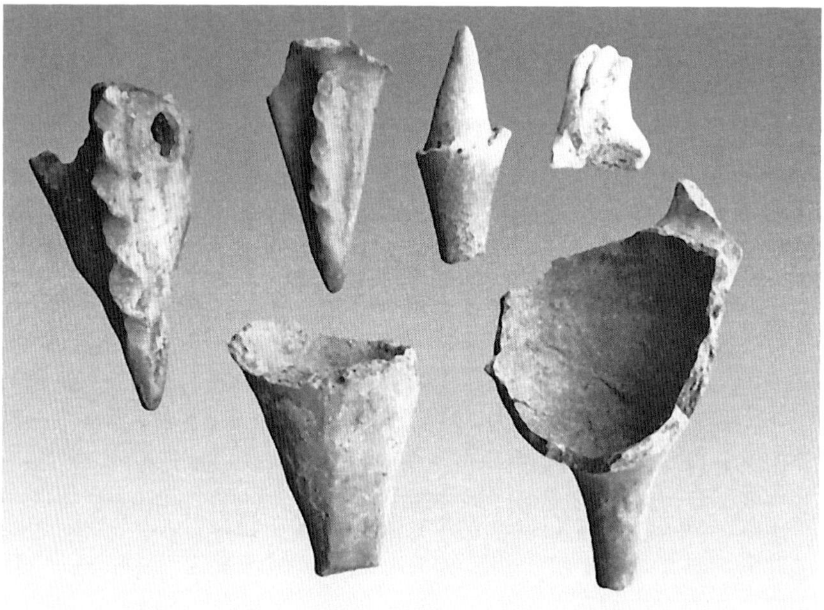

FIGURE 3.135. Longshan period sherds (Middle Longshan, *top row, left to right*: two *ding* tripod feet, *gui* tripod foot attachment, white *gui* tripod handle; Early Longshan, *bottom row, left to right*: *yan* steamer foot, *gui* tripod foot) from Yaowangcheng (DG-YWC-1[CAAI]/GaJL-1).

FIGURE 3.136. Artifacts (*top row, left to right*: two stone *chan* [铲] shovel fragments, unfinished ceramic *fanglun* spindle whorl; *bottom row*: two stone *fu* axes, ceramic *fanglun* spindle whorl) collected from Yaowangcheng (DG-YWC-1[CAAI]/GaJL-1).

Site: LS-ZhuY-1 (Year 11)

County: Lanshan

Town: Zhuyuan (竹园)

Map: Mazhan (马站) [1-50-35-(45)]

Period and Period Number: Longshan 460; Zhou 1030; Han 1391

Cultural Layer: Longshan period

Site Description: The site is located on flat ground in the alluvium, at an elevation of 7.8 m, less than 50 m northwest of the town of Zhuyuan. It is south of the highway and on the west side of a smaller road. It is 900 m north of the Xiuzhen River. We found mostly Han sherds, covering about 1.4 ha, and we made three collections. The Lanshan Cultural Relics Bureau brought us a collection of sherds that were found on the west side of the site. This collection contained Middle Longshan and Han sherds, and only few Zhou sherds.

Site: Zhengjiajiezhuang LS-ZJJZ-4 (Year 11)

County: Lanshan

Town: Zhengjiajiezhuang (郑家结庄)

Map: Hushanpu (虎山铺)[1-50-35-(30)]

Period and Period Number: Longshan 443; **Zhou 985**, 972; **Han 1312**, 1326

Cultural Layer: Multiple

Site Description: The site is located on a slight slope at the base of a broad low piedmont slope that grades into alluvium, ranging between 15 and 25 m in elevation. This large site stretches for more than a kilometer from the southeast edge of the town of Zhengjiajiezhuang, across a large tributary stream, and to the north side of the road to Xiaoshanqian. Most of the site is on the west side of the Tongsan Expressway (同三高速) spreading west to within 150 m of Nandazhuang (南大庄村) and 100 m north of Xiaoshanqian. It extends several hundred meters east of the expressway on both sides of the stream. North of the tributary and south of Zhengjiajiezhuang is a low rise where we found sherds in tea fields, winter wheat, and fallow fields. The only Longshan material we found at the site was in this area. The southern part of the rise closer to the stream had been cut down in the past, thus removing cultural deposits that had continued all the way to the river, so our estimate for the Longshan component (3.2 ha) may be less than half of its original size. Farmers told us many sherds were found in the area when the expressway was constructed. South of the river the terrain grades up into the piedmont. Most of this area was planted in winter wheat or was fallow (Figure 3.137).

On the south side of the road to Nandazhuang, near mulberry trees, there was an area of dark soil with large, thick dark gray sherds and unusual decorative Zhou ceramic forms that may have been from burials. This cultural layer may date to the Spring and Autumn period (771–476 BC). The ceramics are strongly characteristic of Ju culture (莒文化). This part of the site may have been a cemetery.

About 250 m farther south, in the bank of a small stream, and about 250 m east of Xiaoxhanqian, we found a 2 m thick cultural layer mostly associated with Zhou sherds. There were relatively dense concentrations of Zhou and Han pottery in the southern part of the site (Figure 3.138). Stone tools, including a possible *chu* (杵) pounder, a *dao* (刀) knife, and a *moshi* (磨石) grinding stone, were found at the site.

FIGURE 3.137. View of crew surveying Zhengjiajiezhuang (LS-ZJJZ-4).

FIGURE 3.138. Western Zhou period sherds (*left to right*: *guan* jar shoulder with *lanwen* basket design, *li* tripod foot, *pen* basin rim) from Zhengjiajiezhuang (LS-ZJJZ-4[CAP]).

We found Han pottery in most areas of the site, covering 23.7 ha. The largest Zhou occupation (Zhou 985) was south of the river, covering 12.3 ha. We found just a small area of Zhou material north of the river. In both the Zhou and Han (especially Han) periods the site was part of a larger community that included LS-XSQ-1, 150 m to the south.

Wulian County (五莲县)

Site: Dantu WL-Dantu-1 (Year 1)

County: Wulian

Town: Dantucun (丹土村)

Map: Dantucun (丹土村) [1-50-24-(9)]

Period and Period Number: Dawenkou 24; **Longshan 1**; Zhou 1, 2; Han 1, 2, 3

Cultural Layer: None

Site Description: Most of the site is located on a low rise in the alluvium, on the south side of a bend in the Beixiao River, and under the town of Dantucun and in surrounding fields, but it also extends to a low piedmont rise south of the town. The river forms the northern and western boundary of the site. The elevation of the site ranges from 19 to 35 m. Many greenhouses on the site today obscure the cultural remains (see Figure 2.1). Within the boundaries of the site are several quarries, and it is possible that the site extended beyond the river. Middle Longshan (but some Early and Late Longshan sherds are present) is the dominant occupation at the site, covering approximately 131 ha; Longshan material is represented in all eight collections at the site. More than twenty stone tools from the Longshan period were collected, mostly *chan* (铲) shovels or spades and *fu* (斧) axes. Zhou period ceramics (mostly Eastern, with only a small area of Western) were found in four collection areas, covering approximately 37 ha in the northern and western parts of the site. The Han and Late Dawenkou occupations were smaller. The Late Dawenkou occupation, covering about 13.4 ha, is situated in the northern and central areas of the site. The Han material is dispersed in three collection areas, covering 17.5 ha in the northeast. We noted reddish burnt soil in one cut in the northeast part of the site, near the northeastern corner of the town.

The site has been surveyed and excavated multiple times (see Chapter 1). Notable remains include a Late Dawenkou period surrounding wall and Longshan period jade items. The site has national-level cultural preservation site status (China Cultural Heritage Bureau 2007:274–275).

Site: WL-CJG-4 (Year 3)

County: Wulian

Town: Chenjiagou (陈家沟)

Map: Liuguanzhuang (刘官庄) [1-50-23-(8)]

Period and Period Number: Han 130

Cultural Layer: None

Site Description: The site is located on the slope of a low piedmont ridge, 300 m east of the southeastern corner of the village of Chenjiagou, 75 m north of a small stream and modern reservoir, and at an elevation of 42 m. The slope was terraced and planted in winter wheat at the time of the survey. The only cultural remains were a Han period tomb. The site may be part of WL-CJG-3, a small Han site (Han 131) 200 m farther west, at the southeastern corner of the village.

Site: Chaohezhen WL-CHZ-12 (Year 3)

County: Wulian

Town: Chaohezhen (潮河镇)

Map: Liuguanzhuang (刘官庄) [1-50-23-(8)]

Period and Period Number: Longshan 91

Cultural Layer: None

Site Description: The site is located on flat alluvium 600 m north of the town of Chaohezhen and 450 m southwest of Caiyuan (菜园村), adjacent to a modern ditch, and 1,000 m east of the Liuguan River (刘官河), a tributary of the Chao River (潮河). The elevation of the site is 38 m. It was fallow at the time of the survey. We found a dense concentration of Longshan sherds in a very small area of less than 0.5 ha, likely the result of recent farming activity that dug into a buried deposit.

Site: Chaohezhen WL-CHZ-14, 8, 9

County: Wulian

Town: Chaohezhen (潮河镇)

Map: Liuguanzhuang (刘官庄) [1-50-23-(8)]

Period and Period Number: Zhou 130; **Han 150**

Cultural Layer: None

Site Description: The site is located on flat alluvium at the northern edge of the town of Chaohezhen, 1,000 m east of the confluence of the Chao River with two tributaries, the Liuguan River and Chaobai River (潮白河). Several modern ditches cross the site. The elevation of the site is 30 to 35 m. It was in winter wheat and fallow fields at the time of the survey. The site was largest in the Han period, covering 11 ha. The Zhou occupation (Eastern Zhou only) was smaller and more dispersed, covering approximately 6.5 ha.

Site: Caiyuan WL-CY-1 (Year 3)

County: Wulian

Town: Caiyuan (菜园)

Map: Liuguanzhuang (刘官庄) [1-50-23-(8)]

Period and Period Number: Zhou 126, 128; Han 155

Cultural Layer: None

Site Description: The site is situated on the top and slopes of a low piedmont ridge, 300 m northwest of the town of Caiyuan, and extends for more than a kilometer west into the alluvium to within 100 m of the Liuguan River (a tributary of the Chao River). A small modern channel crosses part of the site. The elevation is from 35 to 55 m. Most of the site was in winter wheat at the time of the survey, although the southeasternmost section was in an apple orchard. The site was largest in the Han period, covering 27.2 ha. The Zhou occupation was more dispersed, with two separate scatters of sherds. The larger concentraton (Zhou 126), covering 21.5 ha, was occupied in both Western and Eastern Zhou, while the smaller scatter, covering 4.2 ha, was occupied only during Eastern Zhou.

Site: Donghuaya WL-DHY-1 (Year 3)

County: Wulian

Town: Donghuaya (东花崖)

Map: Dujiahe (杜家河) [1-50-23-(16)]

Period and Period Number: Longshan 87; Zhou 106; **Han 113**

Cultural Layer: None

Site Description: The site is located on flat alluvium at the south edge of the town of Donghuaya, extending south to within 50 m of a small bend in a tributary of the Dujia River (杜家河), and at an elevation of 45 m. Most of the site was in vegetable gardens. It was largest in the Han period, covering at least 5.5 ha. It may have been larger in the past, with part of the site now covered by the town. The site probably was part of a larger Han community with WL-DHY-6 on the south side of the tributary. The Longshan (Early only) and Zhou (Eastern only) occupations were smaller, each covering approximately 2.7 ha.

Site: WL-DHY-6 (Year 3)

County: Wulian

Town: Donghuaya (东花崖)

Map: Dujiahe (杜家河) [1-50-23-(16)]

Period and Period Number: Zhou 98, 105; **Han 110**

Cultural Layer: None

Site Description: The site is located on flat alluvium on the south side of a small bend in a tributary of the Dujia River, approximately 400 m southeast of the town of Donghuaya, and at an elevation of 45 m. Most of the site was in fallow fields or planted with winter wheat (Figure 3.139). The site was largest in the Han period, covering 5 ha. The site probably was part of a larger Han community with WL-DHY-1 on the north side of the tributary. The Zhou occupation (Eastern only) was much smaller and dispersed in two small scatters, both less than 1 ha.

Site: WL-DNP-9 (Year 3)

County: Wulian

Town: Dongnanpo (东南坡)

Map: Liuguanzhuang (刘官庄) [1-50-23-(8)]

Period and Period Number: Han 135

Cultural Layer: Han period tomb

Site Description: The site is located on a low piedmont rise 100 m south of the village of Dongnanpo, 350 m west of a small stream, and at an elevation of 45 m. The site was planted

FIGURE 3.139. Crew surveying Donghuaya (WL-DHY-6).

in winter wheat at the time of the survey. The only cultural remains are a Han period tomb, which is likely part of what may have been a larger Han community, as there are several small Han sites on the piedmont ridge south of the tomb and other concentrations of larger Han sites north and east of the village.

Site: WL-DZ-6 (Year 3)

County: Wulian

Town: Dazhuang (大庄)

Map: Dujiahe (杜家河) [1-50-23-(16)]

Period and Period Number: Zhou 97; Han 107

Cultural Layer: None

Site Description: The site is located on a low rise in the alluvium on the east side of the village of Dazhuang, less than 100 m north of a tributary of the Dujia River, and at an elevation of 40 m. The site is approximately 500 m northwest of the confluence of the tributary with the Dujia River. Part of the site is agricultural, part has been disturbed by quarrying, and the western section is covered by the village. The site covered approximately 8.5 ha during both the Han and Zhou (Eastern only) periods. The Han occupation may have been part of a larger Han community with WL-DZ-1 on the west side of the village.

Site: WL-DZ-10 (Year 3)

County: Wulian

Town: Dazhuang (大庄)

Map: Dujiahe (杜家河) [1-50-23-(16)]

Period and Period Number: Zhou 101, 102; **Han 119**

Cultural Layer: None

Site Description: The site is located on a low rise in the alluvium 350 m northeast of the town of Dazhuang, 150 m west of Wangjiabu (王家埠), and at an elevation of 40 m. The site is 750 m north of the confluence of a tributary with the Dujia River; less permanent water would have been available in a small stream 100 m east of the site. It was in fallow fields and winter wheat at the time of the survey. The site was mostly from the Han period, covering 6.2 ha. Two scatters of Zhou (both Eastern) sherds were smaller, each covering about 1.7 ha.

Site: WL-GST-1 (Year 4)

County: Wulian

Town: Gusitou (崮寺头)

Map: Dayulin (大榆林) [1-50-11-(63)]

Period and Period Number: Zhou 159

Cultural Layer: Zhou period

Site Description: The site is located defensively on the end of a piedmont ridge above the flat floodplain of the Yatou River (崖头河) at an elevation of 54.5 m. A tributary of the Yatou River separates the site from the modern town of Gusitou, which is less than 100 m to the east. Most of the site was in fallow fields at the time of the survey; however, some areas were planted in winter wheat. The site was terraced for farming and a 2 m thick cultural layer was exposed in one cut. The site has the typical artificially flattened top of small, defensively located Shang and Zhou period sites that we found along the western edges of our survey region (Figures 3.140 and 3.141).

Site: WL-JZ-6 (Year 4)

County: Wulian

Town: Jingzhuang (京庄)

Map: Kouguan (叩官) [1-50-11-(64)]

Period and Period Number: **Longshan 105**; Shang 18; Zhou 169; Han 189, 190

Cultural Layer: None

Site Description: The site is located on flat terrain in the alluvium and the adjacent low piedmont slope to the west, at elevations from 45 to 55 m, 100 m west of the Liuguan River, and 200 m north of the town of Jingzhuang. It is on both sides of a small stream with several small modern reservoirs. The slope was terraced for farming and the site was in fallow fields and winter wheat at the time of the survey. The site was largest in the Longshan period (Early only), covering approximately 18.3 ha. We found Zhou sherds (Western and Eastern) along the eastern edge, covering 6 ha, all in low terrain near the river. Shang pottery was noted in a small area in the southeastern corner of the site, covering an area of approximately 1 ha. Han pottery (Han 190), covering 1.4 ha, was noted in the same area. A second smaller scatter of Han pottery (Han 189) was found at the western edge of the site on the piedmont slope.

FIGURE 3.140. Two Western Zhou period *li* tripod feet from WL-GST-1[CAC].

FIGURE 3.141. View of Zhou site WL-GST-1 on top of low piedmont spur.

Figure 3.142. View of WL-LQ-2, 6 on the top and upper slopes of a low piedmont spur.

We collected one stone tool. The site was part of a larger Longshan community (with WL-XJZ-1–8) that may have been as large as 200 ha in Early Longshan and 120 ha in Middle Longshan.

Site: WL-LQ-2, 6 (Year 3)

County: Wulian

Town: Linquan (林泉)

Map: Liuguanzhuang (刘官庄) [1-50-23-(8)]

Period and Period Number: Longshan 90; Shang 7; **Zhou 113**; **Han 126**

Cultural Layer: Han period tomb

Site Description: The site is located on the top and slopes of a piedmont spur that rises steeply from the alluvium, 50 m south of the Chao River. It is approximately 200 m north of the town of Linquan, at an elevation of 40 m, and with a commanding view of areas to the north, east, and south (Figure 3.142). The highest part of the site is covered with pine forest, with tea fields to the south. The site was largest during the Han (2.1 ha) and Zhou (1.9 ha, both Western and Eastern) periods, and there is a Han tomb at the top of the rise. Three deep pits had been dug into the tomb. The Shang and Longshan periods were less well represented, both covering less than 1 ha. Two stone tools found at the site are from the Longshan period; one is a finely made *yue* (钺) axe.

Site: Wangjiayao WL-WJYa-6, 7 (Year 2)

County: Wulian

Town: Wangjiayao (王家窑)

Map: Dantucun (丹土村) [1-50-24-(9)]

Period and Period Number: **Longshan 34**; Zhou 30, 31; Han 31

Cultural Layer: Longshan period

Site Description: The site is located on moderate slopes of a low piedmont ridge 350 m north of the town of Wangjiayao and 600 m northwest of the Beixiao River. It extends around a modern reservoir, at an elevation of 25 to 40 m. Part of the site is in fallow fields; there was a pear orchard in one section and some areas were planted in winter wheat. The entire site was occupied in the Longshan period (Middle only), covering 13.7 ha. A Longshan cultural layer was observed in the side of a shallow ditch at the edge of the site, approximately 0.3 m below the modern surface. Small scatters of Han and Zhou sherds were observed in several areas dispersed across the site, all covering less than 1 ha.

Site: Wangjiayao WL-WJYa-10 (Year 2)

County: Wulian

Town: Wangjiayao (王家窑)

Map: Dantucun (丹土村) [1-50-24-(9)]

Period and Period Number: **Longshan 40**; Han 33

Cultural Layer: None

Site Description: The site is located on flat alluvium on the north side of the Beixiao River and Dantucun, 600 m east of the town of Wangjiayao, and at an elevation of 20 m. It was in fallow fields and planted in winter wheat at the time of the survey. Relatively dense scatters of Longshan sherds (both Early and Middle) were found in a 4.2 ha area. A very small scatter of Han sherds covered an area of less than 0.5 ha.

Site: Wangshitou WL-WST-1 (Year 4)

County: Wulian

Town: Wangshitou (王石头)

Map: Kouguan (叩官) [1-50-11-(64)]

Period and Period Number: **Longshan 95**; Yueshi 1; Shang 12; Zhou 156; Han 196

Cultural Layer: Longshan, Yueshi, Shang(?), and Zhou periods

Site Description: The site is located on a flat river terrace in the alluvium, at an elevation of 70 m, on the north side of the village of Wangshitou. The nearest water source is the Liuguan River, 100 m to the east. Much of the site was in vegetable gardens at the time of the survey. A cut in the bank of the terrace at the north edge of the village had exposed 0.5 m of cultural deposits with Longshan, Yueshi, and Zhou sherds and flecks of charcoal. There also were some exposed pits (Figure 3.143). The site was largest in the Longshan period (both Early and Middle), covering 3.4 ha (Figure 3.144), and the Zhou period (Western only), covering 2.1 ha (Figures 3.145 and 3.146). We made minimal collections of Yueshi, Shang, and Han materials.

Figure 3.143. Luan Fengshi and Fang Hui examining exposed profile at Wangshitou (WL-WST-1).

Figure 3.144. Two Early Longshan period *ding* tripod feet collected from Wangshitou (WL-WST-1).

FIGURE 3.145. Two Western Zhou period *li* tripod feet collected from Wangshitou (WL-WST-1).

FIGURE 3.146. Two unfinished stone tools collected from Wangshitou (WL-WST-1).

The Yueshi and Shang components were very small, less than 0.5 ha, and found only near the cut. Han sherds were found only in the western part of the site, covering approximately 1.1 ha.

The site was discovered by a local Cultural Relics Bureau. Workers recorded its size as 1.5 ha and concluded that the site only contains Longshan remains (China Cultural Heritage Bureau 2007:274–275).

Site: Xiajiazhuang WL-XJZ-1 (Year 4)

County: Wulian

Town: Xiajiazhuang (夏家庄)

Map: Kouguan (叩官) [1-50-11-(64)]

Period and Period Number: **Longshan 94**; Zhou 170; Han 191

Cultural Layer: Longshan period

Site Description: The site is located on flat alluvial terrain, at an elevation of 50 m, adjacent to the west side of the Liuguan River and extends to low piedmont ridges to the west. It is situated on the south, west, and north sides of the town of Xiajiazhuang. Most of the site was planted in either winter wheat or mulberry, and parts were fallow at the time of the survey (Figure 3.147). The site was largest in the Longshan period (both Early and Middle), covering just over 30 ha. In the center of the modern town we found several gray-black Longshan cultural layers and a possible platform (Figure 3.148). The modern town clearly covers much of the Longshan component. Zhou (slightly larger in Western than in Eastern Zhou) and Han sherds were found only in fields south of town, with the Zhou component (4.8 ha) slightly larger than the Han (3.9 ha). The site was the core of a larger Longshan community (with WL-XJZ-5–8 and JZ-6) that may have been as large as 125 ha in Early Longshan and 100 ha in Middle Longshan.

Site: WL-XJZ-5 (Year 4)

County: Wulian

Town: Xiajiazhuang (夏家庄)

Map: Kouguan (叩官) [1-50-11-(64)]

Period and Period Number: **Longshan 110**; Han 192

Cultural Layer: None

Site Description: The site is located on a moderate piedmont slope, at elevations of 60 to 80 m, north of two modern reservoirs, and 150 m northwest of the town of Xiajiazhuang. The area is terraced for agriculture, with fields fallow and in winter wheat at the time of the survey. The site is mostly from the Longshan period (only Early), covering 8.3 ha. A small amount of Han material, covering less than 1 ha, was found at the western edge of the site. The site was part of a larger Longshan community (with WL-XJZ-1–8 and JZ-6) that may have been as large as 200 ha in Early Longshan and 120 ha in Middle Longshan.

Site: WL-XJZ-6 (Year 4)

County: Wulian

Town: Xiajiazhuang (夏家庄)

Figure 3.147. Crew surveying the eastern section of Xiajiazhuang (WL-XJZ-1).

Figure 3.148. Exposed Longshan period cultural layers at Xiajiazhuang (WL-XJZ-1).

Map: Kouguan (叩官) [1-50-11-(64)]

Period and Period Number: **Longshan 113**; Han 194

Cultural Layer: None

Site Description: The site is located on flat alluvial terrain, at an elevation of 55 m, on the west side of the Liuguan River, and 300 m north of the town of Xiajiazhuang. The site was in fallow fields at the time of the survey. It was largest in the Longshan period (Early and Middle), covering 7.4 ha. A small area of Han material (less than 1 ha) was found at the north end of the site, on the east side of the river. The site was part of a larger Longshan community (with WL-XJZ-1–8 and JZ-6) that may have been as large as 200 ha in Early Longshan and 120 ha in Middle Longshan.

Site: WL-XJZ-8 (Year 4)

County: Wulian

Town: Xiajiazhuang (夏家庄)

Map: Kouguan (叩官) [1-50-11-(64)]

Period and Period Number: **Longshan 111**; Zhou 171; Han 193

Cultural Layer: None

Site Description: The site is located on a low piedmont ridge, at elevations of 75 to 90 m, between two small streams, and 450 m northwest of the town of Xiajiazhuang. The area was terraced for farming, with fallow fields and winter wheat at the time of the survey. It was largest in the Longshan period (larger in Middle Longshan than in Early Longshan), covering 7 ha. A small area of Zhou (Eastern only) and Han material was found in the south of the site, covering less than 1 ha. The site was part of a larger Longshan community (with WL-XJZ-1–8 and JZ-6) that may have been as large as 200 ha in Early Longshan and 120 ha in Middle Longshan.

Site: Yaogou WL-YG-1 (Year 3)

County: Wulian

Town: Yaogou (尧沟)

Map: Liuguanzhuang (刘官庄) [1-50-23-(8)]

Period and Period Number: Shang 6; **Zhou 114**; Han 129

Cultural Layer: Present

Site Description: The site is located on top of a low piedmont spur that rises steeply above the alluvium, 250 m west of the small village of Yaogou, about 350 m south of the Chao River, and at an elevation of 40 m (Figure 3.149). From the site there are clear views to the north. Most of the site was terraced and in fallow fields at the time of the survey, although there was some winter wheat. The site covers 1.6 ha and most of the collected sherds are from the Zhou period (Western and Eastern) with only a few Shang and Han sherds. Sherds from all three periods were recovered from a deep cultural layer (more than 1 m thick) in the southern part of the site (Figure 3.150).

FIGURE 3.149. View of Yaogou (WL-YG-1) on the top and terraced slopes of the piedmont rise in the center of the photograph.

FIGURE 3.150. Luan Fengshi and Fang Hui examining an exposed cultural layer at Yaogou (WL-YG-1).

Site: Yatou WL-YT-1 (Year 4)

County: Wulian

Town: Yatou (崖头)

Map: Dayulin (大榆林) [1-50-11-(63)]

Period and Period Number: **Longshan 96**; Zhou 158; **Han 186**

Cultural Layer: None

Site Description: The site is located on flat alluvial terrain, at an elevation of 41 m, under and on all sides of the town of Yatou, and 50 m north of the Yatou River. The part of the site not under the town was planted in winter wheat and vegetables. The site was largest in the Han period (19.6 ha) and then in the Longshan period (larger in Early Longshan than in Middle Longshan), covering 14.4 ha. There is a small area of Eastern Zhou material north of the town, covering less than 1 ha.

Site: WL-ZJG-1 (Year 4)

County: Wulian

Town: Zhujiagou (朱家沟)

Map: Dongjiawa (董家洼) [1-50-12-(57)]

Period and Period Number: Zhou 189; Han 216

Cultural Layer: Han period tomb?

Site Description: The site is located along the slope of a low piedmont ridge, at an elevation of 55 m, running from 50 m northeast of the town of Zhujiagou to 100 m southeast of Xicaijia village (西蔡家村), and 75 m east of a small stream. It was small in both the Zhou (Eastern only) and Han periods, covering less than 1 ha. A Han tomb was exposed in a gully that runs to the northeast corner of town. The tomb was visible as a small opening in the north side of the gully and has several chambers located off a central corridor. We did not find any artifacts associated with the tomb.

Zhucheng City (诸城市)

Site: ZC-DTY-3 (Year 13)

County: Zhucheng

Town: Dongtaoyuan (东桃园)

Map: Sanlizhuang (三里庄) [1-50-12-(50)]

Period and Period Number: Zhou 1209; Han 1650

Cultural Layer: Han period boundary stones

Site Description: The site is located on top of a long, low piedmont ridge, at an elevation of 58 m, and 750 m south of the town of Dongtaoyuan. It is 200 m north of the modern administrative boundary between Zhucheng and Jiaonan, which is also the boundary between Weifang and Qingdao. On the eastern part of the ridge is a possible artificial platform; this feature has been greatly disturbed and plowed down, and so is difficult to identify, although

FIGURE 3.151. A Han period boundary stone from site ZC-DTY-3.

we did find a few Han sherds nearby. Farther upslope on the same ridge, 175 m to southwest, there are three large exposures of natural rock that have been modified into angular shapes with some flat sides (Figure 3.151). The two smaller stones on the east are about 20 m apart. One hypothesis is that these were bases for watchtowers. We found Han sherds nearby. A larger stone is situated 40 m west of the northern area of modified rock. On a flat surface on this stone, part of which has been chiseled, there may be a very eroded inscription (Figure 3.152). We found a large step-like boulder 10 m to the east. There were Han sherds on top of the rock when we cleaned off accumulated soil. The site was 2.8 ha in the Han period.

We found a much sparser scatter of Eastern Zhou sherds in the same area, covering 1.6 ha. Considering its special location, we suspect that the Han site, with possible watchtowers, may have monitored the boundary, along with two other sites in Jiaonan to the south (JN-XDZ-3, 5, and XDZ-6). A boundary in this area may have a long history that can be traced to the Qin–Han period 2,000 years ago—or even earlier. A boundary marker, with inscriptions, used between Qu County (朐县) of Donghai Prefecture (东海郡) and Gui County (柜县) of Langya Prefecture (琅琊郡) found in Lianyungang City (连云港市) is quite similar to the one we found here (F. Liu and Ding 1991; Lianyungang 2001).

Site: Nanzhangjiazhuang ZC-NZJZ-1 (Year 13)
County: Zhucheng

FIGURE 3.152. A partially visible eroded inscription at site ZC-DTY-3.

Town: Nanzhangjiazhuang (南张家庄)

Map: Sanlizhuang (三里庄) [1-50-12-(50)]

Period and Period Number: Dawenkou 29; **Longshan 500**; Zhou 1198; Han 1664

Cultural Layer: Multiple

Site Description: The site is located on the end of a broad low piedmont rise that grades into the alluvium, at an elevation of 31 m, and on the north, west, and east sides of the village of Nanzhangjiazhuang. The site extends 250 m north of the road at the north edge of the village, and to the south within 100 m of the north bank of the Panchi River (蟠池河). The site clearly extends under the modern village. The eastern boundary is a small channel (a tributary of the Panchi River between Nanzhangjiazhuang and Woluozi village [窝洛子村]) that flows into the river. This is a very typical setting for sites in our survey region. Most of the site was in winter wheat and fallow fields, but also in cabbage, mulberries, poplar trees, and haystacks. The richest part of the site was north and west of the village, where we saw four cultural layers. Almost the entire site was Longshan (42 ha, much larger in Early than in Middle). We also found several Late Dawenkou sherds northwest of town, on both sides of the highway, covering 4.4 ha. Han material was found more on the eastern part of the site, including a Han brick, covering 22.9 ha. We found Zhou (Eastern only) materials on the northwestern and western side of the village, covering 8.5 ha. We also found nine Longshan stone tools.

Site: Xiaocaojiazhuang ZC-XCJZ-1, 2, 4 (Year 13)

County: Zhucheng

Town: Xiaocaojiazhuang (小曹家庄)

Map: Sanlizhuang (三里庄) [1-50-12-(50)]

Period and Period Number: Zhou 1206; Han 1656

Cultural Layer: Zhou period

Site Description: The site is located on the first low rise in the alluvium above the Panchi River, at an elevation of 30 m, and on the east side of the village of Xiaocaojiazhuang. The rise is 150 m south of the levee on the south side of the river (Figure 3.153). The richest part of the site was in a poplar grove, where we saw many Zhou sherds in the terrace edge, but we also collected sherds in tea fields to the west. It was an ideal setting for a settlement. Given the richness of the deposits near the village (in ZC-XCJZ-1), we suspect the site extended under the village and was larger than the 0.75 ha area where we collected Zhou sherds (Western and Eastern). Han sherds were dispersed over a larger area (2.6 ha), including the area with Zhou sherds and the scatters in the alluvium closer to the river (ZC-XCJZ-2, 4).

Site: Xiejiazhuangzi ZC-XJZZ-1 (Year 13)

County: Zhucheng

Town: Xiejiazhuangzi (解家庄子)

Map: Sanlizhuang (三里庄) [1-50-12-(50)]

Period and Period Number: Longshan 502; Shang 31; Zhou 1199; Han 1663

Cultural Layer: Probably more than one

Site Description: The site is located on a low alluvial rise, at an elevation of 27 m, on the south side of the Panchi River, and between a bend in the river and the north side of the village of Xiejiazhuangzi. The site most likely extends under the village. Most of the site was planted in winter wheat and cabbage; some fields were fallow. We found a cultural layer and other dense sherd concentrations 50 to 100 m north of the village on both sides of the road. We found Longshan (Early and Middle), local Shang-style, Eastern and Western Zhou, and Han sherds in a relatively small area; the Zhou area was the largest at 4.8 ha and the Shang area was smallest at 1.6 ha. The site may have been part of a larger community north of the river that includes sites at Nanzhangjiazhuang.

Site: ZC-XSL-1 (Year 13)

County: Zhucheng

Town: Xiaoshiling (小石岭)

Map: Sanlizhuang (三里庄) [1-50-12-(50)]

Period and Period Number: Longshan 1504; Han 1733

Cultural Layer: Earthen mound

Site Description: The site is located on the flat top of a low piedmont ridge, at an elevation of 38 m, 130 m northeast of the highest part of the ridge, and 400 m southwest of the town of Xiaoshiling. The area was fallow land. The site is a large earthern mound similar to Han tombs we have found elsewhere. The mound or platform was partly plowed down and had

Figure 3.153. Crew surveying the alluvial terrace where ZC-XCJZ-1, 2, 4 is situated.

a looter's pit dug into it. The mound fill contained very fine yellow sediment; near its base we saw a few Longshan (Early and Middle) sherds. It is likely that the earthen feature was constructed on top of an earlier, small Longshan site (Early and Middle), covering less than 0.5 ha. There were no Longshan sherds on the mound surface.

There were no Han sherds associated with this feature, but the mound is 1,050 m lower on the same piedmont ridge where ZD-DTY-3 is located. We found another possible Han mound or platform that was greatly leveled and possible Han boundary marker stones. We think this feature also dates to the Han period.

CHAPTER FOUR

Regional Settlement Patterns and the Development of Complex Societies

Unraveling long-term changes in ancient complex societies is dependent on the empirical products of archaeological investigation. Although documentary records may also serve this aim in some geographic locales, a dependence on written histories alone often privileges power (e.g., Deetz 1977; Brinkman 1984; Marcus 1992; Feinman 1997) by emphasizing core areas at the expense of outlying domains and underclasses (Wright 2005). Archaeology is most effective for understanding the dynamics of long-term change in early complex societies when we study the past at several analytical scales simultaneously. Systematic settlement pattern survey has been a key component of this multiscalar approach that yields information that is often inaccessible through excavations alone and left unexpressed in written texts.

This volume presents the findings and illustrates the contributions of thirteen seasons of systematic settlement pattern survey in a coastal region of southeastern Shandong Province, China. We argue that these survey findings are important for understanding the long-term changes in early complex societies in this region, as well as for the significant role that this field procedure can have for the investigation of early Chinese civilization more generally. These findings also support the growing recognition that early Chinese civilization did not have one core, but rather was multicentric (e.g., Wright 2005). There is abundant evidence for the development of complex societies during the late prehistoric period in several areas of China (see L. Liu and Chen 2012:16–17; Shelach and Jaffe 2014; Shelach-Lavi 2015; Underhill 2017).

In northern China, until recently, most research on the initial rise of complex societies has focused on Henan Province and adjacent regions of the Central Plains of northern China, including the middle and lower Yellow River valley. Much current research there for the Late Neolithic period and the Early Bronze Age emphasizes the process of state formation. After Wright (1986), several researchers proposed a model of state formation during the Late Neolithic period that involves multiple competing chiefdoms. According to the model, chiefdoms gradually developed in several areas of modern Henan, Shaanxi, Shanxi, and Shandong Provinces, culminating in the Longshan period, beginning after about 2500 BC. Later, competition for power in one region, western and central Henan, led to the emergence of the first state at least by phase III of the Erlitou period, around 1700–1600 BC (L. Liu 1996a, 2004, 2009; Lee 2002, 2004; L. Liu and Chen 2003, 2006; L. Liu et al. 2004; Campbell 2014; IA CASS 2014; see also Xia 1985). In conjunction with state formation, according to this framework, there was widespread sociopolitical collapse in other regions of northern China. Furthermore, areas beyond Henan were peripheral to the centralization of power during both the Longshan period and Early Bronze Age (Chang 1980, 1983a, 1983b, 1987; L. Liu 1996a, 2000, 2004; L. Liu and Chen 2001a, 2001b, 2003, 2006, 2012; Fang 2003b). Researchers also have emphasized the degree of power attained by later states in the Central Plains, such as the Shang state (see Chang 1980, 1987; Liu and Chen 2012).

One important challenge is to investigate sociopolitical change in regions commonly regarded as peripheral to processes of state formation and that are not mentioned to any degree in the historical record. To date, the diversity of regional polities that developed in northern China during the Longshan period and Early Bronze Age has not been adequately assessed. Although there is consensus that there were multicommunity polities with emerging social stratification, craft specialization (including for fine ceramics and jade), and large centers, there is little agreement about the nature of the regional polities that emerged (see Chang 1987; L. Liu 1996b, 2004, 2009; Luan 1996; Demattè 1999; Underhill 2002, 2017; Shelach and Jaffe 2014). Settlement pattern and excavation data raise the possibility that early states may have developed in more than one region during the Longshan period (see Underhill 2002:32, 2017; N. He 2013, 2018; Shelach and Jaffe 2014).

To understand the rise of Chinese civilization, it is necessary to investigate variation in sociopolitical landscapes that developed in different regions of northern China during the Late Neolithic and Early Bronze Age. Several scholars have suggested that urbanism emerged in several areas of China during the Late Neolithic period (see Chang 1983b, 1987; Demattè 1999; T. Wang 1999; Flad 2018; Owlett, Liu, and Underhill 2018). Yet to make their cases, many researchers have focused on identifying urbanism from the features of single sites, such as settlement size and earthen walls. From this perspective, the development of urbanism is a prerequisite for state formation. L. Liu et al. (2004) note marked population nucleation at the Erlitou site, the center of the early state during the Erlitou period. They also, however, cite valuable regional data for settlement change at Erlitou that contrast with the settlement patterns they identified for other areas of the Yi-Luo River valley (see also Xu, Chen, and Zhao 2004; Erlitou Team IA CASS 2005; L. Liu 2006; L. Liu and Chen 2006, 2012; L. Liu et al. 2019).

There is a great need for more regional-level data from northern China. The development of urbanism as well as the rise of states and their central places should be investigated from a regional, rather than individual, site perspective (Cowgill 2004; Small 2006; Underhill et al. 2021). The benefits of this approach (e.g., A. Smith 2003:189) are evident from areas like Mesoamerica, where significant changes in sociopolitical landscapes, composed of centers and smaller communities, are revealed by regional settlement pattern data (Kowalewski et al. 1989; Kowalewski 1990; Feinman and Nicholas 2013). Systematic regional settlement data from the Valley of Oaxaca, for example, reveal that urbanization at one site, Monte Alban, was accompanied by abandonment of certain smaller sites and a degree of demographic relocation (Blanton et al. 1999). In this report our focus is not on the specific archaeological correlates of urbanism, or even the state, but rather on the long-term processes of social and settlement pattern change (Wright 2006:316).

Our systematic, full-coverage regional survey of two coastal basins in the Rizhao area of southeastern Shandong (see Figures 1.1 and 1.2) provides evidence for patterns of change that do not conform to previous expectations for areas external to the Central Plains. Scholars have regarded southeastern Shandong as peripheral to centers of power located to the west during the Bronze Age, since historical records scarcely mention the area (Cai et al. 1997; Underhill et al. 1998, 2002; Fang et al. 2002). The results from our thirteen years of survey, covering approximately 1,440 km^2, are informative about the development of complex societies and regional demographic shifts during more than one period. In contrast to earlier views, it is clear that large sociopolitical formations with comparatively large centers developed during the Longshan period and Early Bronze Age. Likewise, contrary to traditional views, we argue that southeastern Shandong was not controlled by historically known states until relatively late in the Bronze Age (Underhill et al. 2008; Fang et al. 2012; Feinman, Fang, and Nicholas 2019a).

Below we describe the evidence for rapid development of a four-tiered regional settlement hierarchy beginning with the Early Longshan period, perhaps around 2400 BC (Table 1.1; see below). Sedentary settlements first appeared in the Rizhao area of southeastern Shandong during the Beixin period (c. 5300–4200 BC) and increased in size and number during the Late Dawenkou period, sometime after about 3000 BC. Archaeologists in China have concluded that the time gap between the Late Dawenkou and Longshan periods in southeastern Shandong was short (China–U.S. Cooperative Archaeological Team 2016; Luan 2019). It is likely that the timing of the transition between the Late Dawenkou and Early Longshan periods differed by region on China's eastern seaboard (Haidai). In southeastern Shandong, relatively isolated from northern and western sites in the Dawenkou cultural area, this transition may have taken place later than in other regions, perhaps as late as 2400 BC or even by 2300 BC.

During the Early Longshan period two large regional centers developed—Liangchengzhen in the north and Yaowangcheng in the south. As discussed below, these were centers of mostly contemporaneous polities. There are different patterns of settlement around each center that may represent different control strategies by the elite. Two large polities, possibly early states, developed in the Rizhao area at that time. We also argue that the process of settlement nucleation in the Rizhao area during the Longshan period differs from that proposed for other areas of northern China. We supplement our settlement pattern findings with other data to argue that there were significant changes in the nature of political organization in the Rizhao region, as well as significant demographic changes during the subsequent Zhou (c. 1045–221 BC) and Han (206 BC–AD 220) periods. We draw on both archaeological and historical data to discuss changes in the nature of interactions with centers of power to the west. Our systematic survey in the Rizhao area reveals more diverse trajectories of sociopolitical change in northern China than was previously considered.

Initial Occupation during the Beixin and Dawenkou Periods

The two earliest sites we have identified in the Rizhao area date to the Beixin period (c. 5300–4200 BC). Both sites are small (less than 1 ha) and are located in a piedmont zone in the southern half of our survey area (Figure 4.1). A few other Beixin sites have been identified in several areas of Shandong Province, but never previously in the Rizhao area (Luan 1996, 1997, 2015; Fang 2003a; F. Wang 2013). Archaeological findings pertaining to the Beixin period in Shandong indicate an established agricultural economy, a range of craft goods (low-fired, thick pottery, and stone and bone tools), and pit burials with few grave goods.

Although local researchers have reported a few late Paleolithic sites in the vicinity of our study region (Luan 1996), the Beixin period appears to mark the beginning of increased movement to the area. In other areas of northern China at this time, population densities were higher (see Hosner et al. 2016). Our working hypothesis is that relatively early in the Neolithic period, higher sea levels and marshy land in eastern China (Stanley and Warne 1997; Stanley, Chen, and Song 1999) inhibited extensive settlement in many parts of the Shandong coast (Fang et al. 2002; Underhill et al. 2002; cf. Bennett 2004). One of the Beixin sites, Nantunling (DG-NTL-4), has sherds characteristic of both the Late Beixin and Early Dawenkou periods.

There was a marked increase in the regional population in our survey region during the Late Dawenkou period. Overall, twenty-nine separate locations were mapped, with settlements found in both alluvial and piedmont settings (see Figure 4.1; Table 4.1). Many of these sites are located where larger Longshan sites later were situated. The largest Dawenkou site in the Rizhao area is Dantu (WL-Dantu-1) in the north, near Liangchengzhen. (During subsequent reanalysis of sherds collected during the first field season, we identified Late Dawenkou sherds in several collections.) In 2001, archaeologists excavated substantial remains from Dantu, including a walled enclosure and moat, and estimated the site size at 9.5 ha (Shandong Provincial Institute of Archaeology 2001; Y. Liu and X. Wang 2002; see also Xu 2017). The spatial extent of the area where we identified Late Dawenkou sherds (13.4 ha) incorporates the excavation area.

The largest Late Dawenkou site (5.8 ha) in the southern part of our survey area is one of five sherd scatters in the western part of Yaowangcheng (DG-YWC-1/GaJL-1) that probably constituted one dispersed community. Late Dawenkou pottery was discovered during earlier investigations at this site (Luan 1996:226). Similarly, other clusters are present at Donghaiyu (DG-DHY-1), Fengjiagou (DG-FJG-2), and Jinggou (LS-JG-3/DXQH-1). Donghaiyu, which was partially excavated more than thirty years ago, has yielded remains from both the Late Dawenkou and Longshan periods (Donghaiyu Excavation Team 1976; Luan 1996). To date, no Late Dawenkou pottery has been recovered at Liangchengzhen through either survey or excavation. Three sites in the south with exposed cultural layers yielded larger than usual quantities of Dawenkou sherds (DG-NTL-4, DG-XLZT-1, and LS-XJC-2, 3). At this point we do not have enough evidence, however, from either excavation or survey data to conclude that there was more than a modest settlement hierarchy in the Rizhao area during the Late Dawenkou period. Given extensive research on Late Dawenkou burials in other parts of Shandong, however, scholars have concluded that there is clear evidence for social hierarchy (Chang 1987; Luan 1996, 1997, 2013; Fung 2000; Underhill 2000, 2002; Allard 2001; L. Liu 2004; L. Liu and Chen 2012; Shelach-Lavi 2015; Shandong University 2018; Dong et al. 2019).

A recent focus on habitation contexts at Dawenkou period sites reveals that there was a significant increase in population on the eastern seaboard as a whole. Three-tiered settlement hierarchies are evident from reconnaissance surveys in areas to the west of our survey region (L. Liu and Chen 2012; Luan 2013; Underhill 2017). Also, relatively large settlements emerged in more than one region during the Late Dawenkou period (Luan 1996, 2013, 2015, 2017; L. Liu 2004:193–194; L. Liu and Chen 2012:183; Underhill 2017). Excavations reveal that walled sites appeared during the Late Dawenkou period in Anhui Province at Gaixia (垓下) (15 ha; Anhui IA 2010; Luan 2013:420) and in south-central Shandong at Xikangliu (西康留) (5 ha; Y. Wang and C. Wang 2016; Xu 2017, 1:76). In addition, there are some Late Dawenkou sites in northern Anhui that are surrounded by moats, such as at Yuchisi (尉迟寺) (see IA CASS 2001, 2007; Luan 2013:426, 2017:651–653). Although no walled enclosure was found at the site of Lingyanghe (凌阳河) in the neighboring Juxian area, about 60 km west of our survey region, there is evidence that this site was the center of a three-tiered settlement hierarchy (S. Wang et al. 1987; Luan 2013:420–422). Most recently, the ongoing, detailed

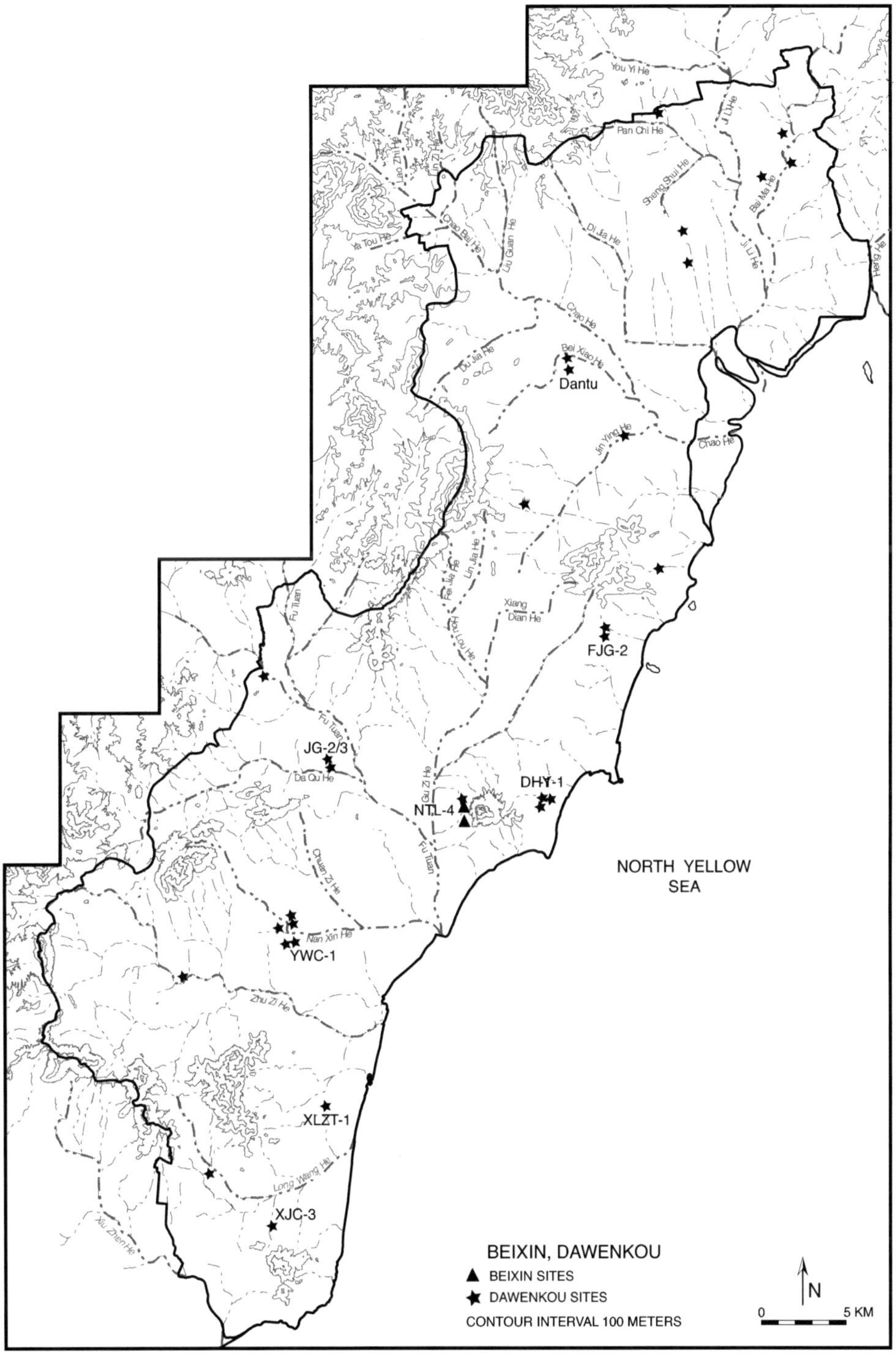

Figure 4.1. Beixin and Dawenkou period sites in the southeastern Shandong survey region.

Table 4.1. Summary of Beixin and Dawenkou sites in the survey region.

Period	Number of sites	Size range (ha)	Total area (ha)	Environmental zone		
				Alluvium	Transitional	Piedmont
Beixin	2	0.5–0.6	1.1	0	0	2
Dawenkou	29	0.1–13.4	53.9	17	7	5

excavations at Jiaojia (焦家) near Jinan, Shandong, have uncovered a walled enclosure, moat, and over one hundred house foundations of various forms within the walled area, in addition to a large cemetery (Shandong University 2018, 2019a, 2019b). At Yuchisi, excavations uncovered row houses (*paifang*, 排房), with each row of compartments possibly representing an extended family (Luan 2013:425). The thorough report for the unwalled Dawenkou site of Jianxin (建新) in southwestern Shandong reveals clusters of houses and burials instead (see Shandong Provincial Institute of Archaeology 1996; Luan 2017, 2:649–650). These diverse remains suggest variation in the ways people organized their settlements in different parts of the eastern seaboard during the Dawenkou period.

The Dawenkou occupation in southeastern Shandong likely was not as extensive as in other regions. Excavations at Dantu (丹土) (Shandong Provincial Institute of Archaeology 2001; see also Luan 2015, 2017) within our survey region recovered a walled enclosure and moat, but Dawenkou period housing remains have not yet been reported. The excavations at Yaowangcheng (尧王城) by the Shandong Provincial Institute of Archaeology should provide more information on Dawenkou period houses and burials.

Based on more abundant survey data for the Dawenkou period, the first substantial migration of people into southeastern Shandong occurred during the Late Dawenkou period. People probably entered this coastal region from the west and south (Feinman, Fang, and Nicholas 2019a). A likely route may have followed the Futuan River, which links to another river in Ju County, where major Dawenkou settlements are known (as discussed above). The Late Dawenkou populations that entered the coastal region of southeastern Shandong likely arrived with an established agrarian economy and social hierarchy. Increased movement into the Rizhao area may have been motivated by social competition with Late Dawenkou communities in areas to the west, or with others to the south. This hierarchical organization was further expanded with demographic growth and full colonization of these fertile but low-lying basins during the Longshan period. Recent radiocarbon dates for Sanlihe and Lingyanghe, two sites beyond our survey region, suggest that the Dawenkou period occupation of southeastern Shandong took place later than in areas farther west (see Dong et al. 2021:277–278).

The Longshan Period

During the Longshan period, likely beginning by about 2400 BC, the pattern of settlement shifted dramatically and the number of sites in our survey area increased to more than five hundred (Figure 4.2; Table 4.2). Although settlements were located in a range of environ-

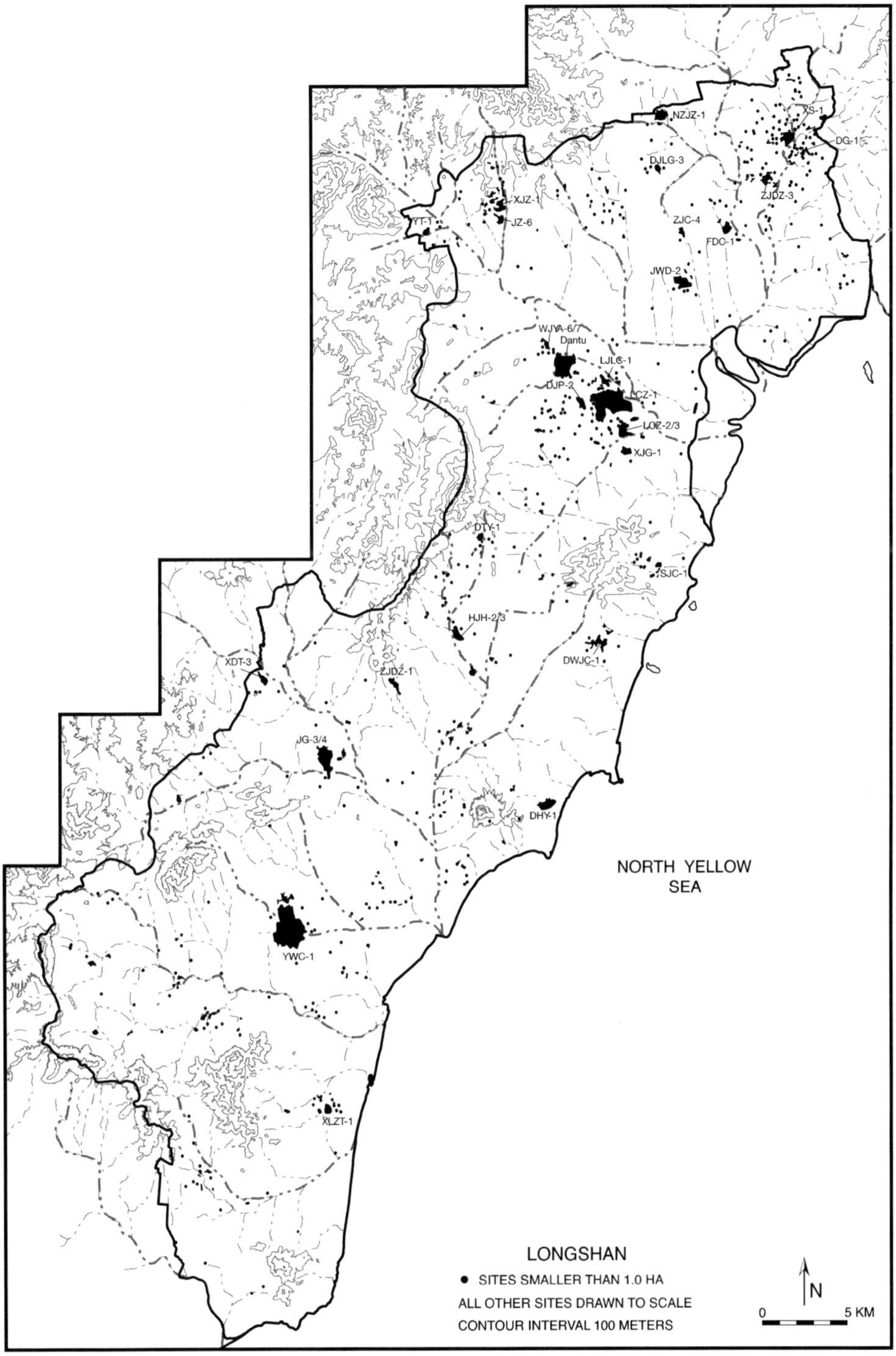

Figure 4.2. All Longshan period sites in the southeastern Shandong survey region.

TABLE 4.2. Summary of all Longshan sites in the survey region by tier in the settlement hierarchy.

Tier	Number of sites	Size range (ha)	Total area (ha)	Average size (ha)	Elevation range (ha)
I	2	272.5–367.5	640.0	320.0	15–18
II	10	41.9–130.7	703.2	70.3	8–35
III	20	10.0–32.6	382.6	19.1	4–65
IV	504	0.1–9.6	571.3	1.1	2–106
Total	536		2,297.1		

	Nearest water source			Environmental zone		
Tier	Small stream	Tributary	Main river	Alluvium	Transitional	Piedmont
I	0	1	1	2	0	0
II	2	4	1	5	1	1
III	12	3	4	11	2	6
IV	286	73	76	261	21	153
Total	300	81	82	279	24	160

		Sites with thin black pottery		
Tier	Average number of vessel forms	Number of sites	Percentage of sites (%)	Total number of vessel forms
I	20.0	2	100.0	40
II	10.6	7	70.0	106
III	8.2	12	60.0	163
IV	1.9	57	11.3	967
Total				

mental zones, two very large centers emerged on or near major river systems: Liangchengzhen (DG-LCZ-1) in the north and Yaowangcheng (DG-YWC-1/GaJL-1) in the south. The systematic regional survey revealed both sites to be considerably larger than prior estimates that were based on excavation and unsystematic reconnaissance (see D. Liu 1958a; 1958b; Shandong Provincial Office 1960; Rizhao City Library and Linyi District Committee 1986; Gao 1995; Cai et al. 1997; Underhill et al. 1998, 2002; Fang et al. 2002). During a resurvey of the western part of Liangchengzhen in 2002 we found the distribution area of surface remains to be slightly larger than what we reported earlier.

Clues about the status of Liangchengzhen were first discovered when archaeologists recovered beautiful jade artifacts and finely made ceramic vessels in 1936 (Yin 1955; Nanjing Museum 1985; Chang 1987; Cai and Luan 1992; Gao 1995; Luan 1996;). Later surveys and test excavations supported these initial interpretations (M. Yuan 1955; D. Liu 1956, 1958a, 1958b, 1972, 1988; Shandong Provincial Office 1960; Rizhao City Library and Linyi District Committee 1986). Similarly, early researchers noted a concentration of finely made goods at Yaowangcheng and estimated it at roughly 52 ha (M. Yuan 1955; D. Liu 1958b). House remains and rice were discovered during other, later brief excavations at the site (Linyi District Office and Rizhao County Library 1985; Shandong Archaeological Team 1994). Results from more recent excavations at Yaowangcheng support our larger estimate (more than 300 ha) for the size of the site (Shandong Archaeological Team, Shandong Province Institute, and Rizhao Bureau 2015; Z. Liang 2016).

Other Longshan sites in our survey region differ markedly in size. We used histograms to order the size of all Longshan settlements. Using natural breaks in these distributions (e.g., Johnson 1973:79; Kowalewski 1990:47), we defined a four-tiered settlement hierarchy in the region as a whole for this period (see Table 4.2). We hypothesize that there were three administrative levels, although any interpretations about the nature of political organization in the region will require adequate supporting data from future excavations. For example, scholars such as Johnson (1973) and Wright (1986) link four-tiered settlement hierarchies to state organization, but there are no artifacts suggestive of a state administration. Nevertheless, some significant changes in regional organization clearly took place during the Longshan period (see below).

Ceramics diagnostic of Early or Middle Longshan were found at roughly half (46%) of the Longshan sites. These sites tend to be larger than those where pottery could only be attributed to Longshan more generally and account for 92% of the Longshan occupied area (Table 4.3). The largest sites were occupied during Early and Middle Longshan. Although we recorded Late Longshan sherds at only thirteen sites, these settlements, including two distinct scatters at Liangchengzhen, tend to be among the largest in our survey area.

The dramatic change in settlement pattern, including the development of a four-tiered site hierarchy, occurred rapidly at the beginning of the Longshan period (Table 4.4; Figure 4.3). Two sites were at the top of this hierarchy. Yaowangcheng grew substantially after the Late Dawenkou period to become the largest center in the region. The other primary (Tier 1) center was Liangchengzhen. During the Early Longshan period these two centers were part of a string of large settlements that extended outside our study region and ran north–south along the coast (Feinman, Fang, and Nicholas 2019a). Although it was not established as early as Yaowangcheng, Liangchengzhen quickly outpaced nearby Dantu (recognized thirty years ago for its fine Longshan period jades; B. Yang 1996). Dantu had been the largest settlement in the region prior to the Longshan period but was now a secondary center to Liangchengzhen. One of the most significant differences between these two major centers (Yaowangcheng

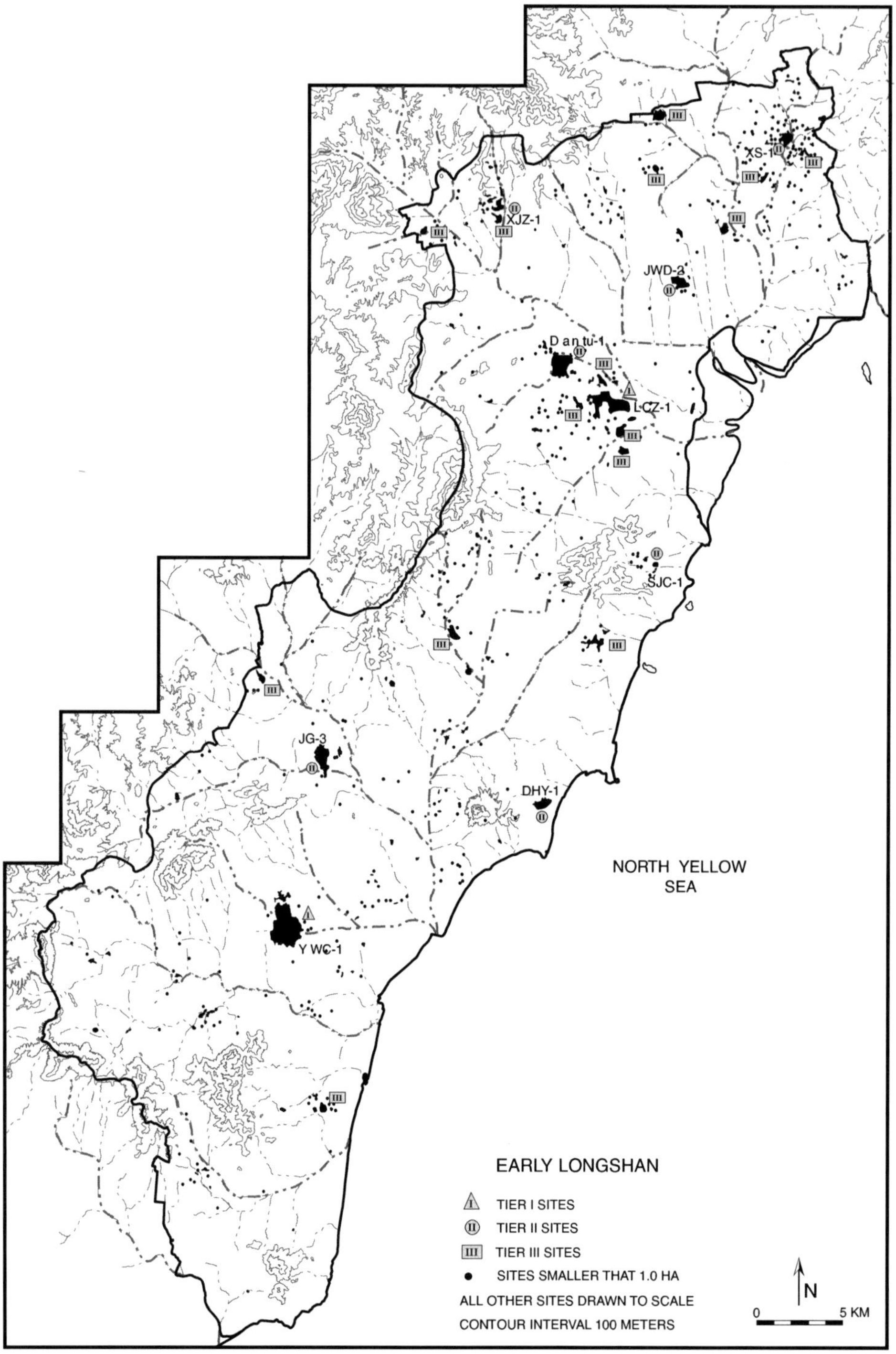

FIGURE 4.3. Early Longshan sites in the southeastern Shandong survey region.

TABLE 4.3. Number and area of Longshan period sites with diagnostic pottery.

Temporal subdivision	Number of sites	Total area (ha)	Average (ha)
Early only	95	140.1	1.5
Middle only	66	75.5	1.1
Late only	1	0.7	0.7
Early and Middle	68	1,309.1	19.3
Early, Middle, and Late	14	584.8	41.8
Unknown	292	186.9	0.6
Total	536	2,297.1	

TABLE 4.4. Summary of Early and Middle Longshan sites by tier in the settlement hierarchy.

Tier	Number of sites	Size range (ha)	Area (ha)	Average (ha)
Early Longshan				
I	2	187.7–367.5	555.2	277.6
II	7	51.0–130.7	562.4	80.3
III	15	13.9–41.9	353.8	23.6
IV	153	0.1–11.68	370.8	2.4
Total	177		1,842.2	
Middle Longshan				
I	2	272.5–367.5	640.0	320.0
II	5	39.9–130.7	361.4	72.3
III	13	12.0–29.2	266.7	20.5
IV	128	0.1–10.0	279.9	2.2
Total	148		1,548.0	

and Liangchengzhen) is the nature of the organization of lower-tier centers around them. Although Yaowangcheng was larger, there was a more developed hierarchy of centers around Liangchengzhen, likely the result of different organizational strategies. The site hierarchy around Liangchengzhen and the greater nucleation of sites in the north are striking patterns that began during the Early Longshan period. A priority for future research should be to trace the possible economic relationships between Longshan settlements of different sizes that are clustered together, such as the flow of tribute from villages to larger settlements.

According to the distribution of Longshan sites with diagnostic pottery, the number of settlements in our study region decreased during the Middle Longshan period, and the overall size of the occupied territory decreased as well (see Table 4.4; Figure 4.4). At the same time, the total number of Middle Longshan sherds in our collections is greater than for the Early Longshan period (Table 4.5). Although we cannot strictly equate sherd quantities with numbers of people, these patterns could indicate that the population of Early Longshan communities was more dispersed. Middle Longshan settlements may have been more densely settled, representing an increase in nucleation of the population. Over half (54%) of the sites with Early Longshan pottery, most of which were very small, did not continue into the Middle Longshan period (see Table 4.3). On the other hand, "Middle Longshan" ceramics may have had a longer duration than Early Longshan diagnostic sherds in the Rizhao area (see the discussion below on Late Longshan and the Early Bronze Age).

The four-tiered site hierarchy continued into the Middle Longshan period, but with some decrease in the number of secondary (Tier II) and tertiary (Tier III) centers (see Table 4.4; Figure 4.4). At the same time, Liangchengzhen increased substantially in size, another possible indication of greater nucleation. This interpretation is supported by excavation and probing data from Liangchengzhen that revealed a densely occupied core area in the center of the site; originally estimated at approximately 100 ha (Luan et al. 2004), this was later revised to around 70 ha (see China–U.S. Cooperative Archaeological Team 2016; Underhill et al. 2021).

Data from both the survey and excavation indicate that the size of the Liangchengzhen settlement increased over time. Another important change during the Longshan period was that the population in the area around Liangchengzhen became increasingly nucleated. The five Tier II and Tier III centers closest to Liangchengzhen maintained or increased in size during the transition from the Early to the Middle Longshan period. Dantu, the largest Tier II center in the region maintained that rank, while DG-LCZ-2, 3 increased in rank from a tertiary to a secondary center. Three Early Longshan Tier III centers close to Liangchengzhen (DG-DJP-2, DG-XJG-1, and DG-LJLC-1) maintained their rank during the Middle Longshan period. We suggest that these changes reflect the increasing power that elites at Liangchengzhen exercised over their immediate region during the Middle Longshan period.

In contrast, only ten of the remaining seventeen smaller centers in the region maintained their rank from Early Longshan to Middle Longshan. And all but three of those ten are estimated to have been smaller in Middle Longshan than they had been earlier. The greatest change was the decline of Early Longshan centers in the area north of Liangchengzhen, where Jiawangdun (JN-JWD-2/LHQ-1), a former secondary center, and three tertiary centers (JN-FDC-1, JN-DJLG-3, and ZC-NZJZ-1) dropped out of the site-size hierarchy altogether. In the northwestern section of our survey area the secondary center of WL-XJZ-1 maintained its rank but lost one of its tertiary centers, WL-JZ-6. The decline of these small clusters of settlements may signal the loss of political rivals in the area. Farther away to the northeast another secondary center, Xisi (JN-XS-1), and two nearby tertiary centers (JN-ZJDZ-3 and JN-DG-1)

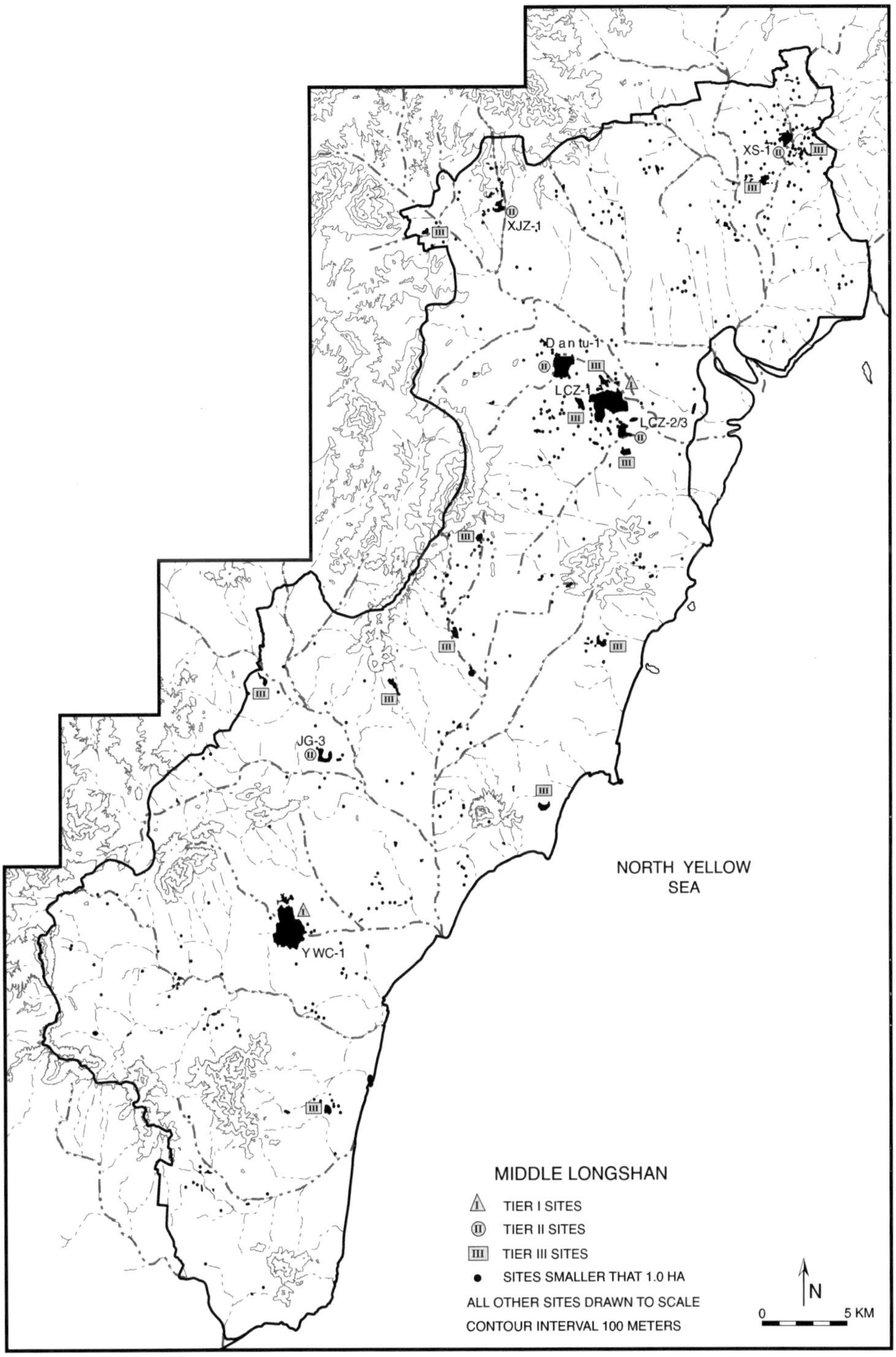

FIGURE 4.4. Middle Longshan sites in the southeastern Shandong survey region.

TABLE 4.5. Total amount of ceramics collected for the Longshan and Zhou periods in the survey region.

Temporal subdivision	Number of sherds	Total area (ha)
Longshan period		
Early	2,926	1,842.1
Middle	3,404	1,548.1
Unknown	13,839	
Late	67	
Early Longshan/ Late Dawenkou	1	
Total	20,237	
Zhou period		
Western	6,490	1,192.5
Eastern	7,778	2,298.3
Unknown	454	
Total	14,722	

maintained their prior ranks. Given the greater distance, these centers may have posed less of a threat (or economic opportunity) to those who wielded power at Liangchengzhen.

Changes in settlement pattern in the Yaowangcheng area to the south are harder to interpret. Secondary and tertiary centers were always more dispersed there, with less nucleation of sites around the primary center. Although Yaowangcheng maintained its size and rank from the Early to the Middle Longshan period, its power over its hinterland may have declined somewhat. Of the three Early Longshan secondary centers between Liangchengzhen and Yaowangcheng (DG-SJC-1, 12, DG-DHY-1, and LS-JG-3/DXQH-1), only Jinggou (LS-JG-3/DXQH-1) maintained its rank, even though it became considerably smaller. Donghaiyu (DG-DHY-1) became a Tier III center and DG-SJC-1, 12 was greatly reduced, no longer a center at all. Four tertiary centers (LS-XDT-3, DG-HJH-2, 3, DG-DWJC-1, and Xilinzitou [DG-XLZT-1] south of Yaowangcheng) maintained their rank during the Middle Longshan period, while two new tertiary centers (DG-ZJDZ-1 and DG-DTY-1/DJZ-3, 5) arose in the western part of this area. These changes in the distribution and number of secondary and tertiary centers likely represent a reorganization of the area between the two largest centers from Early to Middle Longshan.

Regional Sociopolitical Organization in Southeastern Shandong

Our working hypothesis is that Yaowangcheng and Liangchengzhen were centers of politically autonomous, but culturally connected, regional polities during the Early and Middle Longshan periods. An apparent break in the distribution of sites between Yaowangcheng and Liangchengzhen, which is near a natural watershed boundary (between DG-DTY-1 and DG-HJH-2, 3; see Figure 4.2), may represent a buffer zone between two polities. The above-mentioned reorganization of secondary and tertiary centers between the larger ones may indicate that this buffer zone was a contested area. The phenomenon of a buffer zone between polities has been noted for other areas of the world where complex societies developed, such as in Oaxaca, Mexico (Blanton et al. 1999). Another factor to consider is comparative data on the size of late prehistoric polities, given the considerable distance (roughly 34 km) between Liangchengzhen and Yaowangcheng. Hally (1999) cites historical evidence from North America, for example, to propose that Mississippian chiefdoms had a 20 km radius from their centers to their edges.

Another argument in support of two separate polities is based on the difference in the patterns of settlement around Liangchengzhen and Yaowangcheng. Each center has an associated four-tiered settlement hierarchy that developed relatively rapidly. As discussed above, it is likely that Yaowangcheng and at least some of its minor centers developed earlier, and declined earlier, than Liangchengzhen (see China–U.S. Cooperative Archaeological Team [2016] for an expanded discussion about the chronology of Longshan settlements in southeastern Shandong). The contrasting patterns of settlement also suggest different methods of elite control.

As Blanton (2004) notes, the spatial relationship of major to minor centers can reveal significant aspects of regional political and economic organization. The nucleation of settlements near Liangchengzhen during both the Early and Middle Longshan periods is striking and best explained by a deliberate strategy of elites to control labor and possibly the movement of subsistence goods (raw materials, finished goods, or both) to the center. This was a common concern of elites in ancient polities. Steponaitis (1981) predicts efficiency of transport of people and goods when a major center is close to a minor center. The secondary center closest to Liangchengzhen during both Early and Middle Longshan, Dantu, is less than 2 km away. Such clustering of minor centers around a major center suggests a relationship of mutual dependency (Blanton 2004; Pei 2014, 2020). Trigger (1999, 2003) notes this pattern for dynastic Egypt as well. Also, control of labor and subsistence goods was an important strategy of the elite in a key region of northern China during the Early Bronze Age. Oracle bone inscriptions found at Anyang (Yinxu), the Late Shang period capital in northern Henan, reveal that control over labor for farming and craft production was a constant concern of elites (Keightley 1999, 2000, 2012; Underhill and Fang 2004).

The management of labor at both major centers could have centered on the draining of swampy areas for cultivation or the moving of earth to build raised platforms for living areas. An immediate need faced by the people colonizing previously unoccupied parts of the Rizhao area may well have been to coordinate labor for housing and farming. Excavations at Liangchengzhen uncovered raised areas for housing, extensive moats around the settlement, and traces of walls in two locations (Yu 2005; China–U.S. Cooperative Archaeological Team 2016; Luan 2019; Underhill et al. 2021). Phytoliths indicate the presence of aquatic plants (Jin et al. 2004). There may have been some kind of water management for households and for farming, since much rice was recovered in addition to millet (Crawford et al. 2004,

2005; China–U.S. Cooperative Archaeological Team 2016). People who lived in Area 1 at Liangchengzhen prepared the area for housing by adding soil to the surface and creating different features to encourage drainage (see Underhill et al. 2021).

That there was some system of water management for Yaowangcheng is likely as well. Today there is more rice farming in the southern part of our survey region, which has a somewhat milder climate with more available water sources. The management of labor for water control and farming in either the northern or southern sections of our survey region could have been organized by cooperative methods involving kinship networks (see also Underhill 2017; Underhill et al. 2021).

The spatial pattern of secondary centers around Liangchengzhen also would have facilitated the flow of resources to the primary center. The Early Longshan secondary centers within reach of Liangchengzhen in the northeast (especially) are fairly regularly spaced, one at about 7.0 km (Jiawangdun) and another at about 16 km (Xisi, JN-XS-1) from Liangchengzhen. During the Middle Longshan period, when elites at Liangchengzhen consolidated their power, Jiawangdun was largely abandoned, while Xisi, which is farther away, declined only slightly and remained a secondary center.

The clusters of settlements we first noted after five years of survey (Fang et al. 2002; Underhill et al. 2002) remain particularly striking for the northern part of our survey region. The spacing of the secondary and tertiary centers reveals a nested hierarchy of control, particularly in the Liangchengzhen area. Xisi, a secondary center, was close to two tertiary centers (JN-DG-1, 4 and JN-ZJDZ-3), 5.5 km or less, during both the Early and Middle Longshan periods. Also, many tertiary centers served as foci for smaller communities, just as several secondary centers were foci for these same tertiary centers.

Some features of the natural landscape would have been used to transport both people and goods to and from the northern centers. Liangchengzhen is near a main river and most secondary centers are near main rivers or tributaries (see Table 4.2). Secondary centers were situated to access resources from tertiary centers in both piedmont and alluvial settings.

The settlement pattern around Yaowangcheng, in contrast, was more dispersed. There were fewer secondary centers within the reach of elites at Yaowangcheng than for those at Liangchengzhen. There may have been a different strategy of elite control over the area, given the farther distances (over 8 km) to the nearest two secondary centers, Jinggou (Early and Middle Longshan) and Donghaiyu (Early Longshan only). There also were fewer clusters of sites representing smaller site hierarchies, including a less well-defined mini-hierarchy of sites near Jinggou. To the east, Donghaiyu was somewhat more isolated from the tertiary centers in the area, judging from the greater distances.

The natural environment in the Yaowangcheng area would have facilitated the movement of people and goods. Yaowangcheng, Jinggou, and the tertiary (Tier III) center of Dongwangjiacun (DG-DWJC-1) are all near main rivers or tributaries. Given the more dispersed minor centers and lower degree of nucleation of sites around the primary center, however, the settlement pattern in the proposed Yaowangcheng polity indicates less integration than the pattern around Liangchengzhen.

The differential distribution of ceramics provides some evidence for other possible elite strategies in the Rizhao region. In ancient complex societies in Mexico (Feinman, Kowalewski, and Blanton 1984) and other areas, people living in centers tended to have access to a larger range of ceramic vessels. The greatest diversity of vessel forms in our survey region is at Liangchengzhen and Yaowangcheng (see Table 4.2). These include labor-intensive, prestige wares such as thin-walled and polished drinking cups. The diversity of fine-quality ceramic wares also is clear from excavations at these two sites (see Linyi District Office and Rizhao County Library 1985; Nanjing Museum 1985; Luan et al. 2004; China-U.S. Cooperative Archaeological Team 2016; Underhill et al. 2017). Secondary centers have the second highest quantity of forms (average 10.6).

On average, the diversity of ceramic forms is lower at smaller (Tier III and Tier IV) sites, most of which have fewer than eight forms (many of the Tier IV sites have only one or two). A few of these sites, however, have more forms (up to eleven) than other sites, and one Tier III site (Xilinzitou) in the south has fifteen. Furthermore, although fine wares (thin, black, and polished) are more frequently found at primary and secondary centers, they are not restricted to those centers; several smaller sites have those wares as well. Many of these small sites are in the northern half of our survey region within the proposed Liangchengzhen polity, especially in the northeast. The anomalous ceramic diversity at Xilinzitou (DG-XLZT-1), in the south, is indicative of greater importance than would be indicated by site size alone. The only center south of Yaowangcheng, Xilinzitou is roughly equal in distance to that larger center as are the Tier II settlements (DG-DHY-1 and LS-JG-3/DXQH-1) in the southern part of our survey region. Because of its location and ceramic diversity, Xilinzitou may have functioned similarly to the Tier II sites around Yaowangcheng.

On the basis of our preliminary assessment (including discussions with a modern potter who has surveyed clay sources in the area), there are good-quality clays suitable for production of fine black wares in the vicinity of Liangchengzhen (see also Druc et al. 2018). The presence of fine ceramics in small sites could represent the giving of gifts by elites to lower ranking elites in outlying areas. Elites at Liangchengzhen could have occasionally sponsored production of fine wares to give to subordinates in exchange for desired goods or as a reward for services, such as labor and defense. We expect that Longshan elites used a political strategy to maintain and expand their political networks (sensu Blanton et al. 1996). In our ongoing work we are investigating whether Liangchengzhen or Yaowangcheng, or both, were regional centers for production of fine black wares.

The primary centers of Liangchengzhen and Yaowangcheng also would have provided some services to ordinary households in outlying communities, especially those nearby. Elites at these major centers probably legitimized their authority in part through their powerful ancestors, claiming they could offer subordinates spiritual protection as well as physical protection. This argument has been made for Longshan centers in other areas of northern China (Underhill 2002, 2017). It is likely that Liangchengzhen and Yaowangcheng were ritual centers where important ceremonies for the prosperity of the region took place. The excavations at Liangchengzhen uncovered large vessels that may represent feasting activities and other vessels with chemical residues of fermented beverages (McGovern et al. 2005a, 2005b; updated in China–U.S. Cooperative Archaeological Team et al. 2016). For more than one temporal period in China there is evidence to suggest that feasting was a strategy of elites to maintain ties with both commoners and other groups of elites—first with fine ceramic vessels and later with bronze vessels (Underhill 2002, 2018; Reinhart 2015). Elites could have offered feasts in exchange for labor by people from surrounding villages, as first proposed by Dietler (1996, 2001), providing an opportunity to give subordinates gifts of fine vessels.

Broader Implications for Investigation of Regional Polities in China

In our survey region, especially near Liangchengzhen, the nucleation of settlements signals increased interaction between communities. This likely involved a range of households, not just those of elites. Clusters of settlements would have been established to facilitate cooperative relations as well as competitive ones. As McIntosh (1991, 1999, 2005) points out, nucleation of sites at the regional level indicates emerging urbanization, a development that may result in part from efforts to facilitate cooperative relations among households. Cooperative relations among kin groups, especially descent groups, would have formed important economic and social networks during the Late Neolithic period and Early Bronze Age of China (Jing et al. 2013; Pei 2014, 2020). Historical records clearly indicate this for more than one epoch of the Bronze Age. For example, military units and craft specialists often were organized by descent group (Chang 1980; Underhill 2002, 2006). Such economic networks have been observed among modern specialist potters in southwestern China. In areas with good-quality clay, multiple households of potters who are blood relatives collaborate in production (Underhill 2003).

At the same time, there was a more structurally complex regional organization in southeastern Shandong than others have predicted for the Longshan period, with two at least partially contemporary centers, three administrative levels, and dispersed clusters of sites representing mini-settlement hierarchies. Some of the small areas represented by site clusters are relatively well defined geographically on the basis of physical features such as ridges. This organizational structure no doubt facilitated the provision of resources (like laborers and food) to the two major centers, especially Liangchengzhen.

Some researchers have described the survey results from our first five years, which covered an area of 400 km^2 (Fang et al. 2002; Underhill et al. 2002), as indicating a highly integrated territory, on the basis of the large size of Liangchengzhen in comparison to other sites (L. Liu 2000, 2004; L. Liu and Chen 2006). They propose that such a dominant site indicates temporary regional stability and integration, followed by sociopolitical collapse as the Erlitou state rose to power in Henan. We argue that an assessment of the degree of sociopolitical integration in the Rizhao area requires consideration of several factors.

The issue of spatial scale especially is significant. First, expansion of our survey area to the south has shown that there probably were two regional polities in southeastern Shandong, not just one. Relations between Liangchengzhen and Yaowangcheng likely fluctuated, from being competitors in some phases to allies in others. Second, we have already noted the contrasting settlement patterns within the proposed polity areas for Liangchengzhen and Yaowangcheng. Third, the relationship between sites in the northern part of our study area and Liangchengzhen remains unclear, but the degree of integration may not have been great given the distances involved. The more distant clusters of sites (around Xisi in the northeast, for example) may have been partially autonomous.

Some scholars expect that there was a high degree of regional integration in early Chinese states (Demattè 1999; L. Liu and Chen 2001b, 2003; Trigger 2003; L. Liu et al. 2004). For example, it is argued that there was a highly integrated state territory during the Erlitou and Early to Middle Shang periods attributable to elite control over production and long-distance distribution of craft goods such as utilitarian stone tools (L. Liu and Chen 2001b, 2003; Lee 2004; L. Liu et al. 2004) and such resources as salt (L. Liu and Chen 2001b). We suggest that more systematic regional survey in these areas could identify other clusters of sites and provide more possible strategies of elite control. The method also should be useful for untangling relations between the two partially contemporary centers of Erlitou and Yanshi (see Lee 2002, 2004). Political and economic relations between major centers and outlying minor centers even in well-developed states may not be stable. This may be a relevant caveat for interpreting intersettlement relations during the Late Shang period too. Campbell (2009) argues effectively that we should focus on different networks of power in early states, rather than assuming firm control over specific territories. Oracle bone inscriptions reveal that relations between the Late Shang elites at Anyang and people in outlying territories fluctuated considerably. They were allies in some phases and enemies in others (see also Underhill and Fang 2004).

Decline of the Middle Longshan Regional System and the Early Bronze Age

We have found comparatively few ceramics diagnostic of the Late Longshan period and Early Bronze Age (Yueshi and Shang periods) in the Rizhao area and in eastern Shandong south of the Shandong Peninsula more generally (Feinman, Fang, and Nicholas 2019a). All but five of fourteen locations with Late Longshan pottery are in the northern half of our survey region and most are part of or near Liangchengzhen (Figure 4.5). Late Longshan pottery tends to be present in very low numbers at some of the larger sites. Although these sites continue to represent a four-tiered hierarchy, the full significance of the Late Longshan settlement pattern is difficult to interpret at present.

Similarly, we have recorded only a few sites—nineteen—with diagnostic sherds from the Early Bronze Age Yueshi period (c. 1800–1450 BC; see Underhill and Fang 2004; Fang 2013; Shandong University 2016). These sites are dispersed throughout our survey region (see Figure 4.5). Although we found only a few pieces of Yueshi pottery at most of these sites, there were greater quantities of Yueshi sherds at five sites with exposed cultural layers (JN-XS-1, WL-WST-1, DG-QJGZ-1, LS-LCG-1, and LS-GW-1) from disparate parts of our survey region.

The largest concentration of Yueshi pottery extends over 9 ha at Xisi in the northeastern corner of our survey region. No other scatter of Yueshi ceramics covers more than 2.5 ha, and most are much smaller. Elsewhere in Shandong Province, Yueshi sites likely represent small-scale polities independent of political developments in Henan, where the Erlitou state developed sometime after about 1800 BC (Fang 1998, 2003b, 2013; Lee 2004; IA CASS 2014). Given the scarcity of sites with Yueshi pottery in our area and the small number of Yueshi diagnostic sherds present at these sites, it is unclear whether this interpretation applies to our study region. More AMS radiocarbon dates from excavated contexts are needed to clarify the transition between the Yueshi and earlier (Longshan) and later (Shang) periods in different regions of Shandong.

Shang period ceramics also are not well represented in eastern Shandong. From both archaeological and textual data, the main centers of power for both the Early (Erligang) to Middle (c. 1600–1300 BC) and Late Shang (c. 1300–1045 BC) periods were in Henan Province. Sometime during the Middle Shang period another center was established in western Shandong, at Daxinzhuang. This important center continued to be occupied during the Late Shang period and probably represents a colony, judging from the discovery of inscribed oracle bones there (OARC 2003, 2004). Other sites in Shandong with Late Shang-style burials and prestige goods include Subutun and Qianzhangda (Chang 1980; Shandong Archaeological Team 2000; Underhill 2002; F. Li 2006; L. Liu and Chen 2012; Fang 2013; Shelach-Lavi 2015). Based on archaeological and historical data, Late Shang elites aimed to control sea salt in northern Shandong (Fang 2004). Southeastern Shandong, however, most likely was beyond their reach.

We found Late Shang ceramics at only thirty-one sites, dispersed across the Rizhao

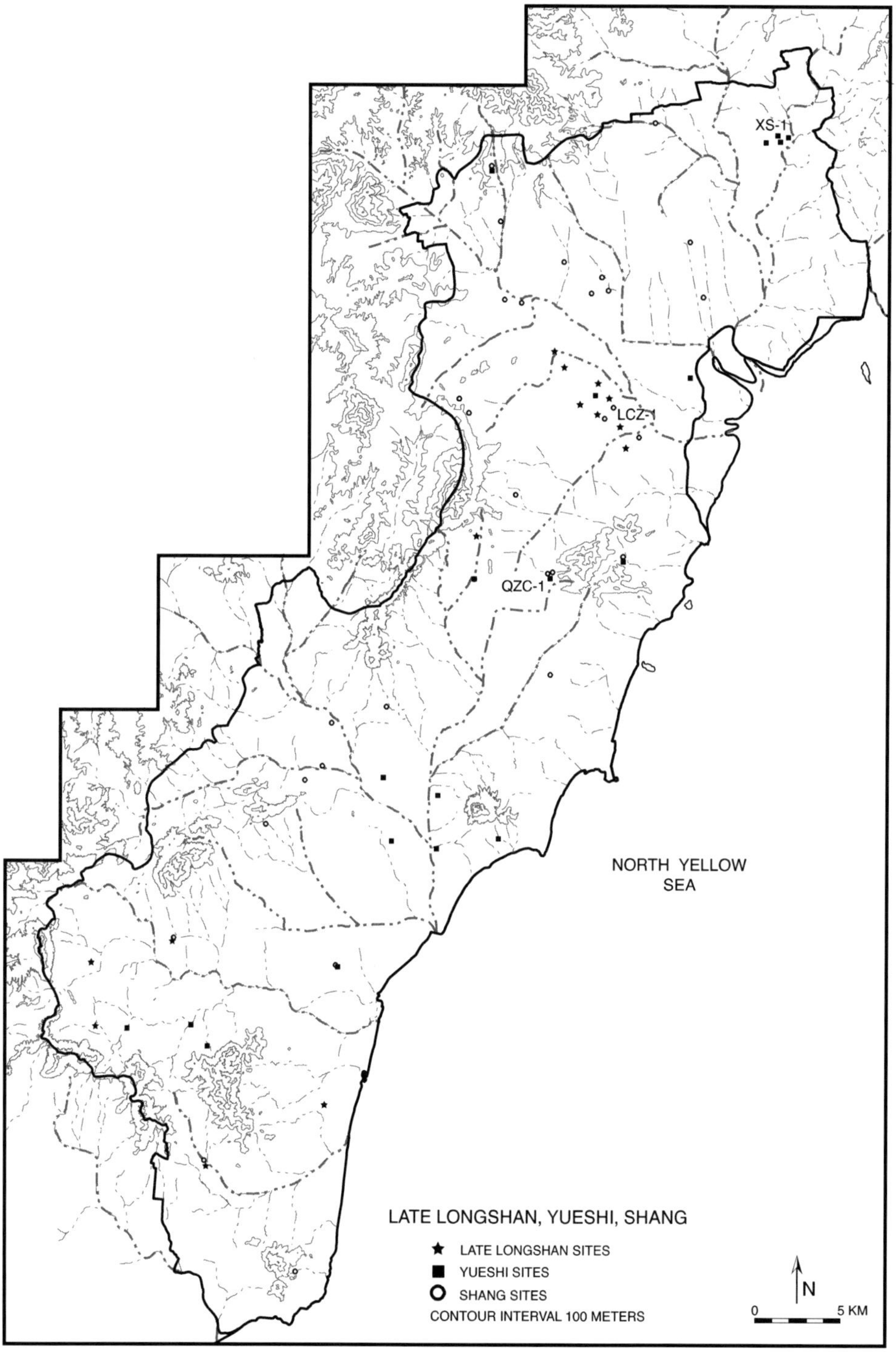

FIGURE 4.5. Late Longshan, Yueshi, and Shang period sites in the southeastern Shandong survey region.

area (including two discrete scatters at both Liangchengzhen and Qianzhucun [DG-QZC-1/WLZ-2]; see Figure 4.5). None of these sherd scatters covered more than 2.5 ha (more than half were less than 1 ha), nor did we find any prestige goods such as bronze vessels. Neither was any of these scatters associated with intact cultural layers, as at several of the sites with Yueshi pottery. It is not likely that these settlements were controlled by the center of power either at Daxinzhuang or Subutun.

We hypothesize that Middle Longshan diagnostic ceramics may have persisted longer in the relatively isolated Rizhao area than in western areas of Shandong. The decline of the Middle Longshan regional system in southeastern Shandong probably occurred later there than in western Shandong (c. 1900 BC). There would have been a time lag for the Late Longshan and Early Bronze Age ceramic complexes (as defined farther west) in southeastern Shandong. In addition, some or all of the Late Longshan, Yueshi, and Shang ceramic complexes as identified from sites in western Shandong may not represent discrete occupational phases in our study region. In the Rizhao area there is very little overlap in the distribution of ceramics from these three complexes (see Figure 4.5). Resolution of this problem will require excavation of more sites in the Rizhao area that span this era and additional radiocarbon dates (see Long, Wagner, and Tarasov 2017). What we can say at this point is that regional population levels declined at the end of the Longshan period and did not bounce back until the Zhou period (Fang et al. 2004).

The Western and Eastern Zhou Periods: Encroaching State Powers

Settlement patterns in the Rizhao region were markedly different for Western (c. 1045–771 BC) and Eastern Zhou (771–221 BC) compared with what we found for earlier periods (Figure 4.6). The Western Zhou population was dispersed into many more small sites at the bottom of the site hierarchy, a pattern that only intensified during Eastern Zhou (Figures 4.7 and 4.8; Tables 4.6 and 4.7). During Western Zhou, many of the larger Longshan centers, including Liangchengzhen and Yaowangcheng, lost population as new centers emerged. The settlement pattern was more decentralized and there was less nucleation of the population in and around the largest centers.

We initially identified a three-tiered hierarchy for all Zhou period sites (Western and Eastern Zhou combined) after five years of survey in southeastern Shandong (Fang et al. 2002; Underhill et al. 2002). During the subsequent eight years of survey we discovered hundreds more Zhou period sites. We now recognize a four-tiered hierarchy for both Western and Eastern Zhou (Table 4.8). We also can identify significant changes in regional sociopolitical organization from Western Zhou to Eastern Zhou.

In the Western Zhou period, the organization of the regional system in the Rizhao area was quite different than it had been during the Middle Longshan period. We had considered Yaowangcheng and Liangchengzhen to be the primary centers, even though they were much smaller than they had been during the Longshan period, because they still were the largest two settlements in our survey region (Fang et al. 2008; Underhill et al. 2008). In the subsequent two field seasons, and during reanalysis, we discovered two other sites that are larger than either of these earlier centers. Given the natural breaks in the histogram of site sizes in Western Zhou, these two new centers—one in the south (Xinliu, LS-XL-1–7) west of Yaowangcheng and one near the buffer area between Liangchengzhen and Yaowangcheng (Qianzhucun,

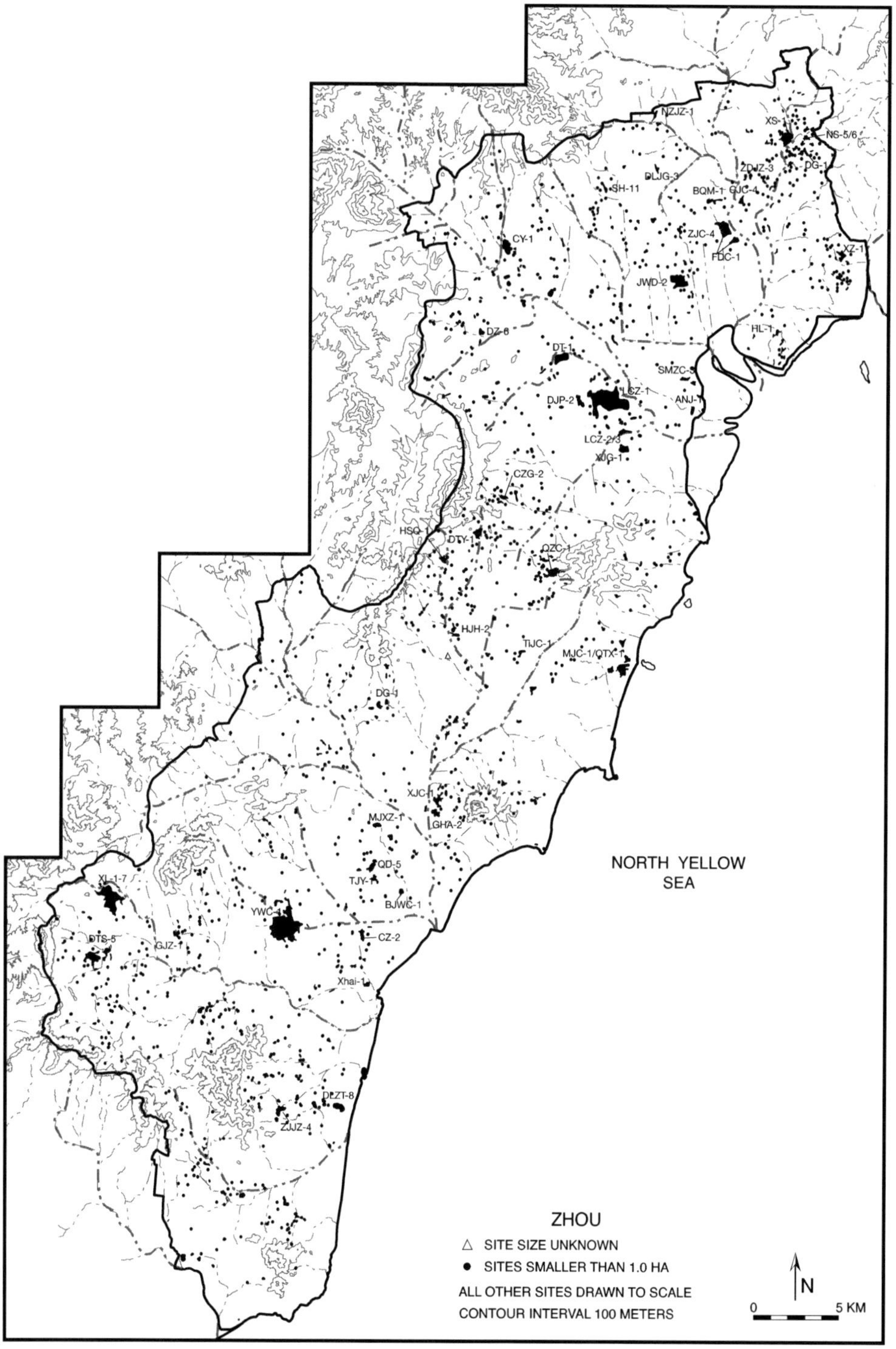

FIGURE 4.6. All Zhou period sites in the southeastern Shandong survey region.

Table 4.6. Summary of all Zhou period sites in the survey region by tier in the settlement hierarchy.

Tier	Number of sites	Size range (ha)	Total area (ha)	Average size (ha)	Elevation range (ha)
I	3	138.7–241.4	606.7	202.2	15
II	10	33.0–110.0	636.6	63.7	4–70
III	17	11.2–28.1	276.3	16.3	2–65
IV	1,198	0.1–7.0	1,191.4	1.0	2–135
Unknown	1	?	?		
Total	1,229		2,711.0		

	Nearest water source			Environmental zone		
Tier	Small stream	Tributary	Main river	Alluvium	Transitional	Piedmont
I	0	1	1	1	1	0
II	3	4	0	5	0	2
III	25	7	6	20	6	12
IV	707	156	119	508	36	438
Unknown	0	1	0	1	0	0
Total	735	169	126	535	43	452

Tier	Average number of vessel forms	Total number of vessel forms
I	7.0	21
II	5.3	53
III	4.1	70
IV	1.5	1,793

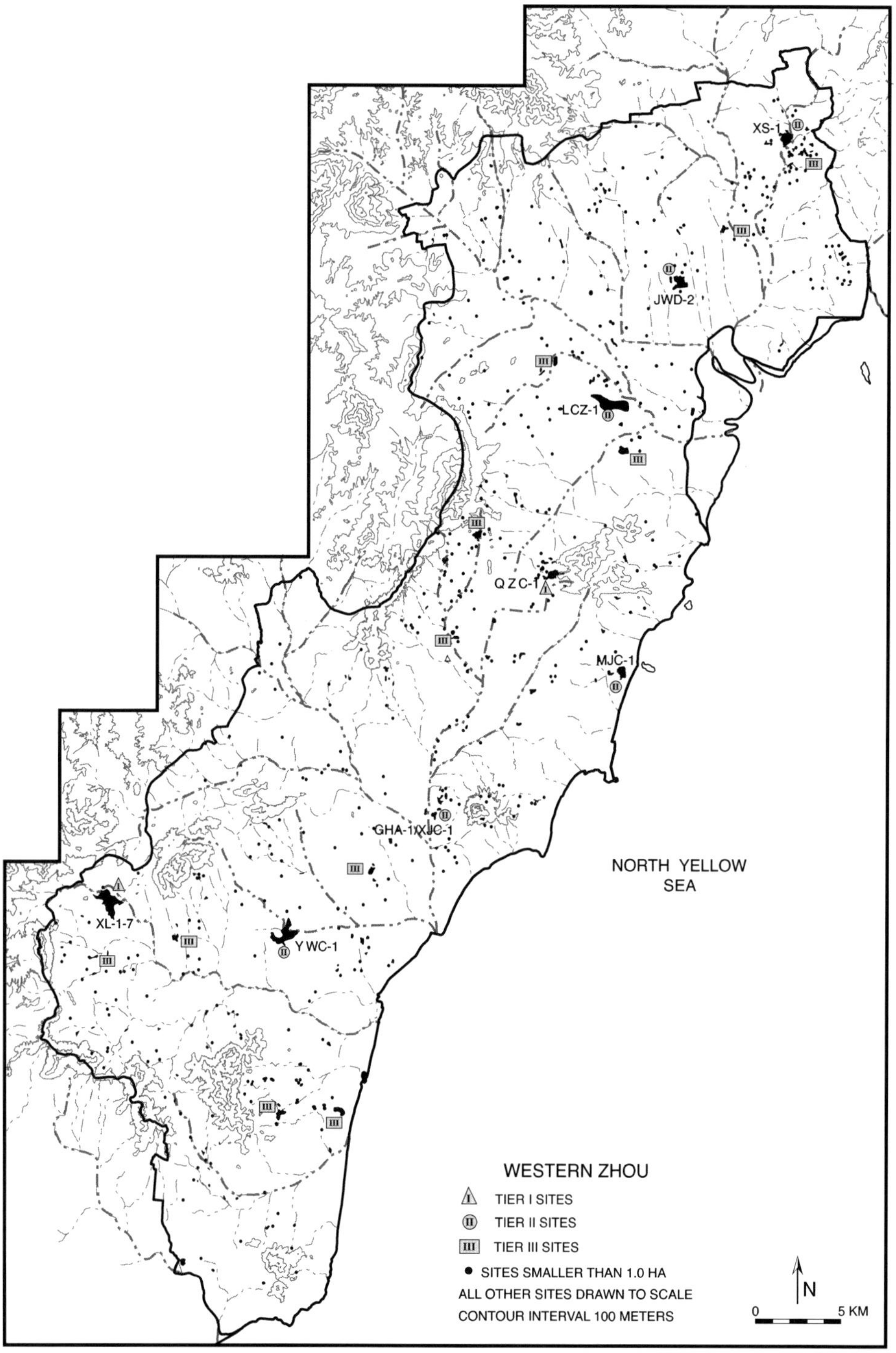

FIGURE 4.7. Western Zhou sites in the southeastern Shandong survey region.

Table 4.7. Number and area of Zhou period sites with diagnostic pottery.

Temporal subdivision	Number of sites	Total area (ha)	Average (ha)
Western only	222	132.1	0.6
Eastern only	705	599.8	0.9
Western and Eastern	241	1,948.9	8.1
Unknown	61	30.1	0.5
Total	1,229	2,710.9	

Table 4.8. Summary of Western and Eastern Zhou sites by tier in the settlement hierarchy.

Tier	Number of sites	Size range (ha)	Area (ha)	Average (ha)
Western Zhou				
I	2	110.0–129.3	239.3	119.7
II	6	32.0–78.6	292.5	48.7
III	11	11.3–21.3	163.4	14.9
IV	443	0.1–9.7	497.4	1.1
?	1			
Total	463		1,192.6	
Eastern Zhou				
I	3	134.3–241.4	595.9	198.6
II	9	29.5–96.4	487.6	54.2
III	12	12.0 –25.7	212.9	17.7
IV	921	0.1–10.6	1,002.0	1.1
?	1			
Total	946		2,298.4	

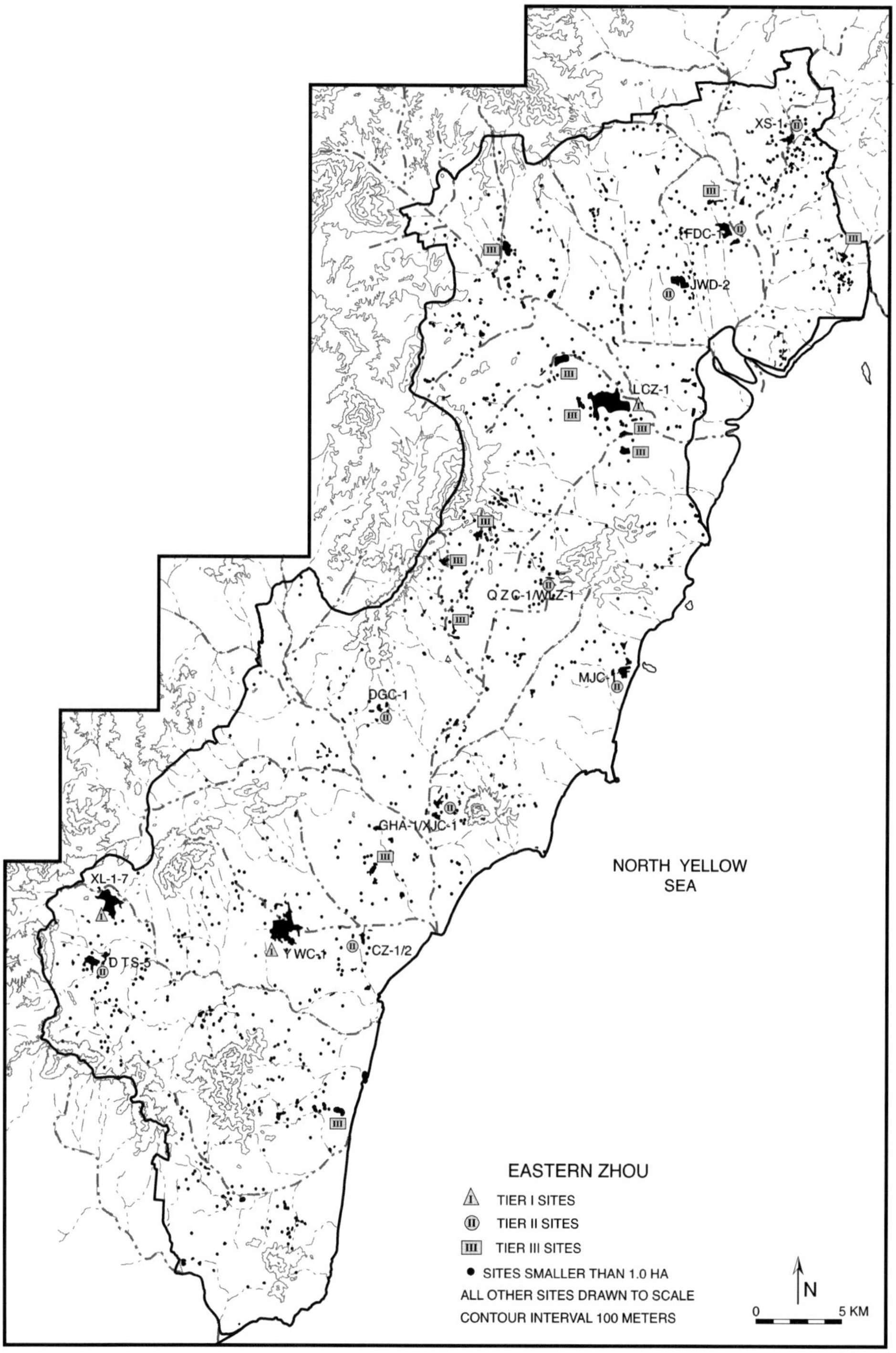

FIGURE 4.8. Eastern Zhou sites in the southeastern Shandong survey region.

DG-QZC-1/WLZ-2)—became the region's two primary centers, and Liangchengzhen and Yaowangcheng became secondary centers (see Figure 4.7). Yet none of these centers was as large as Liangchengzhen and Yaowangcheng had been during the Longshan period. The settlement pattern was more decentralized, thus it may be more realistic to consider the new centers to have been rivals of the earlier centers. Neither of the two later centers had any significant Longshan occupation, and both were in locations with some defensive features. In general, all centers in Western Zhou, but especially the larger ones, were more evenly dispersed across the landscape than they had been during the Longshan period. There also were more smaller sites along the western edge of our survey region.

In the north, around and north of Liangchengzhen, there was greater continuity of centers from Longshan times than in the south. In addition to Liangchengzhen, Xisi (JN-XS-1) continued as an important secondary center, while Jiawangdun (JN-JWD-2/LHQ-1) reemerged as a secondary center. Dantu continued as a center, although it was now a smaller tertiary center. Three tertiary centers retained their rank from Middle Longshan (Dataoyuan [DG-DTY-1/DJZ-3, 5], Xiangjiagou [DG-XJG-1], and Dagou [JN-DG-1]), and Fengduncun (JN-FDC-1) reemerged as a tertiary center, after having that position during Early Longshan. These five tertiary centers were dispersed among the larger centers.

In contrast, most of the Longshan secondary and tertiary sites in the south did not retain their ranks from the Middle Longshan period. In addition to Yaowangcheng, two other secondary centers emerged: Xujiacun (DG-XJC-1)-Guheya (DG-GHA-2; see Chapter 3) and Miaojiacun (DG-MJC-1)-Qiantanxi (DG-QTX-1; see Chapter 3). Except for the more northerly site of Huangjiahe (DG-HJH-1) near the Longshan buffer zone between Yaowangcheng and Liangchengzhen, all the tertiary centers were replaced, including DG-QD-5, LS-DTS-5/CG-9, LS-GJZ-1, DG-DLZT-8, and LS-ZJJZ-4.

In both Western and Eastern Zhou a greater percentage of sites were situated in piedmont zones (see Table 4.6), likely reflecting an effort to exploit more diverse resources or signaling a greater concern with defense. In addition, one secondary center (DG-MJC-1) and a few more tertiary centers and smaller settlements were in coastal zones, indicating increased exploitation of marine resources. Consistent with the Longshan pattern, smaller settlements tended to be near small streams, while the larger centers were near main rivers and tributaries. During Western and Eastern Zhou these centers may have been distribution points for resources exploited from different environmental zones. In contrast with Longshan sites, the diversity of ceramic forms at both Western and Eastern Zhou sites was low, regardless of settlement tier (see Table 4.6). It is not likely that any ceramics we found were prestige goods in the Zhou communities. At that time other materials were more prestigious, especially bronze vessels (see Chang 1987; Underhill 2002; Q. Wang 2002; Shelach-Lavi 2015). Zhou period elites in southeastern Shandong would have focused their attention on controlling other kinds of economic activities.

A greater percentage of sites from the Early Bronze Age (Yueshi, Shang, and Zhou), compared with other periods, are in defendable locations with commanding views of the countryside (Table 4.9). We have no evidence for intercommunity conflict in southeastern Shandong, but defense must have been a greater concern after the Middle Longshan polities disintegrated. Many of these sites are located on the western edge of our survey region. Political relations among communities may have been relatively unstable until the Eastern Zhou period.

There are historical data that are useful for interpreting the nature of Western Zhou polities in the Rizhao area and relations with centers of power to the west. Historical records

TABLE 4.9. Sites in defendable locations for the Longshan period through Han.

Period	Number of defendable sites	Total number of sites	Percentage of sites that are defendable (%)	Total area of defendable sites (ha)	Total occupied area (ha)	Area of defendable sites as percentage of total occupied area (%)
Longshan	16	536	3.0	118.1	2,297.1	5.1
Yueshi	3	19	15.8	4.9	29.6	16.6
Shang	8	31	25.8	6.4	23.8	26.8
Zhou	73	1,229	5.9	197.6	2,711.0	7.3
Han	60	1,681	3.6	118.2	4,337.5	2.7

show that Zhou period rulers of states based in the Zhouyuan and Fenghao areas of the Guanzhong Basin in modern Shaanxi Province conquered the Shang state at Anyang in northern Henan in around 1046 BC (see Xia-Shang-Zhou Chronology Group 2000; Qiu and Cai 2001; Lee 2002; Shelach-Lavi 2015). A key question is the degree of control that state officials had over different areas of Shandong (hundreds of kilometers away) after the Shang conquest and the establishment of the Western Zhou dynasty. One possibility is that Western Zhou settlements in southeastern Shandong were controlled by Zhou elites based in Shaanxi. Based on archaeological research, a statement in the early historical text *Shijing* (诗经) (see Legge 1960)—that everything under heaven is controlled by the Son of Heaven, *tianzi* (天子)—is misleading, since there is evidence for more than one Zhou period state (see F. Li 2013; Shelach-Lavi 2015:265–266). The settlement hierarchy we identified in the Rizhao area could represent either one or two independent, local polities.

One study concludes, using archaeological and historical data, that the Western Zhou state officials based in Shaanxi did not have effective control over eastern Shandong. From inscriptions that refer to political boundaries, X. Wang (1983) infers that the area was largely independent. In areas beyond our survey region, during the early Western Zhou period, state officials established small, initially dependent, polities at Qi, Ji, Xiang, and other locations (see also Tan 1982; Shaughnessy 1999). As control over these areas became unwieldy, such polities became more independent of the central Zhou state over time. X. Wang (1983) concludes that there were several small polities in eastern Shandong. No polities of this kind were mentioned for the Rizhao area, which is separated from the west of Shandong by high mountains.

The comprehensive study by F. Li (2006) concludes that Western Zhou state officials did not succeed in controlling southeastern Shandong. Li explains that the vast Western Zhou state included two kinds of polities: those ruled by people from the royal descent group and those of nonroyal descent allied with the Zhou court. In addition, there were independent states in Shandong that were not part of the Zhou state. Historical texts mention that there were many small states allied to the Zhou court, but ruled by nonroyals, that controlled access to various parts of Shandong and helped the Zhou rulers expand their influence farther east.

Several are known for Shandong Province, but none from the relatively isolated Rizhao area.

F. Li (2006) also shows that the Western Zhou state aimed to control the Jiaodong Peninsula in northeastern Shandong. Western Zhou bronze vessels (some inscribed with explicit reference to the Zhou royal court) and extensive settlement remains were found in several locations along the coast of the Bohai Sea. Li argues that the Zhou state intended to use this area as a staging ground to expand into eastern Shandong. Zhou state officials may have tried to penetrate southeastern Shandong from the south, too; there are records that mention efforts at expansion into the Huai River region of northern Jiangsu Province, which encountered much local resistance. They also may have used the route from Juxian, west of Yaowangcheng. The Zhou officials probably wanted access to marine resources, including salt, like their Shang forbearers.

The four-tiered settlement hierarchy in the Rizhao area may have been organized as one or two polities. Likewise, the political relationships between the centers may have been fluid (e.g., Feinman 1998; M. Smith 2005). The Western Zhou court may have chosen not to record any polities in the Rizhao area that refused to ally themselves to the state, either economically or politically.

The Eastern Zhou text, the *Zuozhuan* (see Durrant, Li, and Schaberg 2016) may refer to an area that includes our survey region. During the Spring and Autumn period, two states outside the Rizhao area, Ju to the north and Chu to the south, fought for control of territory that possibly included where the Xinliu (LS-XL-1–7) site, a primary (Tier I) center in Eastern Zhou, is situated (see Chapter 3). Xinliu probably also was an important and contested site during Western Zhou, judging from the size of the Western Zhou center and the variety of Western Zhou ceramics we recovered. Western Zhou officials may have regarded Xinliu as one of the few important *yi* (邑) settlements (interpreted as cities, with surrounding earthen walls) in the Rizhao area (B. Yang 1981:845).

The degree of social complexity represented by the regional polity or polities in our survey region cannot be definitively determined at present. As we found for the Longshan period, there are smaller clusters of Western Zhou communities in different areas of our survey region that may have had a degree of political autonomy. Even though no Zhou texts mention the Rizhao area as having local states, that possibility cannot be ruled out. A state organization may have been established by local people in part to defend themselves against the Western Zhou threat encroaching on their territory (F. Li 2006:313, 317).

Western Zhou records do mention military campaigns against the "*Dongyi*" people (东夷, a generic term that includes diverse peoples to the east), who were regarded by Zhou officials as eastern barbarians (Luan 1996; F. Li 2006). Yet these records must be tempered by the reality that courtly texts were often distorted in the service of propaganda (e.g., Marcus 1992). It is likely that some locations where these people lived eventually were controlled by the Western Zhou state, while others remained independent (F. Li 2006:307, 313). The Rizhao area probably represents one of these stubbornly independent polities that the Zhou court did not want to commemorate.

During Western Zhou, concern with defense in the Rizhao area is evidenced by the number of sites at high elevations in the west of our survey region and the well-organized clusters of sites in the northeast. The local Rizhao people probably had to make a great effort to control the north, judging from the strong Zhou state presence in the Jiaodong Peninsula and even closer along the Jiao River (Feinman et al. 2021). The south in the vicinity of Yaowangcheng also was strategically important for defense, given the allied Zhou state at Xiang in Juxian County to the west. This southern cluster of settlements included the Guzi

River area south of Rizhao, near its confluence with the Futuan River. It was in this area where the new Western Zhou period secondary center at DG-XJC-1–DG-GHA-2 was established. Two burials, discovered there in 1976 and 1983, contained several late Western Zhou-style bronze vessels (S. Yang 1984; F. Li 2006). Western Zhou state officials may have presented these gifts to local rulers in an effort to create alliances. Whether that effort succeeded remains unclear. Another possibility is that the bronzes were cast locally and emulated Zhou styles (see Sun [2017] for assessment of similar issues for another Western Zhou area).

Historical texts are clear that after 771 BC in northern China the large Western Zhou state disintegrated and local elites in several regions competed for power. Warfare was common and smaller states developed in several regions. Another trend was increased urbanization (Shen 2003). According to historical texts, several states that developed in western Shandong during the Western Zhou period, such as Lu and Qi, continued into Eastern Zhou (Hsu 1999; Lewis 1999; Barnes 2015; Shelach-Lavi 2015). Again southeastern Shandong is not mentioned. In neighboring Juxian, the Ju state (discussed above) was the most powerful in the coastal areas of southeastern Shandong at that time (Y. Liu 2002; Q. Wang 2002). Nothing in the documents, however, precludes the development of independent states in Rizhao or other areas.

Based on the findings of our systematic regional survey, there was tremendous growth in the Rizhao area, and along the entire southern Shandong coast (Feinman, Fang, and Nicholas 2019a; Feinman et al. 2021), from the Western to Eastern Zhou periods. Although many small Western Zhou settlements were abandoned, many new settlements, large and small, were established during Eastern Zhou. Not only was there an increase in the number of centers, but the distribution of those centers across the region also changed during Eastern Zhou (see Table 4.8). Yaowangcheng and Liangchengzhen expanded and reemerged as primary centers. Xinliu (LS-XL-1–7) likely continued as a primary center (albeit considerably smaller than either Yaowangcheng or Liangchengzhen), but DG-QZC-1/WLZ-2 was reduced to a small secondary center (see Figure 4.8).

In the north, JN-JWD-2/LHQ-1 and Xisi (JN-XS-1) both continued as secondary centers in Western Zhou, although Xisi was somewhat diminished in size. An earlier tertiary center located between them, Fengduncun (JN-FDC-1), grew to become one of the largest secondary centers in the region. The other Western Zhou tertiary center in the north dropped out of the hierarchy, while three new ones were established (WL-CY-1, JN-XZ-1, and JN-BQM-1). There also was increased nucleation around Liangchengzhen, as the two nearby Western Zhou centers (Dantu and DG-XJG-1) continued as tertiary centers and two earlier Longshan centers regained their tertiary rank (DG-DJP-2 and DG-LCZ-2, 3).

There also were changes in the area between Liangchengzhen and Yaowangcheng as new centers were established in the Eastern Zhou period. Although two secondary centers north of Yaowangcheng retained their Western Zhou rank (Xujiacun-Guheya), DG-QZC-1/WLZ-2 was much smaller and dropped to a secondary center. A new secondary center emerged at Dagucheng (DG-DGC-1/XSLP-2/QEZ-1, 3, 4, 5). Dagucheng became even more important during the succeeding Han period (see below). The two settlements in this area that had been tertiary centers in Western Zhou (DG-DTY-1/DJZ-3, 5 and DG-HJH-2, 3) continued to be so, while DG-HSQ-1 grew to become a small tertiary center.

In the south, and closer to Yaowangcheng, there were still fewer centers than in other parts of the region. In this area it was not so much the number of centers that changed, but that there were fewer tertiary centers and more secondary centers than there had been during the Western Zhou period. Although Yaowangcheng and Xinliu continued as the two most important centers in the south, Datushan (LS-DTS-5/CG-9) increased in importance from a tertiary to a secondary center, while a new secondary center was established close to Yaowangcheng at Chuanzi (DG-CZ-2). Two earlier settlements continued to be tertiary centers (DG-DZLT-8 and DG-QD-5), while two prior tertiary settlements dropped out of the hierarchy (LS-GJZ-1 and LS-ZJJZ-4).

The Eastern Zhou settlement pattern likely indicates the presence of a more integrated state than existed earlier in the Rizhao region (Feinman, Fang, and Nicholas 2019a, 2019b). Each major center had the potential for interactions with more than one secondary center, and each secondary center had the potential to interact with more tertiary centers than during earlier periods. This more lattice-like pattern indicates greater regional interaction. The region's new secondary and tertiary centers were situated in diverse areas, so that the immediate agricultural catchment potential of certain centers likely was limited to facilitate intercommunity communication and minimize travel costs. Greater economic integration seems likely. As we saw for earlier periods, however, the degree of integration was probably not high for the region as a whole, given the distances between secondary centers and primary centers. Before the Eastern Zhou period, small clusters of sites may have been partially autonomous.

Our Zhou period findings exemplify the value of considering archaeological data in addition to historical data. Although texts exist for northern China at that time, they scarcely mention the Rizhao area. Yet we found over 1,200 sites during our survey that provide a more complete picture of organizational variation and change during this era. The presence of two of the three primary Eastern Zhou centers in the south, and the increase in secondary centers in the southern part of our survey area during the Eastern Zhou period, reflects proximity to the powerful Ju state in Juxian County to the west. The probable contested center of Xinliu (LS-XL-1–7) is approximately 40 km east of Juxian. Since the Eastern Zhou ceramics we found at Xinliu are Ju-style ceramics, the Ju state probably controlled the site for most of the Eastern Zhou period.

A Stronger Western State Presence

These trends intensified during the Han period. The Han empire (206 BC–AD 220) represents considerable expansion of state control over vast areas of China. For this point southeastern Shandong is mentioned more in historical texts, although the implication is that few people inhabited the area. Again, our survey data provide a previously missing perspective; notably, more than 1,600 Han sites were located in diverse zones of our coastal study area (Table 4.10). Not only were there more large sites in the Han period, but the number of small rural sites also increased considerably from Eastern Zhou.

The Han settlement pattern (Figure 4.9) more clearly indicates the presence of a centralized government, whose paramount center was outside the surveyed region. Langyatai, a large Han site to the northeast, likely exercised administrative control over these two coastal basins (Sima 1975; Bodde 1986; Kern 2007; Feinman, Nicholas, and Fang 2010). The most significant change between the Eastern Zhou and the Han period is the increased number of large centers that were fairly evenly dispersed across the survey area. There continued to be a four-tiered settlement hierarchy. Both Liangchengzhen and Yaowangcheng continued as primary centers. Yet these settlements were not as dominant as they had been in the Longshan period. They were only two of seven primary centers that were quite evenly spaced across the

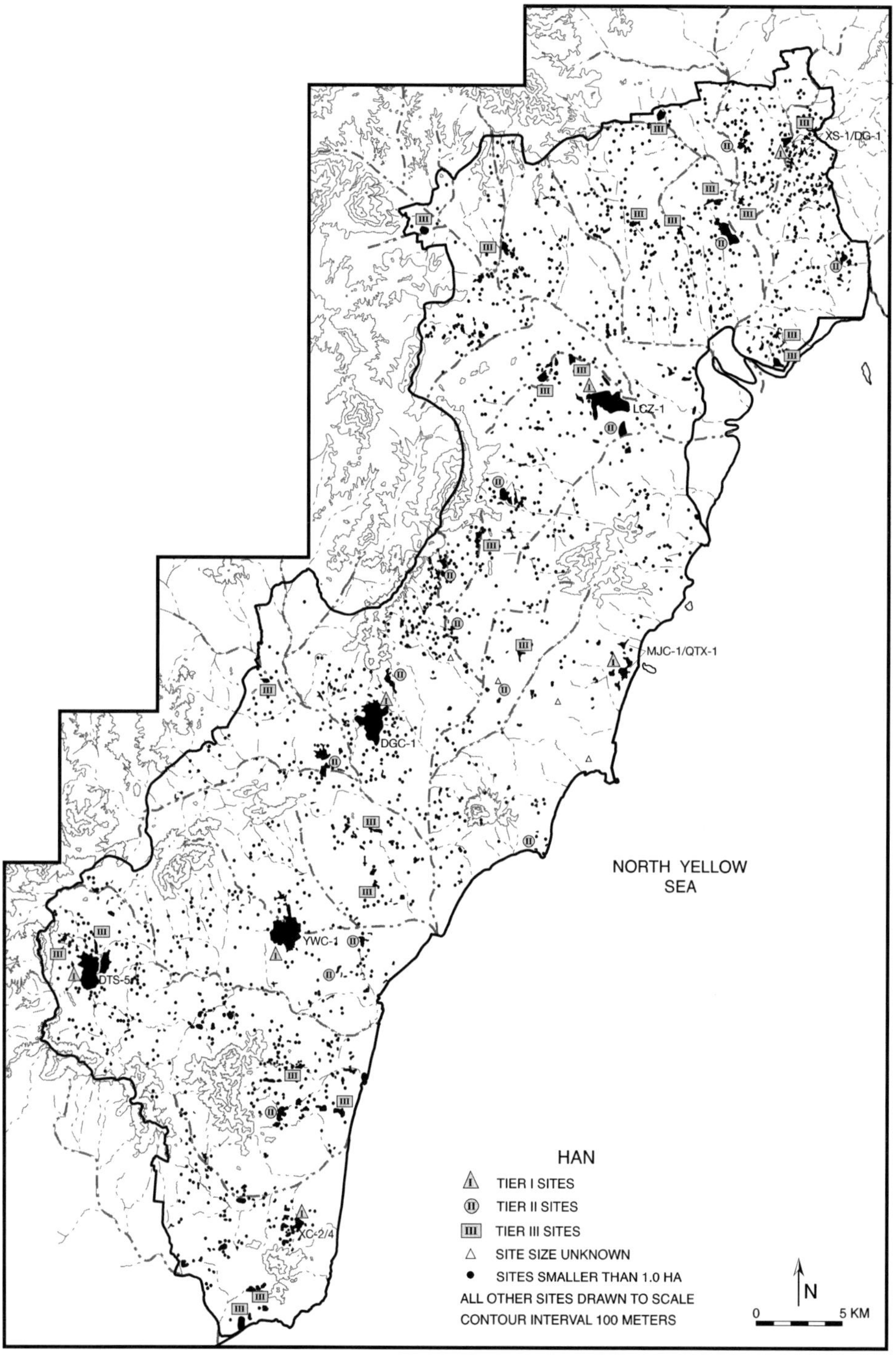

FIGURE 4.9. Han period sites in the southeastern Shandong survey region.

landscape. This higher number of primary centers is a change from what we reported earlier (Fang et al. 2008; Underhill et al. 2008), yet our overall interpretation has not changed and is even strengthened.

The five new primary centers in the Han period were Datushan (LS-DTS-5/CG-9), Dagucheng (DG-DGC-1/XSLP-2/QEZ-1, 3, 4, 5), Xiaocun (LS-XC-2, 4; see Chapter 3), Miaojiacun (DG-MJC-1), and Xisi (JN-XS-1)-Dagou (JN-DG-1, 4; see Chapter 3). All but Xiaocun, in the far south, had been secondary centers during Eastern Zhou. Dagucheng and Datushan, replacing the earlier Eastern Zhou center of Xinliu, were situated near the two easiest passages into these coastal basins from the west and likely were so positioned to control entry into the area. Dagucheng, in the piedmont, and Miaojiacun, on the coast, were positioned in the area between Yaowangcheng and Liangchengzhen, which likely had been contested in the past. The northernmost primary center, at Xisi-Dagou, is the only one of the five that had been a secondary center throughout its occupation, beginning in Early Longshan. This settlement clearly was in a strategic location along the Baima River, one of the major waterways in the north of our survey region. Most other Eastern Zhou secondary centers did not remain at the same rank but became tertiary centers or dropped out of the hierarchy altogether in the Han period. Clearly the location and distribution of the primary Han centers was an intentional effort to control the area.

Another indicator of stronger control over the entire region is a large increase in the number of secondary centers, from nine in Eastern Zhou to fourteen in the Han period (Table 4.10). As noted above, only two of these centers had been secondary centers in Eastern Zhou (JN-FDC-1 and DG-CZ-1). Four sites (DG-HJH-2, 3; DG-HSQ-1 and DG-HSQ-13/QSQ-1; JN-XZ-1; and DG-LCZ-2, 3) that had been tertiary centers in Eastern Zhou grew to become secondary centers in the Han period. The remaining eight were new centers, although several had been secondary (LS-JG-3/DXQH-1) or tertiary (DG-ZJDZ-1 and LS-ZJJZ-4) centers before Eastern Zhou, either in the Western Zhou or the Longshan period. With the greater number of primary and secondary centers, there likely was a more even distribution of the population. This pattern of more major centers of near-equal size may be because the main center was outside the study region (see Johnson 1980:241). Han provincial capitals were located outside the Rizhao region (see Lewis 2007; Barnes 2015; Shelach-Lavi 2015).

A more centralized polity also is evident from the more regular spacing of the seven primary centers (see Figure 4.9). There are roughly equal distances (c. 10 to 15 km) between each primary center and the two nearest primary centers. From Dagucheng to Liangchengzhen (DG-LCZ-1) is about 20 km. In addition, for the first time there were clear architectural symbols of state power at the major centers. At each major center there are elite tombs in the form of large mounds; the large, earthen city walls are still visible at Dagucheng (see Figure 3.2). Isolated Han tombs symbolic of state power are found in other parts of the survey region as well. We also found several examples of glazed and decorated ceramics at Dagucheng and Datushan.

Secondary centers were fairly evenly distributed to control several areas, including the coast. This more carefully situated and comprehensive layout of primary and secondary centers probably helped Han officials control the flow of raw materials and goods from the area. In other areas of the world, more widely but regularly spaced centers can mean more efficient transportation for developing markets (Blanton 2004). Independent forms of commerce may have developed as well. During later historical eras in China settlement patterns varied and changed over time, indicating different linkages between rural populations and market towns (Skinner 1964, 1965).

Archaeological and historical data make it clear that, after the Zhou period, state of-

TABLE 4.10. Summary of all Han period sites in the survey region by tier in the settlement hierarchy.

Tier	Number of sites	Size range (ha)	Total area (ha)	Average size (ha)	Elevation range (ha)
I	7	145.0–309.1	1,556.0	222.3	8–4
II	14	30.0–95.7	705.7	50.4	8–55
III	23	12.5–27.7	428.9	18.6	3–65
IV	1,634	0.1–11.4	1,646.8	1.0	2–120
Unknown	3	?	?		
Total	1,681		4,337.4		

	Nearest water source			Environmental zone		
Tier	Small stream	Tributary	Main river	Alluvium	Transitional	Piedmont
I	1	2	1	2	1	1
II	7	4	2	7	4	2
III	16	5	4	12	3	10
IV	936	240	183	747	55	557
Unknown	2	2	0	2	0	2
Total	962	253	190	770	63	572

Tier	Average number of vessel forms	Total number of vessel forms
I	4.9	34
II	2.9	40
III	2.4	55
IV	0.8	1,343

ficials from the west controlled at least parts of eastern Shandong. According to the Han historical text, the *Shiji*, during the earlier, short-lived Qin dynasty (221–206 BC) the emperor visited the Langya region north of Rizhao in 219 BC; afterward he reportedly ordered 30,000 families to migrate there (Sima 1975; Bodde 1986:65; Feinman, Nicholas, and Fang 2010; Fang, Feinman, and Nicholas 2015). Later, the Han emperor had more opportunity to control such distant regions. He divided his empire into several kingdoms or territories and was the overseer of the entire empire (Loewe 1986a:123). At first the Rizhao area was part of the local Qi territory; in 143 BC it became part of the territory called Langya (Loewe 1986a:146).

We conclude that by Han times our entire survey area had been engulfed by a larger regional polity (Feinman, Nicholas, and Fang 2010; Fang, Feinman, and Nicholas 2015; Feinman and Nicholas 2018; Feinman, Fang, and Nicholas 2019a, 2019b). Only at this point do we have officially commissioned, written records that link the Rizhao region to areas of state power. An historical text called the *Han Shu* (汉书; Ran and Chen 1962) relates that the Han set up a sea salt administrative unit in Haiqu County, the Dagucheng site in our survey area (Fang 2004). A state monopoly on salt and iron was maintained throughout the empire for much of the Han period, with brief periods of respite (Loewe 1986a:202). A clear indicator of solid control over the region by Han officials can be seen from excavations at Dagucheng. Bamboo slips—official state records—were recovered from a large tomb (National Bureau of Cultural Relics 2003). Significantly, Dagucheng is near a pass that is used today by both an expressway and the railroad to connect the Rizhao area to western Shandong Province.

The Han era *Shiji* describes central government officials sent to take charge of distant counties to collect taxes (in the form of money and crops) and coerce labor for building city walls and roads, defense, and other purposes (see Sima 1975). The largest kind of Han settlement mentioned in texts is the *xian* (县), or county seat. Given the presence of large tombs, glazed ceramics, and high densities of sherds at most of the primary centers in our survey region, as well as the even distribution of these centers across the landscape, we suspect that all these centers were *xian* in Langya Province during the Han period; however, only the two westernmost centers, Datushan (LS-DTS-5/CG-9) and Dagucheng (DG-DGC-1/XSLP-2/QEZ-1, 3, 4, 5), are mentioned in the Han era documents and may have been somewhat more important than the others. We hypothesize that all the secondary centers were regarded as *xiang* (乡) towns during the Han period. The tertiary centers probably were considered *xiang* (乡) or *li* (里) villages, where officials lived to enforce security and collect taxes.

Once again, the survey data amplify the picture of life during the Han period that we have from the official state records and elite tombs. A striking pattern in the Rizhao area is an abundance of small Han sites (see Figure 4.9). Compared with the Zhou period, there was a significant growth of small rural communities, representing greater exploitation of diverse areas, especially the coast. It is likely that economic diversity among communities increased, forming the foundation for the kind of community specialization we see today, including fishing and quarrying villages. The two new primary centers on or near the coast (DG-MJC-1 and LS-XC-2, 4) may have been positioned to control the production of salt and other marine resources.

Although the archaeological literature for several periods of ancient China tends to focus on the development of urbanism, our regional survey data for southeastern Shandong reveal another dimension of social change. We have documented a marked trend toward ruralization (sensu Blanton 2004) rather than ever increasing nucleation, since the percentage of the population in rural communities increased at the expense of the cities. Indeed, today there are many hamlets and isolated farmsteads in the Rizhao area (Fang et al. 2004).

The records of Han administrators make it clear that the hamlet was the smallest formal sociopolitical unit recognized by the state. These settlements tended to include about one hundred families and often existed in isolation (Loewe 1986b; Sadao 1986:551–552). Officials focused on managing larger sociopolitical units such as counties. There was no direct bureaucratic administration for hamlets (Loewe 1986b; Sadao 1986:553). In some areas of China the state opened up land through flood control and irrigation, making it possible for farmers to live in new areas (Sadao 1986:554). After people arrived they rarely interacted with state officials. A limited elite presence is evident from the humble range of artifacts we find at Han sites. At most sites there are only a few forms of thick jars or ceramic roof tile fragments (see Table 4.10). The rare exception is decorated brick from elite tombs. The activities of ordinary households in southeastern Shandong during the Han period, therefore, were probably quite isolated from those of the state. The Han state nevertheless likely secured resources from these households through its monopoly on such necessities as iron and salt (Barnes 2015:292).

Conclusions

During the past decade, surveys and excavations in different areas of northern China have identified the development of several regional polities during the Late Neolithic and Early Bronze Age. The nature of these polities and their interrelationships are not adequately understood. The challenge that remains is to identify variation in the nature of these polities and how their leaders amassed economic, social, and ideological power in each region. Scholarship on the rise of complex societies in northern China has emphasized areas where the Erlitou, Shang, and Zhou states emerged. As a consequence there has been a tendency to regard the Late Neolithic and Early Bronze Age polities that developed in other areas of northern China as marginal in importance. Furthermore, it is often assumed that sociopolitical changes in peripheral areas were similar, with the common denominators being collapse of weak Longshan polities and subsequent control by state polities with official records of dynastic history.

Systematic, full-coverage regional survey is a valuable tool for investigating large-scale demographic and sociopolitical changes (Feinman and Nicholas 2018; Feinman, Fang, and Nicholas 2019a). By using this method during the past decades in southeastern Shandong, we have identified significant changes for the Longshan, Zhou, and Han periods. We found thousands of settlements, despite little mention of the area in historical texts. The regional survey has enabled us to define the settlement pattern of a broad, contiguous area with a foundation for investigating development and cycling in regional polities and interactions between centers and smaller sites in southeastern Shandong. Such data derived from systematic regional survey are necessary to investigate changes in degree of regional economic or social integration, in strategies of sociopolitical organization and control, and to identify possible boundaries of regional polities.

The nature of changes we have documented does not fit previous expectations for an area commonly regarded as peripheral. For the Early and Middle Longshan periods in southeastern Shandong we found evidence for a four-tiered hierarchy and two largely contemporary major centers, Liangchengzhen and Yaowangcheng. At present we believe these two Longshan sites were centers of separate polities. One pattern in support of this hypothesis is a distinct area between the two centers with few sites, or a buffer zone. Another significant pattern not identified elsewhere in northern China is the distinctive nucleation of sites around

Liangchengzhen. The nucleation around Liangchengzhen most likely represents a deliberate effort by leaders to control labor and subsistence goods from nearby communities.

In addition, we documented that this Late Neolithic regional sociopolitical system developed rapidly. During the Late Dawenkou and Longshan periods, migrants likely entered southeastern Shandong, bringing with them an established hierarchical sociopolitical organization and a developed agricultural economy. Once they arrived in this coastal domain, these migrants were successful, colonizing the area quickly and expanding in numbers.

One topic for future research in the Rizhao area is the nature of social and economic interactions between settlements, including Yaowangcheng and Liangchengzhen. One possibility is that there were competitive relations between the two centers, especially during the Early Longshan period. The new center at Liangchengzhen could have competed with the previously established settlement at Yaowangcheng for control over resources (including human labor) in the region.

Another important issue to study is the nature of regional ceramic production and exchange during the Early and Middle Longshan periods. We continue to investigate the hypothesis that production of prestige wares took place mainly at major and minor centers. Elites from these centers may have occasionally given gifts of fine wares to local leaders in outlying settlements in exchange for loyalty and services, such as provision of goods. Thus one elite control strategy was gift exchange to enhance personal networks.

Additional research should examine the nature of sociopolitical change from the Middle Longshan to the Western Zhou period. It is possible that the Middle Longshan polities developed and/or persisted later than in areas farther west. The likelihood of some degree of lag in the persistence of Middle Longshan ceramics raises the possibility that a state developed in the Rizhao area in response to centralization of power in one or more areas to the west. But any western states could not easily expand into southeastern Shandong, a naturally protected and isolated area.

The four-tiered settlement hierarchy we identified for Western Zhou in southeastern Shandong using archaeological and historical data most likely represents a polity that was independent of the powerful, literate state to the west. We conclude that there was at least one state, but not one that was formally recognized by the Zhou state officials or their allies who tried to penetrate the area. During the Eastern Zhou period there was a marked increase in the number of centers. Given the political instability throughout Shandong during this period, more than one state would have tried to control the Rizhao area. Our study region possibly began to cede its political autonomy by the end of this period.

During the Han period, in contrast, there was more centralized control over the Rizhao area from an external source. A key change was the establishment of more primary centers that more effectively integrated the entire region. Two of these, Dagucheng and Datushan, grew rapidly and were placed to monitor travel into the region from areas to the west. Dagucheng, with its complex of mounded tombs and an earthen defensive wall, and Datushan may have been linked to more powerful centers situated outside the area, to the west. In the northeast, at Xisi-Dagou, another primary center with a large complex of mounded tombs and platforms, may have had similar links to the east, most notably to Langya. In addition, there is clear historical evidence to show that Qin and Han imperial officials controlled southeastern Shandong. Thus, for the first time, the Rizhao area was fully engulfed in a wider polity centered to the west (Feinman, Nicholas, and Fang 2010; Fang et al. 2015; Feinman, Fang, and Nicholas 2019a, 2019b).

Even though population density increased over time in our survey region, significant changes were not restricted to the Early Longshan period, when more nucleation of settlement began. A different type of change took place during the Zhou period, and especially the Han period, with a distinct increase in rural settlements. Our survey data have revealed this relatively "hidden" aspect of the Han presence in Shandong.

Systematic, full-coverage regional survey, then, has yielded key findings that may also serve as a foundation for further studies of sociopolitical change in northern China. Our results provide a diachronic and scalar vantage on China's past that could not be achieved with excavations or the available textual records alone. Through these findings, we clearly document that there were diverse pathways to social complexity in northern China.

References

ALLARD, FRANCIS. 2001. Mortuary ceramics and social organization in the Dawenkou and Majiayao cultures. *Journal of East Asian Archaeology* 3(3/4):1–22. https://doi.org/10.1163/156852301760238256

AN, ZUOZHANG, ED. 1993. *Shandong tongshi* [*History of Shandong*]. Volume 2, *Qin-Han juan* [*Qin-Han section*]. Jinan: Shandong renmin Press. 547 pp.

[ANHUI IA] ANHUI PROVINCIAL INSTITUTE OF ARCHAEOLOGY. 2010 February 5. "Anhui Guzhen Xian Gaixia faxian Dawenkou Wenhua wanqi chengzhi" ["Discovery of a Late Dawenkou culture city at Gaixia in Guzhen County, Anhui"]. *Zhongguo Wenwu Bao*, p. 1.

BARNES, GINA L. 2015. *Archaeology of East Asia: The Rise of Civilization in China, Korea and Japan.* Havertown, PA: Oxbow Books. 492 pp.

BENNETT, GWEN P. 2002. "The Organization of Lithic Tool Production During the Longshan Period (ca. 2600–2000 BC) in Southeastern Shandong Province, China" [dissertation]. University of California, Los Angeles. 455 pp. ProQuest Dissertations & Theses Global, 3059593. https://www.proquest.com/

—2004. Haidai diqu zhi jingguan kaogu yanjiu [Archaeological research on landscapes of the Haidai region]. *Dongfang Kaogu* (2004)1:217–225.

—2007. Context and meaning in Late Neolithic lithic production in China: The Longshan Period in southeastern Shandong Province. In: *Rethinking Craft Specialization in Complex Societies: Archaeological Analyses of the Social Meaning of Production*, special issue, edited by Zachary X. Hruby and Rowan K. Flad. *Archaeological Papers of the American Anthropological Association* 17(1):52–67. https://doi.org/10.1525/ap3a.2007.17.1.52

BILLMAN, BRIAN R., AND GARY M. FEINMAN, EDS. 1999. *Settlement Pattern Studies in the Americas: Fifty Years Since Virú.* Washington, DC: Smithsonian Institution Press. 246 pp.

BLANTON, RICHARD E. 1976. Anthropological studies of cities. *Annual Review of Anthropology* 5:249–264. https://doi.org/10.1146/annurev.an.05.100176.001341

—2004. Settlement pattern and population change in Mesoamerican and Mediterranean civilizations: A comparative perspective. In: Susan E. Alcock and John F. Cherry, eds. *Side-by-Side Survey: Comparative Regional Studies in the Mediterranean World.* Oxford: Oxbow Books. pp. 206–240. https://www.jstor.org/stable/j.ctt1s474xp

BLANTON, RICHARD E., GARY M. FEINMAN, STEPHEN A. KOWALEWSKI, AND LINDA M. NICHOLAS. 1999. *Ancient Oaxaca: The Monte Albán State.* New York: Cambridge University Press. 153 pp. https://doi.org/10.1017/CBO9780511607844

BLANTON, RICHARD E., GARY M. FEINMAN, STEPHEN A. KOWALEWSKI, AND PETER N. PEREGRINE. 1996. A dual-processual theory for the evolution of Mesoamerican civilization. *Current Anthropology* 37(1):1–86. https://doi.org/10.1086/204471

BLANTON, RICHARD E., STEPHEN A. KOWALEWSKI, GARY M. FEINMAN, AND LAURA M. FINSTEN. 1993. *Ancient Mesoamerica: A Comparison of Change in Three Regions.* 2nd ed. New York: Cambridge University Press. 300 pp.

BODDE, DERK. 1986. The state and empire of Ch'in. In: Denis Twitchett and Michael Loewe, eds. *The Cambridge History of China.* Volume 1, *The Ch'in and Han Empires, 221 BC–AD 220.* Cambridge: Cambridge University Press. pp. 20–102. https://doi.org/10.1017/CHOL9780521243278.003

BRINKMAN, JOHN A. 1984. Settlement surveys and documentary evidence: Regional variation and secular trend in Mesopotamian demography. *Journal of Near Eastern Studies* 43(3):169–181. https://doi.org/10.1086/373078

CAI, FENGSHU, AND FENGSHI LUAN, EDS. 1992. *Shandong Longshan wenhua yanjiu wen ji [Collection of essays about research on the Shandong Longshan culture]*. Jinan: Qilu shushe Press. 362 pp.

CAI, FENGSHU, HAIGUANG YU, FENGSHI LUAN, HUI FANG, CHENGFU SUN, ANNE UNDERHILL, GARY FEINMAN, LINDA NICHOLAS, AND GWEN BENNETT. 1997. Shandong Rizhao shi Liangcheng diqu de kaogu diaocha [Archaeological survey in the Liangcheng region of Rizhao City, Shandong]. *Kaogu* 1997(4):1–15.

CAMPBELL, RODERICK B. 2009. Toward a networks and boundaries approach to early complex polities: The Late Shang case. *Current Anthropology* 50(6):821–848. https://doi.org/10.1086/648398

—2014. *Archaeology of the Chinese Bronze Age: From Erlitou to Anyang*. Los Angeles: Cotsen Institute of Archaeology Press. 232 pp. (Monograph 79.)

CHANG, KWANG-CHIH. 1980. *Shang Civilization*. New Haven: Yale University Press. 417 pp.

—1983a. Sandai archaeology and the formation of states in ancient China: Processual aspects of the origins of Chinese civilization. In: David N. Keightley, ed. *The Origins of Chinese Civilization*. Berkeley: University of California Press. pp. 495–522. https://doi.org/10.1525/9780520310797-020

—1983b. *Art, Myth, and Ritual: The Path to Political Authority in Ancient China*. Cambridge: Harvard University Press. 142 pp.

—1987. *The Archaeology of Ancient China*. 4th ed. New Haven: Yale University Press. 450 pp. https://www.aaeportal.com/publications/-20247/the-archaeology-of-ancient-china

CHEN, MAO, TINGSHI ZHANG, AND YU LI. 2004. Guangxu Rizhao xianzhi, yange [Outline of Rizhao County annals of the Guangxu period]. In: Fenghuang chubanshe, ed. *Zhongguo difangzhi jicheng, Shandong fuxian zhiji [Compilation of local Chinese chronicles, collections of Shandong provincial and county annals]*. Volume 58. Nanjing: Fenghuang Press. pp. 342–503.

CHEN, XUEXIANG. 2007. Shandong Rizhao Liangchu Xinshiqishidai yizhi fuxuan tuyang jieguo fenxi [Results of flotation for two Neolithic sites in Rizhao, Shandong]. *Nanfang Wenwu* 2007(1):92–94. http://dx.chinadoi.cn/10.3969/j.issn.1004-6275.2007.01.014

CHEN, XUEXIANG, HUI FANG, GARY FEINMAN, LINDA NICHOLAS, AND ANNE UNDERHILL. 2009. Ludongnan jichu xiantao yizhi diaocha caiyang fuxuan jieguo fenxi [Analytical results from flotation of carbonized seed samples from selected sites from the survey in southeastern Shandong]. *Dongfang Kaogu* 6:354–357.

CHEN, XUEXIANG, SHIYONG YU, ANNE P. UNDERHILL, AND HUI FANG. 2017. Radiocarbon dating and stable carbon isotopic analyses of Neolithic and Bronze Age staple crops in the lower Yellow River area and their paleodietary implications. *Geoarchaeology* 33(3):307–313. https://doi.org/10.1002/gea.21659

[CHIFENG PROJECT] THE CHIFENG INTERNATIONAL COLLABORATIVE ARCHAEOLOGICAL RESEARCH PROJECT. 2003. *Neimenggu dongbu (Chifeng) quyu kaogu diaocha jieduanxing baogao [Regional archaeology in eastern Inner Mongolia: A methodological exploration]*. Beijing: Kexue Press. 219 pp.

—2011. *Settlement Patterns in the Chifeng Region*. Pittsburgh: University of Pittsburgh Center for Comparative Archaeology. 153 pp. https://sites.pitt.edu/~ccapubs/pdfdownloads/PITTca02-ChifengInternlCollabArchResearchProj_2011.pdf

CHINA CULTURAL HERITAGE BUREAU. 2007. *Zhongguo wenwu dituji, Shandong fence [Atlas of cultural relics in China, Shandong volume]*. Beijing: Zhongguo ditu Press. 572 pp.

CHINA–U.S. COOPERATIVE ARCHAEOLOGICAL TEAM. 2016. *Liangchengzhen—1998–2001 nian fajue baogao [Liangchengzhen: 1998–2001 excavation report]*. Fengshi Luan, Anne P. Underhill, Haiguang Yu, Hui Fang, Fengshu Cai, Fen Wang, and Geoffrey E. Cunnar, eds. Beijing: Wenwu Press. 4 volumes.

Cobb, Charles R. 2003. Mississippian chiefdoms: How complex? *Annual Review of Anthropology* 32:63–84. https://doi.org/10.1146/annurev.anthro.32.061002.093244

Cowgill, George L. 2004. Origins and development of urbanism: Archaeological perspectives. *Annual Review of Anthropology* 33:525–549. https://doi.org/10.1146/annurev.anthro.32.061002.093248

Crawford, Gary, Anne Underhill, Zhijun Zhao, Gyoung-ah Lee, Gary Feinman, Linda Nicholas, Fengshi Luan, Haiguang Yu, Hui Fang, and Fengshu Cai. 2005. Late Neolithic plant remains from northern China: Preliminary results from Liangchengzhen, Shandong. *Current Anthropology* 46(2):309–316. https://doi.org/10.1086/428788

Crawford, Gary, Zhijun Zhao, Fengshi Luan, Haiguang Yu, Hui Fang, Fengshu Cai, Anne Underhill, Gyoung-ah Lee, Gary Feinman, and Linda Nicholas. 2004. Shandong Rizhao shi Liangchengzhen yizhi Longshan wenhua zhiwu yicun de chubu fenxi [Analysis of plant remains unearthed from the Longshan culture site of Liangchengzhen in Rizhao City, Shandong]. *Kaogu* 2004(9):73–80.

Cunnar, Geoffrey E. 2007. "The Production and Use of Stone Tools at the Longshan Period Site of Liangchengzhen, China" [dissertation]. Yale University, Department of Anthropology. 881 pp. ProQuest Dissertations & Theses Global, 3267234. https://www.proquest.com/

—2013. A study of *lian* sickles and *dao* knives from the Longshan culture site of Liangchengzhen in southeastern Shandong. In: Anne P. Underhill, ed. *A Companion to Chinese Archaeology*. Malden, MA: Wiley-Blackwell Press. pp. 459–472. https://doi.org/10.1002/9781118325698.ch22

—2014. Lu dongnan yanhai diqu kaogu diaocha faxian shiqi yanjiu [Research on stone tools discovered from the regional survey in southeastern coastal Shandong]; translated by Kunyang Fang and Dong Yu, proofread by Hui Fang. *Dongfang Kaogu* 10:336–372.

Deetz, James. 1977. *In Small Things Forgotten: The Archaeology of Early American Life*. 1st ed. Garden City, NY: Anchor Press/Doubleday. 184 pp.

Demattè, Paola. 1999. Longshan-era urbanism: The role of cities in predynastic China. *Asian Perspectives* 38(2):119–153. http://www.jstor.org/stable/42928454

Dietler, Michael. 1996. Feasts and commensal politics in the political economy: Food, power and status in prehistoric Europe. In: Polly Wiessner and Wulf Schiefenhövel, eds. *Food and the Status Quest: An Interdisciplinary Perspective*. Oxford: Berghahn Books. pp. 87–125.

—2001. Theorizing the feast: Rituals of consumption, commensal politics, and power in African contexts. In: Michael Dietler and Brian Hayden, eds. *Feasts: Archaeological and Ethnographic Perspectives on Food, Politics, and Power*. Washington, DC: Smithsonian Institution Press. pp. 65–114.

Dong, Yu, Liugen Lin, Xiaoting Zhu, Fengshi Luan, and Anne P. Underhill. 2019. Mortuary ritual and social identities during the Late Dawenkou period in China. *Antiquity* 93(368):378–392. https://doi.org/10.15184/aqy.2019.34

Dong, Yu, Songtao Chen, Stanley H. Ambrose, Anne Underhill, Xue Ling, Mingkui Gao, Zhenguang Li, Fengshi Luan, and Guiyun Jin. 2021. Social and environmental factors influencing dietary choices among Dawenkou culture sites, Late Neolithic China. *The Holocene* 32(2):271–284. https://doi.org/10.1177%2F0959683620970273

Donghaiyu Excavation Team, Shandong Provincial Museum, and Rizhao County Office for Protection of Cultural Relics. 1976. Yijiuqiwu Nian Donghaiyu yizhi de fajue [Excavation of the Donghaiyu site in 1975]. *Kaogu* 1976(6):377–382.

Drennan, Robert D., and Xiangming Dai. 2010. Chiefdoms and states in the Yuncheng Basin and the Chifeng region: A comparative analysis of settlement systems in North China. *Journal of Anthropological Archaeology* 29(4):455–468. https://doi.org/10.1016/j.jaa.2010.09.001

Druc, Isabelle, Anne Underhill, Fen Wang, Fengshi Luan, and Qingyu Lu. 2018. A preliminary assessment of the organization of ceramic production at Liangchengzhen, Rizhao, Shandong: Perspectives from petrography. *Journal of Archaeological Science: Reports* 18:222–238. https://doi.org/10.1016/j.jasrep.2017.12.050

DRUC, ISABELLE, ANNE UNDERHILL, FEN WANG, FENGSHI LUAN, QINGYU LU, QITAO HU, MINGJIAN GUO, AND YANCHANG LIU. 2021. Late Neolithic white wares from southeastern Shandong, China: The tricks to produce a white looking pot with not much kaolin. Results from petrography, XRD and SEM-EDS analyses. *Journal of Archaeological Science: Reports* 35:102673. https://doi.org/10.1016/j.jasrep.2020.102673

DURRANT, STEPHEN, WAI-YEE LI, AND DAVID SCHABERG, TRANSLATORS. 2016. *Zuo Tradition/ Zuozhuan: Commentary on the Spring and Autumn Annals.* Seattle: University of Washington Press. 3 volumes.

EDITING COMMITTEE OF RIZHAO, LOCAL CHRONICLES. 1994. *Rizhao shi zhi* [*Rizhao City annals*]. Jinan: Qilu shushe Press. 826 pp.

EMERSON, THOMAS E. 1997. *Cahokia and the Archaeology of Power*. Tuscaloosa: University of Alabama Press. 318 pp.

[ERLITOU TEAM IA CASS] ERLITOU TEAM, INSTITUTE OF ARCHAEOLOGY OF THE CHINESE ACADEMY OF SOCIAL SCIENCES. 2005. Henan Luoyang pendi 2001–2003 nian kaogu diaocha jianbao [Preliminary report of the archaeological survey from 2001–2003 in the Luoyang Basin, Henan]. *Kaogu* 2005(5):18–37.

FANG, HUI. 1998. Yueshi wenhua de fenqi yu niandai [Periodization and dating of the Yueshi culture]. *Kaogu* 1998(4):55–71.

—2003a. Rizhao diqu quyu xitong kaogu diaocha [Systematic, regional survey in the Rizhao area]. In: Chinese Archaeology Association, ed. *Zhongguo kaoguxue nianji* [*Yearly record of archaeological work in China*]. Beijing: Wenwu Press. pp. 200–201.

—2003b. Yueshi wenhua shuailuo yuanyin lice [Hypotheses about the decline of the Yueshi culture]. *Wen Shi Zhe* 2003(3):139–143.

—2004. Shang Zhou shiqi lubei diqu haiyanye de kaoguxue yanjiu [Archaeological research on the sea salt industry in northern Shandong during the Shang and Zhou periods]. *Kaogu* 2004(4):53–67.

—2009. Cong xinfaxian de jifeng shuxin shuoji Liangchengzhen deng yizhi faxian yuanqi [Origin of the discovery of Liangchengzhen and related sites from several newly found letters]. In: Fengshi Luan, ed. *Liangchengzhen yizhi yanjiu* [*Research on the Liangchengzhen site*]. Beijing: Wenwu Press. pp. 358–368.

—2013. The eastern territories of the Shang and Western Zhou: Military expansion and cultural assimilation. In: Anne P. Underhill, ed. *A Companion to Chinese Archaeology*. Malden, MA: Wiley-Blackwell Press. pp. 473–493. https://doi.org/10.1002/9781118325698.ch23

FANG, HUI, GARY M. FEINMAN, AND LINDA M. NICHOLAS. 2015. Imperial expansion, public investment, and the long path of history: China's initial political unification and its aftermath. *Proceedings of the National Academy of Sciences* 112(30):9224–9229. https://doi.org/10.1073/pnas.1419157112

FANG, HUI, GARY M. FEINMAN, ANNE P. UNDERHILL, AND LINDA M. NICHOLAS. 2004. Settlement pattern survey in the Rizhao area: A preliminary effort to consider Han and pre-Han demography. In: *The Taipei Papers*, Volume 2, edited by Peter Bellwood and Doreen Bowdery. *Bulletin of the Indo-Pacific Prehistory Association* 24:79–82. https://doi.org/10.7152/bippa.v24i0.11873

FANG, HUI, FENGSHI LUAN, HAIGUANG YU, FENGSHU CAI, ANNE UNDERHILL, GARY FEINMAN, LINDA NICHOLAS, AND GWEN BENNETT. 2002. Shandong Rizhao diqu xitong quyu diaocha de xin shouhuo [New results from the systematic, regional survey in the Rizhao district of Shandong]. *Kaogu* 2002(5):10–18.

FANG, HUI, ANNE UNDERHILL, GARY M. FEINMAN, LINDA M. NICHOLAS, FENGSHI LUAN, AND HAIGUANG YU. 2008. Lu dongnan yanhai diqu juluo xingtai bianqian yu shehui fuzahua jincheng yanjiu [Research on the development of complexity and change in regional settlement patterns in the southeastern coastal area of Shandong]. *Dongfang Kaogu* 4:253–287.

Fang Hui, Anne Underhill, Gary M. Feinman, Linda M. Nicholas, Fengshi Luan, Haiguang Yu, and Fengshu Cai. 2012. *Ludongnan yanhai diqu xitong kaogu diaocha baogao* [*Report of the systematic archaeological regional survey in the coastal region of southeastern Shandong*]. 2 volumes. Beijing: Wenwu Press. 506 pp.

Feinman, Gary M. 1997. Thoughts on new approaches to combining the archaeological and historical records. *Journal of Archaeological Method and Theory* 4(3/4):367–377. https://doi.org/10.1007/BF02428069

—1998. Scale and social organization: Perspectives on the archaic state. In: Gary M. Feinman and Joyce Marcus, eds. *Archaic States*. Santa Fe, NM: School of American Research Press. pp. 95–133.

—2001. Settlement and landscape archaeology. In: Neil J. Smelser and Paul B. Baltes, eds. *International Encyclopedia of the Social and Behavioral* Sciences. Oxford: Pergamon Press. pp. 13937–13941. https://doi.org/10.1016/B0-08-043076-7/02073-8

—2015. Settlement and landscape archaeology. In: James D. Wright, ed. *International Encyclopedia of the Social and Behavioral Sciences*. 2nd ed. Oxford: Elsevier. pp. 654–658. https://doi.org/10.1016/B978-0-08-097086-8.13041-7

Feinman, Gary M., Hui Fang, and Linda M. Nicholas. 2019a. Coastal Shandong, China: The longue durée. *Journal of Anthropological Archaeology* 55:101076 https://doi.org/10.1016/j.jaa.2019.101076

—2019b. Political unification, economic synchronization, and demographic growth: Long-term settlement pattern shifts in eastern Shandong. In: Lorenz Rahmstorf and Edward Stratford, eds. *Weights and Marketplaces from the Bronze Age to the Early Modern Period*. Proceedings of Two Workshops. Funded by the European Research Council (ERC). Kiel: Wachholtz Verlag; Hamburg: Murmann Publishers. pp. 355–376. (Weight & Value 1.)

Feinman, Gary M., Stephen A. Kowalewski, and Richard E. Blanton. 1984. Modelling ceramic production and organizational change in the pre-Hispanic Valley of Oaxaca, Mexico. In: Sander E. van der Leeuw and Alison C. Pritchard, eds. *The Many Dimensions of Pottery: Ceramics in Archaeology and Anthropology*. Amsterdam: Albert Egges Van Giffen Institute for Pre-and Proto-history. pp. 297–333. (Cingula 7.)

Feinman, Gary M., and Joyce Marcus, eds. 1998. *Archaic States*. Sante Fe, NM: School of American Research Press. 427 pp.

Feinman, Gary M., and Linda M. Nicholas. 1990. At the margins of the Monte Alban state: Settlement patterns in the Ejutla Valley, Oaxaca, Mexico. *Latin American Antiquity* 1(3):216–246. https://doi.org/10.2307/972162

—1999. Reflections on regional survey: Perspectives from the Guirún area, Oaxaca, Mexico. In: Brian R. Billman and Gary M. Feinman, eds. *Settlement Pattern Studies in the Americas: Fifty Years Since Virú*. Washington, DC: Smithsonian Institution Press. pp. 172–190.

—2013. *Settlement Patterns of the Ejutla Valley, Oaxaca, Mexico: A Diachronic Macroscale Perspective*. Chicago: Field Museum of Natural History. 330 pp. (Fieldiana: Anthropology 43.) https://doi.org/10.3158/0071-4739-43.00.1

—2017. *Settlement Patterns in the Albarradas Area of Highland Oaxaca, Mexico: Frontiers, Boundaries, and Interaction*. Chicago: Field Museum of Natural History. 162 pp. (Fieldiana: Anthropology 46.) https://doi.org/10.3158/0071-4739-46.1.1

—2018. Population, scale, and the framing of long-term history. In: Marcella Frangipane and Linda R. Manzanilla, eds. *Rethinking Urbanization and Its Living Landscapes from the Inspiring Perspective of a Great "Maestro."* Rome: Gangemi Editore. pp. 227–258. (Origini: Preistoria e Protostoria delle Civiltà Antiche 42.)

Feinman, Gary M., Linda M. Nicholas, and Hui Fang. 2010. The imprint of China's first emperor on the distant realm of eastern Shandong. *Proceedings of the National Academy of Sciences* 107(11):4851–4856. https://doi.org/10.1073/pnas.0914961107

Feinman, Gary M., Linda M. Nicholas, Zhengliang Wang, Xiao Long, and Hui Fang. 2021. A local perspective on China's initial unification: Archaeological survey and historical documents from southeastern Shandong. *Archaeological Research in Asia* 27:100294. https://doi.org/10.1016/j.ara.2021.100294

Fish, Suzanne K., and Stephen A. Kowalewski, eds. 1989. *The Archaeology of Regions: A Case for Full-coverage Survey*. Washington, DC: Smithsonian Institution Press. 277 pp.

Flad, Rowan. 2018. Urbanism as technology in early China. In: *Emerging Approaches to the Development of Urbanization in Early China,* special issue, edited by Li Liu, Tricia Owlett, and Anne P. Underhill. *Archaeological Research in Asia* 14:121–134. https://doi.org/10.1016/j.ara.2016.09.001

Fung, Christopher. 2000. The drinks are on us: Ritual, social status, and practice in Dawenkou burials, North China. *Journal of East Asian Archaeology* 2(1–2):67–92. https://doi.org/10.1163/156852300509808

Gao, Guangren. 1995. Shandong shiqian kaogu de jige xin keti [Some new topics in the prehistoric archaeology of Shandong]. In: Institute of Archaeology of the Chinese Academy of Social Sciences, ed. *Zhongguo kaoguxue lun cong* [*A collection of essays on Chinese archaeology*]. Beijing: Kexue Press. pp. 63–71.

Hally, David J. 1999. The settlement pattern of Mississippian chiefdoms in northern Georgia. In: Brian R. Billman and Gary M. Feinman, eds. *Settlement Pattern Studies in the Americas: Fifty Years Since Virú*. Washington, DC: Smithsonian Institution Press. pp. 96–115.

He, Deliang, Tongxiu Zheng, and Shengkuan Cui. 2003. Rizhao Haiqu Handai mudi kaogu de zhuyao shouhuo [Main archaeological discoveries from the Haiqu Han tombs in Rizhao]. *Wenwu Shijie* 5:41–46.

He, Nu. 2013. The Longshan period site of Taosi in southern Shanxi Province. In: Anne P. Underhill, ed. *A Companion to Chinese Archaeology*. Malden, MA. Wiley-Blackwell Press. pp. 255–277. https://doi.org/10.1002/9781118325698.ch13

—2018. Taosi: An archaeological example of urbanization as a political center in prehistoric China. *Archaeological Research in Asia* 14:20–32. https://doi.org/10.1016/j.ara.2017.03.001

Hosner, Dominic, Mayke Wagner, Pavel E. Tarasov, Xiaocheng Chen, and Christian Leipe. 2016. Spatiotemporal distribution patterns of archaeological sites in China during the Neolithic and Bronze Age: An overview. *The Holocene* 26(10):1576–1593. https://doi.org/10.1177%2F0959683616641743

Hsu, Cho-yun. 1999. The Spring and Autumn period. In: Michael Loewe and Edward L. Shaughnessy, eds. *The Cambridge History of Ancient China: From the Origins of Civilization to 221 BC*. New York: Cambridge University Press. pp. 545–586. https://doi.org/10.1017/CHOL9780521470308.010

[Huan He River Team] Huan He River Archaeological Team, Institute of Archaeology of the Chinese Academy of Social Sciences, and Archaeometry Laboratory, University of Minnesota. 1998. Huan He liuyu quyu kaogu yanjiu chubu baogao [Initial report of archaeological research in the Huan He Valley region]. *Kaogu* 1998(10):13–22.

Hui, Xiping. 2016. *Lu dongnan yanhai diqu juluo xuanzhi yu juluo bianqian yanjiu* [*Research on location of settlement and social change in the southeastern Shandong coastal area*]. Beijing: Kexue Press. 166 pp.

[IA CASS] Institute of Archaeology of the Chinese Academy of Social Sciences. 2001. *Mengcheng Yuchisi—wanbei xinshiqi shidai juluo yicun de fajue yu yanjiu* [Excavation and research on the Neolithic settlement of Yuchisi in Mengcheng, northern Anhui]. Beijing: Kexue Press.

—2007. *Mengcheng Yuchisi* (*di er bu*) [Second report for Yuchisi in Mengcheng]. Beijing: Kexue Press.

—ed. 2014. *Erlitou (1999-2006)*. Beijing: Wenwu Press. 5 volumes.

Jin, Guiyun, Fengshi Luan, Fengshu Cai, Haiguang Yu, Hui Fang, and Anne P. Underhill. 2004. Shandong Rizhao shi Liangchengzhen yizhi turang yangpin zhi guiti yanjiu [Research on phytolith soil samples from the Liangchengzhen site in Rizhao City, Shandong]. *Kaogu* 2004(9): 81–85.

Jing, Zhichun, Jigen Tang, George Rapp, and James Stoltman. 2013. Recent discoveries and some thoughts on early urbanization at Anyang. In: Anne P. Underhill, ed. *A Companion to Chinese Archaeology.* Malden, MA: Wiley-Blackwell Press. pp. 343–366. https://doi.org/10.1002/9781118325698.ch17

Johnson, Gregory A. 1973. *Local Exchange and Early State Development in Southwestern Iran.* Ann Arbor: Museum of Anthropology, University of Michigan. 205 pp. (Anthropological Papers 51.) https://doi.org/10.3998/mpub.11396443

—1980. Rank-size convexity and system integration: A view from archaeology. *Economic Geography* 56(3):234–247. https://doi.org/10.2307/142715

Kantner, John. 2008. The archaeology of regions: From discrete analytical toolkit to ubiquitous spatial perspective. *Journal of Archaeological Research* 16(1):37–81. https://doi.org/10.1007/s10814-007-9017-8

Keightley, David. 1999. The Shang: China's first historical dynasty. In: Michael Loewe and Edward L. Shaughnessy, eds. *The Cambridge History of Ancient China: From the Origins of Civilization to 221 BC.* New York: Cambridge University Press. pp. 232–291. https://doi.org/10.1017/CHOL9780521470308.006

—2000. *The Ancestral Landscape: Time, Space, and Community in Late Shang China (ca. 1200–1045 BC).* Berkeley: Institute of East Asian Studies, University of California. 209 pp. (China Research Monograph 53.)

—2012. *Working for His Majesty: Research Notes on Labor Mobilization in Late Shang China (ca. 1200–1045 BC), as Seen in the Oracle-Bone Inscriptions, with Particular Attention to Handicraft Industries, Agriculture, Warfare, Hunting, Construction, and the Shang's Legacies.* Berkeley: Institute of East Asian Studies, University of California. 507 pp.

Kern, Martin. 2007. Imperial tours and mountain inscriptions. In: Jane Portal, ed. *The First Emperor: China's Terracotta Army.* London: The British Museum Press. pp. 105–113.

Kowalewski, Stephen A. 1990. The evolution of complexity in the Valley of Oaxaca. *Annual Review of Anthropology* 19:39–58. https://doi.org/10.1146/annurev.an.19.100190.000351

—2008. Regional settlement pattern studies. *Journal of Archaeological Research* 16:225–285. https://doi.org/10.1007/s10814-008-9020-8

Kowalewski, Stephen, Gary Feinman, Laura Finsten, Richard Blanton, and Linda Nicholas. 1989. *Monte Albán's Hinterland, Part II: Prehispanic Settlement Patterns in the Tlacolula, Etla, and Ocotlan, the Valley of Oaxaca, Mexico.* Ann Arbor: Museum of Anthropology, University of Michigan. 2 volumes. (Memoirs 23.) https://doi.org/10.3998/mpub.11395313

Lee, Yun Kuen. 2002. Building the chronology of early Chinese history. *Asian Perspectives* 41(1): 15–42. https://doi.org/10.1353/asi.2002.0006

—2004. Control strategies and polity competition in the lower Yi-Luo Valley, North China. *Journal of Anthropological Archaeology* 23(2):172–195. https://doi.org/10.1016/j.jaa.2004.01.002

Legge, James. 1960. *The Chinese Classics.* Volume 4, *The She King.* Hong Kong: Hong Kong University Press. Originally published as *The She King, or, The book of ancient poetry,* Trübner, London, 1876. 587 pp. [In Chinese and English.] https://hdl.handle.net/2027/hvd.32044060119468

Lewis, Mark. 1999. Warring states political history. In: Michael Loewe and Edward L. Shaughnessy, eds. *The Cambridge History of Ancient China: From the Origins of Civilization to 221 BC.* New York: Cambridge University Press. pp. 587–650. https://doi.org/10.1017/CHOL9780521470308.011

—2007. *The Early Chinese Empires: Qin and Han*. Cambridge, MA: The Belknap Press of Harvard University Press. 321 pp.

LI, FENG. 2006. *Landscape and Power in Early China: The Crisis and Fall of the Western Zhou 1045–771 BC*. Cambridge: Cambridge University Press. 405 pp. https://doi.org/10.1017/CBO9780511489655

—2013. *Early China: A Social and Cultural History*. Cambridge: Cambridge University Press. 346 pp. https://doi.org/10.1017/CBO9781139034395

LI, FENG, AND ZHONGHE LIANG, EDS. 2018. *Longkou Guicheng: Jiaodong bandao diqu qingtong shidai guojia xingcheng guocheng de kaoguxue yanjiu (gongyuanqian 1000–qian 500 nian) [Guicheng at Longkou: An archaeological study of the formation of states on the Jiaodong Peninsula in late Bronze Age China, 1000–500 BCE]*. Beijing: Kexue Press. 2 volumes.

LI, YUNG-TI. 2005. 1930 Niandai Zhongyanyuan Shiyusuo Shandong diqu Longshan Wenhua de fajue yu diaocha gongzuo [Introduction of archaeological excavations and surveys at sites of the Longshan culture in Shandong by the Institute of History and Philology of Academia Sinica in the 1930s]. In: Hui Fang, ed. *Dongfang Kaogu Yanjiu Tongxun* [Oriental Archaeological Research Bulletin]; Volume 5, Proceedings of the International Conference on The Longshan Time and Early States, 2005, Rizhao China; Jinan: Oriental Archaeology Research Center of Shandong University. p. 13. https://www.history.sdu.edu.cn/__local/4/D9/5C/AD879AE60CB1EF8A30961F2DE5B_22912360_1705B3.pdf?e=.pdf

—2009. Liu Yao "Shandong Rizhao Liangchengzhen fujin shiqian yizhi" zhengli houji [Postscript after review of Liu Yao's "Prehistoric Sites near Liangchengzhen, Rizhao, Shandong"]. In: Fengshi Luan, ed. *Liangchengzhen yizhi yanjiu [Research on the Liangchengzhen site]*. Beijing: Wenwu Press. pp. 20–24.

LIANG, SIYONG. 1954. Longshan Wenhua—Zhongguo wenming de shiqianqi zhiyi [Longshan culture—A prehistoric period of Chinese civilization]. *Kaogu Xuebao* 1954(1):5–14.

—1959. *Kaoguxue Yanjiu Ji [Collected works on archaeological research]*. Beijing: Kexue Press. 162 pp.

LIANG, ZHONGHE. 2016. Yaowangcheng: Lu dongnan shiqian chengzhi xin moshi [Yaowangcheng: New patterns of prehistoric city sites in southeastern Shandong]. *Zhongguo Shehui Kexuebao* 5:1–3.

[LIANYUNGANG] LIANYUNGANG CULTURAL RELICS MANAGEMENT OFFICE AND LIANYUNGANG MUSEUM. 2001. Lianyungang Shi Dongliandao Donghai Langya Jun jieyu keshi diaocha baogao [Survey report on carved stone boundary marker for the east coast Langya Commandery at Donglian Island, Lianyungang City]. *Wenwu* 2001(8):22–30.

LINDUFF, KATHERYN M., ROBERT D. DRENNAN, AND GIDEON SHELACH. 2004. Early complex societies in NE China: The Chifeng International Collaborative Archaeological Research Project. *Journal of Field Archaeology* 29:45–73. https://doi.org/10.1179/jfa.2004.29.1-2.45

LINYI DISTRICT OFFICE FOR THE PROTECTION OF CULTURAL RELICS AND RIZHAO COUNTY LIBRARY. 1985. Rizhao Yaowangcheng Longshan wenhua yizhi shijue jianbao [Brief report of the test excavation of the Longshan culture site at Yaowangcheng in Rizhao]. *Shiqian Yanjiu* 1985(4):51–64.

LIU, DUNYUAN. 1956. Du "Rizhao xian Liangchengzhen deng qi ge yizhi chubu kancha" hou de yixie buchong yijian [Additional opinions after reading "The preliminary survey of seven sites, including Liangchengzhen, in Rizhao County"]. *Wenwu Cankao Ziliao* 1956(6):50.

—1958a. Rizhao Liangchengzhen Longshan wenhua yizhi diaocha [A survey of the Longshan culture site of Liangchengzhen at Rizhao]. *Kaogu Xuebao* 1958(1):25–42.

—1958b. Shandong Wulian, Jimo Xian Liang Chu Longshan Wenhua yizhi de diaocha [A survey of Longshan culture sites in Wulian and Jimo Counties in Shandong]. *Kaogu Tongxun* 1958(4):14–22.

—1972. Ji Liangchengzhen yizhi faxian de liang jian shi qi [Discovery of two stone objects from the Liangchengzhen site]. *Kaogu* 1972(4):56–57.

—1988. Youguan Rizhao Liangchengzhen yu keng yu qi de ziliao [Concerning jade objects from a jade pit at Liangchengzhen in Rizhao]. *Kaogu* 1988(2):121–123.

Liu, Fenggui, and Yizheng Ding. 1991. Lianyungang Shi Xihan jieyu keshi de faxian [Discovery of Western Han boundary carved stone markers in Lianyungang City]. *Dongnan Wenhua* 1991(1): 232–236.

Liu, Li. 1996a. Settlement patterns, chiefdom variability, and the development of early states in North China. *Journal of Anthropological Archaeology* 15(3):237–288. https://doi.org/10.1006/jaar.1996.0010

—1996b. Mortuary ritual and social hierarchy in the Longshan culture. *Early China* 21:1–46. https://doi.org/10.1017/S0362502800003394

—2000. The development and decline of social complexity in North China: Some environmental and social factors. In: *The Melaka Papers,* Volume 4, edited by Peter Bellwood. *Bulletin of the Indo-Pacific Prehistory Association* 20:14–34. https://doi.org/10.7152/bippa.v24i0.11873

—2004. *The Chinese Neolithic: Trajectories to Early States.* Cambridge: Cambridge University Press. 310 pp. https://doi.org/10.1017/CBO9780511489624

—2006. Urbanization in China: Erlitou and its hinterland. In: Glenn R. Storey, ed. *Urbanism in the Preindustrial World: Cross-cultural Approaches.* 1st ed. Tuscaloosa: The University of Alabama Press. pp. 161–189.

—2009. State emergence in early China. *Annual Review of Anthropology* 38:217–232. https://doi.org/10.1146/annurev-anthro-091908-164513

Liu, Li, and Xingcan Chen. 2001a. Settlement archaeology and the study of social complexity in China. *The Review of Archaeology* 22(2):4–22.

—2001b. Cities and towns: The control of natural resources in early states, China. *Bulletin of the Museum of Far Eastern Antiquities* 73:5–47.

—2003. *State Formation in Early China.* London: Bristol Classical Press. 189 pp.

—2006. Sociopolitical change from Neolithic to Bronze Age China. In: Miriam T. Stark, ed. *Archaeology of Asia.* Malden, MA: Blackwell Press. pp. 149–176. https://doi.org/10.1002/9780470774670.CH8

—2012. *The Archaeology of China: From the Late Paleolithic to the Early Bronze Age.* Cambridge: Cambridge University Press. 475 pp. https://doi.org/10.1017/CBO9781139015301

Liu, Li, Xingcan Chen, Yun Kuen Lee, Henry Wright, and Arlene Rosen. 2004. Settlement patterns and development of social complexity in the Yiluo region, North China. *Journal of Field Archaeology* 29(1–2):75–100. https://doi.org/10.1179/jfa.2004.29.1-2.75

Liu, Li, Xingcan Chen, Henry Wright, Hong Xu, Yongqiang Li, Guoliang Chen, Haitao Zhao, Habeom Kim, and Gyoung-ah Lee. 2019. Rise and fall of complex societies in the Yiluo region, North China: The spatial and temporal changes. *Quaternary International* 521:4–15. https://doi.org/10.1016/j.quaint.2019.05.025

Liu, Yanchang. 2002. Ju wenhua de yanjiu [Research on the Ju culture]. In: Society of Pre-Qin History Studies, ed. *Ju wenhua lunwen ji* [*Collected works of Ju culture*]. Jinan: Shandong renmin Press. pp. 80–104.

Liu, Yanchang, and Xueliang Wang. 2002. Wulian Xian Dantu Dawenkou wenhua, Longshan wenhua chengzhi he Dong Zhou shiqi muzang [Dawenkou and Longshan culture city site and Eastern Zhou period burials]. In: The Society of Chinese Archaeology, ed. *2002 Zhongguo Kaoguxue Nianjian* [*2002 Yearbook of Chinese archaeology*]. Beijing: Wenwu Press. pp. 182–184.

Liu, Yao. 2009. Shandong Rizhao Liangchengzhen fujin shiqian yizhi [Prehistoric sites in the vicinity of the Liangchengzhen site in Rizhao, Shandong]. In: Fengshi Luan, ed. *Liangchengzhen Yizhi Yanjiu* [*Research on the Liangchengzhen site*]. Beijing: Wenwu Press. pp. 1–19.

Loewe, Michael. 1986a. The former Han dynasty. In: Denis Twitchett and Michael Loewe, eds. *The Cambridge History of China.* Volume 1, *The Ch'in and Han Empires, 221 BC–AD 220.* Cambridge: Cambridge University Press. pp. 103–222. https://doi.org/10.1017/CHOL9780521243278.004

—1986b. The structure and practice of government. In: Denis Twitchett and Michael Loewe, eds. *The Cambridge History of China.* Volume 1, *The Ch'in and Han Empires, 221 BC–AD 220.* Cambridge: Cambridge University Press. pp. 463–490. https://doi.org/10.1017/CHOL9780521243278.009

LONG, TENGWEN, MAYKE WAGNER, AND PAVEL E. TARASOV. 2017. A Bayesian analysis of radiocarbon dates from prehistoric sites in the Haidai Region, East China, for evaluation of the archaeological chronology. *Journal of Archaeological Science: Reports* 12:81–90. https://doi.org/10.1016/j.jasrep.2017.01.024

LUAN, FENGSHI. 1996. *Dongyi kaogu* [*Archaeology of the eastern Yi*]. Jinan: Shandong University Press. 370 pp.

—1997. *Haidai diqu kaogu yanjiu* [*Archaeological research in the Haidai region*]. Jinan: Shandong University Press. 414 pp.

—ED. 2009. *Liangchengzhen yizhi yanjiu* [*Research on the Liangchengzhen site*]. Beijing: Wenwu Press. 368 pp.

—2013. The Dawenkou culture in the lower Yellow River and Huai River basin areas. In: Anne P. Underhill, ed. *A Companion to Chinese Archaeology.* Malden, MA: Wiley-Blackwell Press. pp. 411–434. https://doi.org/10.1002/9781118325698.ch20

—2017. Haidai diqu de shiqian juluo yanbian yu zaoqi wenming [Changes in prehistoric settlements and early civilization in the Haidai area]. In: *Luan Fengshi kaogu wenji* [*Collected archaeological works by Luan Fengshi*], Volume 2. Beijing: Wenwu Press. pp. 594–698.

—2019. Liangchengzhen de Longshan Wenhua chengzhi he huanhao [The moats and city of the Longshan culture at Liangchengzhen]. *Dongfang Kaogu* 16:274–288.

LUAN, FENGSHI, HUI FANG, AND GUIYUN JIN. 2002. *Kaoguxue lilun, fangfa, jishu* [*Archaeological theory, methods, and techniques*]. Beijing: Wenwu Press. 322 pp.

LUAN, FENGSHI, HAIGUANG YU, HUI FANG, FENGSHU CAI, AND ANNE P. UNDERHILL. 2004. Shandong Rizhao shi Liangchengzhen yizhi 1998–2001 nian fajue jianbao [Short report of 1998–2001 excavations at the Liangchengzhen site in Rizhao City, Shandong]. *Kaogu* 2004(9):7–18.

LUAN, FENGSHI, HAO WU, FEN WANG, GEOFFREY CUNNAR, AND ANNE UNDERHILL. 2021. Shandong Rizhao Liangchengzhen yizhi Longshan Wenhua de shiqi shengchan [Stone tool production at the Longshan Culture site of Liangchengzhen in Rizhao, Shandong]. *Kaogu* 2021(8):82–91.

MARCUS, JOYCE. 1992. *Mesoamerican Writing Systems: Propaganda, Myth, and History in Four Ancient Civilizations.* Princeton: Princeton University Press. 495 pp.

MARCUS, JOYCE, AND KENT V. FLANNERY. 1996. *Zapotec Civilization: How Urban Society Evolved in Mexico's Oaxaca Valley.* New York: Thames and Hudson. 255 pp.

MCGOVERN, PATRICK E., HUI FANG, FENGSHI LUAN, HAIGUANG YU, ANNE P. UNDERHILL, CHEN-SHAN WANG, FENGSHU CAI, GRETCHEN R. HALL, GARY M. FEINMAN, AND ZHIJUN ZHAO. 2005. Shandong Rizhao shi Liangchengzhen yizhi Longshan wenhua jiu yicun de huaxue fenxi: jiantan jiu zai shiqian shiqi de wenhua yiyi [Chemical identification and cultural implications of a mixed fermented beverage from late prehistoric China]. *Kaogu* 2005(3):73–85.

MCGOVERN, PATRICK E., ANNE P. UNDERHILL, HUI FANG, FENGSHI LUAN, GRETCHEN R. HALL, HAIGUANG YU, CHEN-SHAN WANG, FENGSHU CAI, ZHIJUN ZHAO, AND GARY R. FEINMAN. 2005. Chemical identification and cultural implications of a mixed fermented beverage from late prehistoric China. *Asian Perspectives* 44(2):249–275. https://doi.org/10.1353/asi.2005.0026

MCINTOSH, RODERICK J. 1991. Early urban clusters in China and Africa: The arbitration of social ambiguity. *Journal of Field Archaeology* 18(2):199–212. https://doi.org/10.1179/009346991792208272

—1999. Clustered cities and alternative course to authority in prehistory. *Journal of East Asian Archaeology* 1(1–4):63–86.

—2005. *Ancient Middle Niger: Urbanism and the Self-organizing Landscape.* New York: Cambridge University Press. 278 pp.

McIntosh, Roderick J., and Susan Keech McIntosh. 2003. Early urban configurations on the Middle Niger: Clustered cities and landscapes of power. In: Monica L. Smith, ed. *The Social Construction of Ancient Cities*. Washington, DC: Smithsonian Institution Press. pp. 103–120.

Murowchick, Robert E. 1997. The state of Sino-foreign collaborative archaeology in China. *Orientations* 28(6):26–33.

Nanjing Museum, ed. 1985. *Rizhao Liangchengzhen taoqi* [*Pottery from the Liangchengzhen site in Rizhao*]. Beijing: Wenwu Press. 23 pp.

National Bureau of Cultural Relics. 2003. *Zhongguo Zhongyao kaogu faxian* [*Major archaeological discoveries in China in 2002*]. Beijing: Wenwu Press. 168 pp. [In Chinese and English.]

National Museum of China Center for Field Archaeology and Shandong University Department of Archaeology. 2016. *Shandong Xuehe liuyu xitong kaogu diaocha baogao* [*Report for the systematic archaeological survey in the Xue River valley, Shandong*]. Beijing: Kexue Press. 420 pp.

[OARC] Oriental Archaeology Research Center at Shandong University, Shandong Provincial Institute of Archaeology, and Archaeology Institute of Jinan City. 2003. Jinan shi Daxinzhuang yizhi chutu Shang dai jiaguwen [Discovery of Shang period inscribed oracle bones from the Daxinzhuang site in Jinan City]. *Kaogu* 2003(6):3–6.

—2004. Jinan shi Daxinzhuang Shang dai juzhi yu muzang [Burials and settlement remains from the Shang period site of Daxinzhuang in Jinan City]. *Kaogu* 2004(7):25–33.

Owlett, Tricia E., Li Liu, and Anne P. Underhill. 2018. Emerging approaches to the development of urbanization in early China. *Archaeological Research in Asia* 14:1–6. https://doi.org/10.1016/j.ara.2017.12.003

Pei, Anping. 2014. *Zhongguo shiqian juluo qunju xingtai yanjiu* [*Research on clusters of settlements from the prehistoric period of China*]. Beijing: Zhonghua shuju Press. 435 pp.

—2020. *A Study of Prehistoric Settlement Patterns in China*. Singapore: Springer. 458 pp. https://doi.org/10.1007/978-981-15-3060-9

Peterson, Christian E., and Robert D. Drennan. 2005. Communities, settlements, sites, and surveys: Regional-scale analysis of prehistoric human interaction. *American Antiquity* 70(1):5–30. https://doi.org/10.2307/40035266

Peterson, Christian E., Xueming Lu, Robert D. Drennan, and Da Zhu. 2014. *Hongshan Regional Organization in the Upper Daling Valley*. Pittsburgh: Center for Comparative Archaeology, University of Pittsburgh. 102 pp. [In Chinese and English.]

Qiu, Shihua, and Lianzhen Cai. 2001. Xia Shang Zhou duandai gongcheng zhong de tanshisi niandai kuangjia [A ^{14}C chronological framework for the Xia–Shang–Zhou chronology project]. *Kaogu* 2001(1):90–100.

Ran, Zhaode, and Zhi Chen, eds. 1962. *Han Shu Xuan* [*Selections of the Han histories*]. Beijing: Zhonghua shuju Press. 300 pp.

Reinhart, Katrinka. 2015. Ritual feasting and empowerment at Yanshi Shangcheng. *Journal of Anthropological Archaeology* 39:76–109. https://doi.org/10.1016/j.jaa.2015.01.001

Rizhao City Library and Linyi District Committee for Management of Cultural Relics. 1986. Shandong Rizhao Longshan wenhua yizhi diaocha [Survey of Longshan culture sites in Rizhao County, Shandong]. *Kaogu* 1986(8):680–702.

Rizhao Museum. 2006. Shandong Rizhaoshi Dagucheng hanmu fajue jianbao [Brief excavation report of Han tomb at Dagucheng, Rizhao City, Shandong]. *Dongnan Wenhua* 2006(4):18–27.

Rothman, Mitchell S., ed. 2001. *Uruk Mesopotamia and Its Neighbors: Cross-cultural Interactions in the Era of State Formation*. 1st ed. Santa Fe, NM: School for Advanced Research Press. 556 pp.

—2004. Studying the development of complex society: Mesopotamia in the late fifth and fourth millennia BC. *Journal of Archaeological Research* 12(1):75–119. https://doi.org/10.1023/B:JARE.0000016695.21169.37

SADAO, NISHIJIMA. 1986. The economic and social history of Former Han. In: Denis Twitchett and Michael Loewe, eds. *The Cambridge History of China.* Volume 1, *The Ch'in and Han Empires, 221 B.C.–A.D.* 220. Cambridge: Cambridge University Press. pp. 545–607. https://doi.org/10.1017/CHOL9780521243278.012

SANDERS, WILLIAM T., JEFFREY R. PARSONS, AND ROBERT S. SANTLEY. 1979. *The Basin of Mexico.* New York: Academic Press. 575 pp.

SHANDONG ARCHAEOLOGICAL TEAM OF THE INSTITUTE OF ARCHAEOLOGY OF THE CHINESE ACADEMY OF SOCIAL SCIENCES. 1994 January 23. Yaowangcheng yizhi di er ci fajue you zhongyao faxian [Important discoveries from the second excavations at the Yaowangcheng site]. *Zhongguo Wenwu Bao.*

—2000. Shandong Tengzhou shi Qianzhangda Shang Zhou mudi 1998 nian fajue jianbao [Brief report of excavations in 1998 at the Shang and Zhou period cemetery at Qianzhangda village, Tengzhou, Shandong]. *Kaogu* 2000(7):13–28.

SHANDONG ARCHAEOLOGICAL TEAM OF THE INSTITUTE OF ARCHAEOLOGY OF THE CHINESE ACADEMY OF SOCIAL SCIENCES, SHANDONG PROVINCIAL INSTITUTE OF ARCHAEOLOGY, AND RIZHAO BUREAU OF CULTURAL RELICS. 2015. Shandong Rizhao Shi Yaowangcheng yizhi 2012 nian de diaocha yu fajue [Survey and excavation of the Yaowangcheng site in 2012 in Rizhao City, Shandong]. *Kaogu* 2015(9):7–24.

SHANDONG PROVINCIAL INSTITUTE OF ARCHAEOLOGY, ZAOZHUANG CITY BUREAU OF CULTURAL RELICS; DELIANG HE AND ZHIMIN LIU, CHIEF EDS. 1996. *Zaozhuang Jianxin: Xinshiqi shidai yizhi fajue baogao* [*The site of Jianxin at Zaozhuang: Excavation report of a Neolithic site*]. Beijing: Wenwu Press. 80 pp.

SHANDONG PROVINCIAL INSTITUTE OF ARCHAEOLOGY. 2001 January 17. Wulian Dantu faxian Dawenkou Wenhua chengzhi [Discovery of a Dawenkou culture city at Dantu in Wulian]. *Zhongguo Wenwu Bao,* p. 1.

SHANDONG PROVINCIAL OFFICE FOR THE PROTECTION OF CULTURAL RELICS. 1960. Shandong Rizhao Liangchengzhen yizhi kancha jiyao [Summary of investigations at the Liangchengzhen site in Rizhao, Shandong]. *Kaogu* 1960(9):10–14.

SHANDONG PROVINCIAL OFFICE FOR THE PROTECTION OF CULTURAL RELICS AND SHANDONG PROVINCIAL MUSEUM. 1959. *Shandong wenwu xuanji: pucha bufen* [*Catalog of cultural relics in Shandong for part of the cultural relics survey*]. Beijing: Wenwu Press. 134 pp.

SHANDONG UNIVERSITY, DEPARTMENT OF HISTORY, ARCHAEOLOGY SPECIALTY. 1990. *Sishui Yinjiacheng* [Excavation report of the Yinjiacheng site at Sishui]. Beijing: Wenwu Press. 363 pp.

SHANDONG UNIVERSITY, DEPARTMENT OF ARCHAEOLOGY, SCHOOL OF HISTORY AND CULTURE. 2013. Shandong Rizhao Sujiacun yizhi diaocha kantan jianbao [Preliminary report on the survey and exploration of the Sujiacun site in Rizhao, Shandong]. *Zhongyuan Wenwu* 4:8–13, 30.

—2016. Shandong Rizhao Shi Liujiazhuang yizhi 2007 fajue jianbao [Preliminary excavation report for the Liujiazhuang site in Rizhao, Shandong]. *Kaogu* 11:26.

SHANDONG UNIVERSITY, DEPARTMENT OF ARCHAEOLOGY AND MUSEOLOGY, SCHOOL OF HISTORY AND CULTURE, AND CHENGZIYA SITE MUSEUM AT ZHANGQIU DISTRICT, JINAN CITY. 2018. Jinan Shi Zhangqiu Qu Jiaojia xinshiqi shidai yizhi [The Neolithic site of Jiaojia in the Zhangqiu area of Jinan City]. *Kaogu* 7:28–43.

SHANDONG UNIVERSITY, DEPARTMENT OF ARCHAEOLOGY AND MUSEOLOGY, SCHOOL OF HISTORY AND CULTURE, AND CHENGZIYA SITE MUSEUM AT ZHANGQIU DISTRICT, JINAN CITY. 2019a. Jinan Shi Zhangqiu qu Jiaojia yizhi 2016-2017 nian juluo diaocha yu fajue jianbao [Initial report for the excavation at the Jiaojia site and survey in the Zhangqiu District of Jinan City 2016–2017]. *Kaogu* 12:3–19.

—2019b. Jinan shi Zhangqiu Jiaojia yizhi 2016–2017 nian daxing muzang fajue jianbao [Initial report for the 2016–2017 excavation of large burials at the Jiaojia site in Zhangqiu, Jinan City]. *Kaogu* 12:20–48.

Shandong University, Department of Archaeology and Museology, and Shandong Provincial Institute of Archaeology. 2021. Shandong Rizhao Shi Liangchengzhen Yizhi 2018 Nian Fajue Jianbao. [Initial report for the 2018 excavation of the Liangchengzhen site in 2018 in Rizhao City, Shandong]. *Kaogu* 2021(10):16–37.

Shaughnessy, Edward L. 1999. Western Zhou history. In: Michael Loewe and Edward L. Shaughnessy, eds. *The Cambridge History of Ancient China: From the Origins of Civilization to 221 BC*. New York: Cambridge University Press. pp. 292–351. https://doi.org/10.1017/CHOL9780521470308.007

Shelach, Gideon. 1998. A settlement pattern study in northeast China: Results and potential contributions of western theory and methods to Chinese archaeology. *Antiquity* 72(275):114–127. https://doi.org/10.1017/S0003598X00086324

—1999. *Leadership Strategies, Economic Activity, and Interregional Interaction: Social Complexity in Northeast China*. New York: Kluwer Academic/Plenum Publishers. 295 pp.

Shelach, Gideon, and Yitzhak Jaffe. 2014. The earliest states in China: A long-term trajectory approach. *Journal of Archaeological Research* 22(4):327–364. https://doi.org/10.1007/s10814-014-9074-8

Shelach-Lavi, Gideon. 2015. *The Archaeology of Early China: From Prehistory to the Han Dynasty*. New York: Cambridge University Press. 373 pp. https://doi.org/10.1017/CBO9781139022682

Shen, Chen. 2003. Compromises and conflicts: Production and commerce in the royal cities of Eastern Zhou, China. In: Monica L. Smith, ed. *The Social Construction of Ancient Cities*. Washington, DC: Smithsonian Institution Press. pp. 290–310.

Sima, Qian. 1975. *Shiji* [*Records of the grand historian*]. Edited by Zhonghua shuju. *Qin shi huang benji* [*History of the Qin emperor*], Volume 6. Beijing: Zhonghua shuju Press. 72 pp.

Skinner, G. William. 1964. Marketing and social structure in rural China, part I. *The Journal of Asian Studies* 24(1):3–43. https://doi.org/10.2307/2050412

—1965. Marketing and social structure in rural China, part II. *The Journal of Asian Studies* 24(2): 195–228. https://doi.org/10.2307/2050562

Small, David B. 2006. Factoring the countryside into urban populations. In: Glenn R. Storey, ed. *Urbanism in the Preindustrial World: Cross-cultural Approaches*. 1st ed. Tuscaloosa: University of Alabama Press. pp. 317–329.

Smith, Adam T. 2003. *The Political Landscape: Constellations of Authority in Early Complex Polities*. Berkeley: University of California Press. 346 pp. https://hdl.handle.net/2027/heb.32137

Smith, Monica L. 2003. Introduction: The social construction of ancient cities. In: Monica L. Smith, ed. *The Social Construction of Ancient Cities*. Washington, DC: Smithsonian Institution Press. pp. 1–36.

—2005. Networks, territories, and the cartography of ancient states. *Annals of the Association of American Geographers* 95(4):832–849. https://doi.org/10.1111/j.1467-8306.2005.00489.x

—2014. The archaeology of urban landscapes. *Annual Review of Anthropology* 43:307–323. https://doi.org/10.1146/annurev-anthro-102313-025839

Spencer, Charles S., and Elsa M. Redmond. 2004. Primary state formation in Mesoamerica. *Annual Review of Anthropology* 33:173–199. https://doi.org/10.1146/annurev.anthro.33.070203.143823

Stanley, Daniel J., Zhongyuan Chen, and Jian Song. 1999. Inundation, sea-level rise and transition from Neolithic to Bronze Age cultures, Yangtze Delta, China. *Geoarchaeology* 14(1):15–26. https://doi.org/10.1002/(SICI)1520-6548(199901)14:1%3C15::AID-GEA2%3E3.0.CO;2-N

Stanley, Daniel J., and Andrew G. Warne. 1997. Holocene sea-level change and early human utilization of deltas. *GSA Today* 7(12):1–7. https://repository.si.edu/bitstream/handle/10088/7448/JD_stanley_4.pdf

STEIN, GIL J. 1998. Heterogeneity, power, and political economy: Some current research issues in the archaeology of Old World complex societies. *Journal of Archaeological Research* 6(1):1–44. https://doi.org/10.1007/BF02443149

—2001. Understanding ancient state societies in the Old World. In: Gary M. Feinman and T. Douglas Price, eds. *Archaeology at the Millennium: A Sourcebook.* New York: Kluwer Academic/Plenum Publishers. pp. 353–379.

STEPONAITIS, VINCAS P. 1981. Settlement hierarchies and political complexity in nonmarket societies: The Formative Period of the Valley of Mexico. *American Anthropologist* 83(2):320–363. https://doi.org/10.1525/aa.1981.83.2.02a00030

SUN, YAN. 2017. Inscribed bronzes, gift-giving and social networks in the Early Western Zhou: A case study of the Yan cemetery at Liulihe. In: Edward L. Shaughnessy, ed. *Imprints of Kinship: Studies of Recently Discovered Bronze Inscriptions from Ancient China.* Hong Kong: The Chinese University of Hong Kong Press. pp. 47–70.

TAN, QIXIANG, ED. 1982. Zhongguo lishi ditu ji [*The historical atlas of China*], Volume 1. 1st ed. Shanghai: Ditu Press.

TRIGGER, BRUCE G. 1999. Shang political organization: A comparative approach. *Journal of East Asian Archaeology* 1:43–62.

—2003. *Understanding Early Civilizations: A Comparative Study.* New York: Cambridge University Press. 757 pp. https://doi.org/10.1017/CBO9780511840630

UNDERHILL, ANNE P. 2000. An analysis of mortuary ritual at the Dawenkou site, Shandong, China. *Journal of East Asian Archaeology* 2(1):93–127. https://doi.org/10.1163/156852300509817

—2002. *Craft Production and Social Change in Northern China.* New York: Kluwer Academic/Plenum Publishers. 346 pp.

—2003. Investigating variation in organization of ceramic production: An ethnoarchaeological study in Guizhou, China. *Journal of Archaeological Method and Theory* 10(3):203–275. https://doi.org/10.1023/A%3A1026035706326

—2006. Warfare and the development of states in China. In: Elizabeth N. Arkush and Mark W. Allen, eds. *The Archaeology of Warfare: Prehistories of Raiding and Conquest.* Gainesville: University Press of Florida. pp. 253–285.

—2013. Introduction: Investigating the development and nature of complex societies in ancient China. In: Anne P. Underhill, ed. *A Companion to Chinese Archaeology.* Malden, MA: Wiley-Blackwell Press. pp. 3–12.

—2017. The Middle and Late Neolithic Periods of China: Major themes, unresolved issues, and suggestions for future research. In: Junko Habu, Peter V. Lape, and John W. Olsen, eds. *Handbook of East and Southeast Asian Archaeology.* New York: Springer. pp. 483–502. https://doi.org/10.1007/978-1-4939-6521-2_29

—2018. Urbanization and new social contexts for consumption of food and drink in northern China. In: *Emerging Approaches to the Development of Urbanization in Early China,* special issue, edited by Li Liu, Tricia Owlett, and Anne P. Underhill. *Archaeological Research in Asia* 14:7–19. https://doi.org/10.1016/j.ara.2017.07.004

UNDERHILL, ANNE P., GEOFFREY E. CUNNAR, FENGSHI LUAN, GARY CRAWFORD, HAIGUANG YU, HUI FANG, FEN WANG, AND HAO WU. 2021. Urbanization in the eastern seaboard (Haidai) area of northern China: Perspectives from the late Neolithic site of Liangchengzhen. *Journal of Anthropological Archaeology* 62:101288. https://doi.org/10.1016/j.jaa.2021.101288

UNDERHILL, ANNE P., AND HUI FANG. 2004. Early state economic systems of China. In: Gary M. Feinman and Linda M. Nicholas, eds. *Archaeological Perspectives on Political Economies.* Salt Lake City: University of Utah Press. pp. 119–132.

UNDERHILL, ANNE P., GARY M. FEINMAN, LINDA NICHOLAS, GWEN BENNETT, FENGSHU CAI, HAIGUANG YU, FENGSHI LUAN, AND HUI FANG. 1998. Systematic, regional survey in SE Shandong

Province, China. *Journal of Field Archaeology* 25(4):453–474. https://doi.org/10.1179/009346998792005315

UNDERHILL, ANNE P., GARY M. FEINMAN, LINDA M. NICHOLAS, GWEN BENNETT, HUI FANG, FENGSHI LUAN, HAIGUANG YU, AND FENGSHU CAI. 2002. Regional survey and the development of complex societies in southeastern Shandong, China. *Antiquity* 76(293):745–755. https://doi.org/10.1017/S0003598X00091195

UNDERHILL, ANNE P., GARY M. FEINMAN, LINDA M. NICHOLAS, HUI FANG, FENGSHI LUAN, HAIGUANG YU, AND FENGSHU CAI. 2008. Changes in regional settlement patterns and the development of complex societies in southeastern Shandong, China. *Journal of Anthropological Archaeology* 27(1):1–29. https://doi.org/10.1016/j.jaa.2006.11.002

UNDERHILL, ANNE P., FEN WANG, AND FENGSHI LUAN. 2017. Longshan Shidai taoqi de shengchan, fenpei he xiaofei: Liangchengzhen yizhi taobei yanjiu [The production, distribution, and consumption of pottery during the Longshan Period: Analysis of *bei* cups at Liangchengzhen]; translated by Shiwei Jiang. In: Fengshi Luan, Fen Wang, and Yu Dong, eds. *Longshan wenhua yu zaoqi wenming—Di 22jie guoji lishi kexue dahui Zhangqiu weixing huiyi wenji* [Longshan Culture and Early Civilization—Proceedings from the International Conference of the 22nd International Historical Sciences, Satellite Meeting at Zhangqiu]. Beijing: Wenwu Press. pp. 66–76.

WANG, FEN. 2013. The Houli and Beixin cultures. In: Anne P. Underhill, ed. *A Companion to Chinese Archaeology*. Malden, MA: Wiley-Blackwell Press. pp. 387–410. https://doi.org/10.1002/9781118325698.ch19

WANG, QING. 2002. *Haidai diqu Zhou dai muzang yanjiu [Research into the burials of the Zhou Dynasty in the Haidai region]*. Jinan: Shandong University Press. 218 pp.

WANG, SHAOZENG. 1994. Rizhao Wang Xiantang xiansheng shilue [Biographical sketch of Mr. Wang Xiantang]. *Shandong Tushuguan Jikan* (1):51–55.

WANG, SHUMING, SHANDONG PROVINCIAL INSTITUTE OF ARCHAEOLOGY, JUXIAN OFFICE FOR THE PROTECTION OF CULTURAL RELICS, AND SHANDONG PROVINCIAL MUSEUM. 1987. Shandong Juxian Lingyanghe Dawenkou Wenhua muzang fajue jianbao [Short report on the excavation of the Dawenkou culture burials at Lingyanghe, Juxian, Shandong]. *Shiqian Yanjiu* 3:62–82.

WANG, TAO. 1999. A city with many faces: Urban development in pre-modern China. In: Roderick Whitfield and Tao Wang, eds., translators. *Exploring China's Past: New Discoveries and Studies in Archaeology and Art*. London: Saffron Books. pp. 111–122. (International Series in Chinese Art and Archaeology 1.)

WANG, XIANTANG. 1983. *Shandong guguo kao [Study of ancient states in Shandong]*. Jinan: Qilu Press. 280 pp.

WANG, YONGBO, AND CHUANCHANG WANG. 2016. *Shandong gu cheng gu guo kaolue* [Preliminary analysis of ancient cities and states in Shandong]. Beijing: Wenwu Press.

WILKINSON, T. J. 2000. Regional approaches to Mesopotamian archaeology: The contribution of archaeological surveys. *Journal of Archaeological Research* 8(3):219–267. https://doi.org/10.1023/A:1009487620969

WRIGHT, HENRY T. 1986. The evolution of civilizations. In: David J. Meltzer, Don D. Fowler, and Jeremy A. Sabloff, eds. *American Archaeology Past and Future: A Celebration of the Society for American Archaeology 1935–1985*. Washington, DC: Smithsonian Institution Press. pp. 323–365.

—2005. The polycentricity of the archaic civilizations. In: Vernon L. Scarborough, ed. *A Catalyst for Ideas: Anthropological Archaeology and the Legacy of Douglas W. Schwartz*. Santa Fe, NM: School of American Research Press. pp. 149–167.

—2006. Early state dynamics as political experiment. *Journal of Anthropological Research* 62(3):305–319. https://doi.org/10.3998/jar.0521004.0062.301

XIA, NAI. 1985. *Zhongguo Wenming de Qiyuan [Origins of Chinese civilization]*. Beijing: Wenwu Press. 131 pp.

Xia–Shang–Zhou Chronology Specialists Group. 2000. *Xia Shang Zhou duandai gongcheng 1996–2000 nian jieduan chengguo baogao: jian ben [A brief report on results from the 1996–2000 stage of the Xia-Shang-Zhou Chronology Project]*. Beijing: World Library Press. 118 pp.

Xu, Hong. 2017. *Xian Qin Chengyi Kaogu [The archaeology of enclosure settlements in the pre-Qin Period (7000–221 BC)]*. Beijing: Xiyuan Press. 2 volumes.

Xu, Hong, Guoliang Chen, and Haitao Zhao. 2004. Erlitou yizhi juluo xingtai de chubu kaocha [Preliminary analysis of the settlement pattern of the Erlitou site]. *Kaogu* 2004(11):23–31.

Yang, Bo. 1996. Shandong Wulian xian Dantu yizhi chutu yuqi [Jades unearthed from the Dantu site in Wulian County, Shandong]. *Gugong Wenwu Yuekan* 158(1996):84–94.

Yang, Bojun, ed. 1981. *Chun Qiu Zuozhuan Zhu [Comments on "Commentary of Zuo, Spring and Autumn Period"]*. 1st ed. Beijing: Zhonghua Press. 4 volumes.

Yang, Shenfu. 1984. Shandong Rizhao Guheya chutu yi pi qingtongqi [Bronze vessels unearthed from Guheya in Rizhao, Shandong]. *Kaogu* 1984(7):594–597, 606, 674.

Yang, Shenfu, Ying Hu, and Shubin Xu. 1990. Shandong Rizhao shi Zhou dai Wenhua Yicun [Preserved cultural traditions from the Zhou Period in Rizhao, Shandong]. *Wenwu* 6:72–79.

Yang, Shenfu, and Shi'an Wang. 2005. Shandong Rizhao Han dai Haiqu shi kaolue [A brief study of the history of Haiqu County during the Han period in Rizhao, Shandong]. *Dongnan Wenhua* 6:35–38.

Ye, Guishou. 1997. *Xu Shandong kaogu lu [Sequel to an investigation of Shandong's past]*. Jinan: Shandong Wenyi Press. 865 pp.

Yin, Da. 1955. *Zhongguo xinshiqi shidai [The Neolithic Age of China]*. Beijing: Xinzhi Sanlian Shudian Press. 256 pp.

Yu, Haiguang. 2005. Shandong Rizhao Liangchengzhen Longshan wenhua yizhi weicheng yiji de faxian he fajue [Probing and excavation of city wall remains at the Longshan culture site of Liangchengzhen in Rizhao, Shandong]. *Newsletter of the Center for East Asian Archaeology at Shandong University* 5:5–6.

Yuan, Ming. 1955. Rizhao Xian Liangchengzhen deng qi ge yizhi chubu kancha [Preliminary survey of seven sites, including Liangchengzhen, in Rizhao County]. *Wenwu Cankao Ziliao* 1955(12):20–41.

Yuan, Xingyun. 1983. *Xu Han nian pu [Annals of Xu Han]*. Jinan: Qilu Press. 386 pp.

Zheng, Tongxiu, and Shengkuan Cui. 2003. Beifang zui mei de 500 jian Qiqi: Shandong Rizhao Haiqu Hanmu [Five hundred pieces of lacquer in northern China from Haiqu Han tomb, Rizhao, Shandong]. *Wenwu Tiandi* (3):22–27.

Zhou, Zhenhe, ed. 2006. *Han Shu dilizhi huishi [Book of Han: Geographic annals collection]*. Hefei: Anhui Jiaoyu Press. 540 pp.

Zhouyuan Archaeological Team. 2005. Shaanxi Zhouyuan Qixing He liuyu 2002 nian kaogu diaocha baogao [Report of the archaeological survey in 2002 in the Qixing River valley at Zhouyuan, Shaanxi]. *Kaogu Xuebao* 2005(4):449–484.

Index

A

Academia Sinica, 7
adobe walls, 9
adzes, 8, 105, 106, 131, 209
agricultural cultivation, 2, 283–284
alluvial terrain
  Donggang District archaeological sites, 70
  general survey methods, 14–15
  Jiaonan County archaeological sites, 149, 190
  Lanshan District archaeological sites, 190, 249
  settlement patterns, 272, 284
  systematic full-coverage regional surveys, 13, 45–46
  Wulian District archaeological sites, 249, 263
  Zhucheng District archaeological sites, 266
Andongwei, 6, 190, 192
Anhui Province, 272
animal masks, 8
Anjiahu, 192
Anjialing archaeological site, 7, 21, 70–71
Anjiayaowangcheng, 243, 245
Anyang, 283, 287, 296
aquatic plants, 283
arrowheads, 106, 152
Atlas of Cultural Relics in China, Shandong Volume, 9
axes, 82, 105, 106, 200, 209, 233, 249, 255

B

Baima River
  geographical setting, 1
  Jiaonan County archaeological sites, 150
  1995-2007 survey summary, 27, 29, 45
  settlement patterns, 301
Baiyun archaeological site, 40, 192–193
Balizhuang, 78
Baoquanmiao archaeological site, 30, 149
Baozibu archaeological site, 36, 149–150, 190
basins, 9, 135
Bei Chengzi, 199
Bei County, 200
Beidacun archaeological site, 31, 71
Beifanjiacun
  See Gaoxing City
Beijng Road, 94
Beikuo, 42
Beiwangjiacun, 72
Beixiao River
  Dajiepai archaeological site, 80
  Dantu archaeological site, 249
  Liangchengzhen archaeological site, 105
  Liangjialuochuan archaeological site, 170
  Luohuaqian archaeological site, 107
  Qianbianzhuang archaeological site, 116
  Wangjiayao archaeological site, 256
  Xiuqiyuan archaeological site, 184
Beixin period, 37, 82–84, 271–272
ben (adze), 8, 105, 106, 131, 209
Bennett, Gwen, xvi
black pottery, 99
black sediment, 99, 163, 179, 207, 219, 233, 259
black ware, 285
body sherds
  See sherds
Bohai Sea, 297
boundary marker stones, 46, 180, 264, 267
bowls, 117, 187
bricks (Han period)
  Donggang District archaeological sites, 76, 140
  elite populations, 304
  Jiaonan County archaeological sites, 162, 187
  Lanshan District archaeological sites, 203, 229
  Zhucheng District archaeological sites, 265
Bronze Age
  economic and labor strategies, 283
  historical archaeological surveys, 9
  kinship networks, 286
  settlement pattern studies, 3–4, 269–271
  systematic full-coverage regional surveys, 13, 304
bronze artifacts
  adzes, 131
  arrowheads, 106
  burial sites, 298
  dagger-axes, 106, 125
  Dagucheng archaeological site, 77
  Dongjiatan archaeological site, 82
  economic strategies, 295, 297
  feasting activities, 285
  Guheya archaeological site, 94
  historical archaeological surveys, 9
  jars, 131, 215
  knife coin, 117
  Liangchengzhen archaeological site, 106
  Liujiazhuang archaeological site, 215
  Qianzhucun archaeological site, 123
  Qingdun archaeological site, 117
  ritual vessels, 82, 131
  spears, 106
  Sujiacun archaeological site, 125
  swords, 146, 148
  Taojiacun archaeological site, 131
  tripod vessels, 131
  Yaowangcheng archaeological site, 245
  Yujiacun archaeological site, 146
  Zhengjiadingzi archaeological site, 148
buffer zones, 283, 289, 295, 304
burial sites
  bronze artifacts, 298
  Donggang District archaeological sites, 88, 94, 99, 102, 105, 123, 135
  Han period, 74, 75–77, 80, 202–204, 216, 228
  historical archaeological surveys, 7, 9, 274
  Jiaonan County archaeological sites, 187
  Zhou period, 9, 125, 146, 247
  See also Han tombs; tombs

burned earth, 102, 123, 140
burnt clay
 Dongjiawa archaeological site, 153
 Fenshuizhen archaeological site, 205
 Liangchengzhen archaeological site, 106
 Majiazhuang archaeological site, 112
 Qianlianghe archaeological site, 120
 Xujiacun archaeological site, 233
burnt soil, 123, 140, 157, 209, 212, 249

C

Cai Fengshu, xv, 9, 12
Caijiacun archaeological site, 36, 150
Caijia village, 149
Caiyuan archaeological site, 26, 29, 150, 250–251
Central Plains region, 269–270
ceramic artifacts
 basins, 9, 135
 black pottery, 99
 cup base, 187
 cups, 209, 284
 distribution and diversity, 284–285, 305
 feasting activities, 285
 field investigations and collection, 17–19
 food bowls, 117
 general survey methods, 14–15
 recording methods, 20–21
 roof tiles, 74
 settlement pattern studies, 272, 287, 289, 305
 systematic full-coverage regional surveys, 305
 tripod artifacts, 9, 237
 See also diagnostic artifacts
Cha'an, 92
Chang, K.-C., 11
chan (shovel), 100, 107, 209, 233, 249
Chaobai River, 250
Chaohezhen archaeological site, 21, 26–27, 250
Chao River
 Donggang District archaeological sites, 70–71, 105
 geographical setting, 1
 Jiaonan County archaeological sites, 163, 175
 1995-2007 survey summary, 27, 28
 transportation networks, 6
 Wulian District archaeological sites, 250, 261
charcoal, 106, 212, 256
Chegou archaeological site, 43, 199
Chengyang Commandery, 4
Chengzicun archaeological site, 7
Chengzigou archaeological site, 73–74
Chengziya, 7
Chenjiagou, 249–250
Chenjiahu, 193
Chenjiazhuang, 140
Chifeng River, 13
chisels, 190, 200, 205, 209, 215, 233
Chouqiyuan archaeological site, 7
Chuanzi archaeological site, 40, 72–73, 299
Chuanzi River, 40, 144–145, 195
chui (hammer), 105, 209
Chunqiu, 237
chu (pounder), 247
Chu state, 3, 297
city walls, 21, 75, 76
climatic conditions, 1
coastal zones, 295, 299, 301, 303
collection methodologies, 17–19
complex society development
 ceramic artifact distribution and diversity, 284–285, 305
 community interactions, 285–286, 295, 297–299, 301, 303, 305
 economic and labor strategies, 283–284, 285, 286–287, 301, 303, 305
 regional sociopolitical organization, 283–287, 304–305
 research methodologies, 11–14
 settlement patterns, 272, 274, 305–306
 social hierarchies, 277, 280, 282, 283–285, 295
 state formation, 269–271
copper artifacts, 9
cultural layers
 field investigations and collection, 17–19
 recording methods, 20–21
 settlement pattern studies, 272
 soil characteristics, 73–75, 83, 99, 107, 147
Cultural Preservation Bureau, 124, 125
Cultural Relics Bureau
 Donggang District, 88, 140, 147
 Jiaonan County, 156, 163, 168, 187, 190
 Lanshan District, 192, 214, 228, 237, 247
 Wulian District, 259
cup base, 187
cups, 209, 284

D

Dabuluo archaeological site, 43
Dacaopo archaeological site, 74–75
Dachang, 45
Dachangwang'ai, 136
Dachangzhen area, 27, 29
Dacun, 45, 228
dagger-axes, 106, 125
Dagou archaeological site
 1995-2007 survey summary, 36
 regional sociopolitical organization, 305
 settlement patterns, 295, 301
 site descriptions, 150–151, 187
Daguanzhuangdongshan, 194
Dagucheng archaeological site
 elite control strategies, 303
 1995-2007 survey summary, 36
 regional sociopolitical organization, 305
 settlement patterns, 298, 301
 site descriptions, 75–76, 147
Dagudui earthen mound, 7
Daguzhen, 77
Dahoucun archaeological site, 45
Dajiepai archaeological site, 80, 82
Dalan archaeological site, 30, 153–154
Dalingnantou archaeological site, 38, 83
Dalutuan village, 154–155
Dantu archaeological site
 historical archaeological surveys, 7, 8, 9, 274
 jade objects, 8
 settlement patterns, 272, 277, 280, 295, 298
 site descriptions, 249
Danuanzhang archaeological site, 85
dao (knife), 70, 105, 106, 125, 152, 190, 200, 209, 247
Dapengding, 196–197
Dapo archaeological site, 43, 195–196
Daqianli, 198
Daquhe, 40, 197
Daqu River, 208, 221, 232
Dashihekou village, 157
Dashiqiaocun archaeological site, 31, 86–87
Dataoyuan archaeological site
 historical archaeological surveys, 8
 1995-2007 survey summary, 28
 settlement patterns, 295
 site descriptions, 87–88
Datushan archaeological site
 elite control strategies, 303
 1995-2007 survey summary, 43, 44

regional sociopolitical organization, 305
settlement patterns, 299, 301
site descriptions, 198–201
Dawacun archaeological site, 7, 8
Da Wang Fen (tomb), 75, 76
Dawenkou period
Dantu archaeological site, 249
Dashihekou, 157
Donghaiyu archaeological site, 78, 80
Fengjiagou archaeological site, 92
importance, 11
jade objects, 8
Jinggou archaeological site, 208–209
Liangchengzhen archaeological site, 106
Matuan archaeological site, 219
Nantunling archaeological site, 114
Nanzhangjiazhuang archaeological site, 265
1995-2007 survey summary, 37, 40–41, 43–44
Qianshuichegou archaeological site, 223
regional sociopolitical organization, 305
settlement patterns, 11, 12, 271–272, 274
Tashan, 178
Xiaodaituan archaeological site, 230
Xilinzitou archaeological site, 140
Xisi archaeological site, 185, 187
Xujiacun archaeological site, 233–234
Yaowangcheng archaeological site, 243, 245
Zhangjiadazhuang archaeological site, 189–190
Zhoujiacun archaeological site, 189
Daxiangdian, 30, 89, 91, 121
Daxinzhuang, 287, 289
Dayangjuan archaeological site, 91
Dayaowangcheng, 243
Dazhuang, 252–253
Dazhuangzi, 202–203, 229
defense strategies, 297–298
descent groups
See kinship networks
diagnostic artifacts
field investigations and collection, 18, 68
Longshan period, 245, 277, 280, 287, 289
recording methods, 20–21
Shang period, 144, 287, 289
site characterization, 11
Yueshi period, 144, 287
Zhou period, 73
Dijia River Reservoir, 153, 170, 172
Dingjialiugou archaeological site, 46, 152
Dingjiazhuang archaeological site, 28, 82
Dingliuzhoushan village, 200
Dinglutushan, 199
Dingshiqiao archaeological site, 46, 157–158
ding (tripod) vessel, 9, 131
dogs, 245
Dongdingjiazhuang, 158
Donggang District
geographic setting, 1
historical archaeological surveys, 9
1995-2007 survey summary, 21, 26–31, 36–46
site descriptions, 70–148
Dongguan Commandery, 4
Donghai Prefecture, 264
Donghaiyu archaeological site
historical archaeological surveys, 8, 9
importance, 11
1995-2007 survey summary, 37
settlement patterns, 272, 282, 284
site descriptions, 78, 80
Donghu, 83
Donghuaya archaeological site, 26, 251
Dongjiatan archaeological site, 31, 82
Dongjiawa archaeological site, 27, 153
Donglianghe archaeological site, 37, 82–83
Donglinzitou archaeological site, 42, 83
Dongmujiacun, 194–195
Dongnanpo, 251–252
Dongnanshan, 195
Dongnanying, 83, 85
Dongshanqian archaeological site, 85–86, 116
Dongshizilu, 158, 166
Dongsi, 155–156
Dongtaoyuan, 263–264
Dongwangjiacun archaeological site, 29, 88–89, 284
Dongxiaoquhe village, 208
Dongxiaozhuang, 190
Dongyi people, 3, 297
Dong Yu, 124
Dongzaozi archaeological site, 91
Dong Zuobin, 7
drinking cups, 284
Dujia River, 251–253

E

Early Beixin period, 83
Early Bronze Age
diagnostic artifacts, 287
economic and labor strategies, 283
intercommunity conflict, 295
kinship networks, 286
settlement pattern studies, 269–271, 289
sociopolitical change, 304
Early Dawenkou period, 114, 272
Early Longshan period
ceramic artifact distribution and diversity, 11, 305
community interactions, 305
regional sociopolitical organization, 304
settlement patterns, 271, 277, 280, 282, 283–284, 305–306
Early Shang period, 286, 287
earthen mounds, 267
earthen platforms, 99, 151
earthen tombs, 133, 158
earthen walls, 75, 270, 297, 301, 305
Eastern Han period, 4, 70, 114, 160, 162, 171, 189
Eastern Yi people, 3, 297
Eastern Zhou period
regional sociopolitical organization, 289, 295–296, 305
settlement pattern studies, 289, 295, 298–299, 301
social hierarchies, 289, 296, 299
economic strategies, 283–284, 285, 286, 295, 297, 301, 303, 305
elite control strategies, 283, 284–287, 295, 296, 298, 301, 303, 305
Erlitou period, 68, 269, 286, 287, 304
Er Wang Fen (tomb), 75

F

Fang Hui, xvi, 12
fangkong shi chu (hoe), 116
fanglun (spindle whorl), 200, 225, 234
Fanjiaguanzhuang archaeological site, 28, 92
Fanjiahe archaeological site, 91–92
Fanjiazhuang village, 154
feasting activities, 285
Feijiacun, 72
Feijiaguanzhuang, 92, 203
Feijia River, 71, 103, 120
Feinman, Gary, xv, 12
Fengduncun archaeological site
1995-2007 survey summary, 29
settlement patterns, 295, 298

site descriptions, 158–159
Fenghao area, 296
Fenghuang Mountain, 75
Fengjiagou archaeological site, 29, 92, 272
Fengjiaguanzhuang, 173
Fenshui, 42
Fenshuizhen archaeological site, 41, 42, 204
fine-quality ceramics, 284–285, 305
fishery resources, 2
flat stones, 76, 99
food bowls, 117
four-tiered settlement hierarchies, 277, 280, 283, 289, 297, 299, 304, 305
fu (axe), 82, 105, 106, 200, 209, 233, 249
Fu Sinian, 7
Futuan archaeological site, 40, 93
Futuan River
Dagucheng archaeological site, 75
Daquhe archaeological site, 197
geographical setting, 1
Hou'ezhuang archaeological site, 99
migration patterns, 274
1995-2007 survey summary, 28, 31, 39–41, 45
Qianjiangshuigou archaeological site, 119
settlement patterns, 298
transportation networks, 6
Xiaochangwang'ai archaeological site, 136
Xiaodaituan archaeological site, 230

G

Gaixia, 272
Ganyu, 4
Gaoguang County, 200, 201
Gaojiagou archaeological site, 26, 95
Gaojialing archaeological site, 30–31, 93–94, 97, 242–243
Gaowangzhuang archaeological site, 97
Gaoxiang County, 201
Gaoxing City, 40, 192
Gaoxingzhen area, 39
Gaoyang County, 201
ge (dagger-axe), 106, 125
Gengjialan, 159–160
geographic settings, 1–2, 14–15
gift exchanges, 284–285, 305
glazed ceramics, 77
Gouwa archaeological site, 43, 44, 205
granite quarries, 2
gray sediment
Donggang District archaeological sites, 99, 107, 140
Jiaonan County archaeological sites, 158, 163, 177, 179, 182
Lanshan District archaeological sites, 192, 199, 205, 207, 223, 228–230, 233, 245, 247
Wulian District archaeological sites, 259
grinding stones, 82, 200, 233, 247
groundstone tools, 152
guan (jar), 100, 121, 237
Guanjiacun archaeological site, 37, 94–95
Guanjia village, 95
Guanzhong Basin, 296
Guhe'ai, 94
Guheya archaeological site
historical archaeological surveys, 9
1995-2007 survey summary, 38
settlement patterns, 295, 298
site descriptions, 94
Gui County, 264
gui (food bowl), 117
Gumu County, 200
Guojiaqiao, 160
Guojiazhuang archaeological site, 40, 205
Guozhuang, 73, 97
Gusitou, 253
Guzi River
Donggang District archaeological sites, 83, 114, 130, 143
1995-2007 survey summary, 28, 29, 37
settlement patterns, 297–298

H

Haiqing, 45, 162–163
Haiqingzhen area, 21, 27
Haiqu County, 4, 44, 75, 200, 303
Haiting County, 4
Haizhou Bay, 1
hammers, 105, 209
Han dynasty, 4, 264
hangtu rammed earth layers, 105
Hanjiacun, 228, 229
Han period
burial sites, 74, 75–77, 80, 202–204, 216, 228
ceramic artifacts, 82, 301, 303–304
community interactions, 301, 303
economic and labor strategies, 303–304
elite control strategies, 301, 303–304
historical surveys, 9
1995-2007 survey summary, 26–28, 30, 31, 36, 38, 40, 42–45
platform tombs, 75–77, 80, 110
regional sociopolitical organization, 303, 304, 305
settlement patterns, 11, 12, 19, 299, 301, 305–306
tiles, 74, 242
See also bricks (Han period)
Han Shu, 303
Han Shu Xuan, 4
Han tombs
Chenjiagou archaeological site, 250
Chenjiahu archaeological site, 193
Dagou archaeological site, 151
Dagucheng archaeological site, 75–77
Dajiepai archaeological site, 80
Dalutuan archaeological site, 155
Dazhuangzi archaeological site, 203
Dongnanpo archaeological site, 252
Dongshizilu archaeological site, 158
Dongsi archaeological site, 156
Feijiaguanzhuang archaeological site, 204
Guojiaqiao archaeological site, 160
Haiqing archaeological site, 162
Jiangjiacun archaeological site, 164
Jiawangdun archaeological site, 168–169
Jilihe archaeological site, 165
Jintouling archaeological site, 166
Liangchengzhen archaeological site, 105
Linquan archaeological site, 255
Liujiaguanzhuang archaeological site, 169, 216
Luohuaqian archaeological site, 107
Mahugou archaeological site, 170
Miaojiacun archaeological site, 110
Mingwangtai archaeological site, 114
Nanxinzhuang archaeological site, 171–172
Qianlaowo archaeological site, 174
Qigudun archaeological site, 173
Shaojialan archaeological site, 176–177
Shuanghe archaeological site, 175

as state power symbols, 301, 303
Sunjiayingzi archaeological site, 127
Tashan archaeological site, 178
Tuogou archaeological site, 177–178
Wujiatai archaeological site, 133
Xiaojiawa archaeological site, 183
Xiaoliuzhuang archaeological site, 140
Xiaolutuan archaeological site, 184
Xiaoshihekou archaeological site, 188
Xujiaguanzhuang archaeological site, 182
Xujiawa archaeological site, 182–183
Yaowangcheng archaeological site, 243, 245
Zhujiagou archaeological site, 263
Zhujiayao archaeological site, 148
hard earth surfaces, 152
Heiqicun archaeological site, 100
Henan Province, 13, 269–270, 286, 287, 296
Henggoucun, 201
Heshandian archaeological site, 27, 73, 102
He Shan Mountains, 1, 2, 28
Heshanzhen area, 27, 28
hoes, 116
Houbianzhuang, 116
Houcun, 40, 45
Houe'zhuang, 40, 75, 97
Houguzi archaeological site, 38, 99, 138
Houhedong, 180
Houhuangbu, 205, 207
Houjiawa, 158
Houlan archaeological site, 30, 160, 162
Houlaowo archaeological site, 27, 162
Houlianghe village, 94
Houlouhe River, 71
Houlouhe village, 71
Houlou River
Dashiqiaocun archaeological site, 86
Dataoyuan archaeological site, 87
Fanjiahe archaeological site, 92
Huangjiahe archaeological site, 97, 99, 100
Xujialou archaeological site, 143
Yingzi archaeological site, 146
Houmazhuang archaeological site, 45, 208
house foundations, 9, 274, 283–284
Houshanqian archaeological site, 31, 102–103
Houshaopo, 43, 207–208
Huai River, 297
Huanggudunling archaeological site, 160
Huangjiahe archaeological site, 28, 99–100, 295
Huangjiatang Bay, 1
Huan He River, 13
Huashan archaeological site, 100, 102
Huigudui, 164
hu (jar), 9, 131, 215
Hushan, 42
Hushanzhe area, 41

I

intercommunity conflict, 295, 297–298
iron artifacts, 77
iron-smelting production, 76

J

jade objects, 8, 140, 277
jars, 9, 100, 131, 215
Jiajiahu, 212
Jiangjiacun, 164
Jiangjiazhuang, 217
Jiangsu Province, 1, 14, 297
Jianxin, 274
Jiaodong Peninsula, 13, 297
Jiaokezhuang archaeological site, 38, 104
Jiaonan City, 69
Jiaonan County
administrative district, 4
boundaries, 177, 180, 263
geographic setting, 1
historical archaeological surveys, 9
1995-2007 survey summary, 21, 26–31, 45
site descriptions, 149–190
Jiao River, 297
Jiaoxian County, 6, 7
Jiaozhou District, 4
Jiawangdun archaeological site
1995-2007 survey summary, 27
settlement patterns, 284, 295
site descriptions, 160, 167, 168–169, 188
Jijiagou archaeological site, 43, 212
Jilicun village, 166
Jilihe archaeological site, 164–166
Jili River, 29, 45, 149–150, 158, 165, 166, 180
Jimeicun, 166
Jinan City, 7, 274
Jin dynasty, 4
Jinggezhuang, 163
Jinggou archaeological site
1995-2007 survey summary, 40
settlement patterns, 272, 282, 284
site descriptions, 208–209
Jingzhuang archaeological site, 27, 253, 255
Jintouling archaeological site, 166
Jinyin River
Heshandian archaeological site, 102
Liangchengzhen archaeological site, 107
1995-2007 survey summary, 27, 28
Qianzhucun archaeological site, 123
Qingganggou archaeological site, 118
Suijiaguanzhuang archaeological site, 125
Ju County, 6, 274
Jufeng, 6, 40, 42, 45
Jufengzhen area, 41
Jufen highway, 223
Junan County, 6, 201
Ju state, 3, 4, 44, 247, 297, 298, 299
Juxian, 6, 272, 297, 299

K

Kailai Hotel, 143
Kangtou
See Baiyun archaeological site
Kaogu, 8
Kaogu Xuebao, 8
kinship networks, 284, 286
knives, 70, 105, 106, 125, 152, 190, 200, 209, 247
Kouguanzhen area, 27
Kui Shan area, 37, 82–83, 86, 114
Kuishanzhen area, 37

L

labor strategies, 283–284, 285, 303, 305
lacquered artifacts, 77
Lai Bo, 94
Langya County, 44
Langya Jun Commandery, 200–201
Langya Prefecture, 3–4, 264, 303, 305
Langyatai archaeological site, 7, 299
Lanshan, 6
Lanshan District
geographic setting, 1
historical archaeological surveys, 9
1995-2007 survey summary, 39–42, 45

site descriptions, 190–249
Lanshan Mountains, 240
Lanshantou, 6
Late Beixin period, 114
Late Dawenkou period
Dantu archaeological site, 249
Donghaiyu archaeological site, 78, 80
Fengjiagou archaeological site, 92
Jinggou archaeological site, 209
Matuan archaeological site, 219
Nanzhangjiazhuang archaeological site, 265
Qianshuichegou archaeological site, 223
regional sociopolitical organization, 305
settlement patterns, 271, 272, 274
Xiaodaituan archaeological site, 230
Xilinzitou archaeological site, 140
Yaowangcheng archaeological site, 245
Zhoujiacun archaeological site, 189
Late Longshan period
Dajiepai archaeological site, 80
Dantu archaeological site, 249
Dataoyuan archaeological site, 87–88
diagnostic artifacts, 287
Guojiazhuang archaeological site, 205
Liangchengzhen archaeological site, 106
Liujiagou archaeological site, 216
Qianshuichegou archaeological site, 225
settlement patterns, 277, 287, 289
Xiangjiagou archaeological site, 138
Late Neolithic Period, 269–270, 286, 304–305
Late Shang period, 189, 198, 223, 242, 283, 286–287
Liangchengzhen archaeological site
administrative district, 4
ceramic artifact distribution and diversity, 284–285
community interactions, 285–286, 305
diagnostic artifacts, 289
economic and labor strategies, 305
excavation reports, 49, 67
historical archaeological surveys, 7–9, 277, 280
importance, 11
jade objects, 8, 277
1995-2007 survey summary, 21, 26–27
regional sociopolitical organization, 283–286, 289, 298–299, 304–305
research methodologies, 11–12
settlement patterns, 11–12, 272, 277, 280, 282–284, 289, 298
site descriptions, 104–106
social hierarchies, 280, 282, 283–285
transportation networks, 4, 6
Liangjialuochuan, 170
Liangshuiwang village, 108
Liang Siyong, 7
Lianhuaqian, 167
lian (sickle), 105, 205
Lianyungang City, 4, 264
Licheng area, 7
Li Ji, 7
Lijiacun, 72
Lijiatan'ai, 107
Lijiawa archaeological site, 45
Lijiazhuangzi archaeological site, 31, 108
Lingkou archaeological site, 42, 216–217
Lingmen County, 200
Lingyanghe, 272, 274
Linjia River, 71, 87, 92, 97, 144
Linquan archaeological site, 26, 255
Linyi City, 4, 6, 9
Linzitou archaeological site, 7
li (tripod) vessel, 9, 82, 131, 237
Liu Dunyuan, 8
Liuguan River, 250, 253, 256, 259, 261
Liuhangdazhuang archaeological site, 38, 169
Liujiadazhuang, 185
Liujiagou archaeological site, 43, 216
Liujiaguanzhuang, 199, 216
Liujialou archaeological site, 7, 8
Liujiazhuang, 41, 91, 214–215, 217
Liuxiaozhuang, 240
Liu Yao, 8
li (villages), 303
Liwuguan, 45
Longshan period
community interactions, 285–286, 295, 305
cultural significance, 11
diagnostic artifacts, 245, 277, 280, 287, 289
historical archaeological surveys, 7, 9
intercommunity conflict, 295
1995-2007 survey summary, 21, 26–31, 36–46
regional sociopolitical organization, 283–287, 289, 304–305
settlement patterns, 11–12, 274, 277, 280–289, 295, 298, 301, 305–306
state formation, 269–271
Longwang River, 42, 140, 207, 223, 225, 233, 241
looter's pits, 110, 176, 267
Louzidi, 218
Luan Fengshi, xvi, 12
Luochuangou archaeological site, 44, 212, 214
Luohuaqian archaeological site, 26, 107
Lu state, 3, 298

M

Ma'er Mountains, 1
Magou River, 175
Majiacun archaeological site, 40, 108, 110
Majiazhuang archaeological site, 27, 112
mao (spear), 106
Matuan archaeological site, 40, 218–219
Mengjiaguanzhuang archaeological site, 41, 215
metal artifacts, 9, 77
See also bronze artifacts
Miaohou archaeological site, 36, 170, 188
Miaojiacun archaeological site
1995-2007 survey summary, 29, 31
settlement patterns, 295, 301
site descriptions, 110
Miaoshanhou, 112
Miaowangzhuang, 116
Middle Beixin period, 83
Middle Longshan period
ceramic artifact distribution and diversity, 11, 305
intercommunity conflict, 295
regional sociopolitical organization, 304
settlement patterns, 277, 280, 282–284, 289, 295
Middle Shang period, 286, 287
migration patterns, 274, 305
mineral resources, 2
Ming dynasty, 4, 6, 148, 240
Mingwangtai, 114
moats, 49, 67–68, 272, 274, 283
moshi (grinding stones), 82, 200, 233, 247
Mujiacun River, 195
Mujiaxiaozhuang archaeological site, 40, 112

N

Nandazhuang, 247
Nanhu, 45
Nanjing City, 8
Nanjing Museum, 8
Nansi archaeological site, 36, 171
Nantunling archaeological site, 37, 114, 137, 272
Nanxiaozhuangzi, 114
Nanxin River, 72, 108, 112, 146, 243
Nanxinzhuang, 171–172, 243, 245
Nanzhangjiacun archaeological site, 38, 116
Nanzhangjiazhuang archaeological site, 46, 264–265
National Cultural Heritage Bureau, xv
national cultural relics surveys, 9
National Highway No. 204, 6
National Museum of China, xv
natural resource management, 284
Neolithic Period
  historical archaeological surveys, 9
  kinship networks, 286
  settlement patterns, 3
  state formation, 270–271
  systematic full-coverage regional surveys, 13, 269, 304
New Technology Development Zone, 37
Nicholas, Linda, xv, 12
Nitiangou, 140
North Jiangsu Plain, 1

P

paifang (row houses), 274
Paleolithic Period, 271
Panchi River, 265, 266
pan (plate), 9
*pen (*basin), 9, 135
phytolith analyses, 283
Pi County, 200
piedmont ridges/spurs, 272, 284, 295
Pingshang, 6
pits
  Chengzigou archaeological site, 74
  Linquan archaeological site, 255
  looter's pits, 110, 176, 267
  sacrificial pits, 245
  Wangshitou archaeological site, 256
  Xiaoshiling archaeological site, 267
  Yaowangcheng archaeological site, 245
plates, 9
platforms
  Dagou archaeological site, 151
  Dagucheng archaeological site, 76
  Datushan archaeological site, 199
  Dongtaoyuan archaeological site, 263
  earthen platforms, 99, 151
  Fengduncun archaeological site, 159
  Houguzi archaeological site, 99
  Jiawangdun archaeological site, 167
  Jilihe archaeological site, 166
  labor strategies, 283
  Miaojiacun archaeological site, 110
  Xiajiazhuang archaeological site, 259
  Xiaoshiling archaeological site, 266–267
  Xisi archaeological site, 187
  Yaowangcheng archaeological site, 245
platform tombs
  Dagou archaeological site, 151
  Dagucheng archaeological site, 75–77
  Dajiepai archaeological site, 80
  Jilihe archaeological site, 165–166
  Jintouling archaeological site, 166
  Miaojiacun archaeological site, 110
  Xisi archaeological site, 187
points, 105, 152, 209
polishing tools, 71, 118
potsherds
  See sherds
pottery
  See ceramic artifacts
pounders, 247
pouring vessels, 82
precipitation, 1
prestige goods, 284–285, 305
primary population centers, 277, 282, 284, 297–299, 301, 305

Q

Qian'aixia, 221
Qianbianzhuang archaeological site, 26, 116
Qiancaochang, 172
Qiane'zhuang, 75
Qianjiangshuigou archaeological site, 40, 118–119
Qianlaowo, 174
Qianlianghe archaeological site, 28, 119–120
Qianmaojiazhuang, 174
Qianpolou archaeological site, 27, 175
Qianshanqian, 103, 120
Qianshaopo, 225
Qianshuichegou archaeological site, 42, 223, 225
Qiantanxi, 120, 295
Qianwulihe archaeological site, 30, 121
Qianzhangda, 287
Qianzhucun archaeological site
  diagnostic artifacts, 289
  1995-2007 survey summary, 28
  settlement patterns, 289, 295
  site descriptions, 123, 127, 134
Qiaodongtou archaeological site, 117–118
Qi County, 200
Qigudun, 173, 179
Qingdao City, xv, 4, 7, 8, 12, 14, 187, 263
Qingdaolu highway, 89
Qingdun archaeological site, 40, 116–117, 172–173
Qing dynasty, 4, 6, 200, 240
Qingganggou archaeological site, 118
Qinguanzhuang archaeological site, 7
Qingzhou state, 4
Qinjiaguanzhuang archaeological site, 28, 118
Qinjiajiezhuang, 221
Qinjialouxiang area, 28, 29
Qin state, 3–4, 200, 264, 303, 305
Qi state, 296, 298, 303
Qixing River, 13
Qi Yanpei, 7
Quanzigou village, 100
quarries
  Baoquanmiao archaeological site, 149
  Daguanzhuang archaeological site, 196–197
  Dalan archaeological site, 154
  Dantu archaeological site, 249
  Dazhuang archaeological site, 252
  Dazhuangzi archaeological site, 202
  Dongwangjiacun archaeological site, 89
  general survey methods, 15
  granite quarries, 2
  Heshandian archaeological site, 102
  Miaoshanhou archaeological site, 114
  Nantunling archaeological site, 114
  Qianlaowo archaeological site, 174

serpentine quarries, 2, 43–44, 196–197
Taojiacun archaeological site, 130–131
Tianjiacun archaeological site, 130
Xiwangjialiugou archaeological site, 188
Xujiacun archaeological site, 137
Xujialou archaeological site, 143
Yantaishan archaeological site, 242
Qu County, 264
Qulingnantou archaeological site, 40, 221, 223
Quqiu Cheng, 237
Quqiuyi polity, 44

R

rammed earth layers
Dagou archaeological site, 151
Dongsi archaeological site, 156
Liangchengzhen archaeological site, 105
1995-2007 survey summary, 21
Yaowangcheng archaeological site, 245
regional sociopolitical organization
Han period, 303, 305
Longshan period, 283–287, 289, 304–305
Zhou period, 289, 295–299, 305
Republican Period, 4
research methodologies, 11–12
See also systematic full-coverage regional surveys
residential areas, 49
rhyolite, 2
ritual vessels, 82, 131
river basins, 2
river transportation, 284, 295
Rizhao area
community interactions, 305
geographic setting, 1–2
historical and administrative perspective, 3–4, 6
historical archaeological surveys, 7–9
intercommunity conflict, 295, 297–298
regional sociopolitical organization, 303–305
research methodologies, 13–15, 17–19
settlement patterns, 270–272, 274, 296–298
transportation networks, 4, 6
See also settlement pattern studies; site descriptions
Rizhao City, xv, 1, 4, 6
Rizhu highway, 180
road systems, 4, 6
roof tiles, 74
row houses, 274
ruralization, 303–304

S

sacrificial pits, 245
salt-making industry, 145, 242, 286, 303
sand dunes, 83
Sanhetuan, 123
Saniugou, 130
Sanlihe, 274
Sanzhuang, 6
Seagard, Jill, 21
secondary population centers, 280, 282, 283–285, 295, 298–299, 301, 303
sedentary settlements, 271
serpentine quarries, 2, 43–44, 196–197
settlement pattern studies
ceramic artifact distribution and diversity, 284–285, 305
community interactions, 285–286, 297–299, 305
excavation reports, 49, 67–68
Han period, 19, 299, 301, 305–306
historical and administrative perspective, 3–4, 6
Longshan period, 11–12, 274, 277, 280–289, 295, 305–306
map preparation, 20–21
social hierarchies, 272, 274, 277, 280, 282, 283–285, 295
spacing patterns, 301
state formation, 269–271
systematic full-coverage regional surveys, 13–15, 17–21, 271–272, 298–299, 304–306
Zhou period, 11, 12, 19, 289, 295–299, 301, 305–306
Shaanxi Province, 13, 269, 296
Shandong area
diagnostic artifacts, 287
historical archaeological surveys, 7–9, 11–12
intercommunity conflict, 295
regional sociopolitical organization, 283–287, 289, 295–299, 303–305
research methodologies, 11–15, 17–19
See also settlement pattern studies
Shandong Province, 4, 14, 269–271
Shandong Road, 94
Shandong University, xv
Shanghai, 4
Shanglijiazhuang, 129–130
Shang period
Baiyun archaeological site, 193
Chengzigou archaeological site, 73
community interactions, 286–287
Dagucheng archaeological site, 75–76
Daqianli, 198
diagnostic artifacts, 287, 289
economic and labor strategies, 283
Guojiazhuang archaeological site, 205
Gusitou, 253
intercommunity conflict, 295
Jinggou archaeological site, 208–209
Jingzhuang, 253
Liangchengzhen archaeological site, 104–105
Linquan, 255
Majiacun archaeological sites, 108, 110
1995-2007 survey summary, 27–28, 40, 46
Qianzhucun archaeological site, 123
Qinjiaguanzhuang archaeological site, 118
Qulingnantou archaeological site, 221, 223
regional sociopolitical organization, 287, 289, 304
settlement patterns, 11, 287, 289
Wangshitou archaeological site, 256, 259
Xiejiazhuangzi archaeological site, 266
Xinzhuangzi archaeological site, 144
Yangjiazhuang archaeological site, 241–242
Yaogou archaeological site, 261
Yinjiazhuang, 189
Shang state, 270
Shankoucun, 127, 129
Shanxi Province, 269
Shanyu, 225–226
Shaojialan, 176–177
Shengshui River, 166, 188
Shenhai Expressway, 207
Shenjiapo, 127
Shentuan, 6
sherds
field investigations and collection, 17–19
recording methods, 20–21
settlement pattern studies, 272, 277, 280, 289
See also diagnostic artifacts
Shiji, 303
Shijialing, 75

Shijiazhuang, 190, 192
Shijing, 296
Shijiusuo, 4, 6
Shimenkou, 221
Shimiaozicun archaeological site, 26, 177
Shizilu Town, 201
shovels, 100, 107, 209, 233, 249
shrimp ponds, 72–146, 154
Shuanghe archaeological site, 46, 175–176
Shuichegou archaeological site, 44
Shuipozi, 177
Shun legendary ruler, 3
Shuqi, 6
sickles, 105, 205
Si Shan Mountains, 2, 28
site descriptions
  Donggang District, 70–148
  Jiaonan County, 149–190
  Lanshan District, 190–249
  naming conventions, 69–70
  Wulian District, 249–263
  Zhucheng District, 263–267
skeletal remains, 245
slag samples, 76, 157, 163
smelting furnaces, 9, 76
sociopolitical change
  collapsed states, 270, 286, 304
  intercommunity conflict, 295, 297–298
  ruralization, 303–304
  state formation, 270–271
  systematic full-coverage regional surveys, 14, 304–305
soils
  burnt soil, 102, 123, 140, 157, 212
  Chengzigou archaeological site, 73
  color significance, 73–75, 76
  Dalingnantou archaeological site, 83
  Dantu archaeological site, 249
  Dashihekou archaeological site, 157
  Dongjiawa archaeological site, 153
  Fenshuizhen archaeological site, 205
  Hou'ezhuang archaeological site, 99
  Huashan archaeological site, 102
  Jijiagou archaeological site, 212
  Jinggou archaeological site, 209
  Liangchengzhen archaeological site, 106
  Majiazhuang archaeological site, 112
  Qianlianghe archaeological site, 120
  Qianwulihe archaeological site, 123
  Xiaoliuzhuang archaeological site, 140
  Xujiacun archaeological site, 233
Songshuyuan, 225
Song Yanbo, 106, 124
Songzhucun archaeological site, 9, 123
spades
  See shovels
spears, 106
spindle whorls, 200, 225, 234
spouted vessels, 9
Spring and Autumn period, 9, 82, 123, 125, 131, 148, 215, 247, 297
State Administration of Cultural Heritage, xv
state formation, 269–271
stone artifacts/tools
  adzes, 8, 105, 106, 209
  axes, 82, 105, 106, 200, 209, 233, 249, 255
  boundary markers, 46, 180, 264, 267
  chisels, 190, 200, 205, 209, 215, 233
  community interactions, 286
  field investigations and collection, 17–19
  flat stones, 76, 99
  general survey methods, 14–15
  grinding stones, 82, 200, 233, 247
  groundstone tools, 152
  hammers, 105, 209
  hoes, 116
  jade objects, 8, 140, 277
  knives, 70, 105, 106, 125, 152, 190, 200, 209, 247
  points, 105, 152, 209
  polishing tools, 71, 118
  pounders, 247
  shovels, 100, 107, 209, 233, 249
  sickles, 105, 205
Subutun, 287, 289
Suijiaguanzhuang archaeological site, 21, 125
Sujiacun archaeological site, 28, 123–125
Sun Chengfu, xvi
Sunjiayingzi, 127
Suoluoshu serpentine mine, 43–44
survey methodologies, xv–xvi
swords, 146, 148
systematic full-coverage regional surveys
  complementary publications, 46–49
  excavation reports, 49, 67–68
  field investigations and collection, 17–19
  general survey methods, 14–15, 17
  importance, 13–14, 269, 303–306
  map preparation, 20–21
  1995-2007 survey summary, 21, 26–31, 36–46
  recording methods, 20–21
  settlement pattern studies, 271–272, 274, 277, 280, 298–299
  state formation, 269–271

T

Taizhuang archaeological site, 7
Tang dynasty, 4
Taojiacun archaeological site, 29, 130–131
Taoluo, 6, 132–133
Taoluozhen area, 39, 41
taotie (animal mask), 8
Tashan archaeological site, 36, 178, 190
tax collection, 303
temperature, 1
terrain survey methodologies, 14–15, 17
tertiary population centers, 280, 282, 283–285, 295, 298–299, 301, 303
three-tiered settlement hierarchies, 272, 289
Tianjiacun archaeological site, 29, 130
Tianjiayuan archaeological site, 8, 40, 131–132
tianzi (Son of Heaven), 296
Tiejue Mountains, 1
tiles
  Han period, 74, 242
  recording methods, 20
tombs
  earthen tombs, 133, 158
  historical archaeological surveys, 7
  Ming dynasty, 148
  as state power symbols, 301
  Zhou period, 125
  See also Han tombs
Tongjiang-Sanya Expressway, 77
Tongsan Expressway, 6, 218, 240, 247
tools
  See stone artifacts/tools
topographic maps, 17
topography, 1
transportation networks, 4, 6
Tuogou archaeological site, 46, 155–156, 177–178
Tushandongzhuang, 227

U

Underhill, Anne, xv
urbanization, 270, 298, 303

W

walls/walled enclosures
  city walls, 21, 75, 76
  Dagucheng archaeological site, 75–76
  earthen walls, 76, 270, 297, 301, 305
  elite control strategies, 301
  excavation reports, 49, 283
  1995-2007 survey summary, 21
  research methodologies, 67–68
  settlement pattern studies, 272, 274
Wangdong, 159
Wangjiabu, 253
Wangjiacun, 136
Wangjiayao archaeological site, 21, 256
Wangjiazhuang, 242
Wangshan, 173, 178–179
Wangshitou archaeological site, 27, 256, 259
Wang Xiang, 7
Wang Xiantang, 7, 8
Wangzhuang archaeological site, 38, 179–180
warfare, 298
watchtowers, 264
water management systems, 283–284
Weifang City, xv, 263
Weixingying archaeological site, 45
Wendeng Road, 108
Wenwu, 8
Western Han period, 4, 70–71, 77
Western Zhou period
  burial sites, 9
  elite control strategies, 296
  regional sociopolitical organization, 289, 295–296, 305
  settlement pattern studies, 19, 289, 295–298, 301
  social hierarchies, 289, 296–297, 305
Woluozi archaeological site, 123, 127, 134–135, 265
Wujiatai archaeological site, 27, 133
Wulian District
  historical archaeological surveys, 8, 9
  1995-2007 survey summary, 21, 26–31, 45
  site descriptions, 249–263
Wulian Mountains, 1–2

X

Xia dynasty, 3
Xiajiazhuang archaeological site, 27, 259, 261
xian (county seat), 303
Xiangdian River, 91, 120, 121, 143
Xiangjiagou archaeological site
  1995-2007 survey summary, 21
  settlement patterns, 295
  site descriptions, 138, 147
Xiangjialou River, 214
Xiangjiazhuang, 147
Xiang state, 296, 297
xiang (towns), 303
Xiangyang village, 73
Xiaobianjiazhuang archaeological site, 135
Xiaocaojiazhuang archaeological site, 46, 266
Xiaocaopo, 135
Xiaochangwang'ai, 136
Xiaocun archaeological site, 227–229, 301
Xiaodaituan archaeological site, 40, 229–230
Xiaodianzi, 180
Xiaogucheng, 75
Xiaoguzhen, 136
Xiaohai, 136
Xiaojiawa archaeological site, 36, 173, 182–183
Xiaolijiacun, 138
Xiaolingnantou archaeological site, 138–139
Xiaoliuzhuang archaeological site, 139–140
Xiaolutuan, 183–184
Xiaonuozhuang archaeological site, 7
Xiaoqu River, 208
Xiaoshanhou, 142–143
Xiaoshanqian archaeological site, 42, 240–241, 247
Xiaoshihekou village, 167, 188
Xiaoshiling, 266–267
Xiaoxiangdian, 143
Xiasi archaeological site, 240
Xicaijia, 263
Xiejialing, 130
Xiejiazhuangzi archaeological site, 46, 266
Xihai County, 4
Xihezhuang, 232
Xihuangshanqian archaeological site, 45
Xikangliu, 272
Xilinzitou archaeological site
  historical archaeological surveys, 9
  settlement patterns, 282, 285
  site descriptions, 140, 142
Xingfang archaeological site, 40, 232
Xinliu archaeological site
  intercommunity conflict, 297
  1995-2007 survey summary, 44
  settlement patterns, 289, 295, 298–299
  site descriptions, 234, 237
Xinmang period, 4
Xinshan County, 201
Xinxing village, 208
Xinyangzhen area, 29
Xinzhuangzi archaeological site, 28, 144
Xiquan County, 201
Xishilipu archaeological site, 31, 75, 76
Xisi archaeological site
  diagnostic artifacts, 287
  1995-2007 survey summary, 38
  regional sociopolitical organization, 298, 305
  settlement patterns, 280, 282, 284, 295, 298, 301
  site descriptions, 151, 185, 187
Xitushan, 199, 216
Xiuqiyuan archaeological site, 184–185
Xiuzhen River, 42, 193, 204, 242, 247
Xiwangjialiugou, 188
Xizhuang archaeological site, 36, 188
Xue River, 13
Xu Han, 7
Xujiacun archaeological site
  1995-2007 survey summary, 41
  settlement patterns, 295, 298
  site descriptions, 137–138, 232–234
Xujiaguanzhuang, 180, 182
Xujialou archaeological site, 36, 143
Xujia village, 94
Xujiawa archaeological site, 26, 154, 182
Xujiayao, 183
Xujiayuan village, 116
Xuzhou area, 3, 4

Y

Yangjiazhuang archaeological site, 43, 241–242
Yang Shenfu, 146
Yanhai Highway, 104
Yanshi, 286
Yan Shigu, 4
Yantai, 4
Yantai Mountain (Yantaishan), 242
Yantaixi, 242
Yanzhou, 6
Yaogou archaeological site, 26, 261
Yao legendary ruler, 3
Yaowangcheng archaeological site
  ceramic artifact distribution and diversity, 284–285
  community interactions, 286, 297, 305

historical archaeological surveys, 7, 8, 9, 274, 277
1995-2007 survey summary, 21, 39–41, 43–44
regional sociopolitical organization, 283–286, 298–299, 304
settlement patterns, 272, 277, 280, 282, 283, 284, 289, 298
site descriptions, 242–243, 245
social hierarchies, 280, 282, 283–285
Yatou archaeological site, 27, 263
Yatou River, 253, 263
Yaxiashangzhuang, 170
Yayue village, 243, 245
Ye Guishou, 200
Yellow River valley, 269
Yellow Sea, 1, 14
yellow sediment, 245
Yi-Luo River, 13
Yin Da, 7, 9
ying tu mian (hard earth surfaces), 152
Yingzi archaeological site, 28, 146–147
Yinjia'aotou, 144–145
Yinjiacheng archaeological sites, 9
Yinjiazhuang, 189
Yinxu, 68, 283
Yishui administrative district, 4
yi (spouted pouring vessel), 9, 82
Yongzheng (Emperor), 4
Yousuo, 146
Yuchisi, 272, 274
yue (axe), 255
Yueshi period
Daguzhen, 77
Futuan archaeological site, 93
Gouwa archaeological site, 205
historical archaeological surveys, 9
intercommunity conflict, 295
Liangchengzhen archaeological site, 104–105
Luochuangou, 212, 214
Majiacun archaeological sites, 108, 110
Nanzhangjiacun archaeological site, 116
1995-2007 survey summary, 26–28, 43, 44
Qianzhucun archaeological site, 123
Qinjiaguanzhuang archaeological site, 118
settlement patterns, 11, 287, 289
Shimiaozicun archaeological site, 177
Wangshitou archaeological site, 256, 259
Xinzhuangzi archaeological site, 144
Xisi archaeological site, 185, 187
Xujiacun archaeological site, 137–138
Yue state, 3
Yugong, 3
Yu Haiguang, xv, 9, 12
Yujiacun, 146
Yu legendary ruler, 3

Z

Zangjiazhuang, 190
zao (chisel), 190, 200, 205, 209, 215, 233
Zhaike, 131
Zhangjia'aotou, 145
Zhangjiadazhuang archaeological site, 36, 189–190
Zhangjiazhuangzi, 40, 243
Zhang Jingzhai, 8
Zhang Zhibo
Dashiqiaocun archaeological site, 87
Daxiangdian archaeological site, 91
Dongjiatan archaeological site, 82
Gaojialing archaeological site, 30, 94
Lijiazhuangzi archaeological site, 108
Miaojiacun archaeological site, 110–111
Qianwulihe archaeological site, 121
site surveys, 70
Xiaolingnantou archaeological site, 139
Zhang Zhihan, 8
Zhengjiadingzi archaeological site, 31, 40, 147–148
Zhengjiajiezhuang archaeological site, 42, 247, 249
Zhoujiacun archaeological site, 29, 189
Zhou period
bronze artifacts, 82
burial sites, 125, 146, 247
diagnostic artifacts, 73
elite control strategies, 296, 298
historical and administrative perspective, 3
historical archaeological surveys, 9
intercommunity conflict, 295, 297–298
1995-2007 survey summary, 26–31, 36, 38, 40, 42–45
regional sociopolitical organization, 289, 295–299, 304, 305
settlement patterns, 11, 12, 19, 289, 295–299, 301, 305–306
social hierarchies, 289, 296–297, 299, 305
Zhouyuan area, 296
Zhucheng City, 4, 6, 69
Zhucheng County, 4, 7
Zhucheng District
boundaries, 180, 263
1995-2007 survey summary, 45, 46
site descriptions, 69, 263–267
Zhujiagou, 263
Zhujiayao, 148
Zhuluxiang, 201
Zhuyuan, 247
Zhuziling ridge, 138
Zhuzi River
Donggang District archaeological sites, 107, 142
geographical setting, 1
Lanshan District archaeological sites, 199, 203, 234
1995-2007 survey summary, 40, 42, 44
Zuozhuan, 237, 297
zu (point/arrowhead), 105, 106, 152, 209